Marxism in the Chinese Revolution

State and Society in East Asia Series
Elizabeth J. Perry, Series Editor

Marxism in the Chinese Revolution

Arif Dirlik

ROWMAN & LITTLEFIELD PUBLISHERS, INC.
Lanham • Boulder • New York • Toronto • Oxford

ROWMAN & LITTLEFIELD PUBLISHERS, INC.

Published in the United States of America
by Rowman & Littlefield Publishers, Inc.
A wholly owned subsidiary of The Rowman & Littlefield Publishing Group, Inc.
4501 Forbes Boulevard, Suite 200, Lanham, Maryland 20706
www.rowmanlittlefield.com

P.O. Box 317, Oxford OX2 9RU, UK

British Library Cataloguing in Publication Information Available

Library of Congress Cataloging-in-Publication Data
Dirlik, Arif.
  Marxism in the Chinese revolution / Arif Dirlik.
     p. cm. — (State and society in East Asia series)
  Includes bibliographical references and index.
  ISBN 0-7425-3069-8 (cloth : alk. paper)
  1. Communism—China. 2. Socialism—China. 3. Ideology—China. 4. China—Eco-
nomic policy—1976–2000. 5. China—Politics and government—1976–2002. I. Title.
II. Series.
  HX418.5.D58 2005
  335.43'45—dc22
                                                                    2005003075

Printed in the United States of America

⊗™ The paper used in this publication meets the minimum requirements of American
National Standard for Information Sciences—Permanence of Paper for Printed Library
Materials, ANSI/NISO Z39.48-1992.

To Mauri Meisner and the Memory of William Hinton

Contents

Part III   The Cultural Revolution in Historical Perspective

Part IV   After the Revolution

Acknowledgments

The author gratefully acknowledges the following publications for permission to reprint the essays below:

"Socialism and Capitalism in Chinese Socialist Thinking: The Origins," *Studies in Comparative Communism* 21, no. 2 (Summer 1988): 131–52.

"National Development and Social Revolution in Early Chinese Marxist Thought," *China Quarterly* 58 (April/June 1974): 286–309. Reprinted with permission.

"Mao Zedong and 'Chinese Marxism,'" in *Companion Encyclopedia of Asian Philosophy*, ed. Indira Mahalingam and Brian Carr, 593–619 (London: Routledge, 1997).

"Modernism and Anti-Modernism in Mao Zedong's Marxism," in *Critical Perspectives on Mao Zedong's Thought*, ed. Arif Dirlik, Paul Healy, and Nick Knight, 59–83 (Atlantic Highlands, NJ: Humanities Press, 1997).

"The Predicament of Revolutionary Consciousness: Mao Zedong, Antonio Gramsci, and the Reformulation of Marxist Revolutionary Theory," *Modern China* 9, no. 2 (April 1983): 182–211.

"Revolutionary Hegemony and the Language of Revolution: Chinese Socialism between Present and Future," in *Marxism and the Chinese Experience*, ed. Arif Dirlik and Maurice Meisner, 27–39 (Armonk, NY: M. E. Sharpe, 1989). Copyright © 1989 by M. E. Sharpe, Inc. Reprinted with permission.

"The Two Cultural Revolutions: The Chinese Cultural Revolution in the Perspective of Global Capitalism," *Ershiyi shiji* [Twentieth century], no. 37 (October 1996): 4–15.

"Post-Socialism? Reflections on 'Socialism with Chinese Characteristics,'" in *Marxism and the Chinese Experience*, ed. Arif Dirlik and Maurice Meisner, 362–84 (Armonk, NY: M. E. Sharpe, 1989). Copyright © 1989 by M. E. Sharpe, Inc. Reprinted with permission.

"*Looking Backward* in the Age of Global Capital: Thoughts on History in Third World Cultural Criticism," in *Contemporary Cultural Politics in East Asia*, ed. Xiaobing Tang and Stephen Snyder, 183–215 (Boulder, CO: Westview Press, 1996).

"Markets, Power, Culture: The Making of a 'Second Cultural Revolution' in China," *Asian Studies Review* 25, no. 1 (March 2001): 1–33.

1

Introduction

The essays included in this collection were published over three decades, in publications that range widely over the globe, from the United Kingdom to the United States, Hong Kong, and Australia. The very first essay that I ever wrote on socialism in China was published in 1974, in the *China Quarterly* in the United Kingdom. It appears here as chapter 3. The last one, which appears here as the final chapter, was published only last year, in the *Asian Studies Review* in Australia. I underline the publication history of the chapters in this collection because it suggests an explanation—if not any self-evident justification—for the republication of the essays in a collection such as this one. Unpacking this explanation is the task I undertake in the introduction.

The essays are drawn from publications that are scattered over a broad temporal and spatial range, and bringing them together between the two covers of a book makes them available to a readership that may not have access to those publications. While this is quite gratifying for the author, however, it is not sufficient for the reader who might wonder why this particular set of essays might deserve republication; especially on a subject—Chinese socialism—which, to be blunt, is history. Even historians have to account for what they choose to deal with in the past, and how they do so.[1]

I would like to think that there are three good reasons for republishing the essays. The fact that socialism in China is history is not the least aspect of the matter, as it is relevant to all three reasons I will take up here; namely, forgetfulness not only in the reading but also the writing of the past, the importance of comprehensiveness in historical explanations, even when comprehensiveness consists of contradictory fractures rather than organic wholes, and the issue of socialism itself, both in history and in politics—which, to this author at least, are not easily distinguishable. In the final analysis, it is up to the readers to decide whether these chapters in any way contribute to the achievement of the goals which, at any rate, have been the intended goals in the mind of this author. But it seems important to spell out the intentions anyway.

The issue of forgetfulness is almost of necessity the point of departure here. Professors of history frequently complain about the forgetfulness of their students, but rarely do they examine (or so it seems) their own forgetfulness either as teachers or as historians. The problem struck me forcefully for the first time nearly fifteen years ago, in the comments of a reviewer on a manuscript of mine. This reader complained that I made too much of the historical problematic offered by a book (by Joseph Levenson) that had been published quite some time ago—two decades earlier! It seemed that even for historians (which I took this person to be), two decades marked the difference between history and prehistory. The comment could be attributed to the shallowness of this particular individual, but by the 1980s, forgetfulness had become pervasive in the China field, as in Chinese society itself. With the opening of China to capitalism, the revolutionary past became increasingly questionable. Many a scholar of China who had once been sympathetic to the Chinese Revolution—especially those whose sympathies had been marked by a singular absence of critical judgment—rushed to erase memories of their sympathies by taking the revolution out of history, more often than not by degrading what it had been about. Two decades later, the revolutionary past, and socialism in its various guises that it empowered, have all but disappeared from the scholarship.

Forgetting the "losers" in history is an almost inevitable concomitant of a progressivist and teleological historiography, which has little regard for what is cast by the wayside as the past marches on toward the present, and *its* future. It also guarantees the ideological assumption that what has come to pass had to come to pass; a "naturalized" history, sort of to speak, that is shared in common by modern progressivist ideologies regardless of political preference. It may also show up in more mundane forms, as in the case of revolutionary histories such as the Chinese, where historians (Chinese and foreign) have over and over again proven to be captives at the mercy of twists and turns of the revolution, to turn against it once and for all once the Communist leadership turned their backs on their own revolutionary legacy. Politics here shows up in the most vulgar (and opportunistic) form, but its plausibility rests ultimately in the teleology of a naturalized history, bolstered by the hegemonic power of a global status quo.

The kind of forgetfulness to which I am referring here is intentional forgetting (premeditated amnesia, as Alexander Woodside, with his inimitable wit, once put it), for whatever reason. Forgetting is not always bad, as being mired in the past is not a virtue in itself. It is in some ways built into the scholarly enterprise, demanded by the very economy of research, writing, teaching, and the marketplace. Intentionally forgetting itself, in other words, may be due to reasons of professional progress. But all this should not lead us to overlook the strong ideological element in forgetting, whether it is political ideology in evaluating the relative merit of historical events, etc., or the hubris of progress in the understanding of learning, which in some perceptions relegates to oblivion what appears to be superseded in terms of prevailing standards of scholarship. It is inevitably in the present that all this happens, and when forgetfulness becomes an accepted standard of an ideologically dominated professional and public domain, the present dominates the past, as the future no longer is of much concern, and we are left with an ongoing rewriting of the past in accordance with the interests of whoever would claim it. The only cure to the manipulation of the past, for whatever reason, all along has been to reclaim the past, to assure the continued appearance in history of pasts that are "forgotten." Forgetting and memory go hand in hand, but also against one another. In remembering what is forgotten, we also recognize the past not just as the teleological source of the present, as in its ideological manipulations, but also as a source of critical insights in its very grounding of issues of memory and forgetting.

These chapters, then, may be read as part of the ground which they analyze. They deal with the historical circumstances and consequences of what are generally considered to be important issues in Chinese socialism. But they do so not just descriptively and analytically, I hope, but also as critical reflections on socialism, in China and elsewhere, as well as on the scholarship on socialism. I believe, for the same reason, that their publication at the present is intended both to stir up some memories in scholarship, place the present in some kind of perspective, and counter some of the ideological motive forces that drive contemporary scholarship on China and socialism—both within and without China.

A sense of the history of one's professional and intellectual work is a necessity of any critical scholarship not only as a source of knowledge and insight but, most importantly in my view, as a storehouse of possibilities of explanation in its particular domain. Explanations do not merely chase one another into oblivion. They crowd the intellectual field, calling forth judgments of comparative merit, but also more complicated explanations that relate them to one another. The view that an explanation may be discarded as soon as it has been overtaken, where it is not driven simply by ideology or the market, goes along with a reductionist understanding of what constitutes an explanation. It lacks, one might say, a sense of the dialectical interplay of competing problems and explanations, an interplay that may produce totalities of various scope, but also expose significant fractures which, while they may defy the very idea of totality, nevertheless derive meaning from shared historical spaces. What is important is to keep in mind the complex dynamics at work, which is lost to sight as scholarly fashions, and ideologically fashionable explanations supersede one another, and what is left is the chaos that is characteristic of the contemporary market.

The particular issue raised by these chapters is the relationship between revolution and socialism over the century-long history of socialism in China. I don't think it is very controversial to suggest that this was the issue that drove the historiography of China, across disciplines, over the half-century after World War II. The issue has practically disappeared from scholarship over the last decade, and when it is taken up, it is usually to debunk either socialism, or revolution, or both, under the guise of "new interpretations." But the subject has gone out of fashion, and, while there is much work to be done to understand the revolution or socialism, the conscientious advisor does not push it on graduate students.

New departures during this same period have done much to enrich our understanding of modern China, as they have brought to the surface important historical phenomena, events, and persons that did not receive much attention, or were erased, earlier in the preoccupation with revolution and socialism. How these new phenomena relate to the histories of revolution and socialism is a question that begs attention. These chapters hopefully contribute to that end, by reintroducing into the contemporary discussion issues which, as I see it, are revived to provoke a new kind of discussion, rather than to claim some kind of contemporary relevance. If they are relevant, it is in critique of contemporary forgetfulness, and its ideological underpinnings, which also make for reductionist scholarship.

The ordering of the articles here requires some explanation, as it is tied in with my own historiographical inclinations. It was not easy to decide between an ordering in terms of the chronological unfolding of the issues discussed, as they are here, or an ordering in terms of the chronology of writing. The present choice does not imply a pretension, which would be quite unconvincing anyway, to the construction of a historical narrative of Chinese socialism out of the issues and events discussed, which go from the origins of socialism in the late Qing to its final decline if not, as yet, fall, under the Communist Party after 1992. I am not forgetful of the circumstances that turned me from one issue to another, that were in response to historical developments that highlighted issues from the past but, were in the end, of my choosing and formulation. Nevertheless, this volume is not about the unfolding of my understanding of Chinese socialism, which the alternative ordering would have suggested, but about Chinese socialism as I have understood it. The historian's agency is very much in all of these chapters, but it is an agency that is qualified and restricted by the very narrative it constructs. I think it is an important difference.

I should note, secondly, that I have understood socialism in China most importantly as a Third World socialism in identifying the problematics of the narrative. Most historiography of Chinese socialism seeks to find reasons for the particularities of Chinese socialism in past legacies. I do not deny the importance of intellectual legacies from the past in the acceptance and shaping of socialism. My approach is informed by a methodological assumption that the past itself, however powerful, is subject to constant change, and while it may endow the present with some meaning, it is itself the subject of rereading and interpretation in changing historical contexts, whose structure also restructures the past. The issue of structure versus history is in my opinion crucial in the study of modern China, and the Third World in general, to escape both an Orientalist historicism and a crude presentism. Structuralism and historicism do not present themselves as alternative, and mutually exclusive, explanatory strategies. The challenge, rather, is to grasp structures in their historical motions, and history in its structural articulations. The structurings represented by capitalism, socialism, or modernity underwent transformations in their transplantations within a Chinese context. On the other hand, the changing meanings of the Chinese past over the century covered by these chapters should serve as sufficient warning against the uses of the past as an explanation of the present when it is itself part of the problem. Chinese socialism was very much a product of its present, and as that present has given way to other presents, including those of its own creation, it recedes into the past. But the problems it addressed persist, now under different circumstances.

I will say a few words here about the individual essays, and the circumstances under which they were written, to give a sense of their historiographical implications. Unlike in their ordering below, therefore, here I will discuss them in the order in which they were written. My first essay on Chinese socialism, which appears here as chapter 3, "National Development and Social Revolution," is probably the clearest statement of my understanding of Chinese socialism within the context of the problematics of national liberation movements in the 1960s and 1970s. The argument seeks to overcome the opposition between nationalism and socialism that in those years characterized most discussions of Chinese socialism ("is it socialist or nationalist?"). The opposition itself was often driven by an urge to show that Chinese socialism was not "real" socialism. The chapter does not deny the importance of nationalism in the Chinese Revolution, but argues only that this was a nationalism that expressed itself through the categories of socialism, most importantly class, which distinguished it from other nationalisms. Socialism was not merely a plaything at the hands of nationalism, but shaped its contours. The unfolding of nationalism in the People's Republic of China since the abandonment of revolutionary socialism or, for that matter, revolutionary nationalism, may serve as a testament to this distinction.

It is worth mentioning here two articles written in the early 1980s that are not included in this collection, but provide a context for the two articles on the question of revolutionary hegemony reprinted here as chapters 6 and 7, and the article entitled, "Postsocialism" (chapter 10). Together, these articles document and analyze the retreat from revolution and, ultimately, socialism, in the course of that decade. "Spiritual Solutions to Material Problems" addressed the crisis created by the Communist Party's turn away from the revolutionary past while continuing to claim socialist commitments.[2] Socialist ideology, rather than expressing developments in the material sphere, now appeared as ideological in another fundamental sense, as a disguise to cover up the abandonment of revolutionary socialism. The phenomenon the article dealt with, "the socialist ethic and courtesy month," resonated with the New Life Movement of the Guomindang in the 1930s, which I had analyzed some years earlier as an expression of ideological counterrevolution. The New Life Movement had shifted attention from social conflict to bodily cleanliness as it abandoned the revolutionary vision that lay at its origins. This is what the Communist Party now undertook as it launched its own brand of counterrevolution—but in the name of revolution, much as the Guomindang under Chiang K'ai-shek had done in the 1930s. This article continued my inquiry into the contradictions presented by "socialism without revolution," which I had first undertaken two years earlier in an article of that title.[3] That article had drawn the ire of afficionados of the Chinese Revolution who were not yet ready to recognize a distinction between Mao Zedong and Deng Xiaoping; but subsequent events during the 1980s, and what has happened since then, obviously leave little doubt that the beginning of the so-called reforms in 1978 also meant the beginning of the end for socialism in the People's Republic of China.

The article, reprinted here as chapter 6, was written just about the same time. It was my first venture toward an analysis of Mao Zedong. Mao had died in 1976, and his policies of the Cultural Revolution were abandoned after 1978. The contrast between Mao's notion of the relationship between the Party and the people, developed first in the 1930s, reaching their full articulation during the so-called Yan'an Period, and revived once again from the late 1950s, and the more centralized, elitist bureaucratic, and *dirigentist* approach of Deng Xiaoping was very much on my mind as I wrote this essay. I do not know if I would now repeat the statement that "Mao did what Gramsci thought," but I think Antonio Gramsci's Marxism, with its unabashed nationalism, and commitment to the cause of the "backward" in Italy, still resonates in its concerns with many of the issues of the Chinese Revolution as perceived by Mao and the Maoists. Gramsci's notion of "hegemony" also allows a contrast that is important, I think, in distinguishing Mao from the more bureaucratic Bolshevik factions within the Communist Party of China.

The talk from which the article was derived had been entitled, "Gramscian Peregrinations in Mao Zedong Thought." This article also raises a question that is developed more fully in the Mao essays that are included in this volume, especially, "Mao Zedong and 'Chinese Marxism.'" The question is that there is more than one Mao Zedong Thought, just as there is more than one Marx or Marxism. The Maoism of "New Democracy" (1940) in Yan'an was one that had secured the hegemony of the Communist Party and its revolutionary policies, which had been overshadowed by the Maoism of the Cultural Revolution. Yan'an was very important to understanding the latter as well, as the political organicism demanded by the Cultural Revolution had been visible during the Yan'an Period as well. But now it was unchecked by other considerations, and mistook coercion and dictatorship for hegemony, which would bring about its downfall, and the discrediting of the whole Maoist enterprise.

If there was some doubt in the early 1980s about where socialism in China might have been headed, there was little question by the late 1980s that socialism was on its way out. The essays from this period, included in this collection, are devoted to a consideration of the historical sources and implications of the Deng Xiaoping turn in Chinese socialism. The article that leads the volume as chapter 2, "Socialism and Capitalism in Chinese Socialist Thinking," traces the relationship that became very evident in the late 1980s as *the* problem of Chinese socialism, back to the origins of socialism in China in its Sun Yat-sen and Guomindang version, which had first pointed to a "third way" that sought to transcend the opposition between socialism and capitalism, and sought to synthesize the two. Hence it was arguable that there was a line connecting Deng Xiaoping's policies to the earliest considerations that had attracted Chinese radicals to socialism. Indeed, it was also arguable that the connection was mediated by Mao Zedong's idea of "New Democracy," which was in many ways a rephrasing of Sun Yat-sen's ideas of socialism within a teleology of Marxian Communism and Communist victory.

It was in this essay that I first took up a theme, which is visible in subsequent writings; that we need to historicize Mao Zedong Thought to overcome the ideological reductionism that has sought to render one or another interpretation of it into orthodoxy. In addition to the revolutionary Maoism that had come forth during the Cultural Revolution, that made class struggle into the central datum of history, there is also the Mao of "New Democracy," that sought not struggle but class alliance in the national cause. In fact, it was not socialism but "New Democracy" that had emerged victorious in 1949. Equally "Maoist," these two versions of revolution coexisted in Mao Zedong Thought which, I suggest in several of the chapters here, was remarkable for its ability to accommodate contradictions.

"Postsocialism," published originally in 1989, was a concept that I had coined back in 1986, on the occasion of a conference held at Duke University on "Marxism and the Chinese Experience," which was the basis for the book of the same title. This was when "posts" were beginning to proliferate, and not just under the sign of the "postmodern." Socialism was coming to an end by this time, not just in China but globally, and postsocialism appeared in 1989 as another word for post-Communism, coined by a prolific coiner of such terms, Zbigniew Brzezinski. It is important, however, to underline the intention that informs the term. Postsocialism, at least in my usage, was intended to overcome another either/or approach to Chinese socialism; this time, either capitalist or socialist. The article, reprinted here as chapter 10, argues that these are not the only choices that are available; that, in fact, the weight of the socialist revolution—what we might call the revolutionary tradition—in China, shaped the incorporation of China into global capitalism and the incorporation of global capitalism into China. China scholars usually worry about the Chinese cultural tradition, and overlook the many historical traditions that in fact give meaning to the so-called Chinese tradition, conceived in terms of nineteenth-century Orientalist preoccupation with civilizations. The revolutionary tradition had more lasting power than many have been willing to recognize, and so has the experience of socialism—postsocialism as concept was intended to recognize the importance of these pasts, while also marking their passing.

These considerations are also important, I think, in the shaping of the other article from this period, included here as chapter 7, "Revolutionary Hegemony and the Language of Revolution." As with the "Postsocialism" article, it is also possible to see in this article shifting concerns of scholarship in general in interpreting events in China; namely, the importance of the cultural or the linguistic turn, that stressed the importance of language in our understanding of socialism, or what it promised to achieve. How the future is to be named is a question that is taken up in this chapter, which concludes that one of the reasons for the failure of the Cultural Revolution was that it did not have a language with which to describe what it sought to achieve, and was mired in a language of the past that at all points undercut its aspirations. The article is an inquiry in the last instance into the impossibility of revolution—

which the Chinese Cultural Revolution had brought forward dramatically. I would like to think, however, that it does not imply a resignation to what was to follow.

June 1989 was the ultimate expression of the contradictions that had been intensifying throughout the decade, that the articles above had sought to chronicle. Most observers of China in the United States, and in China, had refused to acknowledge these contradictions that had found expression periodically over the decade in instances of popular protest against the Communist Party; blinded by their own rhetoric that sought to erase memories of the revolution by exaggerated, and misleading, portrayals of the Party under Deng Xiaoping as a vanguard of democracy. June 1989 put an end to these false hopes. It also put an end to lingering hopes among some that the People's Republic of China could achieve radical changes in economy and society without repudiating socialism.[4] Of course, 1989 turned out to be eventful globally, as it marked the end of an era of revolution and socialism—and, perhaps, modernity—globally.

The People's Republic of China survived the upheavals of 1989, but more as a caricature of socialism as socialism became a cover for policies of development inspired by capitalism, and the revival of once-rejected national traditions to cement together a society subject to potentially fatal disruptions under a new set of contradictions, created by absorbtion into a global economy. The warning given by the events of 1989, and the global response to them, prompted the Communist Party to speedier accommodation of capitalism, and the creation of a new economic culture that mimicked the practices of advanced consumer society, that they believed might divert attention from politics. But the important event was Deng Xiaoping's imperial trip to the South, followed by a declaration that too much preoccupation with socialism and capitalism obstructed the development of the country. Since then, the Chinese economy has taken off, but so have inequalities between urban and rural areas, classes, and genders. Continuing ferment among the dispossessed and exploited is suppressed by repressions that may not have the dramatic intensity of Tiananmen in 1989, but seems to have become an ongoing phenomenon. If socialism persists in China in an ideological sense, it is because it provides some cover for proliferating inequality. Whatever China's future may be, socialism as it was understood during the years of the revolution is unlikely to be its driving force. As with many other formerly radical Second and Third World societies, developments in China, too, have produced a new class that seeks to combine success in global capitalism with the reassertion of native traditions to assert its identity in globality. The revolutionary traditions, which have not yet disappeared, occupy a slowly narrowing section of the political spectrum.

The last two articles in the volume, chapters 11 and 12, examine these transformations of the last decade. If they have a slightly different tone than earlier articles, it is because they coincide with a turn on my part to cultural studies, and to think out new consequences of confronting the study of China with cultural studies. Intellectual and theoretical approaches associated with Cultural Studies have produced new ways of understanding modern China. On the other hand, the modern Chinese historical experience also enables a critical understanding of these very same intellectual and theoretical approaches. Most important may be the perspective afforded by the Chinese case that Cultural Studies have turned their back on the historical experiences of revolution and socialism that played a major part in their emergence. The essay on Mao and Gramsci and the *"Looking Backward"* essay (chapter 11) deal with this question most directly. Readers interested in this question might read these essays in conjunction with another one (not included here) that was written in the late 1980s, as Cultural Studies was on the emergence to the forefront of intellectual activity. It was in that essay that I first took up the question of culture in relation to its material context; a central theme, in my reading, both in the Chinese Revolution and in Cultural Studies—not coincidentally, as transformations within Marxism occasioned by Third World National Liberation movements were quite significant in the turn to Cultural Studies.[5] Chapter 11 looks at these transformations in light of the predictions in Edward Bellamy's *Looking Backward*, which was one of the first texts to inspire socialism in the late Qing Dynasty. It also relies on my observations of what was happening in post-1989 China in everyday cultural practices, that was just becoming a concern of reporting on China.

The final chapter points to the obliteration of the revolutionary legacy not by suppressing it, but by making it into an object of consumption. It is a new generation that is involved here. One still wonders, however, what if any relationship there was between the political consumption of the revolution, and revolutionary history, under the heady days of Maoism, and the more economically minded consumption practices of the present. And, if so, that in spite of significant differences, there is more of a resonance between the present and its revolutionary past that make the future more complicated than in linear account of progress. It remains to be seen.

A final matter that deserves brief comment is a response to an imaginary question, "how would you have written these essays were you writing in the present?"—quite fashionable among academics, usually as an expression of openness to novelty. I take up the question here because, with minor changes here and there, the chapters that follow are republications of the originals. It is conceivable to me that the essays might never have been published were it not for the immediate circumstances that threw up what seemed to be big questions that demanded analysis. Those circumstances obviously do not exist anymore, which also cuts big questions down to size. For reasons I explained above, it is important to keep the questions of the past in mind in rethinking the present and the future—which may not always yield results that one might wish, but which radicals in particular are in need of these days. And, I hope, for that reason, it is important to publish the originals. It is up to the reader to judge how much they help in preparing the ground for understanding how we got from there to here—and what we have "forgotten" in the process.

The chapters will, hopefully, also serve as reminders of possibilities of resistance to imperialist domination, economic inequality, and exploitation, and class, gender, and ethnic/racial oppression, which, if anything have been exacerbated since the fall of socialism as we have known it, and the end of the Cold War. The "forgetting" of socialism is not accidental; it serves also to erase the possibilities of resistance to power presently by discrediting its past. Socialism as we have had it failed against its own standards, and revolutions were by no means free of criminal acts or unrestrained cruelty. But it is questionable that they were any more criminal or unrestrained in cruelty than those who defeated revolutions, and now seek to erase the possibility of any kind of radical resistance or change by rendering all radical oppositional politics into terrorism. It is necessary to struggle ideologically against this erasure, to re-create the possibilities of new kinds of oppositional politics against what seems to be the promise of perpetual war and unrestrained cruelty without opposition in the name of the most cherished values of modernity such as democracy and universal justice. It is important, to this end, not to cast socialism aside as one of the great failures of history, but to discuss its legacies in their success and failure. We need to remember, against contemporary forgettings of this most recent "loser" in history, that socialism did not just fail, it was also made to fail. And there is a price to be paid for the victory of those who succeeded in defeating the socialist states, tottering under their own ideological weight, and who now seeks to erase the possibility of opposition to their power once and for all—as admitted openly by the ideologues of contemporary U.S. power.

The fall of socialism was greeted with an almost audible sigh of relief, including among scholars of China in the United States, many of whom long have felt uncomfortable with the idea for obvious reasons. Under the circumstances, the escape into ideologies of globalization, into the seductions of culture devoid of social content, and the repudiation of any logic to social relations that hints at a totalistic logic, including the logic of capital, have proven seductive even to those supposedly on the Left. This escape no doubt derived considerable impetus from the repudiation of socialism as it had existed by those who had lived it, and suffered the perversion of socialist goals into state dictatorships of one kind or another.

But the chapters need also to be read as critiques of socialism as it appeared in the Chinese Revolution, before and after 1949—especially after. If I am more sympathetic to the revolutionary socialism of Mao Zedong than to what has followed since the end of the revolution after 1976, it is because of its ability to recognize the contradictions of socialism, which permitted an ideological self-reflexiveness, in contrast to the theoretical poverty and ideological deployment of socialism under Mao's successors. To be sure, there were occasions of descent into political atavism during the Mao years, most notably during the Cultural Revolution, and Party dictatorship has been a feature of Chinese Communism since its appearance in the late 1910s. On the other hand, the tension between national goals of state-building and economic development existed in some kind of a creative tension with the more universal goals of socialism, dynamizing a creative search for alternatives to existing practices of political and economic development. All this has disappeared with the reduction of socialism to some kind of ideological cover for national development under the dictatorship of the Party, and the new class it has fostered.

It is possible to argue that the fall of existing socialisms has been beneficial in releasing socialist thinking from its subservience to regimes that were ideologically and organizationally ossified from the moment they had come into existence. An event such as the Cultural Revolution in China appears in hindsight as the last gasp of revolution rather than its beginning. The globalization of capital with the fall of socialism has also produced new conditions for the search for alternatives in the course of popular struggles for survival and justice, which draw on some legacies of the past while creating new possibilities of their own. Unlike in the past, moreover, when socialist goals were easily yoked to national visions, there are also strong signs of the globalization of dissent and struggle, as more and more people are similarly subjected to the contradictions of capitalist modernity as modernity goes global. But now the search for alternatives looks to solutions that are concretely place-based rather than aspiring to a universal blueprint or even a national solution—which, arguably, was one of the contributions of the Chinese Revolution to Marxist thinking on the subject. Ironically, the search for such alternatives may face greater difficulties in the People's Republic of China where the Communist Party is still in power and, therefore, in a position to dictate what may or may not be considered properly socialist. The Party has been especially wary of alternatives spawned by the very revolutionary legacy it seeks to leave behind which, interestingly, have appeared elsewhere as inspiration for popular struggles.

The vacuum left by the disappearance of socialism has been filled by the resurgence of reactionary ideologies which are now at war with one another. But perhaps socialism, and its legacies, are not as dead as they appear, but persist in less visible everyday forms of struggle for survival and justice. Aijaz Ahmad once wrote that, "socialism is the determinate name for [the] negation of capitalism's fundamental, systemic contradictions and cruelties, and the necessity of this negation will remain, regardless of the fate of the Soviet Union as such."[6] We might add to this the necessity of struggle also against the cruel legacies of the past, and even so-called socialist states which use socialism as a mask for the exploitation of those they claim to represent, as they appear increasingly as contradictory aspects of globalizing capital. But the struggle continues against all these forms of domination and exploitation, and while they do not bear the familiar visage of earlier state-directed struggles for socialism, they owe much in inspiration to the legacies of socialism, and revolutionary traditions of liberation. To recall Milan Kundera in paraphrase, the struggle against "forgetting," always important, is significant presently in new, unexpected, and perhaps unprecedentedly crucial ways.

NOTES

1. I do refer in this introduction simply to socialism, history of socialism, and so forth, but it is important to note that the chapters in this volume deal mostly with Marxism in China. Socialism, however, was much more complicated in the dominance of anarchism in the early part of the twentieth century and the important presence of several kinds of socialism—from state to guild socialism—in the 1930s and 1940s. My own writings on anarchism are intertwined with the chapters included here. As those writings are readily available in collected form, it would have been superfluous to include them here. See Arif Dirlik, *Anarchism in the Chinese Revolution* (Berkeley: University of California Press, 1991). Interest in social democracy has picked up over the last decade, and should yield a better understanding of the relationship between Marxists and socialists.

2. "Spiritual Solutions to Material Problems: The 'Socialist Ethics and Courtesy Month in China,'" *South Atlantic Quarterly* 81, no. 4 (Autumn 1982): 359–75.

3. Arif Dirlik, "Socialism without Revolution: The Case of Contemporary China," *Pacific Affairs* 54, no. 4 (Winter 1981–1982): 632–61.

4. Detailed analysis of responses to June 4, 1989, may be found in an article that I coauthored with Roxann Prazniak, "Socialism Is Dead, So Why Must We Talk about It? Reflections on the 1989 Insurrection in China, Its Bloody Suppression, the End of Socialism, and the End of History," *Asian Studies Review* 14, no. 1 (July 1990): 3–25. This article is not included in this volume, because it was too immediately focused on 1989, but it and the one to which I referred above, "Socialism without Revolution,"

were written at the beginning and the end of this eventful decade and may be viewed, in their specificity, as brackets to the article included.

5. Arif Dirlik, "Culturalism as Hegemonic Ideology and Liberating Practice," in *The Postcolonial Aura: Third World Criticism in the Age of Global Capitalism* (Boulder, CO: Westview Press, 1997), 23–51.

6. Aijaz Ahmad, *In Theory: Classes, Nations, Literatures* (London: Verso, 1992), 316.

I

THE ORIGINS

2

Socialism and Capitalism in Chinese Socialist Thinking: The Origins

Since the beginning of the so-called reforms in 1978, the Communist regime in China has undertaken a restructuring of Chinese socialism. Most dramatic of the changes initiated by the regime is the redefinition of the place of capitalist methods of development within the socialist economy, which has compelled the reevaluation of the entire socialist structure established after 1949. Chinese Communism, the nemesis only two decades ago of anything suggestive of bourgeois thinking and practices, today seeks in capitalist societies answers to problems of socialism.

This turnabout in Chinese socialism raises serious questions about the nature and future of socialism in China and, by implication, globally. The effort of the Communist regime to articulate capitalist methods of development to its socialist goals has invoked hopes (or fears, as the case may be) that the days of socialism in China may be numbered. The further representation of the problems of Chinese Communism as a paradigmatic expression of the dilemmas of socialism in the contemporary world in turn suggests that Chinese success in efforts "to make capitalism serve the cause of socialism" must inevitably beckon other socialist states to follow the Chinese example toward greater accommodation of capitalism in a global retreat from socialism. The attenuation of socialism in China, in other words, erodes faith in the viability of socialism as it rejuvenates hopes in the inevitable victory of capitalism over socialism.[1]

In the discussion below, I offer a historical perspective on the question of capitalism in Chinese socialist thinking that may shed some light on the questions raised by the policies toward capitalism of the contemporary Chinese regime. The discussion focuses on the first decade of the twentieth century when socialism was first introduced into Chinese politics, and immediately provoked a controversy on the relative merits of socialism and capitalism in resolving the problems of state-building and economic development, which were at the time the most urgent problems of Chinese politics and, in modified form, retain their urgency today. My choice of this period is not intended to suggest that the views of China's first socialists on this question have a direct bearing upon the turn Chinese socialism has taken recently; the postrevolutionary Communist regime in China faces vastly different circumstances than those that prevailed around the turn of the century. Rather, I seek to demonstrate that the questions raised by contemporary Chinese socialism have been fundamental to the socialist discourse in China from its very origins. Viewed from this perspective, the premises that underlie policies toward capitalism in Chinese socialism represent not a radical break with the past but rather a revival of a significant current of long standing in Chinese socialist thinking that was suppressed briefly during the Cultural Revolution (taken here to refer to the two decades between 1956 and 1976, and surrounding the "official" Cultural Revolution of 1966–1969).

The redirection of Chinese socialism under the postrevolutionary regime is reminiscent of the earlier experiences of other Communist states, in particular the Soviet Union. Policy changes under Deng Xiaoping have been described in China and abroad as a "second revolution." Indeed, these changes in their political thrust recall Stalin's "second revolution" which replaced old revolutionaries with a managerial bureaucracy better suited to the needs of Communism in power.[2] This "second revolution" is not revolutionary in any strict sense of the word but points to what Robert Tucker has described as the inevitable "deradicalization" of Communism once a Communist Party has established itself in power.[3] In the Chinese case, too, the passing of the revolutionary leadership with the death of Mao Zedong in 1976 signaled not a repudiation of socialism but of a revolutionary Communism of which the Cultural Revolution now appears to have been the last gasp.

I would like to suggest here, however, that because of the differences between Chinese and Russian Communism, which ultimately rest upon the different historical experiences of the two societies, it is misleading to view the "deradicalization" of Communism in China in terms of a model provided by the earlier experience of the Soviet Union. While the process of deradicalization in the two societies may share common features, we still need to explain differences in the speed and direction of deradicalization. One of the most conspicuous, and intriguing, features of the deradicalization of Communism in China under the post-Mao regime is the willingness the regime has displayed in finding an accommodation with capitalism at home and abroad—to the point where China today, in spite of a much later start, leads the Soviet

Union in efforts to "reform" socialism by injecting into it the economic practices of capitalism. Adam Ulam once cynically described Communism as
"capitalism without the capitalists."[4] The Communist regime in China today
acknowledges in word and deed that even capitalists might not be unwelcome
so long as they do not undermine a long-term commitment to socialism.

It may be arguable that the willingness of the Communist regime in China
to compromise its socialism only provides evidence of "hidden" capitalist
tendencies, or at least a shallowness of socialist commitments, among its
leaders, in particular Deng Xiaoping. This was the charge brought against
Deng during the Cultural Revolution and, ironically, it is the view of Deng
that has been cultivated by the American press in recent years.[5]

The discussion below presents a different case. Whatever the truth may be
of this portrayal of Deng and other leaders of the contemporary Communist
regime, the problems presented by Chinese socialism today go beyond individual ideological inclinations to fundamental questions concerning the
meaning attached to socialism in Chinese political thinking in the twentieth
century. During the heyday of the Cultural Revolution, its socialism appeared
to many to be the logical culmination of the historical experience of Chinese
socialism, and the task that faced the student of Chinese socialism was to explain its origins and articulation in the thinking of its architect, Mao Zedong.
Post-Mao developments in Chinese socialism draw our attention to an alternative vision of socialism that may be even more deep-seated than the socialism of the Cultural Revolution and goes back in its origins to the very origins of socialism in China: socialism as an instrument of national economic
and political development which, in the priority it assigns to national interest,
allows for the possibility of capitalist methods within socialist development
so long as they further the national interest; indeed, it renders capitalism into
the dynamic source of national development, and socialism into the guarantee of national unity against the socially divisive consequences of capitalism.
Throughout the history of socialism in China, this understanding of socialism
has coexisted with the more radical utopian-egalitarian strain that came to the
fore during the Cultural Revolution which, while not oblivious to questions
of national development as is falsely claimed today, nevertheless refused to
dissociate national needs from its radical socialist vision.[6] It is even possible
to suggest that these alternative understandings of socialism have coexisted in
uneasy tension in the thinking of individual Communists. This was the case
with Mao Zedong; it is the case today with the older revolutionaries (now
dubbed conservatives) who resist "excessive" compromises with capitalism
and, possibly, even with the architect of the new policies, Deng Xiaoping.
Against the background of the Cultural Revolution, which has played a crucial role in shaping our understanding of Chinese socialism, the changes that

have taken place since the passing of Mao Zedong appear as a fundamental break with the past. A long-term perspective on Chinese socialism reveals that the premises that have guided these changes are as old as the history of socialism in China. With the winding down of the Chinese Revolution, these premises have once again emerged to the forefront of Chinese socialism as its basic ingredients.

ORIGINS OF CHINESE SOCIALISM

Socialism emerged as an issue in Chinese politics for the first time with the founding of the Revolutionary Alliance (Tongmenghui) in 1905. The Revolutionary Alliance, in the founding of which Sun Yat-sen played a central part, was modern China's first authentically revolutionary organization and forerunner to the Nationalist Party (Guomindang), the same party that continues to rule Taiwan today. Its basic goal was to bring about a political revolution: to overthrow the ruling Manchu Dynasty and, more importantly, to replace the monarchy with a republic. On the insistence of Sun and some of his followers, the Alliance incorporated in its program a clause on the "equalization of land rights" as part of its program for a republic. The intention underlying the clause, Revolutionary Alliance ideologues explained, was to use socialism to secure a solid economic and social basis for the republic they envisioned.

This clause would cause considerable dissension in Revolutionary Alliance ranks and, by the time the Alliance was transformed into the Guomindang in 1912, when the anti-Manchu Revolution had succeeded and a republic was established, it was dropped from the political program of the new party. Socialism was not an immediate issue of the Chinese Revolution, as even its proponents conceded, and the leadership of the Party decided to abandon it rather than to risk internal conflicts which would undermine the Party's quest for parliamentary supremacy in the elite-oriented politics of the early Republic. Sun himself did not give up his conviction in the necessity of socialist measures, but found that he was unable to keep his revolutionary program intact as he was shunted aside by the parliamentary leadership of the Party.[7]

The socialist program of the Revolutionary Alliance would be revived in later years as the failure of the republic once again pushed the Guomindang onto the path of revolution, and would form a cornerstone of the Party's revolutionary program in the 1920s. In the program rested the origins of the rather unique socialism of the Guomindang and of Sun Yat-sen, who was not just the "father of the Chinese Republic" but of Chinese socialism as well. Sun's program would serve as the model, remolded in Marxist cast, for the New Democratic program of the Communist Party of China with which the Communists initiated the new regime in 1949. While Sun's heirs in the Guomindang have not been too anxious to publicize the socialist legacy of the Party, at least since the 1930s when the left-wing of the Party was eliminated, these ideas have acquired a renewed significance in the People's Republic of China with the shift in development policies following the death of Mao Zedong.[8]

The sources and implications of these ideas have much to tell us about fundamental issues in Chinese socialism which, first enunciated in the political debates occasioned by the Revolutionary Alliance program, have remained alive during the century-long history of the socialist revolution in China. When the Revolutionary Alliance program was made public in 1905, it came under immediate attack by Liang Qichao, then the chief ideological spokesman for the reform-oriented constitutional monarchists. Liang himself had spoken favorably of socialism in preceding years, but turned against it when the Revolutionary Alliance conjoined socialism with its program for republican revolution. The debate which continued for two years in the pages of the Alliance organ *People's Journal* (*Minbao*) and Liang's own *People's Miscellany (Xinmin congbao)* was the first debate over socialism in Chinese politics. This debate was part of a more general discussion over the revolutionary ideology of the Alliance. The seriousness with which Revolutionary Alliance ideologues took their socialism is evident in the attention they paid to the issues it raised. What they had to say about socialism, and its relevance to China, is revealing of certain basic considerations that have shaped the Chinese discourse on socialism.

The central issue in the debate concerned the path of development that was most suited to China's needs and circumstances: the capitalist path that had accounted for European power versus a socialist path that would guarantee China development without the strains that capitalism had caused in European society. Revolutionary Alliance socialism was not intended to resolve the problems of a society that had already embarked on capitalism; rather, socialism was envisaged as the preferred path of development for a precapitalist society that inevitably faced a choice between capitalism and socialism. In its origins, in other words, Chinese socialism was as much a product of capitalism as socialism elsewhere; what distinguished it was the status of China as a society that was the object of foreign capitalism. This would lead to a peculiar perception of the relationship between socialism and capitalism that has characterized Chinese socialist thinking since then. What the debate between Revolutionary Alliance socialists and Liang Qichao had to say about this relationship not only has much to tell us about the Chinese attraction to socialism around the turn of the century, but also about basic ambiguities in Chinese socialist conceptions of socialism and capitalism that continue to puzzle students of Chinese socialism—and perhaps even its practitioners.

The reasons Chinese intellectuals were first attracted to socialism shed some light on the issues involved in the debate over Revolutionary Alliance socialism. A Chinese historian, Jiao Yihua, has compiled writings from the late nineteenth and early twentieth centuries pertinent to socialism.[9] His compilation shows that socialism was introduced to China through two sources. First were the missionary publications in China which, starting in the 1870s, began to report on the growing socialist movement in Europe, usually within the context of general discussions on European politics. While the knowledge of socialism that the Chinese could acquire through these sources was fragmentary, it did serve to acquaint them with the concept, as well as the social reform ideas favored by Western socialists, especially Christian socialists. Ironically, the most influential work introduced through this source was possibly Edward Bellamy's *Looking Backward,* which would seem to have continued to influence Chinese visions of what a socialist future might look like even after Chinese intellectuals had gained a more sophisticated understanding of socialism. Ideas on land nationalism, and criticisms of the capitalist system for its failure to meet its social responsibilities, also found their way into missionary publications. Martin Bernal has shown that some of this knowledge may have influenced Kang Youwei, the leader of the first radical reform attempt in 1898, whose influential utopian work *Datong shu* (The Book of Great Unity), was composed sometime during this period.[10] Beyond this, however, there is little indication that socialist ideas exerted any significant influence on Chinese thinking on change at this time. Kang's utopia had no bearing on his social and economic reform ideas. As Hsiao Kung-ch'uan has pointed out in his biography of Kang, Kang viewed capitalism as the only alternative for China even as he composed the utopian *Datong shu.* He believed, furthermore, that Western socialism was only a partial approximation of his own ideas, most of which were derivative of native utopianism, even if his sense of time derived its inspiration from the future.[11]

This situation changed as the Chinese came into firsthand contact with developed industrial society in Japan and the West. Much more important as a source for Chinese socialism was Japanese socialism with which Chinese intellectuals became familiar after 1901, when the number of Chinese going to Japan to acquire a modern education increased substantially. Most of the early proponents of socialism in China went through their conversion in Japan. Throughout the early phase of Chinese socialism, and well into the 1920s, Japanese translations and writings on socialism served as the primary source for Chinese understanding of socialism. The modern Chinese term for socialism, *shehui zhuyi,* was itself derived from Japanese (it was different from the term used by the missionaries). By 1903, a number of Japanese works on socialism had been translated into Chinese. And all the articles on Western socialism published in the *People's Voice* and the *People's Miscellany* were either translated from or informed by Japanese views on socialism. These works provided Chinese intellectuals with their first broad, and relatively systematic, glimpse into socialism in the West.

There is evidence that even as Chinese understanding of modern socialism grew, some among Chinese intellectuals continued to associate socialism with ideas from China's past. There was continued interchange, moreover, between the vocabulary of socialism and the vocabulary of premodern Chinese politics. But also evident was a significant shift of attitude toward socialism. Reversing Kang Youwei's attitude toward socialism as an approximation of native political ideals, Chinese intellectuals gradually came to view socialistic ideas and institutions inherited from the past as only partial approximations of modern socialism. When the former were invoked in defense of socialist policies, it was not to establish an equivalence between Chinese and Western ideals, or even to show the relevance of socialism to China, but only to "demonstrate" that socialism could be applied to China without awaiting industrialization. Native communitarian ideals were also reinterpreted from the perspective of Western ideas on community. The case of the anarchists, who used native vocabulary with the greatest frequency, shows that native concepts acquired significantly new associations after 1900. Within the few years following the turn of the century, Chinese intellectuals had become aware of the distinguishing features of modern socialist identity.

Greater acquaintance with foreign radicals and socialists was also an important element in this radicalization of the Chinese conception of socialism. At a time when the popularity of an idea in the West or in Japan sufficed to endow it with intellectual legitimacy, this was an important element in the Chinese interest in socialism. Don Price has shown that the example of the Russian nihilists of the nineteenth century played a significant part in the radicalization of Chinese intellectuals, who associated nihilism with socialism, albeit of an extreme kind.[12] This may have contributed to the interest in anarchism after 1907 but, before then, few Chinese showed genuine interest in "extreme socialism" except as an inspiration to action (the identification of nihilism with anarchism would continue into the 1920s, in the works of the anarchist novelist Ba Jin). Of greater relevance was the rise of a socialist movement in Japan during these years. This, however, occurred within the context of a society that was already beginning to show the strains of the first stages of industrialization, and the influence of Japanese socialists is ultimately indistinguishable as an influence on Chinese intellectuals from the latter's exposure to a capitalist society at work. If Chinese revolutionaries, as revolutionaries, identified with the socialist ideas that seemed to be spreading among radicals in other countries, the identification took place within the environment of a capitalism that signaled trouble for many in society. The radicalization of Chinese intellectuals to the point where they could sense an immediate relevance in socialism for China, in other words, was not simply an intellectual radicalization, but an intellectual radicalization that was nourished by direct encounter with the social strains created by capitalism.

Around the turn of the century, reform-minded Chinese confronted capitalism as a potential reality for China. While there had been a few unorthodox Chinese earlier who had advocated that China move toward an economic system similar to that of Western nations, the view that capitalism might be the only way to develop China gained in respectability only after 1895. The reform proposals of 1898 included state encouragement of commerce and industry, and influential writers began to argue that the source of Western strength lay in the dynamic spirit of desire, competition, and conquest that characterized the Western outlook on life; while "capitalism" itself was not used much as a term, the new values these writers proposed for Chinese emulation were indeed the values of laissez-faire capitalism.[13] Both Kang Youwei, the leader of the 1898 reform movement, and Yan Fu, the first scholar to introduce Western political theory, especially Social Darwinism, to Chinese thought, saw in the emulation of these values the key to China's future strength. Capitalism, in short, loomed large in speculation on China's material future.

This attitude provided the context within which Chinese intellectuals turned to socialism. Socialism, when it appeared in Chinese writings, appeared not as a solution to current economic problems, but as an alternative to capitalism that must be considered in planning for the future. It is not surprising that the first intellectuals who turned their attention to socialism seriously were those who had been exposed to capitalism abroad, where the problems of capitalist society were a good deal more visible than they were in China's Treaty Ports where it appeared mainly as a source of Western efficiency and strength. Sun Yat-sen, who was the first Chinese of stature to proclaim commitment to socialism, dated his conversion to his days in England in the late 1890s. As Schiffrin has written of Sun at this time:

> Contacts such as these (that is, with Western radicals), together with his intensive reading, infused Sun with a new understanding of European political trends. He became convinced that revolution, in some form or another, was a universal process. His first week in London had impressed him with the immensity of Europe's accomplishments, but when he left nine months later, he realized that the industrial revolution had not been beneficial to all segments of Western society. The first visit to the West laid the basis for his future antagonism to laissez-faire capitalism. What he saw and read gave Sun reason to believe that nothing short of a violent upheaval could provide a remedy for the lack of social concern

which had accompanied Western political and economic development. The signs of the coming turmoil and class struggle were all around him; Socialists and Fabians in Britain, Populists and Single-taxers in America—all were protesting against the unjust distribution of wealth. Labor unions were coming into their own and resorting to strikes with ominous frequency. Even non-socialist governments were passing social legislation, and change in the direction of socialism, of further state intervention in the economic order, now appeared inevitable.[14]

Lest this be attributed to Sun's unique disposition, we may look at Liang Qichao's thinking in the early 1900s, soon after he fled to Japan to avoid government persecution following the failure of the 1898 reform movement:

> From ancient times to the present, there have been only two main theories concerning ways of governing; intervention and laissez faire. . . . The trend of free competition led to the thriving of monopoly. The rich became richer, the poor became poorer. As a result, modern socialism arose. . . . It is clear that socialism will reach everywhere in the twentieth century. Therefore, I say that the twentieth century is an age for the complete triumph of intervention.[15]

Ultimately, it was not intellectual influence or the example of other radicals that turned Chinese intellectuals to socialism; it was the conditions of capitalist society. Socialism only showed a way out of those conditions. Around the turn of the century, moreover, it did not take a Chinese intellectual, resentful against the West for what the West had done to China, to perceive in those conditions an outlet for cultural or political frustrations. Social thinkers in the West, especially those who desired to avert a revolution, were gripped with a sense of urgency concerning the need to resolve the problems created by capitalism in society. It was capitalism in Japan, England, and the United States that awakened Chinese intellectuals to the problems of capitalism. It was not Lenin (who was undergoing his own radicalization about the same time) but Japanese, English, and American social thinkers that first made them cognizant of socialism and socialist policies as a possible means to resolving those problems.

What foreign exposure taught Chinese intellectuals was that capitalism was not the unequivocal path to wealth and power that it had seemed earlier. Chinese travelers to the West in the nineteenth century, ensconced in embassies or carefully guided by their Western sponsors, had missed much about Western society. As students or refugees from the Manchus, Chinese intellectuals of the early twentieth century had far greater exposure to the seamier sides of Western development, as well as to its critics. They were convinced quickly that China, in planning for the future, must take precautions to avoid the problems that had been produced by capitalism abroad. It was not incidental that

Sun Yat-sen, who himself was of a lowly class background, perceived these problems more keenly than many of his elite contemporaries abroad.

SOCIALISM AND SOCIAL REVOLUTION IN THE REVOLUTIONARY ALLIANCE

What marks 1905 as a date in the history of Chinese socialism was the inclusion in the Revolutionary Alliance program of precautions intended to ward off the undesirable consequences of capitalism in China. Though intended not as a cure for present ills but rather as a prophylactic against future eventualities, these precautions transformed socialism from a remote issue on which reformers and revolutionaries could agree, into an urgent issue of Chinese politics that provided one more cause for division between the two sides. The significance of the Revolutionary Alliance program did not lie simply in its advocacy of socialism, even if that would turn out to be quite significant in bringing out differences in economic thinking underlying fuzzy expressions of interest in socialism; it lay rather in its call for a social revolution which conjoined socialism to revolution. This was the first time that I am aware of that the term "social revolution" was used in Chinese political language, and over the years it would assume a central role in Chinese political thinking. At this time, its immediate consequence was to bring out serious divisions between reformers and revolutionaries in their economic vision of the future; especially over the issue of how to control capitalism in China without interfering with other developmental needs. The advocacy of social revolution triggered the debate, but it was the issue of the place of capitalism in China's future that provided its grounds.

One of the items incorporated into the Revolutionary Alliance program was "the equalization of land rights." The program did not explain the considerations that had led Sun and his faction in the Revolutionary Alliance to adopt this controversial policy. This was not the first time that Sun had induced his followers to accept it as part of his revolutionary program, and even now, it was not received with great enthusiasm. Over the next two years, the idea gained prominence because of the conspicuous place it held in the debate with Liang Qichao. The debate revealed that "land equalization" was the cornerstone of a socialist vision that included other elements, and was intended as a means of carrying China into a socialist future.

People's Journal writers described their socialism as *minsheng zhuyi*, better known in English as "People's Livelihood," one of Sun's Three Peoples Principles. While Hu Hanmin, one of the most articulate defenders of the program, remarked on one occasion that *minsheng* was better rendered "demosology" (original English) than socialism, there is no question that Sun and his followers viewed it as the equivalent of socialism.[16] They stated openly that *minsheng* was their version of Japanese *shakai shugi (shehui zhuyi),* and also used *minsheng* to describe the policies of European socialist parties.[17] Their policies reveal, moreover, that *minsheng zhuyi* was viewed as a current within world socialism. If they preferred this term, it was probably because, as Scalapino and Schiffrin have suggested, *minsheng* fits in nicely with *minzu* and *minquan* (Ethnicity and People's Sovereignty respectively), to make up the trio of Sun's revolutionary program.[18]

"Land Equalization" owed its inspiration to the American reformer Henry George's "single tax" proposal to resolve the problems of capitalist society. As with George, Revolutionary Alliance theoreticians believed that the problems of late nineteenth century society in the West arose from the private ownership of land, which pauperized the masses and obstructed the fulfillment of the promises of industrial society. Their premises, both ethical and practical, closely paralleled George's own ideas. George, following classical economic theory, believed that land and capital had to be distinguished in economic analysis. Land was natural, which implied both that it was a commodity of limited supply, and that it was not a product of human effort. The increase in its value was a consequence of the advance of civilization, not of any effort on the part of its owner. Capital, on the other hand, was a product of human labor and, therefore, unlimited in supply: its value derived from human effort. It followed that the evaluation of land and capital was subject to different economic and ethical criteria. As a limited commodity, land had a monopoly nature; its owners not only deprived others of their right to a basic resource of nature (comparable to "air and light"), but the concentration of land and capital in the same hands was the basic cause of oppression in capitalist society. For both ethical and economic reasons, land should not be allowed to come under the ownership of individuals who had contributed nothing to its value. George proposed to socialize not land but land rent (rural or urban) which, he believed, would remove a great obstacle to human happiness.[19]

This view was accepted in its totality by Sun and his followers. In the Revolutionary Alliance program, however, George's ideas were blended with those of Land Nationalists who advocated the socialization not just of rent but of property itself. In this scheme, land would come under government ownership to be allotted to the population on demand. The government would abolish all taxes other than the tax (or rent) on land. This, they believed, would not only release funds in society that would otherwise have been taxed, but provide the state with ever increasing income as the value of land went up with the advance of "civilization."[20]

The second component of the Revolutionary Alliance social program was the nationalization of "natural monopolies," which owed more to Richard Ely than to George in inspiration. After 1911, the "control of capital" would come to occupy a place in Sun's thought equal in stature to land nationalization. At this time, it was brought into the discussion as part of the debate over land. Nevertheless, given the fact that *People's Journal* writers saw in monopoly capital the greatest manifestation of inequality in the West, the measure was not an unimportant one. *People's Journal* writers did not argue that monopolies were a product of landownership; rather, they traced the origins of monopoly to economic competition. Nevertheless, they believed that certain resources and enterprises, like land, had a monopoly nature because of their scarcity and utility. Therefore, these, too, should be brought under public ownership (aside from natural resources such as mines, railroads were the primary concern here).[21]

These policies lent the *People's Journal* political argument a strong socialist coloring, especially when viewed in light of its insistence that the ultimate goal was no less than the abolition of classes through these measures. In some cases, such as that of Zhu Zhixin, the program sounded almost Leninist in its insistence on the transformation of the economy by a state that represented the will of the great majority of the people.[22]

Closer reading reveals that this vision was qualified by the process whereby the Revolutionary Alliance intended to achieve its goals. In the first place, the *People's Journal* advocacy of social revolution did not constitute a call for a social *revolution* but was perceived rather as a means to forestall just such an eventuality. As Sun Yat-sen said in a speech in late 1906: "When we undertake the ethnic and political revolutions, we must also think of a way to reform social and economic organization (so as to) forestall a social revolution at a later time. This is our greatest responsibility."[23]

Zhu Zhixin, who was theoretically the most radical of *People's Journal* writers, noted that China's transition to socialism would take a very long time; revolution was systemic change, not just disorder, and required a long period.[24] Hu Hanmin, the major spokesman for the Alliance in this discussion, added that not all revolution connoted upheaval and violence.[25] All *People's Journal* writers who contributed to the debate believed, following Sun, that while a violent revolution had become inevitable in the West (where "civilization" was too advanced), it would be relatively easy to prevent in China if appropriate measures were undertaken from the beginning of industialization. To quote Sun again: "If China undertakes *minsheng zhuyi* at the present, it will be easier to succeed as compared to Europe because social problems are the product of the advance of civilization. If the level of civilization is not high, social problems are not very serious."[26] The basis of this observation was that in backward areas land prices had not yet reached the astronomical levels that they had in the more "civilized" countries and would, therefore, be more amenable to government intervention. Besides, there would be less resistance to the government in the absence of a monopolistic class of wealthy landlords and capitalists.[27]

The key to revolution, secondly, was state socialism. Zhu and Hu both denied that the Revolutionary Alliance advocated "pure Communism." Zhu argued that "pure Communism" could not be achieved at the present but state socialism could be. This, he observed, represented the consensus in contemporary socialist thought, which had advanced considerably since the time of Marx.[28] The argument was echoed by Hu Hanmin and Feng Ziyu. Hu described Revolutionary Alliance socialism as "State Propertyism" *(Guochan zhuyi)*.[29] Feng's associations were even more revealing. Surveying the new trends toward social policy in Western nations and Japan, he pointed to *minsheng* as part of this world tide, emphasizing the benefits to development of policies formulated by the German government beginning with Bismarck.[30]

It was statements such as these which prompted Liang Qichao to observe, justifiably, that if this was the extent of Revolutionary Alliance socialism, it should be called reform through social policy, not socialism. Indeed, the debate between Revolutionary Alliance proponents of socialism and Liang Qichao is somewhat difficult to understand if it is viewed simply as the *People's Journal* defense of socialism against the attacks on socialism of the conservative Liang. Liang himself never repudiated socialism for being irrelevant to China. To be sure, he was wary in these years of any mention of revolution, social, political, or ethnic. And he saw in the advocacy of social revolution the danger of instigating to revolt the "riffraff" in society, "stupid people," as he called them (indeed, he perceived consequences to the Revolutionary Alliance advocacy similar to those of peasant uprisings in the past).[31] What is problematic, however, is the socialism of the Revolutionary Alliance which *People's Journal* writers exaggerated considerably. Liang was erroneous in suggesting that there was no important difference between his policies and those of the Revolutionary Alliance, but he was quite correct in questioning *People's Journal* writers' understanding of or commitment to socialism.

To describe the socialism of the Revolutionary Alliance as Marxist or Social Democratic, as Bernal has done, confuses the issues that were involved.[32] Though there were references to Marx in the debate, and the *People's Journal* published a number of articles dealing with Marx's life and thought within the broader context of European socialism, *People's Journal* writers did not profess any commitment to Marxist ideas of revolution, nor did they display any appreciation of or interest in the problematic nature of the relationship between political theory and political action in Marxism. Discussions of the Materialist Conception of History and class struggle were available in Japanese sources on socialism, such as Kotoku Shusui's *The Essence of Socialism,* even if these sources themselves did not display a grasp of the finer points of Marxism.[33]

These aspects of Marxism were ignored in translations into Chinese. Most of the translations published in the *People's Journal* were from general histories of socialism that made attempts to classify the confusing range of social movements that had arisen by the end of the nineteenth century. These histories, written by moderate or Christian socialists, such as William Bliss, Richard Ely, and Thomas Kirkup, did not give Marx's views a particularly prominent place and were wary, if not outright critical, of Marx's ideas on the revolutionary transformation of society.[34] In these works, democratic socialism and anarchism appeared as the two major currents in contemporary European socialism, with communism associated primarily with anarchism. Social democracy, which was viewed favorably, if not with complete approval, appeared as an improvement over original Marxism to the extent that it had lost its revolutionary thrust.[35]

The question here is not whether or not social democracy is properly Marxist, but rather that the Chinese, in the sources to which they were exposed, were offered a highly partial view of Marxism, one that not only disguised the problems of Marxist political theory, but even tended to portray as relevant only those offshoots of Marxism that fell in with the intentions underlying the social reform movements of the late nineteenth century.

People's Journal writers saw no problem, therefore, in asserting that "pure Communism" had been repudiated in late nineteenth-century scientific thought, or even in referring to social democracy and Bismarckian reforms in the same breath. The social problem was to them a problem of the division of society into the minority rich and the majority poor that could be resolved by appropriate controls over economic individualism, without a necessary transformation of capitalist social relations. By the late nineteenth century, one did not have to be a Marxist or a socialist to endorse such reforms. *People's Journal* writers used their sources eclectically in drawing up plans to avoid the less desirable aspects of capitalism in China; Marxist ideas appeared in their analyses only to the extent that they had become part of a common stock of ideas underlying the social protest movements of the late nineteenth century.

By far the greatest influence on their thinking were Henry George, a one-time mayoral candidate for New York City (and, ironically, an advocate of Chinese exclusion in the United States), and Richard Ely, a professor of economics at Wisconsin, neither of whom was recognized as a socialist in the West, a point that was apparently happily conceded by both individuals. That neither of these authors was anticapitalist per se did not bother Chinese socialists who wholeheartedly endorsed their views. When Liang confronted them with the observation that socialists took land to be a function of capital, and not vice versa, they turned to the defense of George's views with even greater enthusiasm than before. This was not simply a function of the dynamics of debate but an expression of Revolutionary Alliance socialism which, as with George or Ely, sought not to abolish capitalism but to contain it. Their objection was primarily to contemporary monopoly capitalism where one group seemed to toil without reward while the other lived idly off the interest from capital. They viewed as well-deserved capital that which had been accumulated through individual effort: Zhu observed that Marx's views on capital as "plunder" were well suited to explaining contemporary capitalism but was off the mark with regard to early capitalism when capital accumulation had represented individual effort.[36] Capitalism, they agreed with George, was beneficial insofar as it remained untainted by landownership. Consequently, the socialization of the economy that they envisaged did not preclude the continued existence of capitalism, only its dissociation from landownership and monopoly.

Minsheng zhuyi, designed to anticipate problems that would arise in Chinese society with the emergence of capitalism, was fashioned eclectically out of competing, even conflicting, ideas on how to resolve the "social question" in the West. Sun identified causally socialism and sociology.[37] Feng Ziyu completed his discussion of the possibility of socialism in China with an injunction to study "socialism; within socialism, land nationalism; within land nationalism, the single-tax theory."[38] George's ideas were placed within the context of socialism as its most accomplished product. *People's Journal* writers were well aware that the ideas they incorporated in their socialism represented divergent currents in European social thought, as Hu Hanmin hinted when he remarked that *minsheng* was somewhat different from socialism.[39] This eclecticism may have been a product of practical wisdom, naive idealism, or a combination of both. That *People's Journal* writers were not naive visionaries was evident in their emphasis on the practical benefits that would accrue to Chinese society from the institution of their policies. And their socialism makes a great deal more sense if it is understood not as a substitute for capitalism, but as a means of controlling capitalism in a society that was yet to experience capitalist development.

The focal points of the debate between Revolutionary Alliance writers and Liang Qichao further reveal that the real issue was not socialism, but the implications for China's national development of controlling capitalist growth. The basic points of contention were: how serious was the need to incorporate in current political programs policies designed to counteract inequalities that would arise from China's development under capitalism; and what effect would these policies have on the development of production?

On the first point, both sides agreed that China at the present did not suffer from the division between rich and poor that, they believed, would soon bring disaster to European society. On the other hand, they differed widely on how soon such inequalities should be expected to arise, which reflected their differences over the nature and origins of inequality in the West. Both Liang and his Revolutionary Alliance opponents, following their Western sources, especially Ely, saw contemporary capitalism as monopoly capitalism. There was no room for a middle class under conditions of monopoly capital, with the result that society was divided into two camps of rich and poor. They agreed further that the free enterprise system that had come into being in the late eighteenth century had contributed to the exacerbation of this situation. Here they parted ways. Revolutionary Alliance writers saw the contemporary situation as a product of the industrial revolution and laissez faire economics; in other words, industrial capitalism. Liang saw inequality to be endemic in European history; industrial capitalism had only made worse a deep division European society had inherited from its medieval past, when society had been divided into the two classes of noble landowners and commoner peasants. Returning to Chinese history, he argued that the class system in China had broken down two thousand years ago, with the supersession of feudalism by an imperial political system. The absence of monopolistic control over land by the nobility, combined with the equal inheritance system (that is, the equal division of land among offspring), has prevented the accumulation of wealth in the hands of a minority. On the other hand, light taxation by the government has allowed the hard working and the meritorious to accumulate some wealth with the result that a middle class *(zhongchan jieji)* had come into being that comprised the majority of the population. It followed that even with the growth of monopolistic enterprises in China, wealth would be evenly distributed since this middle class would invest in the new enterprises to become a sizable middle class of stockowners.[40]

Revolutionary Alliance writers, who rooted inequality in industrial capitalism, had no such faith, and believed that inequality would arise immediately with China's industrialization under capitalism. Hence the need for socialist policies. The one who went furthest in advocating social revolution was Zhu Zhixin who argued that inequality in China did not match that in the West, but believed that revolution was necessary even at present because of the existence of private property which lay at the basis of inequality.[41] Zhu was possibly the only genuine social revolutionary among Revolutionary Alliance socialists, and would remain so until his death in 1921.

On the second point, Liang argued that China's most urgent need was not distribution but production. If the problem of production was not resolved, not only would there be nothing to distribute but China's economic sovereignty would be threatened. In an era of economic competition (which he compared to war), Liang argued, developed nations in search of markets for their capital would take control of production in China, with the result that the country would end up being divided into two classes of foreign capitalists and Chinese laborers. The only way to prevent this eventuality was to develop capitalism rapidly. The state should take measures to facilitate capitalist activity, while it should enact policies for the protection of labor (e.g., regulation of hours and wages, unemployment insurance, and the like).[42]

Liang's position that capitalism was the only means to develop China hardened as the debate proceeded. He believed, as had his teacher Kang Youwei, that the desire to achieve individual ends was the motive force of economic activity and had been the source of economic development in the West; conversely, equality, in obstructing desire, would serve only to hamper development, and might even lead to the regress of civilization.[43] Secondly, Liang argued that state participation in the economy (except to encourage capitalism) would lead to abuse and inefficiency, especially in the absence of talent. As he saw it, Revolutionary Alliance proposals would only lead to the conversion of the state into a giant monopoly that would oppress the whole society. It certainly would not bring any benefits to the people.[44]

These were arguments in criticism of socialism that have been heard repeatedly in China since Liang's time. Likewise, the Revolutionary Alliance response to Liang enunciated arguments that would become part of a stock of ideas in favor of socialism in ensuing years: that China would develop faster *and* in greater unity under socialism than under an unbridled capitalism.

Hu Hanmin, who offered the most systematic response to Liang, did not dispute the need for increased production, but criticized Liang for overlooking the relationship between production and distribution. Distribution of product involved return to capital (interest), labor (wages), and land (rent). How these were apportioned had enormous influence on production. He himself focused on land rent. The remuneration for land meant that a good portion of the return from production went to those who made no contribution to the productive process (since, in accordance with George's ideas, land represented not human effort but simply a natural resource). The private ownership of land, in other words, had adverse effects not only on distribution but also on production. Capital, which could be used for production was diverted to the purchase of land, which was unproductive and only brought an unearned income to the owner. For the same reason, investment in land led to the fragmentation of capital which was undesirable, especially within the context of a society that needed capital accumulation.[45]

Both of these harmful tendencies could be curtailed if land were nationalized. If the state could become the "big landlord" in society, it would also become, by the same virtue, the big capitalist (though Hu did not use the term, his argument was reminiscent of what Marxists would describe as "primitive accumulation" through state agency two decades later). The state, through landownership, would accumulate capital which it would then invest in productive enterprises. This, in Hu's view, would make for much faster economic development. On the other hand, state ownership of land would prevent the accumulation of two factors of production, land and capital, in the same hands, and thereby prevent the oppression of the third, labor. Not only would labor cease to be dependent on capitalists and landowners because of the new access it would gain to land, but the more rapid development of production would improve the condition of labor as the product would not be distributed only between capital and labor.[46]

Hu's treatment of potential problems that might arise from the institution of equality or the state ownership of land followed a similar reasoning. The redistribution of product, he argued, would create a *tendency* to equality; the equality that the Revolutionary Alliance envisaged according to him was not absolute, or numerical, but rather relative, or "psychological," equality. Hu compared his idea of economic equality to the political equality that existed under a government of laws (constitutional government) where all were equal before the law. The inequality that arose under such a system would be a consequence not of position or monopoly but of differences in talent and effort; in other words, individual merit.[47]

Hu's argument shows readily that Revolutionary Alliance egalitarianism, while genuine, was quite circumscribed. Sun and other Revolutionary Alliance writers shared Liang's belief that egalitarianism would lead to laziness and stagnation, which is not surprising given the hold of social Darwinian ideas of competition and conflict in Chinese thinking around the turn of the century. By egalitarianism they understood equality of opportunity, and believed that their policies would benefit not only the common people but commercial and industrial entrepreneurs as well. That they did not see these views to be inconsistent with their "socialism" was due to their preoccupation with land; they accepted readily the quite "capitalist" premise that the capitalist entrepreneur, like the laborer, produced wealth that accrued to the benefit of the whole society. Zhu's observation that the existence of private property was inconsistent with the achievement of a socialized economy may have been accepted by other Revolutionary Alliance writers;[48] the abolition of private property was pushed so far into the future, however, that it is more proper to speak of it as a component of the Revolutionary Alliance vision than as part of its program of economic reorganization.

Hu also dismissed Liang's fear of the state becoming a despotic monopoly under the Revolutionary Alliance program. He pointed out, in the first place, that in a constitutional system, the state would be representative of the people; hence its activities would be beneficial to all. As with other Revolutionary Alliance writers, Hu believed that the achievement of the goals of Republicanism and socialism were interdependent. Secondly, the state was not to monopolize all economic activity, he explained, but only that which had a tendency toward "natural monopoly." Beyond this, there would be a broad realm of free economic activity with which there would be no interference.[49]

Last, but not least, Hu denied that imperialism presented a threat to China. Accusing Liang of confounding political and economic questions, he argued that international commerce would actually be beneficial to China's development. Foreigners investing in China would take away funds in the form of profit and interest (on capital), but the wages and the rent that they paid would increase China's wealth and, therefore, contribute to development. It was only necessary for China to see to it that foreigners did not use political means to gain economic advantages. Besides, he pointed out, if it came to competition, government monopolies would have greater resources than private enterprises to compete successfully with foreigners.[50] It need not be emphasized that these views on imperialism were also consistent with the Revolutionary Alliance economic outlook. Imperialism as a reason for the institution of socialism in China would not enter the consideration of socialists for another decade.

This was the essence of Hu's refutation of Liang's arguments against socialism. The debate continued over the next few issues of the *People's Journal,* and ceased only toward the end of 1907, when a change in political circumstances in China drew the participants to other activities than publication. Following Hu's long article, it turned into a highly numerical discussion of social policies, focusing on issues of how land value could be fixed and the overall practicality of the program. Hu's article had offered some figures on the increased revenue to the government that would be possible with the institution of the new policies. Liang had argued earlier that without exchange on the market, there would be no way to determine the value of land; now he went on to question Hu's figures. As others rushed to Hu's defense, the question of land values, as well as all other issues, were forgotten as each side generated more elaborate figures to prove that it was closer to the realities of Chinese government finances. There was no refutation, especially since neither side based its figures on any serious investigation. Possibly the only effect of the debate over social policy was to impress on the minds of Revolutionary Alliance ideologues the possibilities that land offered as a means to financing China's development.[51]

THE SIGNIFICANCE OF THE DEBATE

What does the debate reveal concerning differences between Liang and the Revolutionary Alliance, the nature of Revolutionary Alliance socialism, and its implications for socialist thought in later years? The two sides were obviously divided over the issue of capitalism in China's development. They agreed on the historical advance represented by capitalism, and its beneficial contributions as well as divisive consequences. They differed in the way they weighed its advantages against its disadvantages and, therefore, in their evaluation of the tolerable level of limitations to be placed on its practice in China. Their arguments involved both ethical and practical considerations. Liang believed individual desire to be the motive force of economic activity. Since in his view what China needed most was economic development, he disapproved of any limitations on private enterprise beyond what was needed to protect laborers.

Revolutionary Alliance writers insisted that public welfare was the goal of development, and maintained that the redistribution of resources from the private to the public sector would actually speed up development. They advocated extensive state involvement in the economy both in production and distribution, but also favored the retention of a large capitalist sector. The combination, they believed, would develop China faster while keeping away the evils of capitalism. Revolutionary Alliance ambivalence toward capitalism was to be inherited by the Guomindang which, even at the height of its radicalism in the 1920s, would not repudiate capitalism—and even use against its Communist critics arguments similar to those Liang directed at the Revolutionary Alliance at this time. That much of the support for the Revolutionary Alliance came from coastal business, it has been suggested, was a basic determinant of its economic outlook. This is plausible only if we remember that the association did not keep the Revolutionary Alliance from threatening speculation in real estate, which had already emerged as a source of wealth in China's coastal cities.

Secondly, Revolutionary Alliance writers assigned a far greater role to land in development than did Liang, who was more urban development-oriented. Liang did not appreciate the problem of land; as with many economists, socialist or otherwise, he believed that land derived its value from exchange and was, therefore, indistinguishable from capital; its value was simply a function of capitalist development. Revolutionary Alliance writers themselves paid little actual attention to the agrarian problems of China (they were, with George, concerned primarily with land values in urban areas), but they did view land as an independent source of wealth, even of capital. Whatever the merits of their argument, it is apparent that in an agrarian society such as China, it reflected a radical awareness at a time when capitalist economic models had already made a significant impact on Chinese thinking on development.

The debate over capitalism was also revealing of the two sides' conceptualization of the relationship between state and society that they envisaged.

Liang, the constitutional monarchist, favored far more autonomy for society than was allowed for by the Republicans. The latter did not see economic intervention of the state in society as a source of oppression but as an articulation of essential unity, as the promise of Republicanism fulfilled: the expression of a "social state" *(shehuidi guojia).*[52] Liang, however, viewed state intervention as a source of potential despotism. This was not simply out of opposition to state intervention in society or the economy, which he viewed himself as a "world tide" in the contemporary era. He believed, however, that capitalism, which had proven its developmental power in the West, offered the best means to China's development. At the same time, he was possibly more aware than Revolutionary Alliance writers that a policy of socialization would be more likely to breed conflict than harmony and unity; and he could not countenance the prospect of social conflict any more than he could ethnic or political conflict. It is also worth remembering that the elite class in which Liang had his origins had more to lose than gain from government social policies; Liang himself was all for government intervention insofar as it contributed to commercial and industrial activity.

The socialization of the economy reinforced the Republican argument for greater unity between state and society; which implied not only greater state activity, but also greater social involvement in politics. To this, Liang was opposed. The unity that he desired was to be achieved through ideological transformation: the cultivation of a sense of loyalty to state and society. While Liang was more pessimistic than Revolutionary Alliance writers on the divisions created by inequality in the West, he was willing to tolerate inequality in China on the grounds that it would contribute to national development. Unlike the Revolutionary Alliance writers who believed, at least formally, that national ends were interdependent with social justice, Liang held that national development had to take precedence over social justice. His definition of "public morality" as loyalty to polity was more limited than his opponents' view that economic equality was but the fulfillment of the promise of public morality.[53]

In spite of these significant differences, however, Liang and his Revolutionary Alliance opponents were political contemporaries in the common belief they shared in the efficacy of "political solutions to social problems." While this attitude was quite evident in the case of Liang, it was no less true for the Republicans. Zhu Zhixin suggested on one occasion that the social revolution must serve as the foundation for the political; nevertheless, the social and the political were distinguished in the Revolutionary Alliance conception of politics, and the state was placed above society, endowed with the power of autonomous activity to dispose of social problems. Hence Revolutionary Alliance writers were able to ignore the question of interest articulation in the reorganized state that was not only to guide but even to participate in a mixed economy; not just in the sense of extension of the conflicts of civil society into the state, but also in the sense of the emergence of autonomous state interests that might be at odds with the interests of society. Hence also their faith in the ability of politics to control capitalism and to avert a social revolution. Even more revealing was the fact that Revolutionary Alliance writers (with the possible exception of Zhu Zhixin) did not give much thought to finding a means whereby to incorporate in politics the common people for whose future they showed so much concern. Indeed, the control of revolutionary tendencies among the people was as much a concern to them as was the control of capital. Their ambivalence over the question of classes as well as their ambivalence toward capital would become lasting features of the Guomindang conception of revolution as expressed in Sun's Three Peoples Principles. Their reliance on the state to dispose of social problems marked the emergence of a corporatist reasoning that would characterize much of Chinese socialist thinking over the years.

The socialism of the Revolutionary Alliance is better described by a term that has gained currency since then: noncapitalist development. The term is residual as a concept, but then there was much in Revolutionary Alliance socialism that was residual. Significantly, this is the term that Guomindang leaders used in the 1920s to distinguish the Three Peoples Principles from communism. Socialism in the Revolutionary Alliance conception was not an alternative to capitalism but a means to control it. This conception was derived not so much from socialism as from late nineteenth-century reformers in the West who advocated modifications in laissez faire capitalism in order to avert the danger of socialism and social revolution. Unlike with socialism, the Revolutionary Alliance argument denied the central role played by capital in capitalist society. And it ignored questions raised by class conflict and class interest in society. Revolutionary Alliance writers for the most part perceived society not in terms of classes but in terms of rich and poor. This was especially the case with their understanding of Chinese society where, they believed, there was no serious question of class oppression and exploitation because the gap between the rich and poor was not comparable to that in capitalist society. Their land program was intended not to relieve the suffering of the people, but to prevent the emergence of inequality!

Instead Revolutionary Alliance socialism offered the prospect of equitable development that would avoid the pitfalls of capitalism that had become evident in the course of Western development. In a sense, the deficiencies of this socialism as socialism were also its strengths when we consider its relationship to its political and intellectual context. It offered the promise of preventing inequality, but also the prospect of development and unity, two central preoccupations of the period. Indeed, no version of socialism would succeed in Chinese politics then or later that did not address these two questions. On the other hand, the socialism of the Revolutionary Alliance, however wanting it may have been as socialism, introduced significant new problems into Chinese thought on national development: how to secure development without creating severe inequality; the role of capitalism in China's development; the role of land as a source of wealth and inequality; the economic relationship between state and society and its consequences for politics. Above all else, it presented Chinese thinkers with the challenge of a conception of politics that was not merely political, but social and economic as well.

ECHOES

The debate between the Revolutionary Alliance and Liang articulated issues that remain central to Chinese socialist thinking to this day. These involved issues of the relative attention to be given to production and distribution in economic growth, the implications of economic egalitarianism for economic development, the role the state should play in economic activity, both internally and as guarantor of economic autonomy for the nation. These issues crystallized around the question of the relationship of capitalism to socialism, the one perceived generally as the best way to achieve rapid growth of production, the other as a principle of distributive justice that, in guaranteeing social cohesion and stability, would further the goal of national economic development.

These issues would resurface periodically at critical moments of the Chinese Revolution. In the 1920s, in the course of the conflicts over the Guomindang and the Communist strategies of revolution, the Guomindang would bring against the Communists charges that were quite similar to those that Liang Qichao directed against Revolutionary Alliance socialism: that the Communists sought to sacrifice progress in production to a "petit-bourgeois" preoccupation with distribution.[54] After 1940, the Communists were to modify their own pursuit of revolution with the idea of "New Democracy," which presupposed a strategy of development that drew directly on Sun Yat-sen's idea of socialism: the New Democracy idea allowed for the continued existence of "capitalism" in the transition to socialism in order to secure the rapid development of the forces of production.[55] The same issues have resurfaced in recent years with the postrevolutionary interpretation of socialism by the current Chinese leadership which seeks to expand the scope of capitalist methods in economic activity in order to promote rapid advances in production.

This is not to suggest that these issues have carried the same meaning at all times. The sources Chinese socialists drew on to articulate their socialism changed radically over the years, and old problems assumed additional dimensions with the changing circumstances of the revolution. It is possible to make a case, however, that through all these changes, the basic problematic of socialism enunciated in its earliest phase has remained unaltered; indeed, it may not be farfetched to view the Chinese Revolution as one long and tortuous effort to reconcile the contradictions that were first articulated in the debate between the Revolutionary Alliance and Liang. The widespread puzzlement over the nature and future of Chinese socialism in our day is a product of uncertainties concerning socialism in Chinese thinking, including the thinking of the Communist leadership, that are not far removed from the ambivalence toward socialism that lay at the very origins of the socialist discourse in China. The question is not whether Chinese socialists, now or then, have taken their socialism seriously. Contrary to much wishful thinking in China and abroad, China's leaders today are every bit as serious about their socialism as their predecessors in Chinese socialism who, from the very start, saw in socialism "the only way out for China."[56] If anything, they have a greater stake in upholding socialism than before if only because the very legitimacy of the regime they lead rests on sustained faith in the desirability and possibility of socialism. The question, rather, lies in the equivocal status that Chinese socialist thinking has from the start assigned to socialism, not out of hesitation about the necessity of socialism but because of a profound ambiguity which is built into the very conceptualization of socialism.

Socialism first appeared in Chinese thought not as a revolutionary conception of new, postcapitalist, order but as a principle for the control of capitalism, a higher stage of capitalism, as it were, that would correct the deficiencies of laissez-faire capitalism. While China's first socialists conceived of socialism and capitalism as two alternative strategies of development that they were free to choose between, they did not think them to be mutually exclusive alternatives. They hoped, indeed, that capitalism (or private entrepreneurship) could be made to serve China's economic development, while socialist measures would help contain the social divisions that must be created by the inevitable concentration of capital under an unchecked capitalism, and guarantee equitable *and* efficient development. In either case, the considerations that determined choice of strategy had little to do with the virtues of capitalism or socialism as social systems: in this conceptualization, neither socialism nor capitalism appeared as utopianized expressions of alternative visions of the good society, or even as utopian projections of class interest, but as strategies in the fulfillment of a national project.

The conception of socialism (as of capitalism) was an instrumental one: as a means to the realization of the double tasks of state-building and economic development called for by the emergent nationalist conception of China. This conception provided the context for the Revolutionary Alliance argument for socialism which, while it was not oblivious to questions of class oppression and social injustice, nevertheless rested not on conviction in socialism as a goal in its own right but on the promise it offered as a strategy of national development. Hence also its basic conviction that with socialist measures in place, capitalism need not be abolished but could be made to serve developmental needs.

In later years, as the Chinese Revolution unfolded, socialism and capitalism would be distinguished much more sharply, and assume the character of class-based ideologies in inevitable contradiction. And yet socialist ambivalence toward capitalism, paralleled by an ambivalence over the question of class interest versus national interest, would never be too far beneath the surface of socialist thinking as long as socialism remained wedded to a national project of development. It is this same ambivalence that has resurfaced with the winding down of the revolution in China, and the turn of attention once again to national unity and development. What needs to be remembered, as we puzzle over whether or not China is headed for capitalist restoration, is that the revival of "capitalist" strategies of development in order to promote production represents not an unthinking slide into capitalism from a socialism that is its irreconcilable alternative, but a controlled process over which socialism stands guard. On the other hand, recognition of this conception of socialism, which is as old as the history of socialism in China—socialism not as a substitute for but a limit to capital—may help us better appreciate why China's socialists, with all their seemingly "unsocialist" behavior, are very serious about the socialism that they continue to uphold.

NOTES

1. The "re-privatization" of the Chinese economy has encouraged hopes that capitalism is once again on the ascendancy, and would seem to have strengthened the resolve of conservative states people such as Prime Minister Margaret Thatcher to "bury socialism." See David Winder, "Governments Put Themselves Out of Business Worldwide," *Christian Science Monitor* 79, no. 125 (May 26, 1987).

2. John Kautsky, *Communism and the Politics of Development* (New York: John Wiley & Sons, 1969), 93–94.

3. Robert Tucker, *The Marxian Revolutionary Idea* (New York: W. W. Norton & Co., 1969), chapter 6.

4. Adam Ulam, *The Unfinished Revolution* (New York: Vintage Books, 1964), 45.

5. *Time* magazine named Deng Xiaoping "Man of the Year" in 1984 and again in 1985. In the latter year, it was joined by the *National Review*. In each case, Deng's

efforts to bring capitalism into Chinese economy played a prominent part in his choice for the honor.

6. I do not mean to suggest that because the Maoist–Cultural Revolutionary version of socialism was egalitarian in ideology, it therefore achieved or promised to achieve an egalitarian society. Nevertheless, the two understandings of socialism differ radically in their *ideological* stances over the question of equality. The instrumental version of socialism presented equality primarily as "equality of opportunity." Contemporary Chinese socialism has gone even further to declare egalitarianism "the enemy of socialism." See Arif Dirlik, "Socialism without Revolution: The Case of Contemporary China," *Pacific Affairs* 54, no. 4 (Winter 1981–1982): 632–61.

7. For Sun's continued interest in socialism, see the speech he gave before the Chinese Socialist Party in 1912, *Sun Zhongshan shehui zhuyitan* [A Discussion of Socialism by Sun Yat-sen] (n.p., 1912).

8. Chen Keqing, "Shi lun Sun Zhongshandi jingji jianshe sixiang" [Discussion of Sun Yat-sen's Thinking on Economic Reconstruction], *Jingji yanjiu* [Economic Research], no. 2 (1980): 45–51. By the fiftieth anniversary of the founding of the People's Republic, two decades after the beginning of the "reforms," Sun was enshrined by the Communist Party in a status at least equal to that of Mao's.

9. Jiao Yihua, *Shehui zhuyi xueshuo zai Zhongguodi chuqi chuanpo* [The Initial Propagation of Socialist Theories in China] (Shanghai: Fudan University Press, 1983).

10. Martin Bernal, *Chinese Socialism to 1907* (Ithaca, NY: Cornell University Press, 1976), 25.

11. Hsiao Kung-ch'uan, *A Modern China and a New World* (Seattle: University of Washington Press, 1975), 318.

12. Don Price, *Russia and the Roots of the Chinese Revolution* (Cambridge, MA: Harvard University Press, 1973), 125.

13. Hsiao, *A Modern China*, 301–35.

14. Harold Schiffrin, *Sun Yat-sen and the Origins of the Chinese Revolution* (Berkeley: University of California Press, 1970), 136.

15. Liang Qichao, "Ganshe yu fangren" [Intervention and Laissez-faire], in *The Introduction of Socialism into China*, ed. Li Yu-ning, 8–9 (New York: Columbia University Press, 1971).

16. Minyi (Hu Hanmin), "Gao feinan minsheng zhuyizhe" [Response to Opponents of the Principle of People's Livelihood], *Minbao*, no. 12 (March 6, 1907): 45–154, 126.

17. Sun Wen, Speech at the First Anniversary Celebration of the *Minbao* (December 2, 1906). See *Minbao*, no. 10 (December 22, 1906): 7–14.

18. Robert A. Scalapino and H. Schiffrin, "Early Socialist Currents in the Chinese Revolutionary Movement: Sun Yat-sen vs. Liang Ch'i-ch'ao," *Journal of Asian Studies*, 18, no. 3 (May 1969): 334.

19. Charles Gide and Charles Rist, *A History of Economic Doctrines* (London: George C. Harrap and Co., 1964), 588–92.

20. Sun Wen, Speech, 8–12.

21. Xian Jie (Zhu Zhixin), "Cong shehui zhuyi lun tiedao guoyou ji Zhongguo tiedaozhi guanban siban" [A Discussion of Railroad Nationalization from the Perspective of Socialism and the Problem of Official versus Private Management of Chinese Railroads], *Minbao*, no. 4 (June 29, 1906): 45–56.

22. Xian Jie (Zhu Zhixin), "Lun shehui zhuyi geming dang yu zhengzhi geming bingxing" [On the Necessity of the Simultaneous Institution of the Social and Political Revolutions], *Minbao*, no. 5 (June 29, 1906): 43–66.

23. Sun Wen, Speech, 7.

24. Xian Jie, "Lun shehui zhuyi," 49–50.

25. Minyi, "Gao feinan minsheng zhuyizhe," 49.

26. Sun Wen, Speech, 9.

27. Ziyou (Feng Ziyou), "Lun Zhongguo ribao minsheng zhuyi yu Zhongguo zhengzhi geming qiantu" [Reprint from *China Daily* of the Principle of People's Livelihood and the Future of China's Political Revolution], *Minbao*, no. 4 (May 1, 1906): 97–122, 109.

28. Xian Jie, "Lun shehui zhuyi," 45.

29. Hanmin (Hu Hanmin), "Minbaozhi liuda zhuyi" [The Six Great Principles of *Minbao*], *Minbao*, no. 3 (April 18, 1906): 1–22, 11.

30. Ziyou, "Lun Zhongguo," 109.

31. Liang Qichao, "Shehui zhuyi guowei jinri Zhongguo suobiyao hu?" [Does China Need Socialism Today?], *Xinmin congbao*, no. 86 (July 15, 1906): 1–52, 51.

32. Bernal, *Chinese Socialism to 1907*, 225.

33. Kotoku Shusui, *The Essence of Socialism*, trans. Sharon Sievers (Ph.D. diss., Stanford University, 1969).

34. See, W. D. P. Bliss, *Handbook of Socialism* (New York: C. Scribner's Sons, 1895); Richard Ely, *French and German Socialism in Modern Times* (New York: Harper, 1883); and *Socialism: An Examination of Its Nature, Its Strengths, and Its Weaknesses, with Suggestions for Social Reform* (New York: Thomas Y. Crowell and Co., 1894); and Thomas Kirkup, *History of Socialism*, 5th ed. (London: A. C. Black, 1913).

35. Bernal, *Chinese Socialism to 1907*, 78. For George, see George R. Geiger, *The Philosophy of Henry George* (New York: Macmillan, 1933).

36. Shi Shen (Zhu Zhixin), "Deyizhi shehui gemingzhe xiaozhuan" [Brief Biographies of German Socialists], *Minbao*, nos. 2, 3 (November 26, 1905 and April 5, 1906): 1–19 and 1–50, respectively. Citation in no. 2: 15, 17.

37. Quoted in Liang, "Shehui zhuyi guowei," 28. See also Hu's defense of Sun's usage in Minyi, "Gao feinan minsheng zhuyizhe," 145–46.

38. Ziyou, "Lun Zhongguo," 122.

39. Minyi, "Gao feinan minsheng zhuyizhe," 53–66.

40. Liang, "Shehui zhuyi guowei," 10–14.

41. Xian Jie, "Lun shehui zhuyi," 57.

42. Liang, "Shehui zhuyi guowei," 16–19, 20.

43. Liang, "Shehui zhuyi guowei," 23–24. For Kang, see Hsiao, *Modern China*, 318.

44. Liang, "Shehui zhuyi guowei," 24.

45. Minyi, "Gao feinan minsheng zhuyizhe," 30–33.

46. Minyi, "Gao feinan minsheng zhuyizhe," 58.

47. Hu at one point appealed to the authority of Marx and Engels to justify his defense of the retention of private property. See Minyi, "Gao feinan minsheng zhuyizhe," 100.

48. Xian Jie, "Lun shehui zhuyi," 65–66. Also see Hanmin, "Minbaozhi liuda zhuyi," 11.

49. Minyi, "Gao feinan minsheng zhuyizhe," 57.

50. Minyi, "Gao feinan minsheng zhuyizhe," 38.

51. For this debate see Bernal, *Chinese Socialism to 1907,* 162–97.

52. Sun Wen, Speech, 10.

53. Liang Qichao, "Xinmin shuo" [On the New Citizen], in *Xinhai gemingqian shinian jian shilun xuanji* [Selections from Discussions on Current Affairs during the Ten Years Preceding the 1911 Revolution] (Beijing: Sanlian shudian, 1978), vol. 1, pt. 1, 118–56, especially the section entitled "Lun gongde" [On Public Morality], 123–27.

54. Arif Dirlik, *Revolution and History: Origins of Marxist Historiography in China, 1919–1937* (Berkeley: University of California Press, 1978), 78.

55. Mao Zedong, "On New Democracy," *Selected Works,* II (Beijing: Foreign Languages Press, 1965), 339–84.

56. The slogan, "Only Socialism Can Save China," was heard frequently during the 1980s, when Chinese society in transition appeared to be in a constant state of crisis. For an example, see a *Hongqi* [Red Flag] editorial discussion reprinted in *Renmin ribao* [People's Daily], February 15, 1987.

3

National Development and Social Revolution in Early Chinese Marxist Thought

Studies of communism in China reveal a strong element of nationalism in the acceptance and interpretation of communism from Li Dazhao to Mao Zedong. The concern of Chinese Communists with the plight of the Chinese nation has led to two significant revisions of communism in its Marxist-Leninist form: the elevation of national over class struggle and the consequent eclipsing of the proletariat by the "people." Maurice Meisner says of Li Dazhao, whom he regards as the forerunner of Mao, "Li no doubt attached considerable importance to the organization of the proletariat, but he was predisposed from the beginning to look to the potential revolutionary forces of the whole 'proletarian' nation rather than of a single social class forming only a tiny portion of the nation."[1]

An exaggerated emphasis on the Communists' national concerns is liable, however, to distort the nature of Chinese communism and to blur the distinction between Communists and other nationalist groups in China. Few would argue that Chinese Communists were "radish" Communists, willing to sacrifice their social revolutionary aims to their national concerns. Rather, commitment to radical social transformation has been amalgamated with national goals of independence and development. This chapter is an attempt to examine this amalgamation and its consequences for Chinese Communist nationalism; a subject that has so far received little attention from scholars, who tend to regard nationalism and communism as political alternatives rather than possible correlatives.

Meisner, after demonstrating the importance of nationalism for Li Dazhao, notes that "in the Chinese Marxist milieu, nationalism has been identified not with the more moderate and conservative political tendencies but with the most radical and voluntaristic tendencies."[2] If I understand him correctly, what this implies is that the nationalism of Chinese Communists should not be considered apart from their commitment to the radical restructuring of Chinese society. The urgent awareness of China's national plight and a fervent desire to regenerate the Chinese people have not been restricted to Communists in twentieth-century China; they, however, have been the only ones among a number of political groups to couple nationalist goals with demands for social revolution. Though not all of the Communists' political competitors ignored the social aspects of China's problem, those that did consider it tagged it on as a secondary issue to the primary objective of national salvation. This is obvious in the case of Sun Yat-sen whose "principle of people's livelihood" *(minsheng zhuyi)* addressed itself directly to the social problem in China. Li Dazhao's view of China as a "proletarian nation," where proletarianism was a national attribute, was echoed in Sun's statement that "what the Chinese call inequality of wealth is no more than the distinction of the more and the less poor in an [overall] class of poor."[3] Even those members of the Guomindang (GMD) most conscious of the social problem inferred from this that since all Chinese were poor, the essential task was to liberate China from its foreign oppressors. Social revolution was at best secondary and even harmful to the achievement of the primary task. Social reorganization would be necessary after the national revolution but this was to prevent the possible emergence of a social problem in the future, not to resolve an existing one.[4]

In contrast to this, Chinese communism as it evolved in the 1920s came to view the national and social questions as organically related: it would be impossible to achieve national integration and liberation without a social revolution, or vice versa. This same commitment to social revolution also provided the link between Marxism-Leninism and Chinese communism, in spite of the evolution of the latter in ways not anticipated by Marx or Lenin. In its convergence with nationalism in China, communism became sharply limited by national boundaries, losing much of its supranational class character. Internally, too, the class interests of the proletariat were often compromised by considerations of national ends and, even more fundamentally, by the commitment to a notion of the "people" that superseded class. Nevertheless, the Communists preserved intact the commitment to the revolutionary reorganization of society in accordance with the interests of the proletariat and the peasantry and their revisions constituted not an abandonment but a development of Marxism in its Leninist interpretation. That there was a remarkable emphasis on the peasantry in Chinese communism is indisputable, but this does not mean that the Chinese conception of communism was molded merely by some leaders' enchantment with the peasantry. A close examination of the specific arguments that accompanied the Chinese nationalization of

Marxism-Leninism indicates rather that Chinese Communist ideology was more an outgrowth of Lenin's incorporation of non-European nations into the revolution against capitalism in the era of imperialism. If Lenin's strategy took a course in China that he had not intended, the primary reason was that things appeared differently from Shanghai than they did from Moscow; a shift that Lenin would have understood, even though he might not have condoned it.

The synthesis of national and social revolution in Chinese Communist thought reflected the twin predicaments of Chinese society in the 1920s: social and political disintegration, and economic stagnation and deterioration. Marxism, with its basic premise tying social and political to economic phenomena, offered a unified explanation of the diverse problems internal to Chinese society, while Lenin's theory of imperialism permitted the relation of internal problems to imperialist activities in China. This, I think, accounts to a large degree for the popularity Marxism-Leninism enjoyed in China in the 1920s even among those who rejected its revolutionary strategy. It was the Communists alone, however, who drew revolutionary conclusions from the Marxist-Leninist explanations of the Chinese problem.

These observations emerge from a debate about revolutionary goals and strategy between the Chinese Communist Party (CCP) and the GMD after the breakdown of the first United Front in 1927. The discussion included GMD radicals, disheartened by the upsurge of conservatism in their party, disgraced Trotskyites from the CCP as well as those subscribing to the Li Lisan leadership then in charge of the CCP under the guidance of the Stalinist Comintern. With a few exceptions, the participants in the discussion were not official spokesmen for the revolutionary strategies associated with these three groupings. Most were radical intellectuals who regarded the split of 1927 as a failure of the revolutionary movement due to infiltration from the Right or excessive zeal on the Left. Their concern was to find support in Chinese social structure for the revolutionary goals and strategy which they espoused and to convince the many rank-and-file radicals, bewildered by the events of 1927, of the correctness of their position. This, they believed, would rejuvenate the revolutionary movement by refocusing revolutionary energies.[5]

In practice this discussion never achieved these objectives; serving only to make the irreconcilable differences of the participants more explicit. Nevertheless, the verbal battle which ensued provides valuable insights into the goals of Chinese revolutionaries at that period and shows how they related Marxism-Leninism to the problems of Chinese Revolution. Their lack of official status did not preclude their sharing basic presuppositions with the leaders of the revolutionary movement, and much of Chinese Communist behavior since then suggests the acceptance of premises similar to those that underlay the discussion of the 1920s. An examination of the issues involved in these discussions will, I hope, shed some light on the interplay of national and social concerns in Chinese Communist thought and on its place in the Marxist tradition.

BACKGROUND TO THE DEBATES

Throughout the 1921–1926 period, Chinese revolutionaries, Communist and non-Communist alike, agreed that the revolution was directed against "feudal forces" and foreign imperialism. The "feudal forces" referred to in the documents of the period were the warlords (or militarists) who, encouraged by the imperialists, were responsible for the deterioration of Chinese society. The documents make little attempt to elaborate further on the relationship between Chinese society and imperialists, taking the latter as more or less an external force feeding on China's backwardness.[6] Agreement on this basic aim of the revolution made possible the alliance of all the classes within the United Front.

From 1926 onward, with signs of serious tension in the United Front, this facile description of the goals of the Chinese Revolution was challenged first in Moscow and then in China. It is not clear how the various factions in the Comintern reacted to the first coup d'état by Jiang Jieshi (Chiang K'ai-shek) after the Zhongshan incident in March 1926, but it seems likely that some disagreement was responsible for the restatement of the Comintern position on China in the Seventh Plenum of the Executive Committee of the Comintern in December 1926, a few months before Trotsky's open opposition to the Stalinist line in China. This plenary session recognized Chiang as a representative of the big bourgeoisie but decided nevertheless to continue the United Front.[7]

With the launching of the Northern Expedition in mid-1926, it became increasingly evident that the Communists and the Nationalists had different ideas on what constituted "feudal forces" in China. When the Communists began to encourage extensive land reforms and class struggle in the captured areas, the GMD reaction was swift. On April 12, 1927, Jiang, with the acquiescence of the bourgeoisie, slaughtered all the Communists that he could lay hands on in Shanghai. The debacle of the United Front was completed with the split in Wuhan in July 1927 between the Communists and the left-wing GMD under Wang Jingwei. It was in this period that the Comintern controversy on China policy flared up and was soon carried over into China.

Trotsky's challenge to Stalin's policies was based on his own analysis of the Chinese social structure. He argued that, in China, power was not in the hands of "feudal forces" personified by militarists or even landlords, but lay with the bourgeoisie. Rural leadership in China was in fact indistinguishable from the bourgeoisie:

> Large and middle-class landownership (as it exists in China) is most closely intertwined with urban, including foreign, capitalism. There is no landowning caste in China in opposition to the bourgeoisie. The most widespread, generally hated, exploiter in the village is the usurious wealthy peasant, the agent of urban banking capital. The agrarian revolution has therefore just as much of an anti-feudal as it has of an anti-bourgeois character in China.[8]

If the urban and rural elite were inextricably bound together, the relationship between the composite Chinese bourgeoisie and imperialists was no less intimate. In a comprehensive statement on the bonds between imperialists and Chinese society, Trotsky wrote that:

> Imperialism, which violently hampers the economic development of China by its customs, its financial and military policy, condemns the worker to beggary and the peasant to the cruelest enslavement. The struggle against the big landlords, the struggle against the usurer, the struggle against the capitalists for better working conditions is thus raised by itself to the struggles for national independence of China for the liberation of its productive forces from the bonds and chains of foreign imperialism. There is the principal and the mightiest foe. It is mighty not only because of its warships, but also directly by its inseparable connections with the heads of the banks, the usurers, the bureaucrats and the militarists, with the Chinese bourgeoisie, and by the more indirect but no less intimate ties with the big commercial and industrial bourgeoisie.[9]

Hence, Trotsky continued, the anti-imperialist struggle for national liberation in China was also a class struggle. If China were to achieve national liberation and the progress of its productive forces, the proletariat must lead the struggle against imperialists and the bourgeoisie.

Stalin's reaction to this criticism was the reiteration of the feudal nature of Chinese society, and the reaffirmation of the antifeudal anti-imperialist character of the Chinese Revolution. It has been noted in earlier studies of this period that the Stalinist leadership came very close to Trotsky's suggestions concerning China after the disaster of 1927 but had to resort to many face-saving devices to prove the opposition wrong while co-opting its policies.[10] This was the case on the issue of the goals of the Chinese Revolution. In an article in *Pravda* on July 28, 1927, Stalin described the aims of the Chinese Revolution in terms that differed little from Trotsky's, while seemingly rejecting them:

> The opposition forgot that the revolutionary struggle of the Chinese people against imperialism is to be explained above all and in the main, by the fact that

in China, imperialism is that force which supports and inspires the direct exploiters of the Chinese people—the feudalists, the militarists, the capitalists, the bureaucrats, etc., that the Chinese workers and peasants cannot conquer these exploiters of theirs without waging at the same time a struggle against imperialism.[11]

Stalin here pits the workers and peasants against all members of a variegated ruling class in alliance with the imperialists. In other statements, however, he made it clear that the chief internal enemies of the Chinese Revolution were the "feudal forces." These forces he described as the militarists and the bureaucrats as well as "feudal and medieval methods of exploitation and oppression of the peasantry," which later became the basis of Chinese Marxists' arguments that China was a "feudal" society. Furthermore, without denying that mercantile capital played an important role in China, an effective weapon in the Trotskyite arsenal, Stalin argued that this situation existed side by side with feudal methods of exploitation and, presumably, intensified feudal exploitation, as the Chinese Marxists concluded later.[12]

These are the broad outlines of the two major standpoints on the social and economic dimensions of the Chinese Revolution to emerge from the conflict in the Comintern. It was these arguments which Chinese Marxists acquired from Comintern leaders. The controversy in China, however, was complicated from the beginning by the presence of a Left-GMD standpoint which disagreed with that of the Communists and, presenting an alternative, instigated further elaboration of the two Communist positions. Furthermore, all three groups in China, perceiving the problem not from Moscow but from Shanghai, shifted the emphases of the Comintern leaders into new directions.

THE DEBATE OF 1927

The opposing views of these three groups defined the limits of controversy after 1927. *Either* China was predominantly feudal with imperialism supporting (or perpetuating) the feudal social structure in China; *or* China was predominantly capitalist, with imperialism, by its very nature, helping the development of capitalist forces in Chinese society (or, more often, supporting the bourgeoisie); *or* China was neither feudal nor capitalist but a society where the ambiguity of the class structure had enabled parasitic political forces of a feudal nature to retain their power, with these forces, at the time, serving the cause of imperialists.

The debate was initiated by supporters of the third view; Left-GMD radicals associated with Wang Jingwei after the Autumn of 1927, who felt that the revolutionary promises of the 1924 Party reorganization and the United Front had been betrayed both from the Right and from the Left in 1927.[13] These non-Communist radicals started to wage a theoretical struggle from 1928, in a final effort to keep the revolution alive against rightist encroachment and to prevent its dissolution into anarchy under leftist pressure. It was the challenge of their social analysis that gradually forced the Communists to define their own position.[14] Their evaluation of the various strategies of revolution in terms of social structure, even if rigid, raised revolutionary polemics to a new level of sophistication.

The GMD Radicals' Argument

GMD leftists continued after 1927 to describe the dominant powers of Chinese society as feudal. Unlike the Communists, however, they relegated the "feudal forces" to the superstructure of society, in keeping with the assumptions of the earlier period. They argued that the feudal system in China had disappeared long before, from about the middle of the Chou Dynasty (1122–255 B.C.), under the impact of commerce.[15] But though feudalism had come to an end at that time, China, unlike Europe at the end of the medieval period, had never completed the transition to the next historical stage of capitalism and had remained suspended in a transitional stage. The economy throughout this period had been dominated by agriculture, subject to the chronic disintegrative function of commercial capital. The major characteristic of Chinese society through the transitional period had been the ambiguity of its class structure. The developments in Chou that had brought about the downfall of feudalism had led to the fusion of landed wealth and commercial capital so that a new economic elite had arisen which simultaneously invested in land and engaged in mercantile and usurious activities. Commerce, an impetus to capitalism in the West, had subsisted in China on the exploitation of land and the mediation of regional specialization, with little incentive for the development of productive forces. This had produced pernicious results. Commercial capital, constantly encroaching on land, had served periodically to concentrate landownership and impoverish the peasants, leading to the disorders of dynastic changes. It had furthermore perpetuated disunity, as it had a stake in regional differences of production.[16]

The Marxist theory of society expects the political superstructure to reflect the interest of the dominant economic class in society. GMD Marxists were well aware of this but were able to argue that since Chinese society had not had a clearly dominant economic class, no one group, such as landowners or capitalists, had been able to establish its control over the state. At the end of the Chou period, the concentration of economic and political power in the same group had come to an end. While the new landowner-merchant group had established its dominance over the economy, political power had passed to bureaucrats recruited from the gentry *(shidaifu)*, an educational and political elite rather than an economic one. The interests of the bureaucrats often coincided with those of landowners against the peasants, and the two constantly encroached on one another's spheres (bureaucrats buying land and merchant-landowners entering office), but a distinction nevertheless remained between the political and the economic elite.[17]

The bureaucrats with the military, which overshadowed the bureaucracy in times of disorder, constituted the political elite of imperial China. This political elite, which did not engage in economic activities and, on the whole, led a parasitic existence, was feudal in nature.[18] Feudal in this sense ranged from military-bureaucratic localism to patriarchalism in the family and to the dominance of Confucian thought, a product of the feudal period. Confucian emphasis on agriculture as the backbone of society was not a result of altruism, as the Confucians claimed, but a reflection of the subsistence basis of the political elite who feared the effects of mercantile activities on their position in society. Merchants, suppressed by this political elite, were never able to develop into an independent class, establishing instead a symbiotic relationship with the landlords. The net result of this was a confusion of the class structure.

This situation continued into the present century with the addition of a major new external force, imperialism. Whereas the dominant political elite of the past had served the interests of landlords, now this same elite of bureaucrats and militarists, traditionally lacking in national consciousness, served the imperialists and their agents, the compradors, themselves *shidaifu* who had developed new skills.[19] Chinese capitalism was still weak in spite of new economic pressures.

> Because of the intermediacy of the *shidaifu*, the capitalist class has a strong *shidaifu* nature and finds it very easy to ally with military groups. Also, since the development of capitalism was not internal to the Chinese economic structure but was enforced from the outside, the result is that although one sees the establishment of a capitalist class, one does not see the destruction of feudal thought or the success of the democratic revolution.[20]

Not only did capitalism have difficulty in taking root in Chinese soil, but the effects of imperialism, ironically, aggravated the existing situation. China's growth under western pressure was lopsided; appendages of modern industrialism preceded the establishment of an industrial basis—e.g., railroads were introduced before the building of factories, thus contributing to China's centrifugal tendencies by increasing the mobility of warlords. The large feudal state now appeared to be divided into many smaller feudal principalities.[21]

In addition, imperialism augmented the exploitative nature of commercial capital in China. Contemporary imperialism was primarily financial. During the present period, native commercial capital was subordinated to imperialist finance, helping the latter in its exploitation of China. Where once it had been tied to interregional trade, this capital now served to link the Chinese village with the outside world. The exploitation of the Chinese peasant, the worst sufferer, stretched from the remotest corner of China to the bankers in New York and London.[22]

While they regarded foreign and Chinese finance capital as fused together, the GMD Marxists made a distinction between Chinese and foreign industries. They argued that the available finance and the rapidly growing labor force, two preconditions of capitalism, helped only foreign industries, not Chinese ones.[23] As the foreign industries continued to grow, Chinese industries stagnated and in some cases even regressed.[24] The causes of stagnation were numerous: the destruction of native handicrafts due to the spread of foreign commodities, the outflow of China's wealth through opium, indemnities, etc., and the impoverishment of the people, which contracted the market and also played into the hands of militarists by providing them with manpower. The major causes, however, were competition from foreign industries, the strength of commercial and finance capital and the disunity caused by bureaucrats and militarists.

Competition from foreign industries limited Chinese enterprises to light industries while foreigners controlled the more strategic sectors. Chinese industrial development was further limited by the importation of commodities from abroad. Transportation and finance were controlled by foreigners who had technical advantages over their Chinese competitors in the abundance of their capital, their expertise in labor and management and their technological superiority. Added to those were political advantages such as tariff limitations and extraterritoriality which made foreigners immune to the many exactions that Chinese entrepreneurs suffered at the hands of political authorities.[25]

Finance capital not only worked through Chinese merchants to impoverish Chinese society, it also encouraged the flow of capital to unproductive investments. Since industrial growth was slow and erratic, many people preferred to invest in land or engaged in urban speculation where the returns were faster and higher. These were all unproductive, and the capital that flowed into the cities ended up in the hands of foreigners. That which went to the countryside, as of old, furthered the exploitation of the peasant who was the biggest loser, as was obvious from the decline of Chinese agriculture at the time.[26]

Finally, this whole sorry situation was made worse by the disunity of China caused by the uneven development of the Chinese economy for which commerce had been chiefly responsible. GMD writers, though they isolated the state from social classes, stressed the interdependent nature of the political and economic problems in China.[27] The Chinese economy had a regional basis. This not only helped commercial capital but also provided the basis for the political and military power of warlords who, products themselves of disunity, became its agents. Some writers compared China to Germany and Italy in the nineteenth century where the primary task had been unification and not, as in the case of France and Russia, revolution.[28] Given this situation, GMD theoreticians argued, the most suitable strategy for the Chinese Revolution was that devised by Sun Yat-sen in the Three Principles of the People *(san-min zhuyi)*. Chinese Revolution had two tasks, destructive and constructive. The destructive aspect was to be aimed at the traditional exploiters of society, bureaucrats and militarists, who still dominated the political superstructure, as well as at imperialists. Destruction should not extend to class struggle for several reasons. First, because of the ambiguity of class structure, there was no dominant class. Capitalists were weak and suffered themselves from foreign oppression and warlords. Landlords were subject to commercial capital, their only advantage being their ability to pass on their exploitation to the shoulders of the peasants; they were not a ruling class as such.[29] Second, China's greatest need was integration. Class struggle would interfere with political and economic integration, making China more vulnerable than before. As for imperialism, most urgent was the achievement of tariff equality and the abolition of extraterritoriality which were the prime weapons of the imperialist penetration of China.[30]

The task of construction, on the other hand, would consolidate the gains of revolution and establish the foundations of true socialism. Most important in this respect was the development of productive forces and the advance of the industrial sector of the Chinese economy. This would establish the dominance of the cities over the countryside (or of the industrial sector over agriculture) and subordinate commercial capital to industrial capitalism, eliminating the harmful effects of the former, and leading it into productive channels. Charging the Communists with "consumer socialism" much in the fashion of the Confucian bureaucracy, GMD writers argued that true scientific socialism could only be founded upon an advanced industrial basis. What was needed for that was not class struggle but the cooperation of all patriotic forces to develop China's productive forces.

Finally, GMD theoreticians, aware of the problem of class in society, argued, as had Sun Yat-sen, that China's backwardness diminished the importance of class but that, nevertheless, the Party should take measures to prevent this becoming a problem in the future. The GMD should preserve itself as a mass party, thus not only guaranteeing its revolutionary purity against militarists and bureaucrats, always ready to sneak into the party, but also curbing the risk of future class struggle.

The Communists' Argument

Communist disagreement with the ideas of the GMD writers described above revolved around the issue of class. While the latter regarded class struggle as unnecessary and inimical to national integration, Communist writers saw class struggle as a *precondition* to such unification. The Communists, however, differed among themselves as to the nature of the ruling class in Chinese society, and hence on the targets of revolution.

The new leadership of the Communist Party after 1927,[31] in accordance with Stalinist policy, continued to insist that the Chinese Revolution was still antifeudal and anti-imperialist in nature. Writers representative of this position in the controversy argued that Chinese society was feudal or, more commonly, semifeudal and that imperialism strengthened feudal forces in Chinese society. Unlike GMD writers, who relegated "feudal forces" to the political superstructure, they saw feudalism as the essential characteristic of the Chinese socioeconomic structure. Aware of the differences between contemporary China and medieval Europe they justified their use of the term "feudal" by arguing that, though superficially there was no resemblance between the two societies, the basic exploitative structure *(boxue xingshi)* was the same in both.[32] Many conceded, however, that feudalism had been eliminated from the political superstructure, and hence that "semifeudal" was the more appropriate term for China *(ban fengjian)*.[33]

On the other hand, CCP writers did not reject the existence of capitalism in China altogether but relegated it to the foreign-controlled sphere of China's economy, in similar fashion to GMD theoreticians. The European section of the industrial and commercial sector continued to flourish; few Chinese were involved in this sector and, where they were, they were confined to insignificant enterprises which were stagnating, if not deteriorating. The transforming effect of imperialism, "the highest stage of capitalism," did not go beyond a few coastal, urban areas which themselves had become exploiters of the vast majority of the Chinese nation.[34]

The dilemmas involved in describing, in Marxist developmental categories, a society modernizing under outside pressure and the inherently conflicting activities of imperialism in such a society are most obvious in the case of this group of writers who literally had to qualify every one of their statements with some concession to arguments of an opposite nature. Chinese society in the 1920s was suffering from severe economic and social dislocations. To many, economic breakdown in the Chinese countryside, under way for a century, appeared not as a strain created at least partially by economic modernization but wholly as the consequence of imperialist aggression and native ruling class subversion. This impression was magnified by the relative stagnation of Chinese industrial enterprises in the 1920s, after a brief period of rapid growth during the First World War when European activities had been diverted elsewhere. Added to this was the support of foreign powers in the 1910s and 1920s for one or another of the warlord-bureaucratic cliques that dominated China at this time. The latter, engaged in constant internecine strife, plundered and destroyed the countryside as well as making life difficult for the budding Chinese bourgeoisie by their numerous extortions and exactions. Whatever the precise contribution of their activities to economic stagnation and breakdown, they certainly contributed to social disorder and confusion, and helped to create an atmosphere unconducive to economic progress. Imperialism, supporting the warlords, appeared paradoxically as the supporter of backward "feudal" forces in Chinese society which, theoretically, it should have eliminated.

The dilemma is evident in the tortuous arguments offered by CCP writers who theoretically accepted capitalism and imperialism as historically progressive but had difficulty in reconciling this with their resentment of the effects of these forces in Chinese society. Their effort to deal with a complex transitional society was encumbered further by their categorical manner of thinking: they sought to explain what was happening to Chinese society in terms of Marxian historical categories derived from European experience. One of the most illustrative examples of the efforts to deal with these contradictions is the following statement by Pan Dongzhou:

> Because China is a backward agricultural country, the superiority of semi-feudal forces within agriculture [means that] they hold a superior position within the whole of China's economy. . . . When we speak of the totality of economic relations in China, urban capitalism definitely holds a leading (*lingdao*) position; the tendency of the development of the whole economy is toward capitalism. But in their relative weight (*bizhong*) within the whole country, semi-feudal relations are still superior. . . . We are only saying that feudal relations are superior in China's economy; we are definitely not saying that China does not have capitalism. China has not only been subjected to control by finance imperialism in the cities, [but even] in the villages, [class] divisions *fenhua*) have appeared. But no matter what, in the national economy of the whole country [to be distinguished from the foreign sector] feudal relations still hold an extreme degree of superiority. Speaking of capitalism, we cannot but note that imperialism is absolutely superior. Imperialism, using the power of its abundant finances, increasingly assaults the whole of China's economy.[35]

Thus, while capitalism might be the "leading," dynamic force in China's economy, the backward "feudal forces" carried more weight, a seeming play on words vehemently objected to by the Trotskyites who were quick to note the inconsistency and to point out that what is "leading" is also "superior" and that to claim otherwise was to play into the hands of the reactionary bourgeoisie."[36] An ambivalence toward imperialism was also evident in the statement. Thus, while imperialism pushes China toward capitalism, a more progressive stage than feudalism in the historical scheme of things, it also "assaults" China's economy, and becomes simultaneously a regressive force.

What these writers referred to as "feudal relations" can be described as the traditional, agrarian features of Chinese society, ranging from social structure to economic practices. In the statement above by Pan, and in other references, the very dominance of a backward agrarian economy conducted by primitive methods is evidence of "feudalism." A concomitant of this was the regionally uneven development of the Chinese economy or, in other words, the lack of a national market. But the cornerstone of the argument that China was feudal was the mode of exploitation that prevailed in the Chinese village. Most of the basic arguments along this line were formulated in the manifesto of the Fifth Congress of the CCP in May 1927.[37] This manifesto mentions the following specifically as examples of the feudal mode of exploitation: high rate of tenancy, arbitrary and exorbitant rent; political and economic subjection of peasants to landlords; militarists and bureaucrats who control rural China; subjection to merchant's capital and usury which, being in the hands of landlords, was regarded as a tool of feudal exploitation. Pan elaborates these as rents of more than 50 percent of yield, high taxes, and miscellaneous exactions, the power of local despots, etc.,[38] and Zhu Peiwo, a prolific writer subscribing to this view, adds to the list rent-in-kind, forced labor, tribute obligations (in luxury items like poultry and wine), the use of force by the landlord against the peasants as severe as that of the feudal lord against serfs, and status distinctions.[39] All these comprised the definition, for this group, of Marx's reference to feudal exploitation as "extraeconomic" or "noneconomic."[40]

The severe exploitation of the peasant strengthened landlords and supported the military and the bureaucracy all of whom subsisted on such exploitation and had a stake in it. Furthermore, the impoverishment of the peasants played into the hands of feudal political forces when the peasants, trying to find a refuge from their misery, took the course of joining warlords' armies for security.

Imperialism, while by its very nature propelling China toward capitalism, itself benefited from the feudal model of exploitation and therefore supported it.[41] But the situation was more serious than that created by imperialists dumping surplus commodities or their rape of Chinese resources. The developing sector of the economy was under imperialist control, so any further advances would accrue to their benefit. In other words, while China could have developed economically under such circumstances, that would have been at the cost of political enslavement.[42]

Such a view ruled out bourgeois revolution or the development of capitalism in China. The revolution would have to be led by the proletariat leading the peasantry and it would be directed at feudal forces and the imperialists, the two forces obstructing China's development. Furthermore, since the alliance of these two forces depended on the feudal mode of exploitation, the aims of China's revolution could not be achieved without abolishing such exploitation: national liberation could only be achieved through social revolution (or, in this case, land revolution, as it was referred to). China would then embark on a path of "non-capitalist" *(feiziben zhuyi)* development toward socialism. One important consequence of this strategy of revolution should be noted here. Although the native bourgeoisie was deemed incapable, by its very situation, of leading the national revolution, it was not included among the targets of revolution, as it was by the Trotskyites. The bourgeoisie itself, as the native/foreign capitalism distinction implied, was subject to the oppression of feudal forces and imperialism, and might yet join the revolution in a future alliance!

The Trotskyites' Argument

This issue was an important factor in the split of the Communist Party in China after 1927, resulting in the expulsion of Trotskyites from the Party in late 1929.[43] The Trotskyites differed from both of their rivals in the debate in their insistence that the Chinese bourgeoisie could not be distinguished from the foreign and must be included among the targets of the revolutionary struggle for liberation. With greater theoretical consistency, if not political prescience, they contended that imperialism, being the most advanced form of capitalism, had the historical mission of destroying feudal forces and supporting the spread of capitalism everywhere.[44] China was now part of a world dominated by capitalism; it was ludicrous to make distinctions between native and foreign capitalism and declare China feudal on those grounds.

More so than Trotsky himself, the Chinese Trotskyites were quick to deduce from bourgeois dominance in China that Chinese society was already a capitalist society, or at least a transitional society with capitalist forces in a leading position. As has been noted, Yen Ling-feng criticized Fan Tung-chou vehemently for his distinction of "superior" versus "leading" forces,[45] pointing out that if capitalist forces were the "leading" forces in Chinese society, they were also "superior" and hence, the chief target of the revolution.

The Trotskyites, who also differed among themselves, used the manifestations of a modern economy in China to prove their point that China was capitalist. Their works are full of statistics on the increase in the number of factories and steamships and of the mileage of railroads in China in proof of their contention that capitalism had taken root in China and was continually progressing, not regressing. They were often more mechanical in explaining away the complexity of the situation in China than their rivals.[46] But they did challenge their opponents effectively with their argument that self-sufficiency, which they took to be crucial to the definition of feudalism, had disappeared in China with the subjection of even the countryside to a commodity economy. The Chinese peasant was no longer independent of a national, or even a world market. Of course commercial capital played a major role in this but to the Trotskyites commercial capital represented the primitive accumulation of capital *(yüanshi zibendi jilei)*, not an independent element or a tool of feudal exploitation as it did to the other groups.[47]

The Trotskyite argument ultimately hinged on the assumption of the insignificance of national boundaries in economic considerations and the oneness of the world market in the period of imperialism. This is why they regarded the development of capitalism in China as inevitable. Some of them, more cognizant of the complexity of Chinese society, conceded however that, while imperialism "absolutely" *(jueduidi)* encouraged the growth of capitalism in China, it "relatively" *(xiangduidi)* obstructed its development, just as feudal forces obstructed capitalism while their own basis was being eroded by it.[48]

While the Trotskyites differed from the other two groups in their evaluation of what was happening to the structure of Chinese society and economy, their predictions as to China's future differed little from those of the others. Since imperialism was the dominant factor in the dynamics of world society, China must inevitably be drawn under imperialist control as its economy advanced, i.e., the greater the advance of capitalism, the deeper China's colonization. Where the Trotskyites differed radically from their rivals was in their inclusion of the bourgeoisie among the targets of revolution. The Chinese bourgeoisie was indistinguishable from the foreign; hence, as Trotsky had argued, the anti-imperialist struggle for national liberation was also a class struggle against the bourgeoisie, urban and rural, which seemed to include all but the proletariat and the peasantry. It was this uncompromising alienation of all except the proletariat and the peasantry from revolutionary ranks, I think, which earned the Trotskyites the sobriquet "liquidationists" *(quxiaopai)* and made their strategy less popular than it might otherwise have been.

SUMMARY AND CONCLUSION

The controversy on revolutionary strategy in the late 1920s illustrates the confluence of class and nation in Chinese Marxist Thought. There is little reason, from the discussion itself, to question the protagonists' commitments to Marxism-Leninism. Of greater significance is the fact that their attitudes toward class struggle were inextricably bound up with their concerns for China's national liberation and development. Class struggle, an end in itself to Marx and Lenin, appears here as the means to the national ends of Chinese society: the emancipation of the proletariat and the peasantry, however valuable, was also the means with which to eliminate the forces which obstructed China's political integration and economic development. All groups shared this basic conviction; their disagreements stemmed from different evaluations of the scope of the ruling group. Their goals, without exception, entailed independence from foreign, economic, and political control and one or another form of internal social revolution as a means of securing national development. As Marxists they were all committed to the distant goal of an egalitarian, classless society but for the immediate future, class struggle was tied in with national liberation and not taken as a supranational end in itself. This is the unspoken assumption that is implicit in the reasons for and the anticipated results of revolution.

The fundamental question in the controversy concerned China's economic and social development. Many saw Chinese society as stagnating, and even regressing. Traditional economic and political forces, refusing to vanish, were obstructing the development of modern modes of social organization. At the same time, they were no longer powerful enough to fulfill their traditional function in social stability and instead fed on disorder to perpetuate their now parasitic existence. New forces, "powerless to be born," languished or were themselves driven to parasitism in the womb of the old society. While modernity gradually but inevitably destroyed the old, its function seemed to be limited to destruction, with few of its positive aspects in sight. Hence Tao Xisheng's complaint that "although one sees the establishment of a capitalist class, one does not see the destruction of feudal thought or the success of the democratic revolution." The continuation of this situation threatened to destroy the basic subsistence of Chinese society. The new commodity economy destroyed the old agrarian economy day by day and yet industrialization remained insignificant. Chinese radicals no doubt exaggerated China's impending destruction. Most of the crisis they perceived was possibly due to what has been described as the "birth pains of capitalism"; nevertheless, the death-pains of old Chinese society seemed more immediate and therefore more real.[49]

In this situation the crucial element was imperialism. Chinese radicals held imperialism responsible for both the persistence of the old and the inability of the new to emerge. The claims of imperialist support for Chinese feudalists or capitalists were often exaggerated in the discussion. But the exaggeration was more in the refusal to recognize the complexity of imperialist involvement in China than in the search for scapegoats in explaining China's plight. In China, as elsewhere, imperialism was "not only a modernizing influence, but also a conservative force."[50] While it inadvertently brought new ideas and practices and undermined the basis of traditional society, it also supported backward elements in China whose activities were detrimental to the national interests. Chinese radicals responded to this ambiguity of the role of imperialism with a corresponding ambivalence of their own. They recognized the role of imperialism in bringing a new social organization to China but they also noted, with greater urgency, imperialist erosion of the extant socioeconomic organization and imperialist support, for the sake of political stability in the pursuit of profit, of reactionary elements. But regardless of which side they emphasized, they saw imperialism as ultimately harmful. Even those that recognized the economic modernization of China under imperialist pressure, such as the Trotskyites, admitted that further development in that direction must be avoided for every economic advance under imperialist auspices led to greater imperialist penetration of Chinese society. This ruled out development in the direction of capitalism since that would lead to the political enslavement, or the colonization, of Chinese society.

An offshoot of the problem of development in such circumstances, with important consequences for Chinese Marxism, was the "uneven development" of Chinese society.[51] As a result of the interaction between worldwide capitalism and Chinese society, different parts of China developed at different rates with a growing gap between them. The most important polarity was between the modern coastal areas and the backward interior or, what in effect amounted to the same thing, that between urban and rural China. In the eyes of the radicals, urban China, representing a conglomeration of landlords, bourgeoisie and imperialists,[52] was the center of exploitation of the rest of the country. Furthermore, as all agreed that the developing sector of the economy was under imperialist control, urban areas were in effect part of the worldwide capitalist network, with interests inimical to those of the nation: in the presence of imperialism, the distinction between oppressed and oppressor corresponded to the distinction between Chinese and non-Chinese.

The participants in the controversy agreed on these basic problems and believed in the efficacy of Marxism in explaining their nature. Their explanations, and hence the remedies they offered, differed nevertheless in accordance with their political proclivities. As might be expected, the most serious gap was between the GMD Marxists and the Communists. The GMD radicals, though they accepted the relationship between the social and the national questions, regarded social revolution and national integration and development as mutually antagonistic. Social revolution would only exacerbate the traditional centrifugal tendencies of Chinese society. Besides, as the major rift in China was between society and the political superstructure, what was required immediately was a political revolution to bring into power those representative of the nation. Such a government, representing no one class but all the people, would oversee China's integration and development without permitting the rise of social problem.

The Communists, in spite of their internal differences, concluded from their analyses that the rift in China was not between society and the political superstructure but within society itself, among classes with antagonistic interests. The ruling class in China, whether the "feudal" landlords or the bourgeoisie, was allied with imperialists against the rest of the people. Hence to the Communists Marxism promised, through class struggle against oppressors, an end to the disintegration of the country as well as the elimination of oppression. This is not to say that the Marxism of Chinese Communists was a mere cloak for nationalism; rather, as national "bifurcation" and class division appeared to be part and parcel of the same process, the elimination of one simply required the elimination of the other. National liberation and social revolution, as first Lenin and then Trotsky had suggested, had to be achieved simultaneously or not at all.

The question that remains is whether or not this convergence of class struggle and national liberation implied a deviation from Marxism-Leninism. The significance of the answer to this question reaches beyond the Chinese case to the nature of communism in the world today and, in particular, the nature of radical nationalist, or national liberation movements.

Of Lenin's contributions to Marxism, the most relevant in this respect was his incorporation of imperialism and anticolonial liberation movements into the revolution against capitalism. Although this implied the shift of the burden in the anticapitalist struggle to the underdeveloped world, Lenin remained remarkably loyal to the priority of the advanced European proletariat as the vanguard of socialism. His approach to national liberation was basically Europe-oriented, directed at achieving a proletarian socialist revolution in Europe which would form the foundation of worldwide socialism. There is no indication that national liberation was ever an end in itself to Lenin. The anti-imperialist struggles of colonial countries were significant to him to the extent that they affected the fate of the worldwide bourgeois–proletariat struggle. If colonies could be closed off to European capitalism, an economic crisis would be created in Europe and the long-delayed revolution of the European proletariat would follow. After 1917, when the European proletariat failed to respond to the call, the Soviet Union increasingly became the center of the socialist camp with a consequent blurring of national and socialist interests, but the commitment to internationalism persisted as in the activities of the Communist International.

Lenin regarded national revolutionary movements as the response of "nations without history" to being "drawn into the capitalist whirlpool."[53] Imperialism as such was a positive historical force, drawing backward, "feudal" societies out of their traditional cocoons and making them part of a universal socioeconomic system, laying the groundwork for true universal socialism. Within individual societies, however, imperialism also served as an obstruction to development. The native bourgeoisie, a product itself of imperialism, soon discovered that imperialists were unwilling to relinquish their exploitation and, hence, control of the colonies. Under such conditions, the native bourgeoisie could enter an alliance with the native proletariat in spite of the fundamental hostility between the two classes. The participation of the proletariat in such an alliance could, in turn, be condoned because of the contribution of the alliance to the worldwide struggle against capitalism. At an appropriate time, the proletariat would have to reject the alliance, turning to the more basic and universal struggle against the bourgeoisie. In this conception, the national liberation movement was but a passing stage in the grand struggle of classes.[54]

Lenin's interpretation of Marxism has been explained as an adaptation of Marxist socialism to the situation in developing Russia.[55] While this may be true of his conception of party organization and his incorporation of the peasantry into the revolution after 1905, the theory of imperialism and national liberation went beyond the necessities of the Russian situation. Russia differed in its developmental problems from many non-European societies in its independence of imperialist domination; Russian radicals regarded Russia as an imperialist state itself. Furthermore, Russia's proximity to Europe and the European base of the Russian Communist movement gave Russian revolutionaries a close identity with their European counterparts. As a result, they were able to preserve a Europe-centered perspective on revolution, seeing the Russian Revolution as part of a European socialist revolution. Lenin, in his views on imperialism and national liberation, was a spokesman of this tradition. Nevertheless, his interpretation of Marxism provided a bridge between classical Marxist ideas on revolution and twentieth-century developments in Marxist socialism as it spread out of Europe.

The standpoint of radicals outside Europe and North America inverted Lenin's perspective on class struggle and national liberation even as they accepted his analysis in its totality. To them, the most important consideration has been the destructive effect of imperialism on their societies, not the role of imperialism in delaying the proletarian revolution in Europe. Regardless of the extent of their identification with supranational classes, the immediate motivation for their struggle against imperialism has derived not from the desire to quicken the pace of socialist revolution in Europe but from their concerns with national integration and development. From this perspective, national liberation, a mere phase in the international bourgeois-proletarian struggle in Lenin's conception, has emerged as a valuable end in itself, subjecting class struggle to its own purposes. Where internationalistic commitments have been retained, their realization has been pushed so far into the future that they have little effect on present political behavior. However, one must still be wary of describing national liberation movements as a mere degeneration of communism into nationalism.[56] It is true that the fusion of the vocabulary of Marxism with the vocabulary of national ends has blurred the distinctions between Communists and other groups working toward nationalist goals. Marxian assumptions about the relationship between socioeconomic revolution and political revolution have even entered the outlook of movements which do not profess to be Communist and even reject explicitly the Communist strategy of class struggle as a viable alternative for their societies.[57] This was the case with the GMD in China. GMD radicals recognized the existence of a social problem in China but still insisted that national political unification must take precedence over class struggle: the latter was even deemed subversive of the primary goal. In contrast, the Communists, in China and elsewhere, have not rejected class struggle but rather have incorporated it as an integral part of national unification.

It is not surprising to find the classical example of the fusion of national and class struggle in China, the first clearly non-Western environment in which Lenin's theses were put into practice. Chinese society, in the problems it faced in the 1920s, was much more analogous to the contemporary "Third World" than it was either to Europe or to prerevolutionary Russia. From its beginnings, therefore, Chinese communism contained elements characteristic of later national liberation movements, despite the Communists' recognition of Soviet leadership and guidance providing the first instance of the type of revolutionary movement that has replaced orthodox communism as a revolutionary force by the mid-twentieth century in much of the underdeveloped world. Events since the Sino-Soviet split and recent statements by Chinese spokesmen have made it evident not only that the Chinese feel a close affinity with such movements but also that they themselves conceive of international socialism in terms of a collection of independent states each planning socialist development in accordance with its particular national ends.[58] Socialism based on a universal class superseding nations has more than ever been relegated into the far future. This attitude is in no way peculiar to China but represents, I think, the direction that the "Marxian revolutionary idea" has taken in the twentieth century. No statement expresses this trend more cogently than that by Trotsky in 1929, soon after the disaster of the first United Front in China: "The socialist revolution begins on the national arena, it unfolds on the international arena, and is completed on the world arena."[59]

NOTES

1. Maurice Meisner, *Li Dazhao and the Origins of Chinese Marxism* (Cambridge, MA: Harvard University Press, 1967), 223.

2. Meisner, *Li Dazhao*, 194.

3. Sun Yat-sen, *Sanmin zhuyi* [Three People's Principles] (Taipei: Sanmin shuju, 1966), 198.

4. Zhou Fohai, *Sanmin zhuyizhi lilun tixi* [The Theoretical System of the Three Peoples Principles] (Shanghai: Xin shengming yuekan chuban she, 1928), 221–32.

5. Wang Lixi, "Zhongguo shehui shi lunzhan xumu" [Introduction to the Controversy on Chinese Society], *Dushu zazhi* [Readers' Magazine] 1, nos. 4–5 (August 1931): 9–10.

6. This is quite evident from the documents of the various CCP congresses of the 1921–1926 period. See C. Brandt et al., eds., *A Documentary History of Chinese Communism* (Cambridge, MA: Harvard University Press, 1967).

7. See Benjamin I. Schwartz, *Chinese Communism and the Rise of Mao* (New York: Harper Torchbooks, 1967), 58–59.

8. Leon Trotsky, "The Canton Insurrection" in *Problems of the Chinese Revolution,* ed. Max Shachtman, 125 (Ann Arbor: University of Michigan Press, 1967).

9. Trotsky, "First Speech on the Chinese Question," delivered at the eighth plenum of the Executive Committee of the Communist International, Moscow, May 1927. In *Problems*, 110–11.

10. Schwartz, *Chinese Communism*, passim.

11. J. V. Stalin, "Comments on Current Affairs in China," *Pravda* (July 28, 1927). In *Selections from V. I. Lenin and J. V. Stalin on the National Colonial Question* (Calcutta: Calcutta Book House, 1970), 205.

12. Stalin, "Comments on Current Affairs in China," 205–6.

13. In the winter of 1928, the supporters of Wang Jingwei organized themselves into the Reorganization Society [*gaizu tongzhi hui*] to carry on the struggle against the right wing of the GMD. The group was discredited and disappeared after the defeat of their paradoxical alliance with the northern warlords, Yan Xishan and Feng Yuxiang. Among the outstanding leaders were Chen Gongbo and Gu Mengyu.

14. Left-GMD views were explained in a number of journals published from 1928. The more important were *Xin shengming* [New Life], *Shuang shi* [Double Ten], *Geming pinglun* [Revolutionary Review] and *Qianjin* [Forward]. *Xin shengming* became especially popular for its social analyses of historical and contemporary Chinese

society. The foremost author in these areas was Tao Xisheng, who, until 1925, was a relatively unknown legal historian and an editor at the Commercial Press. From 1927 until 1937, when he went into politics, Tao was one of the most imaginative social historians in China, a professor at Beida (after 1931) and the publisher of *Shih huo* [Food and Commodities Monthly] (1933–1937), an outstanding journal of social and economic history.

15. Tao Xisheng, *Zhongguo sheizhi shihdi fenxi* [Analysis of the History of Chinese Society] (Shanghai: Xin shengming shuju, 1929), 26. Also see Yu Zhi [Gu Mengyu], "Nongmin yü tudi wenti" [Peasants and the Land Question], in *Zhongguo wentizhi huigu yu zhanwang* [The Chinese Question: Retrospect and Prospect], ed. Tao Xisheng, 261–62 (Shanghai: Xin shengming shuju, 1930).

16. Many of Tao's works deal with the problem of the role of commercial capital in Chinese society. For a discussion of the early period, see *Zhongguo fengjian shehui shi* [History of Chinese Feudal Society] (Shanghai: Xin shengming shuju, 1929), 41–60.

17. Tao, *Zhongguo sheizhi shidi fenxi*, 83–105. Tao regarded the gentry as a status group intermediating between the formally economic landlords and the formally political bureaucracy. He was somewhat ambiguous on this issue, trying to present them as not belonging to any class. One opponent, an acclaimed expert (in the 1920s) on Marxism, Li Ji, criticized him severely for his views on the gentry.

18. Tao, *Zhongguo sheizhi shidi fenxi*, 83–105. For his distinction between feudal lords and the *shidaifu*, see p. 38 of the same book.

19. Tao Xisheng, "Minzu wenti yu minzu zhuyi" [The National Question and Nationalism], *Xin shengming* 2, no. 7 (July 1929): 1–14.

20. Tao, *Zhongguo sheizhi shidi fenxi*, 42.

21. Tao, *Zhongguo sheizhi shidi fenxi*, 142.

22. Tao Xisheng, "Zhongguozhi shangren ziben ji dizhu yu nongmin"[Merchant Capital in China, Landlords and Peasants], *Xin shengming* 3, no. 2 (February 1930): 7.

23. Tao, "Zhongguozhi shangren ziben," 12.

24. Tao, "Zhongguozhi shangren ziben." See also He Siyuan, "Zhongguo zai shijie jingjidi diwei he Zhongguo weiji" [The Position of China in the World Economy and the Chinese Crisis], *Xin shengming* 2, no. 5 (May 1929): 1–4 and Lin Min, "Ziben zhuyi shehui yanjiu" [Analysis of Capitalist Society], *Xin shengming* 3, no. 12 (December 1930): 1–11.

25. The articles dealing with these issues are too numerous to cite. For a detailed discussion of the advantages of foreign industries over Chinese, see Zhou Gucheng, "Xiandai Zhongguo jingji bianqian gailu" [Discussion of Changes in the Chinese Economy] *Dushu zazhi* 2, nos. 7–8 (August 1932), 1–69, especially 50–55 for these issues.

26. Tao, "Zhongguozhi shangren ziben." GMD leftists played down the exploitative role of the landlord as landlord, blaming exploitation on commercial capital instead.

27. Some important ones are Tao, "Tongyi yu shengchan" [Unity and Production], *Xin shengming* 3, no. 4 (April 1930) and "Changqi hepingzhi zhenduan" [Diagnosis of Long-term Peace], *Xin shengming* 3, no. 11 (November 1930); Sa Mengwu,

"Guomin geming yu shehui geming" [National Revolution and Social Revolution] *Xin shengming* 1, no. 8 (August 1928): 1–15; Sa, "Diyi tongyi, dier shengchan" [First Unity, Then Production], *Xin shengming* 3, no. 5 (May 1930): 1–4; and Sa, "Geming yu tongyi" [Revolution and Unity], *Xin shengming* 3, no. 6 (June 1930).

28. Sa, "Geming yu tongyi."

29. Tao, "Zhongguozhi shangren ziben," 16. Also Yu Chih, "Nongmin yu tudi wenti," 265.

30. Tao, "Minzu wenti yu minzu zhuyi," 13.

31. In the August 7 conference in 1927, Qu Qiubai replaced Chen Duxiu as the secretary-general of the party. Qu retained this position for close to a year, after which it was passed on to Xiang Zhongfa in the Sixth National Congress of the CCP in Moscow in 1928. Finally, the second plenary session of the sixth central committee marked the rise of Li Lisan to leadership within the party. These changes in leadership, however, reflected little more than tactical shifts in party policies. Except for a brief period in 1928 when the party toyed with the idea of China as an "Asiatic society," the estimation of Chinese society as "feudal" and Chinese Revolution as "antifeudal anti-imperialist" was the dominant one. This view was explained, in addition to party documents, in journals such as *Sixiang yuekan* [Thought Monthly], *Shijie yüekan* [World Monthly], *Modeng qingnian* [Modern Youth], and *Xin sichao* [New Thought Tide]. See Wang Yichang, "Zhongguo shehui shi lun shi" [History of Discussions on Chinese Social History] *Dushu zazhi* 2, nos. 2–3 (March 1932): 1–71, 22–23.

32. The mode of exploitation of the peasant by the landlord, described variously as "noneconomic" or "extraeconomic" exploitation, was taken by many holding this view as crucial to the definition of feudalism. Zhu Qihua [Zhu Peiwo], *Zhongguo shehuidi jingji jiegou* (Shanghai, 1932), 277.

33. Li Lisan, "Zhongguo gemingdi genben wenti" [Fundamental Problems of the Chinese Revolution], *Buersaiweike* [Bolshevik] 3, nos. 2–3 (March 15, 1930): 37–83, 60.

34. These views were quite common. For an example, see Pan Dongzhou, "Zhongguo guomin jingjidi gaizao wenti" [The Problem of Transforming the Chinese National Economy], *Shehui koxue jiangzuo* (Shanghai, n.d.), vol. 1, 246–51.

35. Pan, "Zhongguo jingjizhi xingzhi" [The Nature of the Chinese Economy], quoted in Ren Shu, *Zhongguo jingji yanjiu xulun* [Introduction to the Study of the Chinese Economy] (Shanghai, 1932), 23–24.

36. Yan Lingfeng, *Zhongguo jingji wenti yanjiu* (Shanghai: 1931), 50.

37. *A Documentary History*, ed. Brandt et al., 946.

38. Pan, "Zhongguo guomin jingjidi gaizao wenti," 242.

39. Zhu Xinfan, "Zhongguo shehuizhi fengjian xingdi taolun" [On the Feudal Nature of Chinese Society], *Dushu zazhi* 1, nos. 4–5 (August 1931), 45.

40. As noted above, the "non-" or the "extra-" economic nature of the exploitation in Chinese agriculture was crucial to the definition of Chinese society as feudal by advocates of this position. Zhu and others frequently quoted from the third volume of *Das Kapital* to prove that Marx regarded "extraeconomic" exploitation as a characteristic of feudalism. In his discussion of labor rent, Marx says, "It is furthermore evident that in all forms in which the direct labourer remains the 'possessor' of the

means of production and labour conditions necessary for the production of his own means of subsistence, the property relationship must appear as a direct relationship of lordship and servitude, so that the direct producer is not free; a lack of freedom which may be reduced from a serfdom with enforced labour to a mere tributary relationship. The direct producer, according to our assumption is to be found here in possession of his own means of production, the necessary material labour conditions required for the realisation of his labour and the production of his means of subsistence. . . . Under such conditions the surplus-labour for the nominal owner of the land can only be extorted from him by other than economic pressure, whatever the form assumed may be." See Marx, *Das Kapital* (New York, 1970), vol. 3, 790–91. The interpretation of this passage by advocates of the "feudal" China position involves two problems. One, it is not clear from the passage that Marx meant this as a definition of feudalism as such. What is important is a condition where the producer continues to remain the possessor of the means of production. Just after that passage, Marx refers to that condition as existing in Asia, with the state replacing the individual lord. Secondly, by "other than economic pressure" at the end of the passage, Marx would seem to mean that since the laborer possesses the means of production, he is not subject to purely economic (market) competition, like the proletariat, but is economically his own master. That being so, the extortion of surplus labor is political or "extraeconomic." Chinese Marxists who held this position, in interpreting this idea, simply took exorbitant exploitation to mean "extraeconomic" or "noneconomic" exploitation.

41. The ambiguity toward imperialism is evident in the following two passages from Pan Dongzhou. "After imperialism invaded China, it had to build railroads and open up ports there in order to export its commodities into the country. In order to exploit the cheap labor of China and to utilize her natural treasures it had to establish new style capitalist enterprises. China's revolution in production certainly started after the eastward expansion of capitalism. Imperialism brought to China new style capitalist techniques and opened up China. Following this, it dealt a heavy blow to China's feudal economy, guild system and natural economy, driving China's economic organization on to a new path," in *Zhongguo jingji lun* [Discussion of the Chinese Economy], quoted in He Ganzhi, *Zhongguo shehui xingzhi wenti lunzhan* [Controversy on the Nature of Chinese Society] (Shanghai, 1937), 63–64. Though imperialism destroyed the feudal economy, it was unwilling to permit the development of China that would mean an end to its exploitation of the country. In this exploitation, imperialism used the same methods of exploitation as used by the Chinese feudal groups, perpetuating the very mode it was undermining. "The method employed by imperialism in obtaining raw materials from the Chinese peasant is to ally itself with the feudal landlords and the commercial capital of the village. They use their compradors [commercial capital] to purchase raw materials from the landlords, raising the hopes of the latter and leading them to even deeper exploitation of the peasant. Furthermore, [the landlord] taking advantage of the plight of the peasant, uses interest and money to force down the prices of his [the peasant's] products. With all these ties, imperialism uses landlords and Commercial capital to make the exploitation of the peasant harsher under the old methods and relations of production." Quoted in He, *Zhongguo shehui*, 64.

42. "Speaking from the viewpoint of its major forces and its direction of development, the Chinese economy is one that preserves strong feudal forces but has entered the path of capitalism in a colony. This is to say, on the one hand, China has already started developing toward capitalism under the control of international imperialism which is propelling it toward semicolonialism while, on the other hand, she preserves very strong feudal forces." Wang Xuewen in *Shehui kexue jiangzuo* [Roundtable on Social Science], quoted in Ho Ganzhi, *Zhongguo shehui xingzhi wenti lunzhan,* 61–62.

43. The Trotskyites mostly joined the discussion after their expulsion from the CCP in late 1929. The outstanding exponents of this position were Ren Shu and Yan Ling-feng, whose book-length studies cited above became the targets of attacks from the other positions (see notes 38–39). Also in 1930, the Trotskyites published a short-lived journal, *Dongli* [Der Motor], in which they explained their position on Chinese society.

44. Ren Shu, *Zhongguo jingji yanjiu xulun,* 37.

45. See above, note 36.

46. The following tables offered by Ren as "proof" of the victory of capitalism in China indicate this attitude. "If we can say that Chinese junks manifest the means of communication of the feudal economy and steamships represent the means of communication of the capitalist period, then":

	1875	1905	1915	1925	1926
Steamships	85	91	93	97	98
Junks	15	9	7	3	2
Total	100	100	100	100	100

Ren applied a similar reasoning to native banks and modern banks as further proof:

Native banks	68	37
Modern banks	32	63

See Ren, *Zhongguo jingji yanjiu xulun,* 82–83. Ren was attacked severely by his opponents as well as by his fellow Trotskyite Yan Ling-feng.

47. Yan, *Zhongguo jingji wenti yanjiu,* 9–10. A similar argument was offered by Zheng Xuejia, "Ziben zhuyi fazhan zhongzhi Zhongguo nongcun," *Dushu zazhi* 2, nos. 7–8 (August 1932): 9.

48. Yan, *Zhongguo jingji wenti yanjiu,* 10.

49. This confidence in communism as a means of solving problems of development confirms the thesis that communism in developing societies has served as an ideology of national development. Studies on this theme generally agree that the socialism of developing nations represents not so much a single doctrine as a common vocabulary derived from European socialism, especially Marxism, but endowed with a significantly new meaning that reflects the common experiences of these nations. This vocabulary has found particular relevance in those societies exposed to colonialism. See John H. Kautsky, *Political Change in Underdeveloped Countries: Nationalism*

and Communism (New York: Wiley, 1962) and *Communism and the Politics of Development* (New York: Wiley, 1968). For a more theoretical examination of Marxism from the perspective of modernization, see Robert C. Tucker, *The Marxian Revolutionary Idea* (New York: Norton, 1969). One of the earliest works to point out the relationship between Marxism and development was Adam B. Ulam's *The Unfinished Revolution* (New York: Random House, 1960). Ulam's influence is discernible in later works on the same theme. Of these works, the most explicit in developing a relationship between nationalism and communism are the books by Kautsky.

50. Kautsky, *Communism and the Politics of Development*, 60.

51. Tucker has suggested that under conditions of "arrested" and "differential" modernization, which correspond to the "stagnation" and "uneven development" of Chinese Marxists, the glaring polarity between the modern and the premodern sectors of society is very reminiscent of Marx's portrayal of "a totally polarized revolutionary society, a society divided into two hostile camps." This he identifies as Marxism's source of appeal in modernizing societies: "This central theme of Marxism [i.e., social polarity] is intensely meaningful to many members of the radical intelligentsia of a semimodern country because of a salient aspect of society as they perceive it: its bifurcation." (Tucker, *Marxian Revolutionary Idea*, 126.) The Chinese case confirms that social bifurcation was an important concern of radicals and that they looked to Marxism as a means of overcoming it. The explanation offered here differs nevertheless from Tucker's. Tucker suggests that the appeal of Marxism under such circumstances is merely paradigmatic: it is the "theme" of polarization rather than the class analysis in Marxism that is "intensely meaningful" to the radical intelligentsia "guiltily and indignantly conscious of the social cleavage" in their societies (127). The evidence of Chinese Marxists indicates that, whatever the individual reasons for becoming a Marxist, Marxism at the political level answered the important demand for national integration that *was* bound up with the issue of classes.

52. All sides in the discussion agreed on the intimacy of the ties between landlords and urban interests. The disagreements were more on the role of the landlord.

53. V. I. Lenin, *Imperialism* (Peking: Foreign Languages Press, 1969), 147.

54. Lenin's ideas on the national question are not free of ambiguities. On occasion, he does sound as if he condones national liberation as an end in itself: "Victorious socialism must necessarily establish a full democracy and, consequently, not only introduce full equality of nations but also realize the right of the oppressed nations to self-determination." See "The Socialist Revolution and the Right of Nations to Self-Determination," in *Selections from V. I. Lenin and J. V. Stalin on the National Colonial Question*, 31. But this statement itself is preceded by one on revolution in Europe and the United States. On the whole, I think, Lenin's writings on national liberation and imperialism display little evidence that he thought of national liberation independently of the worldwide class struggle between the proletariat and the bourgeoisie or regarded class struggle as an instrument of achieving national goals; rather, the overall thrust was in the direction of regarding national struggles in subordination to class struggle. In the "Preliminary Draft Theses on the National and Colonial Questions" he presented to the Second Congress of the Communist International in 1920, he stated categorically that "petty-bourgeois nationalism," preserving "national self-

interest intact" and not going beyond demands for national equality must be rejected in favor of "proletarian internationalism" that gives priority to the worldwide struggle of the proletariat against the bourgeoisie and "international capital." In *Selections*, 58.

55. Kautsky, *Communism and the Politics of Development*, 69–82.

56. Kautsky, *Communism and the Politics of Development*, 91. Kautsky takes the communism of developing countries as a tool of national development. Although his general analysis of the relationship between Marxism and nationalism has a great deal of merit, his depreciation of the communist commitment to social revolution obscures the differences between the strategies of national development conceived by different groups of nationalists, such as those observed between communists and the GMD in the 1920s. The distinguishing criterion of the three groups discussed here, all of them "nationalists," was their attitude toward social revolution. Marxist premises were accepted by them in different degrees, indicating a tension between those premises and national concerns, rather than the use of one as a cloak for the other.

57. "Every vital revolutionary movement of the twentieth century has been both national and social." Louis L. Snyder, *The New Nationalism* (Ithaca, NY: Cornell University Press, 1968), 33. On the other hand, only communist revolutionary movements have undertaken serious social restructuring.

58. Shih Chun, "On Studying Some History of the National Liberation Movement," *Peking Review* 15, no. 45 (November 10, 1972), 6–10. National liberation appears here as very much the end of history. See p. 10.

59. Leon Trotsky, *The Permanent Revolution and Results and Prospects* (New York: Pathfinder Press, 1970), 279.

II

MAKING MARXISM CHINESE:
MAO ZEDONG

4

Mao Zedong and "Chinese Marxism"

The thought of Mao Zedong (1893–1976) stands at the intersection of two histories: a global history that, beginning in the late nineteenth century, intruded with increasing forcefulness on Chinese thinking, and provided a new frame of reference for thinking about the past, present, and future of Chinese society; and a Chinese history the autonomy of which appeared as an issue as the new world impressed itself on Chinese consciousness. As "Mao Zedong Thought"[1] took shape in the course of the Communist Revolution in the 1930s it drew upon a foreign ideological import—Marxism—for its constituent elements; but it was the crucible of that revolution—Chinese society, with its social formations and quotidian culture—that gave it its form. At the heart of Mao's philosophical formation lies an account of a Third-World revolutionary consciousness seeking to remake itself into an autonomous subject of this new world against the immanent threat of degradation into its marginalized object. The contradictions in Mao Zedong Thought, no less than its contributions, are located in this account.

Mao's philosophy is the articulation of a "Chinese Marxism," at once Marxist *and* Chinese. It is Marxist not only because Mao himself (and Maoism) has placed his thought unambiguously within a Marxist tradition, but more importantly because the categories of his philosophy are derivative of Marxism; indeed, we might suggest that there is no constituent conceptual element of Mao's thought that is not traceable to Marxism. At the same time, there is something ineluctably Chinese about Mao's Marxism. Mao did not just read Marxism in accordance with a Chinese historical experience, as is commonly recognized, but insistently read the Chinese historical experience into Marxism, in the process "re-creating" Marxism.[2] Universally Marxist in its conceptualization of the world, Mao's Marxism is particularly Chinese in expression. One of Mao's greatest strengths as a leader was his ability to translate Marxist concepts into a Chinese idiom; and it was at the level of language (which to Marx represented "practical consciousness") that he read the Chinese historical experience into Marxism. Even at the most abstract exposition of his philosophical ideas, Mao drew his references from Chinese history, past and present, which placed his Marxism within a Chinese world of discourse that in its vocabulary is not readily accessible to the outsider, no matter how thoroughly armed with Marxist concepts.

Three caveats are necessary by way of introduction. First, while it is possible (and necessary) to speak of Mao's philosophy, this should not be taken to suggest that Mao may, or should, be viewed primarily as a philosopher, if by philosophy we understand the pursuit of abstract questions. Mao, who described himself on one occasion as a "graduate of the university of the greenwoods," observed of the pursuit of abstractions: "The way they go about it in the universities at present is no good, going from book to book, from concept to concept. How can philosophy come from books?"[3] First and foremost a practical revolutionary, Mao even at his most abstract had as his goal not to interpret but to change the world. This is not to say that he did not seek to ground practical problems of revolution in abstract principles, or that we may not extract such principles from his discussion of practical problems; but it is important to keep in mind that for Mao the criterion of validity even for abstractions was not their inner logic but whether or not they withstood the test of practice. Mao's was a philosophy of revolutionary practice. All Marxism may be viewed as a philosophy of *praxis* (or practice intended to change the world), as it was Karl Marx himself who stated that the goal of philosophy was not just to interpret but to change the world; but Mao was much more practice-orientated than Marx, and less constrained even than his immediate inspiration, Lenin, by the demands of abstract theory. Philosophy was of value to Mao only to the extent that it was "any good for making revolution."[4]

Second, the focus below on Mao's Marxism as he articulated it in the late 1930s does not imply that Mao had always been a Marxist, or that his thinking remained the same over the years. Mao's thought had a history. Mao was already a mature adult of twenty-seven when he participated in the founding of the Communist Party in 1920–1921, and he did not have any serious familiarity with the basic texts of Marxism until the 1930s, when those texts became available in Chinese. F. Wakeman has provided a catalogue of the diverse sources that went into the making of Mao's thinking ("confused," by Mao's own admission) in his pre-Marxist years.[5] This calls for a distinction between the pre- and post-Marxist phases of Mao's thinking. Moreover, while it is not clear if and how these pre-Marxist sources entered Mao's later reading of Marxism, it seems plausible that his pre-Marxist disposition to a populist approach to the relationship between the leaders and the led, to an anarchist suspicion of centralized power as well as anarchist conceptions of social organization, and even a basic emphasis on the unity of thought and action (theory and practice),[6] played a formative part in his thinking as well as his vision of revolutionary society, predisposed him to one reading of Marxism over other possible readings, and even introduced lasting (and dynamic) contradictions into his Marxism. In later years, too, Mao's thinking went through change, or at least elaborations, with regard to the practice of revolution in postrevolutionary society; especially controversial is the reasoning that was to culminate in the Cultural Revolution of the 1960s.

The analysis offered below is formal, rather than historical. While it is not intended to imply that Mao's thought remained changeless, it does suggest that the mature Mao's articulation of Marxism is representative of his philosophy in its most comprehensive statement, and reveals the characteristic tenor of his thinking as a practicing Marxist revolutionary. The crystallization of the intellectual and experiential sources of his thinking, Mao's articulation of his Marxism in the late 1930s was also to provide the source for the changing (and conflicting) claims to be made on "Maoism" in later years.

Finally, it is important while discussing Mao's philosophy to remember that this philosophy owed much to the contributions of others. The question of whether or not Mao's philosophy was a product of individual creativity or of the collective wisdom of the Party leadership, acquired over the course of revolutionary struggle, is a problematic one; but there is sufficient evidence to indicate that others participated in casting Mao's ideas in philosophical formulations, if not in their evolution in the first place. Those writings of Mao which offer the most systematic exposition of his philosophy are available only in their officially revised form. R. Wylie has suggested that in their origins also these writings owed much to contributions from young revolutionary scholars who served Mao as an unofficial "think-tank."[7]

The discussion below is divided into three parts: the relationship of Mao's Marxism to Marxism in general, especially an elucidation of his "sinification" of Marxism in relationship to the circumstances of the Chinese Revolution, which it sought to illuminate and to guide; a formal discussion of the philosophical premises of Mao's thought as they were articulated during the Yan'an Period (1937–1945) of the Chinese Revolution, especially in the two essays "On Contradiction" and "On Practice," which are commonly recognized as the most important efforts on Mao's part to formulate systematically the abstract principles underlying his revolutionary practice; and an evaluation of these principles with reference to Marxist theory, with particular attention to the contradictions they were to bequeath to revolutionary thinking in China—and to the unfolding of Marxism.

"MAKING MARXISM CHINESE"

Of all the innovations that have been claimed for Mao's Marxism, none is as fundamental, or as far-reaching in its implications, as its "sinification of Marxism" or, more appropriately, "making Marxism Chinese" *(Makesi zhuyide Zhongguohua)*. In its articulation of national to socialist goals, Mao's Marxism represented the epitome of a "Chinese Marxism" (or, even more broadly, a "Chinese socialism"), at once Chinese *and* Marxist. The same procedure lay at the root of Mao's restructuring of Marxism, by demanding a Chinese voice in a global Marxism, which would have far-reaching implications not just for the Chinese Revolution, but for Marxism globally.

Following Mao, Chinese students of Mao have conventionally described the "sinification of Marxism" as "the integration of the universal principles of Marxism with the concrete practice of the Chinese Revolution."[8] This seemingly straightforward formulation conceals the complexity of, not to say the contradictions presented by, the procedures of integrating universal principles (or theory) with revolutionary practice under particular circumstances. Stuart Schram has described "sinification" as "a complex and ambiguous" idea,[9] which is evident in the conflicting interpretations to which "sinification" has been subject. At the one extreme "sinification" appears simply as the "application" *(yunyong)* of Marxism to the revolution in China, with no further implications for theory, or even as the ultimate fulfillment of the fundamental practice orientation of Marxism. At the other extreme it represents the absorption of Marxism into a Chinese national or cultural space, irrevocably alienated from its origins in Europe. In between are a variety of interpretations which hold that while "sinification" left Marxism untouched in its basics, it brought to Marxism a Chinese "air" or "style."[10]

It is arguable that Mao's Marxism accommodated all these different senses of "sinification" (without a sense, however, that a Chinese Marxism thus defined represented an alienation or deviation from Marxism). Sinification was the articulation of Marxism to a historical situation of which Chinese society was the terrain, but a terrain in the process of transformation by global forces. Mao's Marxism was successful politically because it was able to speak to the multifaceted demands of an overdetermined historical situation. And it is of long-term historical significance not because of any profound theoretical contribution Mao made to Marxism, but because it articulated in its structure the problematic of this historical situation, which was to recast Marxism in a global perspective with consequences that were not just political but theoretical as well. As a Chinese *and* a Marxist, Mao sought at once to transform China through the general principles of Marxism, and to transform Marxism to meet the demands of China's specific historical circumstances; the sinification of Marxism presupposed both of these procedures. It is possible to read Mao's Marxism in different, even contradictory, ways because it was structured by these countervailing procedures. For the same reason, those interpretations of Mao that opt for one or another of the above readings, and ignore the contradictions that are built into the very structure of his Marxism (and the contradictions the latter presents to Marxism in general), are likely to fall into an arbitrary reductionism both in their readings of Mao and in their restriction of Marxism to some essence or other against which to evaluate the authenticity of Mao's Marxism.

Mao's Marxism, I should like to suggest here, forces us to rethink Marxism as a global/universal discourse. The tendency often is to think of Mao's Marxism in terms of an original Marxism; it is also possible, however, to rethink Marxism in terms of Mao's Marxism. I shall argue here that Mao's Marxism represents a local (or vernacular) version of a universal Marxism. Mao's Marxism was very much a product of the globalization of Marxism outside Europe (through the agency of the Russian Revolution, and Lenin). While this globalization of Marxism may also be taken as the universalization of a Marxist discourse, it also represents a dispersion of the discourse. Mao (like Lenin) was not a passive recipient of this discourse, but was to rephrase it in a Chinese vernacular. His Marxism, while very much a product of the globalization of Marxist discourse, introduced disruptive contradictions into the discourse in this very process. Mao's Marxism is most significant in the development of Marxism as the first fully articulated Third-World instance. In its insistence on the vernacular, it also represents the first significant challenge to a Marxist hegemony. Perhaps most significantly, it points to a new kind of nonhegemonic universality, in which a genuinely universal Marxist discourse is to be constituted out of various vernacular Marxisms.

Such a perspective becomes evident if we view Mao's Marxism in terms of the historical situation from which it springs. The contradictions in Mao's Marxism are found upon close examination to be implicit in the historical situation in which Chinese society was placed in the twentieth century. It was this situation that rendered Marxism attractive to Chinese revolutionaries. In their efforts to find Marxist resolutions to China's problems, revolutionaries were to restructure Marxism to accommodate the questions thrown up by this multidimensional historical situation. The identity of Mao's Marxism (and of Chinese Marxism), as well as its discursive structure, rests not upon some abstract notion of China conceived in isolation from its historical context, but upon this historical situation which appears with the location within Chinese social structure and consciousness of unprecedented historical forces that displaced Chinese society from its earlier historical context, and relocated it irretrievably within a new global economic, political, and ideological process.

There are three strategic dimensions of China's historical situation in the twentieth century that have been crucial in structuring Chinese Marxism. The first is the global dimension. Beginning in the nineteenth century, China was drawn inexorably into a global history of which the dominant motive force was capitalism. Whether or not China was completely incorporated into a capitalist world-system or became capitalist in the process are moot questions; indeed, a basic goal of most socialists in China was to counteract such incorporation.

The second is the Third-World dimension. The Chinese, unlike Western European or North American societies but like most Asian and African (and to some extent South American) societies, experienced the globalization of history and its motive force, capitalism, not as an internal development but as alien hegemony. While Chinese history was conjoined to global history, in other words, the Chinese experienced the process as one of subjugation, as a Third-World society. Under the circumstances, socialism was not merely an alternative to capitalism, but an alternative that promised national liberation from capitalist hegemony, and the possibility of entering global history not as its object but as an independent subject.

The third dimension is the national dimension: Chinese society itself, which, in spite of its Third-World status in a capitalist world, remained the locus of its own history. The conjoining of China to a global history did not mean the dissolution of Chinese society into a global pool, any more than its identification as a Third-World society implies its reduction to some homogeneous Third-World configuration. The national dimension, while seemingly transparent, is in actuality quite opaque. In a historical situation where the very conception of China is overdetermined by the incorporation of Chinese society into a global structure, it is difficult to distinguish what is pristinely Chinese (which, as an idea, was itself a product of the historical situation since the Chinese did not think of China as a nation among others before this situation came into existence) from what is insistently Chinese in response to global pressures for transformation. The historical situation, in other words, is characterized by mutual incorporation (and contradiction): the incorporation of China into a global structure, and the incorporation into Chinese society of new global forces. It is in the structure of this mutual incorporation that we may discover the multiple dimensions of the historical situation. Our conception of China (as well as the Chinese conception of self), correspondingly, is of necessity overdetermined, a product of the moments in the conjuncture of historical forces that relocated China in a new world situation. Marxism, in its anticapitalism, also promised the possibility of national self-discovery for a society that a capitalist world threatened to consume. In order for the promise to be fulfilled, however, Marxism itself had to be rephrased in a national voice, for a Marxism that could not account for a specif-ically national experience abdicated its claims to universality; worse, under the guise of universalism, it replicated in a different form the hegemonism of capitalism, of which it was historically a product.

These three dimensions were also the structuring moments of Chinese Marxism, which would find its most comprehensive articulation in Mao's "sinification of Marxism." Mao's Marxism is most properly conceived as a reflection upon this historical situation (which must be distinguished from re-flection *of* the situation) if we are to grasp it in its structural complexity. As a discourse, Mao's Marxism bears upon its discursive structure the imprint of the multidimensional historical situation from which it derived its problem-atic. It is at once a reflection upon Chinese society from a universalist Marx-ist perspective and a reflection upon Marxism from the perspective of China as a Third-World society and a nation. The two procedures, while coexten-sive, are also contradictory. Nevertheless, they have with all their contradic-tions structured the discourse that we may call Chinese Marxism.

That this historical situation served as the point of departure in the formu-lation of a Chinese Marxism is in evidence everywhere in the texts (authored by Mao or his close associates) associated with the "sinification of Marxism," of which the culmination was Mao's January 1940 essay "On New Democ-racy," which stands as the classic formulation of the premises of Chinese Marxism.[11] "New Democracy" referred to an economic and political forma-tion (a mixed economy to facilitate economic development, and an alliance across classes—under Communist leadership—in the pursuit of national lib-eration) suitable to China's immediate needs; but more significantly it also represented the insertion of a new stage in historical progress appropriate to all societies placed similarly to China in the world. Its premises were: (a) that the Chinese Revolution is part of a global revolution against capitalism; (b) that it is, however, a revolution against capitalism in a "semifeudal semi-colonial" society to which national liberation is a crucial task; and (c) that it is also a national revolution, a revolution to create a new nation—and a new culture which would be radically different from both the culture inherited from the past and the culture imported from abroad. The latter, significantly, included Marxism:

> In applying Marxism to China, Chinese communists must fully and properly in-tegrate the universal truth of Marxism with the concrete practice of the Chinese revolution or, in other words, the universal truth of Marxism must be combined with specific national characteristics and acquire a definite national form.[12]

In the end, the sinification of Marxism did not achieve an "integration of the universal truth of Marxism with the concrete practice of the Chinese Revolution," if by that we understand a seamless synthesis which dissolved Marxism into China's circumstances, or integrated China's peculiarities into the existing conceptual framework of Marxist theory. Mao's Marxism did not consist of merely applying Marxism to China's circumstances (which suggests too passive a role for what is Chinese in it, that is, contrary to his insistence on the project of sinification in the first place), or of just developing it (which, while arguable, is misleading to the extent that it suggests the absence of any disjuncture between Mao's Marxism and Marxism in general). The very tortured way in which Mao presented the project of "sinification" may offer the most persuasive clue that the "sinification of Marxism" entailed an effort to "integrate" what might not be integrable in the above sense of the term. It is worth quoting at some length the passage in which Mao used the term "sinification" for the first time (and is also one of his fullest descriptions of what he means by it) to convey a sense of the reasoning that, rather than argue out the logic of the project it proposes, seeks instead to suppress the contradictoriness of the project by the force of its metaphors:

> Another task of study is to study our historical legacy, and to evaluate it critically using Marxist methods. A great nation such as ours with several thousand years of history has its own developmental laws, its own national characteristics, its own precious things. . . . The China of today is a development out of historical China. We are Marxist historicists; we may not chop up history. We must evaluate it from Confucius to Sun Zhongshan, assume this precious legacy, and derive from it a method to guide the present movement. . . . Communists are Marxist internationalists, but Marxism must be realized through national forms. There is no such thing as abstract Marxism, there is only concrete Marxism. The so-called concrete Marxism is Marxism that has taken national form; we need to apply Marxism to concrete struggle in the concrete environment of China, we should not employ it in the abstract. Communists who are part of the great Chinese nation, and are to this nation as flesh and blood, are only abstract and empty Marxists if they talk about Marxism apart from China's special characteristics. Hence the sinification of Marxism, imbuing every manifestation of Marxism with China's special characteristics, that is to say applying it in accordance with Chinese characteristics, is something every Party member must seek to understand and resolve. We must discard foreign eight-legged essays, we must stop singing abstract and empty tunes, we must give rest to dogmatism, and substitute in their place Chinese airs that the common people love to see and hear. To separate internationalist content and national form only reveals a total lack of understanding of internationalism.[13]

Rather than resolve the contradiction between "internationalist content and national form," the sinification of Marxism was to produce an ideological construct of which Marxism was a determining moment, but which in turn rephrased Marxism in its own particular grammar. Marxism helped define Mao's vision of a new China; but the vision is not therefore reducible to Marxism, for it retained its fundamental sources outside Marxism. Likewise, a deep awareness of China's national needs conditioned Mao's understanding of Marxism, but did not therefore dissolve Marxism into Chinese nationalism. This *irreducibility* of the moments that went into the making of Mao's Marxism invites its conceptualization in structural terms: structure in Louis Althusser's sense, that is visible in the interaction of the moments constituting it; which, although mutually transformative, are not reducible into one another or dissolvable into the structure, and in their irreducibility retain their contradictory relationship within a context of structural unity.[14] It is just such a structure that the sinification of Marxism produced; and it is this structure that is Mao's Marxism (or Chinese Marxism, as understood here). It is Marxist because Marxism was present in it as a determinant moment; it also broke with the Marxism that informed it because it rendered Marxism into one moment of a structure that had multiple sources in its construction.

The consequences of this new structural context for Marxist theory will be discussed below. Suffice it to say here that Mao's Marxism appears differently depending on the perspective provided by the different moments that constituted it. In their conjuncture these alternative perspectives yield a comprehensive appreciation of its structural complexity.

In its relationship to Marxism worldwide, Mao's Marxism is universal/global, for there is little in its formal-theoretical articulation that is not derivative of European Marxism. The new structural context would have the consequence of opening up ("deconstructing") Marxist theoretical formulations, but neither its political premises nor its theoretical concepts suffice to distinguish Mao's Marxism from Marxism elsewhere. Basic to it was the equation of Marxism with a "social revolution" to which the transformation of class relations was central. As a political discourse, it is also global in compass because, both in its origins and in its unfolding, it has been part of a global discourse on Marxism; in other words, it was global currents in Marxism that nourished it, and Mao's Marxism at all times spoke to issues raised by Marxism globally.[15] It is difficult to identify elements in Mao's theoretical formulations that render his Marxism any the less Marxist than any other. In its global guise, his Marxism appears as a transformative idea, as a reflection in Marxist language upon Chinese society that sought to reshape the terrain upon which it reflected in accordance with universal Marxist aspirations. Mao was even capable of referring to China as a "blank sheet of paper" upon which Marxism could write its agenda!

Within this global discourse, however, Mao's Marxism appears in the guise of a Third-World Marxism that reflects upon socialism from a Third-World perspective. For reasons that should be apparent from China's relationship to capitalism as a Third-World society, socialism in China appears throughout its history as part of a national project; in other words, the socialist struggle for a social revolution against capitalism as well as against the legacy of the past has been obsessively involved with the struggle for national liberation and development: as capitalism appeared in China in the guise of imperialism, the struggle against capitalism likewise has been indistinguishable from the struggle for liberation from imperialist hegemony. This qualification compels us to modify the universality of Mao's Marxism; not only because the commitment to national liberation rendered problematic the theoretical assumption of social change through class struggle (divisive of necessity), but also because socialism as he conceived it had to assume burdens which were of slight concern to socialism in its origins in capitalist Europe: state-building to render China into a viable nation (which ultimately had to face the problem of creating a "civil society" as well), economic development to withstand imperialist hegemony as well as to create a basis for socialism, and not least cultural reconstruction. These burdens, commonly shared by the socialism of Third-World societies, have had far-reaching consequences for socialism in these societies and, by implication, the unfolding of socialism globally. Mao, quite aware of this commonality, explicitly conceived of Marxism in relationship to the problems of such societies.

Mao's Marxism, finally, is a Chinese reflection upon global socialism, spoken in a vernacular voice by a Chinese subject who expressed through Marxism local, specifically Chinese, concerns. From a Chinese perspective, socialism too appears as an alien idea and, in its claims to universality, a hegemonic one, hence the urge to rephrase it in a Chinese vernacular, to assimilate it to a quotidian Chinese consciousness or "structure of sentiment,"[16] in order to guarantee a Chinese voice in a universal socialist language. What is involved here is more than a Third-World assimilation of socialism to a national project. The vernacularization of socialism by Mao does not consist merely of making the national good, or national considerations of wealth and power, into the measure of the relevance of socialism, or the validity of its claims; rather, it represents an authentic nationalization of socialism, bringing into it the voices of its local social and cultural environment. If the one is political and economic in its appreciation of socialism, the other is insistently social and cultural. It seeks to domesticate socialism by endowing its language with the phraseology and nuances of a specifically Chinese historical experience. Vernacular socialism represents the absorption of socialism into a Chinese terrain, the re-presentation of its universal aspirations in the language of native ideals. In Mao's Marxism, this is evident not only in his formal calls for making Marxism Chinese, but more eloquently in the very language in which he presented Marxism to his Chinese audiences, in which Chinese history past and present served as the medium for communicating Marxist abstractions.[17]

These three perspectives, in their conjuncture, are essential to appreciating Mao's Marxism in its structural complexity, and contradictions. The problems which Mao's Marxism presents are largely a consequence of the fact that it is at once locally Chinese and universally Marxist, the one as compellingly significant as the other. The grounding of Mao's Marxism in its historical situation may not resolve the questions it raises, but it allows us to reformulate its *problematic* as a discourse without reductionism, in such a way as to accommodate the contradictions that it presents. As a reflection on China's historical situation, Mao's Marxism is best read as what Jurgen Habermas has described as a "practical discourse."[18] A practical discourse is to be distinguished, on the one hand, from a theoretical discourse that is divorced from practice (and, therefore, its concrete premises) and, on the other hand, from practice (understood as practical activity to change the world) that takes its theoretical premises for granted. This distinction is significantly different from the formal distinction Chinese Marxists (beginning with Mao) have drawn over the years between theory and practice. The latter objectifies Chinese society as a "target" for the "arrow" of theory, or a "blank sheet" upon which Marxism may write its agenda (both, by the way, Mao's metaphors), which privileges theory as a universal over its application in practice, even if in actuality the reverse may have been the case more often than not. The notion of practical discourse recognizes Mao (and Chinese practitioners of socialism) as the subjects who reflect on Marxism; their relationship to a global Marxism appears, therefore, not as a subject–object relationship but as an intersubjective one. It allows, in other words, a genuine Chinese national participation in a global socialist discourse. It is the irreducibility of the national and the global in this practical discourse, and the centrality to resolving its contradictions of the reflecting subject, that lay at the core of Mao's philosophical restatement of Marxism.

CONTRADICTION AND PRACTICE

Mao articulated the philosophical premises of his Marxism in the process—and as an integral part—of the sinification of Marxism. His two essays "On Practice" and "On Contradiction" were delivered as speeches in July and August 1937, respectively, coinciding with his call for a shift in Communist revolutionary strategy in response to Japan's full-scale invasion of China in July 1937. As its most fundamental level of vernacularization, the sinification of

Marxism was a product of revolutionary problems (especially the problem of a Marxist revolution in agrarian China, which theory was ill-prepared to contain); some of the key ingredients that were to go into the making of a "sinified" Marxism had been enunciated earlier in response to these problems, which were quite independent of the national problem.[19] The national problem as a problem in Marxism was also a subject for intensive discussion in Chinese intellectual circles as early as 1936.[20] Nevertheless, the project of sinification was clearly formulated and realized only between 1937 and 1940: there was a direct line connecting the theoretical formulations of Mao's philosophy in these two essays and the reasoning underlying the signified Marxist strategy that Mao was to enunciate in his "On New Democracy" in 1940. Eminently practical and tactical in intention, the two essays nevertheless sought to ground the problems of the Chinese Revolution within Marxist theory, in the process offering Mao's fullest and most comprehensive statement on the philosophical considerations underlying his reformulation of Marxist theory. What Mao wrote in later years of a philosophical nature represented primarily an application and extension of ideas first enunciated in these essays.

There is a further, possibly more intrinsic, connection between the practical project of sinification and Mao's theoretical formulations in these essays. Central to Mao's Marxism as presented in the essays is the concept of contradiction. Norman Levine has suggested that while the concept of contradiction originated in Hegel, and was used extensively by Lenin, it acquired an unprecedented significance and elaboration in Mao's Marxism.[21] I suggested above that sinification produced an explicitly structural reading of Marxism by its very effort to reconcile contradictory demands, which in turn rested upon the irreducibility of the moments that went into its constitution. The centrality of the concept of "contradiction" in Mao's Marxism, I should like to suggest, was a direct product of his reformulation of Marxism to account for China's historical situation, which was defined structurally by the contradictoriness of its various moments, and the articulation of this contradictoriness as a contradiction between theory and practice. We must underline here that while the contradiction between national and social revolutionary needs is the most obvious, the problem went deeper into the very practice of revolution in a social situation that was not anticipated in theory: an agrarian society in which a socialist revolution had to be engineered out of components that theory did not account for; in which the revolutionaries themselves were outsiders to the social situation (and, therefore, in contradiction to it), and had to maneuver with great care in order not to antagonize the population and jeopardize their own existence; and, therefore, could not translate the multifaceted conflicts they encountered readily into *their* theoretical categories, but rather had to recognize them as *irreducible* features of the social situation into which to articulate theory. This is what raised the question of the language of revolution at the most fundamental level. And ultimately, beyond the level of the national struggle, it was this social situation that made the "sinification" of Marxism into a total theoretical project, and called for the reformulation of theory in terms of the multitude of contradictions that revolution faced at the level of practice. This is evident, I think, in the intrinsic relationship Mao establishes in the two essays between a social analysis based on contradictions and the activist epistemology that he sets forth in his analysis of practice.

"The law of contradiction in things, that is the law of the unity of opposites, is the basic law of materialist dialectics."[22] Thus began Mao's discussion of "contradiction." He continued:

> As opposed to the metaphysical world outlook of materialist-dialectics holds that in order to understand the development of a thing we should study it internally and its relations with other things; in other words, the development of things should be seen as their internal and necessary self-movement, while each thing in its movement is interrelated with and interacts on the things around it. (p. 313)

"On Contradiction" depicts a world (and a mode of grasping it) in which not "things" but relationships are the central data. Such relationships are relationships of mutual opposition as well as transformation (difference as well as identity). These relationships do not coexist haphazardly, moreover, but constitute a totality structured by their many interactions, a totality that is nevertheless in a constant state of transformation because the relationships between the whole and the parts that constitute it, no less than the relationships between the parts, are not merely functional but also (and more importantly) oppositional. The idea of "contradiction," as a dialectical idea, encompasses both functionality and opposition ("unity of opposites"); "contradiction" as a constitutive principle of the world (and the cosmos) produces a totality where everything (the parts no less than the whole) contains everything else, and yet nothing is therefore reducible to anything else. As Mao puts it later on in the essay:

> Since the particular is united with the universal and since the universality as well as the particularity of contradiction is inherent in everything, universality residing in particularity, we should, when studying an object, try to discover both the particular and the universal and their interconnection, to discover both particularity and universality and also their interconnections of this object with the many objects outside it. (p. 329)

As a philosophical essay, "On Contradiction" is devoted to an elaboration of the characteristics of "contradictions" in which these general ideas are embedded. These characteristics may be summarized (using Mao's own wording) as follows:

1. Contradiction is universal:

The universality or absoluteness of contradiction has a twofold meaning. One is that contradiction exists in the process of development of all things, and the other is that in the process of development of each thing a movement of opposites exists from beginning to end. . . . There is nothing that does not contain contradiction; without contradiction nothing would exist. (p. 316)

2. Contradiction is also particular:

Every form of motion contains within itself its own particular contradiction. This particular contradiction constitutes the particular essence which distinguishes one thing from another. (p. 320) . . . There is always a gradual growth from the knowledge of individual and particular things to the knowledge of things in general. Only after man knows the particular essence of many different things can he proceed to generalization and know the common essence of things. When man attains the knowledge of this common essence, he uses it as a guide and proceeds to study various concrete things which have not yet been studied, or studied thoroughly, and to discover the particular essence of each; only thus is he able to supplement, enrich and develop his knowledge of their common essence. . . . These are the two processes of cognition: one, from the particular to the general, and the other, from the general to the particular. (pp. 320–21) . . . Qualitatively different contradictions can only be resolved by qualitatively different methods. (p. 321) . . . Contradictions [in Chinese society] cannot be treated in the same way since each has its own particularity; moreover, the two aspects of each contradiction cannot be treated in the same way since each has its own characteristics. We who are engaged in the Chinese revolution should not only understand the particularity of these contradictions in their totality, that is, in their interconnectedness, but should also study the two aspects of each contradiction as the only means of understanding the totality. (pp. 322–23)

3. Principal contradiction and the principal aspect of a contradiction:

There are many contradictions in the process of development of a complex thing, and one of them is necessarily the principal contradiction whose existence and development determine or influence the existence and development of the other contradictions. (p. 331) . . . In any contradiction the development of the contradictory aspects is uneven. (p. 333) . . . The nature of a thing is determined mainly by the principal aspect of a contradiction, the aspect which has gained the dominant position. But this situation is not static; the principal and the non-principal aspects of a contradiction transform themselves into each other and the nature of things changes accordingly. (p. 333) . . . At certain times in the revolutionary struggle, the difficulties outweigh the favorable conditions and so constitute the principal aspect of the contradiction and the favorable conditions constitute the secondary aspect. But through their efforts the revolutionaries can overcome the difficulties step by step and open up a new favorable situation. (p. 355)

4. Identity and struggle of the aspects of a contradiction:

Identity, unity, coincidence, interpenetration, interpermeation, interdependence (or mutual dependence for existence), interconnection or mutual cooperation—all these different terms mean the same thing and refer to the following two points: first, the existence of each of the two aspects of a contradiction in the process of development of a thing presupposes the existence of the other aspect, and both aspects coexist in a single entity; second, in given conditions, each of the contradictory aspects transforms itself into its opposite. (p. 337) . . . How then can one speak of identity or unity? The fact is that no contradictory aspect can exist in isolation. Without its opposite aspect, each loses the condition for its existence. (p. 338) . . . The unity of opposites is conditional, temporary and relative, while the struggle of mutually exclusive opposites is absolute. (p. 342)

5. Antagonism in contradiction:

Antagonism is one form, but not the only form, of a struggle of opposites. In human history, antagonism between classes exists as a particular manifestation of the struggle of opposites. (p. 343) . . . Contradiction and struggle are universal and absolute, but the methods of resolving contradictions, that is, the forms of struggle, differ according to the differences in the nature of contradictions. Some contradictions are characterized by open antagonism, others are not. (p. 344)

"On Contradiction" is a revolutionary hermeneutics; an interpretative strategy, in other words, the premise of which is "making revolution." While it is revealing of a life outlook that may include native philosophical elements in addition to Marxism (of this more below), all these elements are subsumed under, and refracted through, this basic problem.

At one level, it is possible to read the essay simply as a statement in the abstract of specific problems of revolution in the immediate circumstances of Chinese society in 1937. The statements above are interspersed with observations on contemporary developments in China's historical situation that are used in illustration of Mao's various abstractions. It is difficult to say which came first, the abstractions or the illustrations, but there is little question that the historical situation depicted in the illustrations had priority in Mao's thinking.[23] A fundamental goal of Mao in the essay is to provide a theoretical justification for the change in the Party's revolutionary policy in response to the Japanese invasion of China (which shifted the "primary" contradiction from class struggle to national struggle). This also explains why the major part of the essay is devoted to discussion of the "particularity" of contradiction (which includes discussion of primary/secondary contradictions, as well as the discussion of its primary/secondary aspects). It is in the process of this legitimation of change in policy that Mao articulates the priority of practice to theory. As he put it:

> The dogmatists . . . do not understand that conditions differ in different kinds of revolution and so do not understand that different methods should be used to resolve different contradictions; on the contrary, they invariably adopt what they imagine to be an unalterable formula and arbitrarily apply it everywhere, which only causes setbacks to the revolution or makes a sorry mess of what was originally well done. (p. 322)

In spite of the priority of practical questions in Mao's thinking, however, it would be reductionist to read the essay simply as a discussion of practical questions, and ignore the consequences for theory of Mao's theoretical justification of practice. Louis Althusser grasped the significance of this problem when he wrote of "On Contradiction":

> Mao's essay, inspired by his struggle against dogmatism in the Chinese Party, remains generally *descriptive*, and in consequence it is in certain respects *abstract*. Descriptive: his concepts correspond to concrete experiences. In part abstract: the concepts, though new and rich in promise, are represented as *specifications* of the *dialectic* in general rather than as *necessary implications* of the Marxist conception of society and history.[24] (italics in the original)

What Althusser tells us is that while Mao's theoretical formulations remain incompletely theorized, they are nevertheless path-breaking and significant (and are not therefore reducible to descriptive abstractions). The former is evident. While Mao sought in the essay to theorize the particularity of revolutionary practice, he consciously demoted theory: "in the contradiction between theory and practice, practice is the principal aspect" (p. 335). This demotion of theory was also to lead to a restatement of the role of theory: Mao conceived of theory primarily as an abstraction of concrete revolutionary practice, and only secondarily as an abstract formulation of "laws" of social movement. Mao did not repudiate theory, or the necessity of understanding it. On one occasion, responding to an imaginary audience which held that those who were "instinctively" dialectical in their activity did not need to read books to understand theory, he reaffirmed the importance of studying theory because, without such study, there was no possibility of synthesizing the multifaceted phenomena that the revolutionary faced.[25] "Without revolutionary theory," he believed with Lenin, "there can be no revolutionary movement."[26] Indeed, given his revolutionary hermeneutics, theory was to reappear in Mao's thinking as an essential guide to the revolutionary in determining the direction of revolution.

It was another matter, however, with the practice of revolution. The priority that Mao assigned to practice meant that, unlike Althusser, he was only marginally interested in theorizing his abstract formulations; it is even possible to suggest that "On Contradiction" was only "in part abstract" because Mao's historicism (by which I mean his emphasis on concreteness and particularity) did not allow theorization beyond a certain point. What it did produce was a hermeneutics: revolutionary practice was no longer predictable from theory; rather, the latter became a guide to "reading" historical situations in the activity of making revolution. Mao's appreciation of theory was itself "contradictory" in the double meaning he assigned to it at once as a guide and instrument: "guide" in the long-term direction of revolution, "instrument" in immediate analysis. Theory, in other words, was part of the very contradictions that it was intended to unravel and to resolve. This was the key to Mao's restructuring of theory.

The world of "On Contradiction" is a world of ceaseless and endless confrontation and conflict, where unity itself may be understood only in terms of the contradictoriness of its moments, where no entity is a constant because it has no existence outside its contradictions or a place of its own other than in its relationship to other contradictions. It may be that all Marxism is a conflict-based conceptualization of the world. But how ever differently Marxists may have structured conflict or organized the structure of society, conflict in most interpretations of Marxism is conceived of in terms of a limited number of social categories (production, relations of production, politics, ideology, etc.), and there has been an urge to hierarchize these categories in terms of their effectivity in the social structure. Mao's multitude of contradictions resist such hierarchization and, more significantly, reduction to a limited number of categories. Some contradictions are obviously more significant than others in determining social structure or historical direction, but Mao refuses to deny a role in social dynamics to what seem to be the most trivial contradictions (and, therefore, to dissolve them into broader categories) or to hierarchize them except on a temporary basis, for in their interactions they are in a constant state of flux as regards their place in the structure. What he says of the primary categories of Marxist theory is revealing:

> For instance, in the contradiction between the productive forces and the relations of production, the productive forces are the principal aspect; in the contradiction between theory and practice, practice is the principal aspect; in the contradiction between the economic base and the superstructure, the economic base is the principal aspect; and there is no change in their respective positions. This is the mechanical materialist concept, not the dialectical materialist conception. True, the productive forces, practice and the economic base generally play the principal and decisive role; whoever denies this is not a materialist. But it must also be admitted that in certain conditions, such aspects as the relations of production, theory and the superstructure in turn manifest themselves in the principal and decisive role. (pp. 335–36)

This, I think, yields a conception of causation that may best be described in terms of Althusser's notion of "structural effectivity" (or causation); that is, a notion of causation without hierarchy, where the structure is visible only in the interaction of its constitutive moments, which are mutually determinant through the intermediation of the structure as "absent cause." (It is no coincidence that Althusser finds in Mao's idea of contradiction a point of departure for his own reflection on causation.)[27] Causation here is conjunctural and overdetermined: social and historical events are products of the conjuncture of multiple contradictions. Mao's difference from Althusser may be that he conceived of conjunctures in more contingent (and historical) terms than Althusser was willing to do. His notion of causation, therefore, remains less theorized than Althusser's. More importantly, essential to Mao's idea of contradiction was the role of the revolutionary subject. In the first place, an "overdetermined conjuncture" points to a revolutionary alternative as one possibility among others, because such a situation is of its very nature open ended; in other words, open to interpretation. It is up to the revolutionary to interpret it in accordance with revolutionary goals. This is also where the importance of abstract theory as a guide to action comes in; because without the aid of theory, the revolutionary will be at a loss to make choices consistent with long-term goals. Second, while itself a product of contradictions, revolutionary practice is part of the structure of contradictions, and effective in aligning the contradictions in a manner most consistent with revolutionary goals. The role of revolutionary struggle in converting an unfavorable to a favorable situation was part of Mao's analysis of contradiction (see above); it appears most prominently in other places in the context of his discussions of the military strategy of revolutionary struggle.[28]

Mao's companion essay, "On Practice," offers in epistemological form a more direct statement on interpretation as an essential component of revolutionary activity (or, if I may overstate the point, on revolutionary activity *as* interpretative activity). On the surface, the epistemology which "On Practice" offers is an empiricist one. As he presents it, cognition begins with perceptual cognition, which is "the stage of sense perceptions and impressions."[29] As sense perceptions are repeated and accumulate, "a sudden change (leap) takes place in the brain in the process of cognition, and concepts are formed. Concepts are no longer phenomena, the separate aspects and the external relations of things; they grasp the essence, the totality and the internal relations of things" (p. 298). (Mao also describes this as "the stage of rational knowledge.") The knowledge thus acquired is then tested for its validity in actual practice, which leads to further perceptions, conceptual modifications, back to practice in an ongoing cycle of perception-conception-practice-perception.

If Mao's epistemology is empiricist, however, it is the empiricism of an activist who constructs knowledge in the process of reconstructing the world with revolutionary goals. While there is one illustration in the essay which suggests that cognition may be a passive process of the accumulation of perceptions, the essay in its totality points to an activist epistemology. Mao believes that cognition has a class character, and he clearly elevates dialectical materialism over other possible methods in understanding the world (p. 305). Mao begins his discussion of cognition at the stage of perception, but this does not imply that the mind is a blank sheet of paper upon which perceptions rewrite themselves into conceptions, because the mind already has a conceptual apparatus for organizing perceptions (implicit in the class character of knowledge), and a theoretical apparatus (dialectical materialism) for articulating them. His epistemology, furthermore, elevates certain activities over others in the acquisition of knowledge (the struggle for production and class struggle) (pp. 296, 300), and knowledge has a clear goal: "making revolution." Most important is the place of practice (which Mao consistently uses in the sense of praxis, activity to change the world in cognition). While in his discussion of cognition Mao represents "practice" as one stage of the process, "practice" clearly plays a much more important part in his thinking. It is practice, rather than perception, that stands at the beginning of the process of cognition (since different practices lead to different understanding of the world, and Mao elevates those perceptions that arise from the struggle for production and class above all others). Practice also intermediates the transformation of perceptions into conceptions: "The perceptual and the rational are qualitatively different, but are not divorced from each other; they are unified on the basis of practice" (p. 299). The goal of "On Practice" is not to argue for a vulgar empiricism ("seeking truth from facts"), but to assert the priority of practice in cognition against a theoretical dogmatism oblivious to concrete circumstances of revolution. Quoting Stalin, Mao observes: "Theory becomes purposeless if it is not connected with revolutionary practice;

just as practice gropes in the dark if its path is not illumined by revolutionary theory" (p. 305).

"On Practice" may be viewed as a call for the revolutionary hermeneutic
which Mao would elaborate a month later in "On Contradiction." Composed
as parts of a single project, the two discussions illuminate each other in their
intertextuality. Mao's understanding of knowledge as interpretation, as well
as his unwillingness to view it *just* as interpretation, is expressed in the following statement:

> Fully to reflect a thing in its totality, to reflect its essence, to reflect its inherent
> laws, it is necessary through the exercise of thought to reconstruct the rich data
> of sense perception, discarding the dross and selecting the essential, eliminating
> the false and retaining the true, proceeding from the one to the other and from
> the outside to the inside, in order to form a system of concepts and theories—it
> is necessary to make a leap from perceptual to rational knowledge. Such recon-
> structed knowledge is not more empty or more unreliable [than empiricism]; on
> the contrary, whatever has been scientifically reconstructed in the process of
> cognition, on the basis of practice, reflects objective reality. (p. 303)

There is a profound contradiction in Mao's thinking. As a Marxist materialist, Mao believes that there is an "objective reality" against which to judge
the validity of competing forms of knowledge; hence his repeated references
to cognition as a "reflection" of the world in the mind. At the same time, as
the essay "On Contradiction" leaves little doubt, Mao views objective reality
(or the context of thought) itself to be a product of contradictions; which renders it into an object of interpretation and "reconstruction." His foray into the
discussion of "truth" is revealing of this contradiction in its simultaneous assertion of the "relativity" of truth, even of revolutionary truth, and his conviction of the possibility of an "absolute truth":

> Marxists recognize that in the absolute and general process of development in
> the universe, the development of each particular process is relative, and that
> hence, in the endless flow of absolute truth, man's knowledge of a particular
> process at any given stage of development is only relative truth. The sum total
> of innumerable relative truths constitutes absolute truth. . . . Marxism-Leninism
> has in no way exhausted truth but ceaselessly opens up roads to the knowledge
> of truth in the course of practice. (pp. 307–8)

The contradiction between absolute and relative truth presents Mao with an
unresolvable contradiction, which he seeks to overcome by resorting to practice as "the criterion of truth" (p. 305). Practice as activity to change the world
is bound up in Mao's thinking with the notion of contradiction: that is, changing the world is a process of resolving contradictions, which leads to new

contradictions, which leads to new practices and so on in an endless process. This itself is problematic, however, because, as the discussion of "contradiction" tells us, practice in and of itself does not provide a direction to history unless guided by some notion of "truth" (Mao is quite disingenuous in his representation of "absolute truth" as the "sum total of relative truths," since he obviously does not recognize the truthfulness of all relative truths), or any judgment of validity other than "what works, works." The assumption of an "absolute truth," in other words, serves as an ideological closure upon a fluid reality that is hardly an "objective reality," but is itself the product of human activity, which constructs its understanding of the world in the process of reconstructing the world:

> The struggle of the proletariat and the revolutionary people to change the world comprises the fulfillment of the following tasks: to change the objective world and, at the same time, their own subjective world to change their cognitive ability and change the relations between the subjective and the objective world. (p. 308)

This very representation of the world as ongoing revolutionary interpretation and construction, on the other hand, is disruptive of the ideological closure, and exposes the latter as a contradiction between theory and practice, absolute and relative truth, which, in its open-endedness, may be resolved only through the intervention of an omniscient will. For all its effectiveness in practice as a revolutionary hermeneutic, or perhaps because of it, Mao's Marxism could in the end restore a direction to history only through revolutionary will.

GUERILLA SOCIALISM/VERNACULAR MARXISM

Mao did not come to Marxism as a "blank sheet of paper," and there are tantalizing traces in his philosophy of various traditions in Chinese thought. There is, for instance, a parallel between his emphasis on "practice" and the practical orientation of Confucian philosophy; Frederick Wakeman Jr. has pointed to parallels between Mao's thought and the emphasis on the "unity of thought and action" in the Wang Yangming school of Confucianism in which Mao was interested as a young radical.[30] Thomas Metzger suggests, even more directly, that "The Sinification of Marxism . . . came to express and implement the traditional ethos of interdependence."[31] Benjamin Schwartz has observed a continuity with Confucian tradition in Mao's preoccupation with morality in politics.[32] At a more obscure level, it may be possible to perceive in Mao's assertion of the ceaselessness of change traces of more esoteric currents in Chinese thought going back to the *Yijing (Book of Change)* and *yin-yang* naturalism which held that change was the only constant in the universe.[33] Even Mao's dialectic, with its insistence on everything containing everything else, is at times reminiscent more of certain currents in a Buddhist dialectic than the dialectic of Hegel and Marx. These ideas or their traces were part of the political and cultural discourse in Mao's environment, and the possibility of their presence in Mao's discourse on Marxism is not to be denied. It is important nevertheless that such presence, if possible, is informal (that is, Mao made no formal effort to integrate his Marxism with any of these traditions); and any parallels drawn between his Marxism and native traditions is of necessity speculative.

More importantly, if Mao's thinking indeed contained traces of these intellectual traditions, these were mediated by and refracted through the problematic of revolutionary practice.

There is little ambiguity in the direct relationship between Mao's Marxism and the immediate experience of the Chinese Revolution. The above analysis has stressed Mao's vernacularization of Marxism, which may be viewed at two levels. First the national level; that is, his effort to render Marxism relevant to China as a nation, with a problematic identity in a new historical situation. While this already implies a localization of Marxism, what made Mao's Marxism authentically radical (and not just an excuse for nationalism) was his insistence on integrating Marxism into the language of the masses, which he believed should reconstitute China as a nation; in other words, localizing it *within* the nation at the level of everyday life. (This is the major difference between Mao's Marxism and the post-Mao "socialism with Chinese characteristics.") Mao's vernacularization of Marxism was bound up at its most profound (and comprehensive) level with the experience of revolution in China as guerrilla warfare; it is not surprising that the first calls for translating Marxism into the language of the masses coincided with the appearance of a guerrilla strategy of revolution (and not by Mao, but others in the Party).

As the hermeneutic of a guerrilla strategy of revolution, Mao's philosophical abstractions bore the imprint of this historical situation both in its basic concepts and in his mode of presentation. The oppositions in the historical situation, whether at the national level (between China and a hegemonic European culture, including a universalized European Marxism) or at the social level (where the oppositions were much more multifaceted and complex than class oppositions), were irreducible to one another, or the theoretical categories of Marxism—to the point where the relationship between theory and practice itself appeared as an oppositional relationship. The concept of "contradiction" (conceived dialectically as the "unity of opposites") provided Mao with an intellectual instrument for integrating within a structural totality these oppositions between the whole and the parts (including theory and practice), as well as the numerous parts (themselves conceived as contradictory "pairs") that constituted the historical situation that guerrilla struggle sought to transform. Mao's insistence on practice as the ultimate test of validity was also a product of the conjunctural and, therefore, contingent nature of causation in such a situation, which could not be based on predictions from theory but called for interpretation at every step.

Mao's mode of presentation of his ideas was an elaboration of the simultaneously integrative and dispersive implications of relationships characterized by contradiction. Integrative: because everything depends for its existence on everything else and is, therefore, in a state of identity. Dispersive: because everything has its own irreducible particularity and is, therefore, in a state of difference and opposition. Analysis, including the analysis of the relationship between universal Marxist theory and the practice of revolution in China, must at all points remain cognizant of this basic relationship. The relationship, moreover, is not extrinsic but intrinsic: both identity and difference are intrinsic qualities of things that at once exclude and include one another. The whole and the parts, as well as the parts and the parts, may not be reducible to one another. As Althusser suggests, it is possible at one level to read these abstractions as a description of guerrilla warfare: guerrilla struggle, for its success, demands that guerrillas remain part of a unity even as they disperse into different terrains as they respond to local conditions. The vernacularization of Marxism appears here as the abstraction to a paradigmatic level of a guerrilla socialism. At its most comprehensive level, this was the significance of the "sinification" of Marxism.

What are the implications of this procedure for the relationship between Marxism and Mao's Marxism? Mao did not reduce Marxism to a Chinese version of it, or view China merely as another illustration of universal Marxist principles. In its rhetorical trope, his exposition of the relationship is at once metonymic (reducing the Chinese Revolution to "the status of an aspect or function" of Marxism in general, from which it differs nevertheless in a relationship that is extrinsic) and synecdochic (in construing the relationship "in the manner of an *intrinsic* relationship of shared *qualities*").[34] The result was a conception of the relationship that insisted on China's *difference*, and yet represented Chinese Marxism as an embodiment of Marxism. Ai Siqi, one of Mao's close collaborators in the project of "sinification," put it as follows (in an article that followed Mao's "On New Democracy," in the journal *Chinese Culture,* which started publication in January 1940, as an organ of a "sinified" Marxism):

> Marxism is a universal truth *(yibande zhengquexing)* not only because it is a scientific theory and method, but because it is the compass of the revolutionary

struggle of the proletariat. . . . That is to say, every country or nation that has a proletariat or a proletarian movement has the possibility *(keneng xing)* and necessity *(biran xing)* of giving rise to and developing Marxism. Marxism can be sinified *(Zhongguohua)* because China has produced a Marxist movement in actuality *(shiji)*; Chinese Marxism has a foundation in the internal development of Chinese economy and society, has internal sources, it is not a surface phenomenon. . . . The Chinese proletariat has a high level of organization and awareness, has its own strong Party, has twenty years of experience in struggle, has model achievements in the national and democratic struggle. Hence there is Chinese Marxism. If Marxism is a foreign import, our answer is that Marxism gives practice *(shijian)* the primary place. If people wonder whether or not China has its own Marxism, we must first ask whether or not the Chinese proletariat and its Party have moved the heavens and shaken the earth, impelled the masses of the Chinese nation to progressive undertakings. The Chinese proletariat has accomplished this. Moreover, it has on this basis of practice developed Marxist theory. Hence it has its own Marxism. These are the real writings of Chinese Marxism, the texts *(shujue)* of Chinese Marxism. . . . Marxism cannot but assume different forms depending on the different conditions of development of each nation; it cannot assume an international form globally. Presently, Marxism must be realized through national forms *(minzu xingshi)*. There is no such thing as abstract Marxism, there is only concrete Marxism. The so-called concrete Marxism is Marxism that has taken national form.[35]

The Marxism (Marxism-Leninism) that Chinese Communists inherited was a Marxism that had already been "deterritorialized" from its original terrain in European history. Ai's statement metonymically recognizes the difference of Chinese Marxism from an international Marxism, but in the process also restates the relationship between Chinese and European (or any other) Marxism as a part–part relationship within a Marxism that as a whole has now been removed from any territorial associations. Synecdochically, he "reterritorializes" Marxism upon a Chinese terrain, by asserting that Chinese Marxism is "intrinsically" as representative of a whole Marxism as any other.[36] In this simultaneous recognition of a global Marxist discourse as a pervasive unity and the discursive appropriation of Marxism in a Chinese terrain is expressed as the fundamental essence and the contradictoriness of the structure of Mao's Marxism and the procedure of sinification of which it was the product.

CONCLUSION: IN HINDSIGHT

I have discussed above Mao's philosophy, not his politics. In the light of what Mao's politics after 1949 has done to the memory of his philosophy, however, a few words may be in order here concerning the relationship of his philosophy to his politics that may further illuminate his philosophical formulations, as well as the contradictions embedded therein.

Mao's philosophy was a product of the years we have focused upon above. His "philosophical" essays after 1949 added little of a philosophical nature to his earlier statements, and mainly represent applications in a new situation (with the Communist Party having moved from the "greenwoods" into state power) of these earlier formulations.[37] Mao's use of his ideas may have changed after the mid-1950s, but there is little basis for arguing that his philosophical premises or revolutionary assumptions had also changed in the process.

The point at which Mao began to diverge from his colleagues in the Communist Party is revealing also from a philosophical perspective, however. In hindsight the divisions that were to culminate in the Cultural Revolution of the 1960s first appeared in the Eighth Party Congress of 1956, when the Communist Party declared that China had achieved the transition to socialism (from New Democracy), and charted the course for future development to Communism. This Congress also formulated the "primary contradiction" of the present stage of the Chinese Revolution as the contradiction between highly advanced relations of production (socialism) and backward forces of production. This agreement on the identification of the "primary contradiction," however, was not accompanied by an agreement on how to resolve the contradiction. The contradiction was interpreted differently by different factions. Mao was to place a revolutionary interpretation on it, and seek its resolution in a renewed revolutionization of society through further transformation of the relations of production, while others sought to develop the forces of production to align them with relations of production that had already advanced beyond the ability of production to sustain them. For the next twenty years, radical Maoists had their way. Since Mao's death in 1976, the Party has opted for the alternative interpretation, and shifted its emphasis to production, even backtracking from the relations of production that had come into existence by 1956.

I am not concerned here with these developments, but with what they reveal about Mao's philosophical assumptions. The availability of alternative choices in the resolution of a commonly recognized contradiction underlines the interpretative problems raised by an analysis based on contradictions. Such an analysis, in other words, does not automatically point to a single resolution, but merely raises alternative possibilities, where the choice of one resolution over an alternative one depends on considerations exterior to the contradiction, or some long-term ideal of "absolute truth." Mao, in spite of his recognition in theory of the "relativity" of the truths yielded by such analysis, was prepared when it actually came to disagreement to assert the "absoluteness"

of his "relative truth" against others. Depending on our own political pro-
clivity, we may describe this as absolutism or the assertion of "revolutionary
will," but the point here is that the very existence of choice is indicative of a
basic problem (or "contradiction") in Mao's philosophical formulations, and
reveals *their* contingency.

Much the same may be said of the relationship of Mao's Marxism to Marxism, which lay at the heart of those formulations. The Cultural Revolution is
itself quite revealing in this regard, because at the height of the Cultural Revolution an unprecedented national chauvinism coincided with unprecedented
claims on the authenticity of Chinese Marxism to the exclusion of all other
Marxisms. In its very extremeness, the national appropriation of Marxism
during the Cultural Revolution is revealing of the contradictions created by
Mao's Marxism within Marxism in general. The introduction of a Chinese national voice into a global Marxism represented a major contribution to Marxism. It forced an opening up of Marxist categories to reveal a complexity to
revolutionary practice that rendered Marxism a more effective instrument of
revolution in diverse terrains. Politically, it pointed the way to the possibility
of a genuinely universal Marxism in its insistence that a Marxism that refused
to incorporate local voices into its structure reintroduced in a radical form the
Eurocentric hegemony that was built into it in its historical origins.

At the same time, however, this insistence on the national voice, if divorced from its dialectical structure, promised the dissipation of Marxism
into many local contexts, losing all coherence as a theory either of social development or social revolution. This is what happened during the Cultural
Revolution. And it may be the historical fate of Marxism (as it would now appear) unless Marxists are able to formulate a new, universal Marxism out of
the intertextuality of many national experiences.

In the long run, and in spite of the negation of his own philosophical premises that he may have orchestrated after 1949, Mao's significance as a
philosopher of Marxism rests upon his recognition of a problem that was not
just a Chinese problem but would emerge in later years as a global problem
of Marxism, and his articulation of it in a philosophical formulation which remains one of the most comprehensive statements of it in the abstract. Whether
or not this formulation retains its significance beyond that of the merely historical will depend on the future of Marxism in the contemporary world.

NOTES

1. "Mao Zedong Thought" is the official designation for Mao's Marxism. As such,
it is an abstraction, and needs to be distinguished from "Mao's Marxism," because it

refers to a body of thought that was the product of collective effort while the latter refers to the thought of Mao the individual. Thus it is possible for the Communist Party to reject Mao's Marxism while upholding Mao Zedong Thought. While recognizing this distinction, I use the two terms interchangeably here because such a distinction did not become necessary until the 1950s, when (at least officially) consensus broke down over the meaning of the revolution.

2. Norman Levine, *Dialogue within the Dialectic* (London: George Allen & Unwin, 1984), 332.

3. "Talk on Questions of Philosophy" (1964), in *Chairman Mao Talks to the People*, ed. Stuart Schram (New York: Pantheon Books, 1974), 212–30, esp. 213.

4. "Talk on Questions of Philosophy," 214.

5. Frederic Wakeman Jr., *History and Will: Philosophical Perspectives of Mao Tse-tung's Thought* (Berkeley: University of California Press, 1975). For Mao's "confusion," see Edgar Snow, *Red Star over China* (New York: Grove Press, 1961), 147–48.

6. For Mao's "populism," see Maurice Meisner, "Leninism and Maoism: Some Populist Perspectives on Marxism–Leninism in China," *China Quarterly* 45 (1971): 2–36; for "anarchism," see Robert A. Scalapino, "The Evolution of a Young Revolutionary: Mao Zedong in 1919–1920," *Journal of Asian Studies* 42 (November 1982), 29–61; for "thought and action," see Wakeman, *History and Will*, esp. 238–58.

7. Raymond Wylie, *The Emergence of Maoism: Mao Tse-tung, Ch'en Po-ta and the Search for Chinese Theory, 1935–1945* (Stanford, CA: Stanford University Press, 1980). See also Thomas Kampen, "Wang Jiaxiang, Mao Zedong and the 'triumph of Mao Zedong Thought' (1935–1945)," *Modern Asian Studies* 23, no. 4 (October 1989): 705–27.

8. Shu Riping, "Shinian lai Mao Zedong zhexue sixiang yanjiu shuping" [An Account of Research on Mao Zedong's Philosophy over the Last Ten Years), *Mao Zedong zhexue sixiang yanjiu* [Research in Mao Zedong's Philosophical Thought], no. 5 (1989): 4–10, esp. 6. This article also offers a useful survey of discussions of Mao's thought over the preceding ten years; such discussions achieved an unprecedented intensity in the early 1980s but have declined in recent years.

9. Stuart S. Schram, *The Political Thought of Mao Tse-tung* (revised and enlarged edition) (New York: Praeger Publishers, 1971), 112.

10. For differences among Chinese interpretations, see Shu, "Shinian lai Mao Zedong," 6. For different interpretations among Euro-American analysts, see "Symposium on Mao and Marx," *Modern China* 2, no. 3; 3, no. 1; and 2 (October 1976–1977, April 1977).

11. Published originally as "Xin minzhu zhuyide zhengzhi yu xin minzhu zhuyide wenhua" [The Politics and Culture of New Democracy], *Zhongguo wenhua* [Chinese Culture], 1 (January 1940). An English translation is available in *Selected Works of Mao Tse-tung* (4 vols., Beijing: Foreign Languages Press, 1965–1967), vol. 2, 339–84. Hereafter *SWMTT.*

12. *SWMTT,* 380–81.

13. Mao Zedong, "Lun xin jieduan" [On the New Stage]. Speech to the Enlarged Plenary Session of the Sixty Central Committee (October 12–14, 1938), in *Mao*

Zedongji [Collected Works of Mao Zedong], ed. Takeuchi Minoru (10 vols.), vol. VI, 163–263, 260–61 (Hong Kong: Po Wen Book Co., 1976). Hereafter *MZDJ*.

14. For Althusser's statement on structural effectivity (or causality) and an illuminating discussion of the idea, see Fredric Jameson, *The Political Unconscious: Narrative as a Socially Symbolic Act* (Ithaca, NY: Cornell University Press, 1981), 23–28.

15. Accounts of Mao's "influence" outside of China are to be found in Arif Dirlik, Paul Healy, and Nick Knight, eds., *Critical Perspectives on Mao Zedong's Thought* (Atlantic Highlands, NJ: Humanities Press, 1997). For an excellent discussion of Mao's global relevance, see Rossana Rossanda, "Mao's Marxism," *The Socialist Register,* eds. Ralph Milliband and John Savill (London: Merlin Press, 1971), 53–80. See also Arif Dirlik, "The Predicament of Marxist Revolutionary Consciousness: Mao Zedong, Antonio Gramsci and the Reformulation of Marxist Revolutionary Theory," in this volume.

16. For this concept, see Raymond Williams, *Marxism and Literature* (London: Oxford University Press, 1977), 128–35. The term is especially appropriate to the discussion of "sinification," which its authors conceived as a problem not just of material conditions and ideology, but in terms of a Chinese "air" or "style." *Guoqing,* the term used to describe this, ranges in meaning from "national circumstances" to "national sentiment." Whether or not Marxism was consistent with a Chinese *guoqing* was a matter of intense debate during this period. For a statement by one of Mao's close collaborators in "sinification," see Ai Siqi, "Lun Zhongguode teshuxing" [On China's Special Nature], *Zhongguo wenhua* [Chinese Culture] 1 (January 1940): 26–28.

17. Schram has recognized the importance of the issue of language in Mao's Marxism. See *The Political Thought of Mao Tse-tung,* 113. Nick Knight offers a careful analysis of Mao's use of native sources and language even in an abstract essay such as "On Contradiction" in his important textual analysis of Mao's philosophical texts, "Mao Zedong's On Contradiction and on Practice: Pre-liberation Texts," *China Quarterly* 84 (December 1980): 641–68, esp. 658–59. Knight has recently published his textual studies (including, in addition to these two essays, the "Lecture Notes on Dialectical Materialism") in *Mao Zedong on Dialectical Materialism Armonk,* ed. Nick Knight (New York: M. E. Sharpe, 1990). His translations and annotations of Mao's philosophical writings from this period, supplemented with an excellent introduction on the sources of Mao's writings, provide the most up-to-date textual analysis of Mao's philosophical writings.

18. Jurgen Habermas, *Theory and Practice,* trans. John Viertel (Boston: Beacon Press, 1973), 2, 10–16.

19. Indeed, some of the earliest and most important discussions on the need to translate Marxism into the language of the masses were provided not by Mao, or Maoists, but by Qu Qiubai, an earlier secretary of the party and a literary theorist. For a discussion of his ideas, see Paul Pickowicz, *Marxist Literary Thought in China: The Influence of Ch'u Ch'iupai* (Berkeley: University of California Press, 1981). A more direct discussion of Qu's (and the Party's) efforts to accomplish this through literary means in the early part of the agrarian revolution is to be found in Ellen Judd, "Revolutionary Drama and Song in the Jiangxi Soviet," *Modern China* 9, no. 1 (January

1983): 127–60. Early practice is most readily (and comprehensively) apparent in a recently (1982) published account of a local investigation he conducted in 1930, which has just become available in English. See Mao Zedong, *Report from Xunwu,* ed. Roger R. Thompson (Stanford, CA: Stanford University Press, 1990). This essay has justified some Chinese authors in carrying Mao's "sinification" of Marxism past the war years back to 1930. See Shu, "Shinian lai Mao Zedong."

20. These discussions were published under the title of *Xian jieduande Zhongguo sixiang yundong* [The Chinese Thought Movement of the Present] (Shanghai: Yiban shudian, 1937).

21. See Levine, *Dialogue within the Dialectic,* 317–47, 363–91, for the debt Mao owed to "Hegelianized Leninism" for his ideas as well as the ways in which he moved beyond it. Levine does an illuminating job of placing Mao within Marxist discussions of the dialectic. For a contrary view, which stresses the significance of "contradiction" as a *Marxist* break with the Hegelian dialectic, see Louis Althusser, "Contradiction and Overdetermination," in *For Marx* (New York: Vintage Books, 1970), 89–128, esp. 90–94.

22. *SWMTT,* vol. 1, 311. The parenthetical references in the text will all be to this translation, 311–47. Nick Knight has demonstrated that this text is an edited version of the pre-Liberation text of "On Contradiction" (which contained additional passages that were edited out after 1949), but has not otherwise questioned what is given in this translation.

23. Textual analyses by Schram and Knight in the works cited above have revealed (contrary to earlier opinions) that "On Contradiction" and "On Practice," along with "Lecture Notes on Dialectical Materialism," were composed in 1936–1937 and together represented "a single intellectual enterprise." Mao's philosophical effort at the time was part of the struggles for leadership within the Communist Party, as an endeavor to demonstrate his qualification for leadership against theoretically much better-informed opponents. Indeed, Wylie has argued that the "sinification of Marxism" was a product of organizational struggles against "dogmatists" within the Party. While this view has much virtue, it needs to be placed within the broader context of the problem of revolution. I focus on the first two essays, because unlike the "Lecture Notes on Dialectical Materialism," which was mainly copied from other sources, "On Contradiction" and "On Practice" represent original contributions by Mao. While these essays were part of an ongoing philosophical effort that preceded Japan's invasion of China, moreover, they were still rooted in practical considerations, and the texts we have are explicitly devoted to the legitimation of change in political policy in response to the "new situation."

24. Althusser, *For Marx,* 94n.

25. Mao, "Bianzhengfa weiwulun" [Dialectical Materialism], in *MZDJ,* vol. 6, 265–305, esp. 302–3.

26. Mao quotes Lenin in both essays. See *SWMTT,* vol. 1, 304, 336.

27. Althusser, *For Marx.*

28. See, for instance, "On Tactics against Japanese Imperialism" (1935), in *SWMTT,* vol. 1, 152–254.

29. *SWMTT,* vol. 1, 297. References in the text are to this translation, 295–309.

30. Wakeman, *History and Will*, 238–58.

31. Thomas A. Metzger, *Escape from Predicament: Neo-Confucianism and China's Evolving Political Culture* (New York: Columbia University Press, 1977), 233.

32. Benjamin I. Schwartz, "The Reign of Virtue—Some Broad Perspectives on Leader and Part in the Cultural Revolution," *China Quarterly* 35 (1968): 1–17.

33. Joseph Liu, "Mao's 'On Contradiction,'" *Studies in Soviet Thought* 11 (June 1971): 71–89, esp. 78–81.

34. For a discussion of these rhetorical tropes, see Hayden White, *Metahistory: The Historical Imagination in Nineteenth-Century Europe* (Baltimore, MD: Johns Hopkins University Press, 1973), 31–38.

35. Ai, "Lun Zhongguode teshuxing," 31–32.

36. For "deterritorialization" and "reterritorialization," see Gilles Deleuze and Felix Guattari, "What Is a Minor Literature?" *Mississippi Review* 11, no. 3 (1983): 13–33.

37. I am referring here to such essays as "On the Ten Great Relationships" (1956) and "On the Correct Handling of Contradictions among the People" (1957), and his discussions of "permanent" or "uninterrupted" revolution in 1958.

5

Modernism and Antimodernism in Mao Zedong's Marxism

Reviewing Mao Zedong Thought in terms of perspectives afforded by modernism and antimodernism, which is what I propose to do below, is risky but worthwhile. Risky because to my knowledge Mao himself did not employ these terms or think through them, and there is little evidence in his published writings that he addressed with any explicitness the questions that they imply; the risk lies in the ever-present possibility of distortion, or reading what is not there, when concepts are employed in reading a body of thought to which they may be alien.[1] The undertaking is worth the risk, however, for what it may reveal about what is otherwise obscure or contradictory. If Mao did not address explicitly questions of modernism and antimodernism, the problems presented by modernity were integral to his historical context—not just the context of Chinese society but the global context of that society in the twentieth century—as the premise of the Chinese Revolution, and in their sedimentation in the ideology that guided the revolution, Marxism. How Mao responded to those problems may have much to tell us about modernism and antimodernism as formative moments in his thinking. It may also have something to tell us about modernism and antimodernism in Third World, specifically Chinese, perspective. I seek to get at these questions below by examining the relationship of Mao Zedong Thought to Marxism, which is itself expressive of "some of modernist culture's deepest insights and, at the same time, dramatizes some of its deepest inner contradictions."[2]

MODERNIZATION, MODERNITY, MODERNISM, ANTIMODERNISM

In his seminal work, *All That Is Solid Melts into Air*, subtitled *The Experience of Modernity*, Marshall Berman writes:

> There is a mode of vital experience—experience of space and time, of the self and others, of life's possibilities and perils—that is shared by men and women all over the world today. I will call this body of experience "modernity." To be modern is to find ourselves in an environment that promises us adventure, power, joy, growth, transformation of ourselves and the world—and, at the same time, that threatens to destroy everything we have, everything we know, everything we are. Modern environments and experiences cut across all boundaries of geography and ethnicity, of class and nationality, of religion and ideology: in this sense, modernity can be said to unite all mankind. But it is a paradoxical unity, a unity of disunity: it pours us all into a maelstrom of perpetual disintegration and renewal, of struggle and contradiction, of ambiguity and anguish. To be modern is to be part of a universe in which, as Marx said, "all that is solid melts into air."[3]

Rather than a historical "condition," modernity is a historical experience (including the experience of history); or if it is a condition, it is condition as experience, that seeks ceaselessly to transform the very conditions that produce it. As David Harvey puts it in his *The Condition of Postmodernity:*

> Modernity can have no respect for even its own past, let alone that of any premodern social order. The transitoriness of things makes it difficult to preserve any sense of historical continuity. If there is any meaning to history, then that meaning has to be discovered and defined from within the maelstrom of change, a maelstrom that affects the terms of discussion as well as whatever it is that is being discussed. Modernity, therefore, not only entails a ruthless break with any or all preceding historical conditions, but is characterized by a never-ending process of internal ruptures and fragmentations within itself.[4]

Modernization, then, is the historical process (or processes) that have produced (and continue to produce) the condition of modernity: "scientific discoveries, industrial upheavals, demographic transformations, urban expansions, national states, mass movements—all propelled, in the last instance, by the 'ever-expanding, drastically fluctuating' capitalist *world market*,"[5] to which we might add revolutions.

These processes point to a fundamental contradiction imbedded in modernity as its generative source. On the one hand, the immense creativity of science and scientific thinking: rooted in critical reason, and an Enlightenment faith in the ability of human rationality to comprehend and transform the world so as to improve the human condition, and expressed through the productive and social technology of capitalism. On the other hand, the destructiveness that is implicit in this very creativity: that in its conquest of the world destroys the very conditions of human existence, undermines social relations that endow existence with stability and security, and liberates humanity from nature only to imprison it in the "iron cages" of factories, slums, concrete jungles, and the bureaucratic mazes of rationalized states. The experience of modernity, therefore, is also an experience of ceaseless experimentation in efforts to overcome this contradiction that lies at the very source: ranging from the repudiation of the Enlightenment, and its faith in enlightenment through reason, to an affirmation that only further enlightenment may make up for the defects of the Enlightenment (we may substitute for "enlightenment" in this statement any of the terms that in different contexts appear as alternative descriptions of these processes, such as science, capitalism, the market, revolution, socialism).[6] All these experiments (including those which repudiate enlightenment, ironically) are driven by the urge to restore as subjects of history—an Enlightenment promise—the men and women whom modernization has rendered into its objects.

Berman defines modernism as "any attempt by modern men and women to become subjects as well as objects of modernization, to get a grip on the modern world and make themselves at home in it."[7] Modernism is to be distinguished from "modernizationism." The latter is a one-dimensional commitment to the technological, economic, and social processes of modernization. Modernism, on the other hand, is to live with contradiction, with the promise as well as with the destructiveness of modernization, and to carve out of it a subject position that also recognizes the inevitable historical objectification of the subject; something along the lines of that premise of historical materialism which enjoins that the recognition of historical necessity is the prerequisite of liberation from necessity.

Antimodernism, conceived with reference to modernism (and comprehensible only with reference to it), partakes of the same contradiction. "To be fully modern," Berman writes, "is to be antimodern."[8] To be fully antimodern, if I may reverse his statement, is to be modern, not only because antimodernism is incomprehensible without reference to the modern, but more importantly because antimodernism is itself motivated by an urge to realize goals that appeared as possibilities only with the emergence of the modern. In his study of antimodernism in the United States, *No Place of Grace*, Jackson Lears has argued that even when it took the form of escape into the past (as with medievalism or Orientalism), antimodernism in the United States was quintessentially modern in its search for personal authenticity, rather than escapist, premodern, or reactionary. The search of the elite for personal authenticity, the resistance of craft workers to factory discipline, the protest of farmers who countered capitalist expropriation with agrarian utopias, or the antiurbanism of rural dwellers, Lears reminds us, represented not a residual nostalgia for the past but efforts from different class and power positions to overcome the oppressive and alienating consequences of modernity without rejecting modernity per se.[9] Most importantly, antimodernism represents (and is crucial to) a search for an alternative modernity that is not likely to go away so long as modernization in practice postpones (or betrays) the promise of liberation that motivates it in theory.

Socialisms (including Marxism but especially anarchism) are antimodernist but hardly against modernity (or even modernization); the goal of socialist revolution for the last two centuries has been to transcend capitalist modernity to create an alternative modernity closer in its constitution to the Enlightenment vision of human liberation. It is noteworthy that socialism, and not just "utopian socialism," retained in its vision of the future memories of the premodern community, but only in a form reworked by reason and the subjective goals of modernity; the contradiction endowed socialism with a revolutionary dynamism. To the extent that socialist antimodernism may account for this revolutionary dynamism, the contradictoriness of antimodernism, in its socialist guise at any rate, needs to be distinguished from modernism's celebration of the contradictions of modernity, which also disguises or estheticizes social and political resignation.[10] I need to point out that I am referring here to socialism as revolutionary movement. Socialism in state power is another matter. There, socialism appears as an alternative ideology of modernization, guided and controlled by the state; on the one hand abandoning its own utopian vision dynamized by antimodernism, and, on the other hand, vulnerable itself to the disruptive forces of modernization that it seeks to control (which until recently, underlay claims to the superiority of socialist modernization to the "anarchy" of capitalist modernity).[11]

Three aspects of Berman's conceptualization of modernism need to be underlined here because they are directly pertinent to the discussion below. First, Berman's discussion of modernism is motivated by the goal of recuperating the creative dynamism of nineteenth-century modernism, which he believes has been lost in the twentieth century. Nineteenth-century modernists were creative in their visions of the future because they were profoundly ambivalent toward modern life, which dynamized their dialectical appreciation of the contradictions between modernity and modernization, modernism and antimodernism, closing off and opening up the future. "Their twentieth century successors," on the other hand,

> lurched far more toward rigid polarities and flat totalizations. Modernity is either embraced with a blind and uncritical enthusiasm, or else condemned with a

neo-Olympian remoteness and contempt; in either case, it is conceived as a closed monolith, incapable of being shaped or changed by modern men. Open visions of modern life have been supplanted by closed ones, Both/And by Either/Or.[12]

"Going back," therefore, "can be a way to go forward: that remembering the modernisms of the nineteenth century can give us the vision and the courage to create the modernisms of the twenty-first."[13] The distinction Berman draws between the nineteenth and the twentieth centuries also shows up in his analysis of the relationship between Marx and later Marxism (or socialist states). In a highly original (and stimulating) discussion of Karl Marx's thought, Berman tells us that Marx was both a great analyst of modernity, and a modernist himself whose solutions to the problems of modernity embodied the deepest contradictions of modernism (a great analyst precisely because he grasped and internalized "the tragedy of development").[14] Marx's work "mapped out" in all its contradictoriness the relationship between (bourgeois) modernization and modernism as its cultural expression. His panegyrics to the success of the bourgeoisie in breaking with the past (including its own past: the constant revolutionizing of production) were accompanied by a keenly felt recognition of the cultural price that must be paid for such success: "all that is solid melts into air." The tragedy of the bourgeoisie was that it must fall in the end not because of its failure but because of its success.[15] Rather than repudiate the achievements of bourgeois modernization, however, Marx proceeded to appropriate it for another class that itself was the product of modernization, the proletariat, which would seize from modernity the rich possibilities that were closed off to the bourgeoisie by its ideology: "The wounds of modernity," could be healed only "through a fuller and deeper modernity."[16] This assumption of modernity for the socialism of the future, as its historical foundation, would introduce into Marxism the very contradictions that Marx had identified in bourgeois modernization. Perceptively (if not prophetically), Berman concludes (in 1982) that the efforts of socialist states to promote modernization while constricting modernism (reducing Marxism to modernization, denying *its* richest possibilities) is doomed to failure because the disruptiveness of modernity haunts them as much as it haunts bourgeois society. Marx's modernism, ironically, has less to say in socialist than in capitalist society which, for all its oppressiveness, gives free play to the "dialectical dance" of contradictions; Marxism needs to be recalled into capitalist society in the late twentieth century, not as "a way out of the contradictions of modern life but a surer and deeper way into these contradictions."[17]

This statement is worth pondering for what it has to say about a modernist reading of Marxism; and its implications for understanding the role of Marxism in Third World modernity in general and Mao Zedong Thought in particular (indeed, its reference to contradictions, and what it does with them, immediately calls forth contrasts with the thinking of Mao, in which contradictions played a central part, as I will discuss below). Berman's reading brings out a fundamental contradiction in Marxism; it is also revealing of a serious limitation in a modernism thus conceived. This limitation will have to be transcended if modernism is to have any meaning within a Third World historical context—except as a simple extension of European modernism.

This is indeed how Berman conceives of modernism in the Third World, which is the third aspect of his conceptualization of modernism I would like to note. In a chapter entitled "The Modernism of Underdevelopment," Berman examines modernism in nineteenth-century Russia which he describes as "an archetype of the emerging twentieth-century Third World."[18] In Russia, modernization was experienced

> mainly as something that was *not* happening; or else as something that was happening far away, in realms that Russians, even when they travelled there, experienced more as fantastic anti-worlds than as social actualities; or else, where it was happening at home, as something that was happening only in the most jagged, halting, blatantly abortive or weirdly distorted ways.[19]

The experience of modernity, then, took here the form of "the anguish of backwardness and underdevelopment."[20]

While Berman recognizes that, in areas outside of Europe, "the meanings of modernity would have to be more complex, elusive and paradoxical,"[21] to the extent that his work refers to these areas (other than Russia), these references indicate at best a nonparadoxical, one-dimensional appreciation of modernism in Third World societies; comparable to his approach to "actually existing" socialist societies.[22] The representation of nineteenth-century Russia as an "archetype" of the Third World is revealing of a reductionism in Berman's thinking about the Third World: Russia may have been "backward" economically, but its political power cast a shadow over "advanced" Europe; its modernity is hardly comparable to the many Third World societies who were the objects of imperialism, colonialism and neocolonialism, and whose cultural alienness to Europe was not relieved by any of the ambiguities surrounding Russia's relationship to Europe. In these other societies, as Berman represents them, modernism is something that is yet to happen, must happen, if they are to be freed from the "pseudo-Faustian" projects in which they are imprisoned.[23]

Perry Anderson, in his critique of Berman, has offered a conjunctural explanation for modernism, as a characteristic of "societies still at definite historical cross-roads," where the future of modernity is still at issue.[24] For him, "a shadow configuration of what once prevailed in the First World" also has existed in the Third World during the twentieth century. There, too, however, modernism must go the way of modernism in Europe once the historical circumstances that produced it have disappeared.[25]

Anderson's objection to Berman's approach to modernism raises the question of the historicity of modernism, in both a spatial and a temporal sense. Indeed, it is arguable that Berman's reading of modernism, which proceeds on an exclusively esthetic plane, dehistoricizes and depoliticizes the problems of modernity. His Marxist reading of modernism, which bases modernism in historically defined social relationships, is overwhelmed in the end by his modernist reading of both Marxism and modernity, where modernism appears as a set of attitudes or contradictions that cut across all boundaries of nations, classes, genders, etc., and is immune as well to changing temporalities within modernity; as when he invites Marx back into the late twentieth century, not as "a way out of the contradictions of modern life but a surer and deeper way into those contradictions." Needless to say, this is a reading of Marx that deprives Marxism of its political project. Marxism appears in Berman's work to fall from the grace of modernism to the extent that it remains political. Marx, rightly or wrongly, thought that he had some answers to the contradictions of modern life. In Berman's reading, these answers disappear into an estheticized fetishism of contradictions (which provides an interesting contrast to Mao's reading of contradictions).

This same homogenization of spatiality and temporality is evident in Berman's approach to the problem of modernity in the Third World, which makes it possible to render nineteenth-century Russia into an "archetype" of modernity. It is to this problem, as it appears in Mao's Marxism, that I would like to turn now.

MAO ZEDONG, THIRD WORLD MODERNITY, AND "CHINESE MARXISM"

What does it mean to speak of modernism with reference to Mao Zedong Thought? Most immediately, the question invokes an image of Mao Zedong as a historical figure, a real-life Faust who unleashed in Chinese society every possible contradiction that may be inferred from the term "creative destruction" which, David Harvey tells us, "is very important to understanding modernity precisely because it derived from the practical dilemmas that faced the implementation of the modernist project." Harvey has Mao Zedong in mind when he describes these dilemmas:

> You simply cannot make an omelette without breaking eggs, as a whole line of modernist thinkers from Goethe to Mao have noted. The literary archetype of such a dilemma is . . . Goethe's Faust. An epic hero prepared to destroy religious myths, traditional values, and customary ways of life in order to build a brave new world out of the ashes of the old, Faust is, in the end, a tragic figure. Synthesizing thought and action, Faust forces himself and everyone else (even Mephistopheles) to extremes of organization, pain, and exhaustion in order to master nature and create a new landscape, a sublime spiritual achievement that contains the potentiality for human liberation from want and need. Prepared to eliminate everything and everyone who stands in the way of the realization of this sublime vision, Faust, to his own ultimate horror, deploys Mephistopheles to kill a much-loved old couple who live in a small cottage by the seashore for no other reason than the fact that they do not fit in with the master plan. "It appears . . . that the very process of development, even as it transforms the wasteland into a thriving physical and social space, recreates the wasteland inside of the developer himself. This is how the tragedy of development works."[26]

We know how the "tragedy of development" worked for China under Mao. We do not know if the development "recreated a wasteland inside the developer himself." "I am alone," he said to André Malraux in 1958, with "bitterness, perhaps irony, and above all pride."[27] "I am alone with the masses," Mao told Malraux, and just a few years later he would once again launch the masses into action against the very system he had guided into existence, with further tragic consequences for millions in Chinese society—and his own image as the leader of the Chinese Revolution.

There is another sense in which it is possible to speak of modernism with reference to Mao Zedong Thought, that I would like to pursue here; one that may tell us something about Mao the individual, but is more important for what it reveals about modernity as a Third World and Chinese historical phenomenon, and helps us place in historical perspective "the tragedy of development" there—and Mao himself as an agent of development. I am referring here to modernism as an acknowledgment of the contradictoriness of development, which allows a recognition that Mao Zedong Thought has built into it as a structuring moment a deeply ambivalent attitude toward modernity; which informs its account of Chinese modernity as an interplay of contradictions, as well as its own contradictoriness as a strategy for resolving those contradictions. The former is articulated in the structure of Mao's Marxism, which reflects on the contradictions of modernization and modernity, and of the relationship between them, in a Third World national context. The latter is visible in the contradictoriness of Mao's efforts to resolve those contradictions against the grain of his own theoretical conviction that contradictions defy efforts to contain them, articulated in his politics, which then becomes the site for explosive confrontations between alternative (and conflicting) aspects of modernity imbedded in his Marxism. Mao's ambivalence toward modernity was to disrupt teleological notions of society and history, of which the most compelling evidence is to be found in the centrality Mao Zedong Thought assigns to the concept of contradiction as the most appropriate means to grasping a world of impermanence, rupture, and conflict, where the future is as ambiguous as the present is elusive in its multifaceted contradictions. Endowed with generative power as a dynamic principle of both society and nature, "contradiction" renders into an epistemology that cogent expression of modernist irony: "everything is pregnant with its contrary."[28]

Mao's ambivalence toward modernity has long been recognized, but only to be subjected to one-dimensional interpretations that have suppressed the complexity of Mao Zedong Thought. On the eve of the official launching of the Cultural Revolution of the 1960s, Benjamin Schwartz wrote of the "Maoist vision":

> The official view of the present leadership is that the vision—no matter how its interpretation may fluctuate—not only provides the most effective means for achieving modernization, but is also an end in itself. *The only desirable modernization is a modernization which can be incorporated into the Maoist vision.* At the other extreme, we have the view that the vision runs completely athwart the prerequisites of modernization or that it is a sort of rationalization of the failures and difficulties of modernization in China.[29]

Two comments are in order concerning the conflicting interpretations of Mao Zedong Thought that Schwartz identifies. First, antithetical as they are, both interpretations take modernization as the basic criterion in evaluating Mao Zedong Thought, the latter much more uncompromisingly than the former. That Mao's Thought ran "athwart the prerequisites of modernization" has been a widely accepted idea, which has acquired the status of an orthodoxy under Mao's successors; at its most extreme, it takes the form of the portrayal of Mao Zedong as a "feudal" remnant of sorts, and of Maoists as conservatives, who undermined China's modernization. Maoists in their time insisted, to the contrary, that the Maoist vision would lead to a better and more thorough modernization. While this view had the virtue of affirming Mao's modernism (recall what Berman said of Marx above), it nevertheless perpetuated modernization as a basic criterion of evaluation, disguising the contradictions that were integral to Mao Zedong Thought as an account of Third World modernity.

More remarkable, secondly, these interpretive differences, that are seemingly differences in the evaluation of Mao Zedong Thought, are at bottom differences over the meaning of modernity, which are barely disguised by a one-dimensional insistence on the truth of one version of modernization against another, implicit in their either/or approach to the question. From a perspective that recognizes the complexity and contradictoriness of both Mao Zedong Thought and modernization, these seemingly antithetical interpretations are both valid. Mao Zedong Thought did run "completely athwart the prerequisites of modernization"—modernization, that is, that was conceived after existing models of modernity. But Mao Zedong Thought was also irretrievably modern, informed by an alternative vision of modernity, and a modernization that would help usher in such a modernity. We might add, contrary to Maoists who insisted uncompromisingly on the progressive revolutionary nature of Mao's Thought, that this alternative vision of modernity was made possible and informed by a deep antimodernism that infused Mao Zedong Thought; an antimodernism which, far from being a residual "feudal" hindrance to modernity, was itself a product of Chinese modernity as a Third World modernity, that rendered the projects of modernity and modernization far more complex and multidimensional than they had seemed earlier—even in Marxism.

Marxism provided Mao with the language of modernity and modernization; and it is in his Marxism that these complexities and contradictions are most apparent. Mao's Marxism was idiosyncratic *because* in his formulations (or, more accurately, reformulations) of Marxism within a Chinese context, Mao sought to account for a Chinese experience with modernity, which required the rephrasing of the very language of Marxism. His Marxism bears upon it the imprint of the historical situation from which it sprang and offers significant clues, therefore, to the guise modernism assumes in a society that is compelled into modernity not as its subject but as its object; where the problem of modernism presented itself not just as a problem of how "to get a grip on the modern world and make themselves at home in it," but also how to gain admission and feel at home as an autonomous subject in a world that had already been claimed as home by someone else. Marxism itself, ironically, had to be rendered hospitable to the Chinese experience, before it could help usher in a genuinely alternative modernity.

I have discussed my understanding of "Chinese Marxism" at length above, and will only highlight points here that are relevant to the question at hand. The Marxism Mao produced through the "sinification of Marxism" *(Makesi zhuyi Zhongguohua)* is most striking as a reflection on an overdetermined historical situation, but also a reflection on theory that is very much informed by that historical situation. The Chinese experience in the nineteenth and twentieth centuries was an experience that was overdetermined by incorporation in a global history as a Third World society with its own particular history, that would ultimately produce a Chinese nationalism marked with all the contradictions of this situation. To view "sinification" simply as "nationalization," as a one-dimensional and unidirectional process, is quite misleading, as it ignores the transformation of Chinese society even as it gave local form to global processes. We should not exaggerate the national element in Chinese or Third World Marxism either, as Marxism has assumed national form, or been subjected to national considerations, everywhere. Eric Hobsbawm has observed that while capitalism created a global history by drawing other societies within its orbit, the same globalization set in motion a contrary process that was to culminate in the late nineteenth century in political reorganization globally around sovereign nation-states, with their particularistic claims on history.[30] Chinese nationalism, too, was a product of these processes. This emergent nationalism was to dynamize initially revolutionary resistance to the new global order—and its assumption of a universal modernity conceived after the European experience. Following the October Revolution in Russia in 1917, Marxism (in its Leninist version) would provide a powerful language of resistance to capitalist modernity. In its anticapitalism, Marxism promised the possibility of national self-discovery for a society that a capitalist world threatened to consume. But Marxism itself shared in the teleology of capitalist modernity, and its Eurocentrism.[31] In order for its liberating possibility to be fulfilled, Marxism itself had to be rephrased in a national voice, for a Marxism that could not account for a specifically national experience abdicated its claims to universality; worse, under the guise of universalism, it replicated in a different form the hegemonism of capitalism, of which it was historically a product.

Nevertheless, the relationship between Marxist and nationalist concerns assumed different forms in different contexts, not just between First and Third World contexts, but within the historical contexts of different societies. In the case of China (as in the case of other latecomers to nationalism), there has been another aspect to the question of national voice that is significant for all of modern Chinese thought, but is especially crucial to understanding Mao's Marxism: who constitutes the substance of the nation, and provides the language of a national culture? Already by the 1930s, in the midst of national crisis, the question was an urgent one for Chinese intellectuals who had become suspicious of "old" elite culture as well as the Occidentalism of the 1920s, and sought in China's historical experience with modernity the sources of a new culture that would be Chinese because rooted in a Chinese experience, but also contemporary because that experience was irretrievably modern.[32] And not a few believed that the culture of the "people," especially the people in the countryside, offered the best hope for creating a native modern culture.[33] For the Communists, the question was not an abstract intellectual one but was concretely practical. Driven to the countryside in 1927, Chinese Communists were to become the first Marxist revolutionaries historically to confront the contradictions of an agrarian revolution carried out under the banner of Marxist ideology; that brought a modernist Marxism face to face with the premodern local cultures of agrarian society. Whatever the ideological and cultural proclivities of the Communists born out of their nationalism, sheer necessities of survival required the translation of Marxism into the language of the people; especially the language of those agrarian classes and groups (such as women) who were among the most downtrodden in society. The problem of a national language, in other words, was further complicated immensely by questions of classes, genders and ethnicities in an agrarian revolutionary situation that did not lend itself to ready conceptualizations in terms of the categories of an urban modernist Marxism.

This "overdetermined" historical situation helps us identify crucial aspects of Chinese modernity as a Third World modernity: (a) Chinese modernity was a product of the same forces of capitalist modernization that had produced modernity in Europe; this modernity, however, was a product not of Chinese but of European modernization. When Chinese intellectuals first encountered problems of modernity beginning in the late nineteenth century, modernization in any significant material or social sense still lay in the future. "The anguish of backwardness," arising from a sense that modernization was something happening somewhere else was integral to Chinese modernity, to be sure, but so was a sense that "backwardness" in China was a product of European modernity; not a distant modernity but a modernity that forced all others into its orbit, resistance to which might result in national extinction. Such fears were accompanied, ironically, by hopes that learning from the destructiveness of modernity in the European experience, Chinese might be able to create a better modernity drawing not only on the positive aspects of European modernity but on native resources as well. (b) These complexities of modernity came into focus around the question of nationalism, the immediate political product of modernity, which held out the promise at once of serving as an agent of modernization and of resisting and overcoming modernity. Nationalist ideology was at once modernist and antimodernist. It sought to transform China by creating a new politics, but it could do so successfully only by forging a national identity out of a premodern historical legacy that seemed to conflict with the demands of modernity and modernization. In either case, however, the goal was not a return or escape into a premodern past, but the creation of an alternative future for which the nation would serve as a vehicle. Having been assigned this task, nationalism also privileged the collective experience of modernity over the particularism of individual experience or the experience of social classes and groups. (c) The experience of modernity as an invasion from the outside created a suspicion of the values of modernity as tools of domination, and a negation of native values (which would include, ultimately, Marxism). Nationalism, in the very necessity it called forth of invoking native values as a source of national identity, reinforced the antimodernism implicit in such an experience of modernity. But for all its privileging of the collective over partial experience, nationalism could not contain the contradictions of modernity, for the nation remained to be invented and its values consolidated, and different groups in Chinese society made differing claims on the nation as they were mobilized progressively by the ever-deepening incorporation of Chinese society into a modern world. Hence the experience of modernity could be seen as oppressive or liberating, depending on social standing.

Within a matter of decades in the first half of the twentieth century, Chinese would traverse the broad range of cultural and intellectual realms that had been opened up by two centuries of European modernization, throwing the cultural landscape into upheaval as they sought to capture it for their alternative (and conflicting) paradigms of modernity. Chinese struggles with modernity, which appear in the modernizationist perspective of historians as manifestations of a Chinese inability to liberate themselves from the burden of a weighty past, appear in this alternative perspective as the very contradictions of a Chinese modernism, caught up between modernity as hegemonic actuality and liberating project: Enlightenment at once as a means of liberation from the past and a negation of native subjectivity and learning; the past at once as a source of identity and a burden on the present; the individual at once as citizen of a modern nation and a threat to collective national liberation; social revolution at once as a means to liberating classes and social groups to create an authentic nation and a divisive source of national disintegration; the countryside at once as the source of a pristine national identity against the degeneracy of cosmopolitan urban centers and a drag on development; the nation at once as an agent of cosmopolitan universalism and a defense against hegemony that closes out the world in perpetuation of native parochialism. The contradictions could be multiplied endlessly. They appeared differently from different social perspectives, but they are the contradictions of modernity nevertheless, that multiplied the possibilities of those perspectives, and set them against one another.[34]

Mao's Marxism, I suggested in the preceding chapter, is most properly conceived as a reflection upon this historical situation (which must be distinguished from reflection *of* the situation) if we are to grasp it in its structural complexity. As a discourse, Mao's Marxism bears upon its discursive structure the imprint of the multidimensional historical situation from which it derived its problematic. It is at once a reflection upon Chinese society from a universalist Marxist perspective, and a reflection upon Marxism from the

perspective of China as a Third World society and a nation. The two procedures, while coextensive, are also contradictory. They have with all their contradictions structured the discourse that we may call Chinese Marxism.

That this historical situation served as the point of departure in the formulation of a Chinese Marxism is in evidence everywhere in the texts (authored
by Mao or his close associates) associated with the "sinification of Marxism,"
of which the culmination was Mao's January 1940 essay, "On New Democracy," which stands as the classic formulation of the premises of Chinese
Marxism. "New Democracy" referred to an economic and political formation
(a mixed economy to facilitate economic development, and an alliance across
classes—under Communist leadership—in the pursuit of national liberation)
suitable to China's immediate needs; but more significantly it also represented the insertion of a new stage in historical progress appropriate to all societies placed similarly to China in the world. Its premises were: (a) the Chinese Revolution is part of a global revolution against capitalism; (b) it is,
however, a revolution against capitalism in a "semifeudal semicolonial" society to which national liberation is a crucial task; (c) it is also a national revolution, a revolution to create a new nation—and a new culture, that would be
radically different both from the culture inherited from the past and the culture imported from abroad. The latter, significantly, included Marxism: "in
applying Marxism to China, Chinese Communists must fully and properly integrate the universal truth of Marxism with the concrete practice of the Chinese Revolution or, in other words, the universal truth of Marxism must be
combined with specific national characteristics and acquire a definite national
form." To the extent that it was successful in incorporating these contradictory aspirations, Chinese Marxism was itself to become the site for the confrontation between modernism and antimodernism. The confrontation itself
was a direct product of Chinese modernity; and, where the revolutionaries
were concerned, it held out the promise of an alternative modernity, which
would allow for a subjective Chinese presence in a global discourse on
modernity. There was both self-assertion and pathos in Mao's declaration in
September 1949 that "the Chinese people have stood up!"[35]

THE GRAND EXPERIMENTER

"Contradiction" is a, if not *the*, keyword of Mao's Marxism; it not only appears in the titles of two of the four essays that were designated by Maoists
as the philosophical basis of Maoism,[36] but appears everywhere in Mao's
texts as the epistemological key to understanding the world.

Mao's elaboration of "contradiction" in the essay of that title (from a speech he gave in 1937) was very much part of the process of formulating a "Chinese Marxism," and is crucial to understanding the contradictoriness of his own approach to the resolution of contradictions in Chinese society: on the one hand a nearly fetishistic celebration of contradictions as a sign of revolutionary vitality, a condition in their free interplay of revolutionary progress into an open-ended future; and, on the other hand, a willful configuration of contradictions to direct them into a future posited by his own revolutionary vision, premised on faith in his own ability to interpret "the correct resolution" of contradictions. The free interplay of contradictions took the form in actual practice of social experiments in which Mao the interpreter appeared as Mao the experimenter, with Chinese society as the subject of his experiments. The inspiration was all too modern, the results devastating.

In his 1937 essay, "On Contradiction," Mao described a world that was one of ceaseless and endless confrontation and conflict, where unity might be understood only in terms of the contradictoriness of its moments, where no entity was a constant because it had no existence outside of its contradictions or a place of its own other than its relationship to other contradictions. It may be that all Marxism is a conflict-based conceptualization of the world. But however differently Marxists may have structured conflict or organized the structure of society, conflict in most interpretations of Marxism is conceived of in terms of a limited number of social categories (production, relations of production, politics, ideology, and so on), and there has been an urgency to hierarchize these categories in terms of their effectivity in the social structure. Mao's multitude of contradictions resist such hierarchization and, more significantly, reduction to a limited number of categories. Mao, like a good Marxist, sought to contain contradictions within a Marxist narrative of modes of production, but in the end his insistence on the universality and eternity of contradiction called into question any possibility of their containment—even under the professed end of history in Communism.

The concept of contradiction was by no means an invention of Mao's, and his understanding of the concept may have drawn upon a variety of sources, native and foreign,[37] but the meaning Mao assigned to it reconfigured earlier meanings of the concept to account for the Chinese experience with modernity, which is apparent in the expository strategy of his discussion of contradictions where modern Chinese history illustrates and informs the concrete manifestations of "contradiction" as abstraction. The relationship of contradiction to Chinese modernity was not an extrinsic one, as of a heuristic device for analysis, but an intrinsic relationship: contradiction as epistemology was valid only to the extent that the structure of explanation corresponded to the reality of historical social experience. I suggested above that "sinification" produced an explicitly structural reading of Marxism by its very effort to reconcile contradictory demands, which in turn rested upon the irreducibility of the moments that went into its constitution. The centrality of the concept of contradiction in Mao's Marxism, I would like to suggest here, was a direct product of his reformulation of Marxism to account for China's historical situation, which was defined structurally by the contradictoriness of its various moments, and the articulation of this contradictoriness as a contradiction between theory and practice. We must underline here that while the contradiction between national and social revolutionary need is the most obvious, the problem went deeper into the very practice of revolution in a social situation that was not anticipated in theory: an agrarian society in which a socialist revolution had to be engineered out of components that theory did not account for; in which the revolutionaries themselves were outsiders to the social situation (and, therefore, in contradiction to it), and had to maneuver with great care in order not to antagonize the population and jeopardize their own existence; and, therefore, could not translate the multifaceted conflicts they encountered readily into *their* theoretical categories, but rather had to recognize them as irreducible features of the social situation into which to articulate theory. Beyond the level of the national struggle to articulate a Chinese modernity, it was this social situation that called for the reformulation of theory in terms of the multitude of contradictions that the revolution faced at the level of practice.

The problem with "contradiction" as a substitute for a linear mode of production analysis was, obviously, that it did not allow for a future predictable from theory; or, rather, that it pointed to a multiplicity of possible futures. Conceived in terms of contradictions, "objective reality" ceases to be objective, and becomes rather an object of interpretation and construction. A linear direction may be imposed on such a situation from the outside, through revolutionary practice, but revolutionary practice as Mao viewed it is itself open to interpretation since, in order to be successful, it must articulate in its structure the contradictions of its revolutionary environment. A revolutionary vision conceived as a blueprint demands resolution of contradictions, by willful suppression if necessary, in order to achieve its goals. Mao did this on repeated occasions when he asserted his vision in order to sustain *his* interpretation of contradictions against other possible interpretations. What is most remarkable, however, is that Mao conceived of revolutionary practice itself as a means to release contradictions and bring them to the surface of politics, which blurred the difference between the pursuit and the resolution of contradictions, and revolutionary vision as an end (a blueprint) versus a process—the utopianization, in other words, of revolution itself.

Mao's revolutionary practice appears in hindsight as experimentation with contradictions, as "a surer and deeper way" into the contradictions of Chinese society and its relationship to the outside world. While such experimentation was not exactly open ended, it was not entirely bounded by a blueprint of the future either, as the very logic of contradictions precluded any predetermined path into the future, and presupposed that a revolutionary vision could be constructed only in the process of revolution.

The language of experimentation infuses Mao's writings. Two examples will have to suffice, one revealing of the metaphysical assumptions of theory, the other an instance of Mao's practice—as the leader of a state:

> The finite is transformed into the infinite, the infinite is transformed into the finite. . . . The universe, too, undergoes transformation, it is not eternal. Capitalism leads to socialism, socialism leads to communism, and communist society must still be transformed, it will also have a beginning and an end, it will certainly be divided into stages, or they will give it another name, it cannot remain constant. If there were only quantitative changes and no qualitative changes, that would go against dialectics. There is nothing in the world that does not arise, develop and disappear. Monkeys turn into men, mankind arose. In the end, the human race will disappear, it may turn into something else.[38]
>
> There remains a question in my mind about producing, in the course of the second five-year plan, 20 million tons of steel. Is this a good thing, or will it throw everything into confusion? I'm not sure at the present, so I want to hold meetings. We'll meet four times a year, and if there are problems, we will make adjustments. The situation after construction has been carried out must be one of the following: excellent, fairly good, not too good, bad, or great disorder. It looks as though, if disorder results, it won't be all that great, there will just be a spell of disorder, and then things may well move towards "order." The appearance of disorder contains within it some favorable elements, we should not fear disorder.[39]

Whatever the personal elements that went into the making of the worldview expressed in these statements, the contradictions in Mao's thinking, as well as his "commitment" to the pursuit of contradictions in revolutionary practice, were also bound up with the contradictions of Chinese modernity of which Mao's Marxism was an articulation, perhaps the most revealing articulation available. Mao's Marxism in its heyday enjoyed the popularity it did *because* it resonated with the concerns of many in China and abroad, especially in the Third World; and it may be that it has fallen out of favor not because it was a failure but because it was all too successful in achieving what it set out to achieve. It continues to intrigue for its insistence on an alternative modernity to overcome the problems with which modernity presented Chinese society; which since then has been abandoned under his successors, who have settled into accepted notions of modernity, and deny that there is anything problematic about the modernization that they pursue, even when they have to kill to achieve their goals.

In contrast, Mao is the tragic expression of Chinese modernism. Mao was able to inspire in millions of Chinese (and others) a faith that it might be possible to overcome the past and the present to create an alternative modern, only to turn around and inflict upon them the deepest and most tragic contradictions of modernity. What makes Mao appear even more Faustian than Goethe's fictional character was his seeming obliviousness to the human costs of his experiments with revolution, to the living people who were in the end reduced to experimental subjects in a relentless quest for revolutionary vision.

The experience was tragic in another sense. So traumatic was the destruction Mao unleashed in the 1950s and 1960s (the Cultural Revolution) that it discredited totally a vision of revolution of which his may well have been the last historical expression; and, with it, the possibility of overcoming modernity. The Cultural Revolution appears in hindsight as the last agonized historical effort to take a society out of capitalism in search of an alternative modernity. Evidence over the last two decades of societies globally suggests that there may be no "way out of the contradictions of modern life," except to learn to live with its destructiveness as a condition of life.

NOTES

1. My use of Mao Zedong Thought here is subject to the same considerations I noted in the preceding chapter. Indeed, the present chapter is very much a continuation and elaboration of issues raised in that chapter, but from the perspective of modernism, antimodernism, and what has acquired currency since the 1990s as alternative modernity. I have also edited out of the present chapter parts that overlapped with the previous chapter, briefly summarizing points that are discussed at much greater length in the preceding chapter.

2. Marshall Berman, *All That Is Solid Melts into Air: The Experience of Modernity* (New York: Penguin Books, 1988), 89.

3. Berman, *All That Is Solid*, 15.

4. David Harvey, *The Condition of Postmodernity* (Oxford: Basil Blackwell, 1989), 11–12.

5. Perry Anderson, "Modernity and Revolution," *New Left Review* 144 (March–April 1984), 97 (emphasis in the original).

6. Jurgen Habermas, *The Philosophical Discourse of Modernity: Twelve Lectures*, trans. Frederick G. Lawrence (Cambridge, MA: MIT Press, 1990), "Introduction" by Thomas McCarthy, xvii.

7. Berman, *All That Is Solid*, 5.

8. Berman, *All That Is Solid*, 14.

9. Jackson Lears, *No Place of Grace: Antimodernism and the Transformation of American Culture, 1880–1920* (New York: Pantheon Books, 1981), xvi.

10. Anderson, "Modernity and Revolution," 112.

11. Berman, *All That Is Solid*, 75–78, 124–25.

12. Berman, *All That Is Solid*, 23.

13. Berman, *All That Is Solid*, 36.

14. Berman, *All That Is Solid*, chapter 11.

15. Berman, *All That Is Solid*, 94.

16. Berman, *All That Is Solid*, 98.

17. Berman, *All That Is Solid*, 129. For the "dialectical dance," see 90.

18. Berman, *All That Is Solid*, 175.

19. Berman, *All That Is Solid* (emphasis in the original).

20. Berman, *All That Is Solid*. The difference in the Third World experience with modernity as something happening elsewhere, Berman says, is an intensification of the experience of modernity's contradictions: "The modernism of underdevelopment is forced to build on fantasies and dreams of modernity, to nourish itself on an intimacy and a struggle with mirages and ghosts. In order to be true to the life from which it springs, it is forced to be shrill, uncouth and inchoate" (232).

21. Berman, *All That Is Solid*, 77.

22. Berman, *All That Is Solid*, 75–82, 124–26.

23. Berman, *All That Is Solid*, 77.

24. Anderson, "Modernity and Revolution," 109.

25. Anderson, "Modernity and Revolution," 109.

26. Harvey, *The Condition of Postmodernity*, 16. The quotation is from Berman.

27. André Malraux, *Anti-Memoirs* (New York: Holt, Rinehart and Winston, 1968), 388, 390.

28. Berman, *All That Is Solid*, 23.

29. Benjamin I. Schwartz, "Modernization and the Maoist Vision," in *Communism and China: Ideology in Flux* (New York: Atheneum, 1970), 179 (emphasis added).

30. Eric J. Hobsbawm, *Nations and Nationalism since 1780: Programme, Myth, Reality* (New York: Cambridge University Press, 1990), chapter 4.

31. For a further discussion of teleology in Marxism, see Arif Dirlik, "Post-Socialism/Flexible Production: Marxism in Contemporary Radicalism," *Polygraph* 6/7 (1993): 133–69. I may note here that the "sinification" of Marxism, which brought a Third World perspective on Marxism, also helped "deconstruct" Marxism and open up Marxist theory to expose some of its contradictions. Berman is quite right in insisting on Marx's ambivalence toward modernity. On the other hand, Euro-Marxism (including Marx's Marxism) had little ambivalence when it came to the modernization of Third World societies. While Marx did express sympathy for Asian peoples suffering at the hands of British imperialism, for instance, he saw this imperialism as a progressive force that would rescue these societies from their barbarism and "vegetation." Nor is there any evidence that he saw a place for the native subjectivities and historical legacies of these societies in modernity. The problem, needless to say, appeared quite differently to members of these societies.

32. These debates were considerably more complex and sophisticated than discussions of culture in the May Fourth Period (the 1920s), and, in spite of the fetishization of the May Fourth period in historical memory, it is they rather than May Fourth discussions that set the terms for contemporary discussions of culture in China. For two important collections of contributions to these debates, see *Xian jieduande Zhonqquo sixiang yundong* [The Chinese Thought Movement at the Present Stage] (Shanghai, 1937) and *Zhonqguo benwei wenhua jianshe taolun* [Discussion on the Construction of an Indigenous Culture for China] (Shanghai: Wenhua jianshe yuekanshe, 1936).

33. See the interesting and important discussion of this reorientation of Chinese thought in the late 1930s in Chang-tai Hung, *War and Popular Culture: Resistance in Modern China, 1937–1945* (Berkeley: University of California Press, 1994).

34. For a discussion of these problems in the early part of the century, see Arif Dirlik, *Anarchism in the Chinese Revolution* (Berkeley: University of California Press, 1991), chapter 2. Anarchists are especially revealing of these contradictions as they found in anarchism a source both of modernism and antimodernism.

35. Mao Zedong, "The Chinese People Have Stood Up!" in *Selected Works of Mao Tse-tung* (Peking: Foreign Languages Press, 1977), vol. 5, 15–18.

36. The essays are "On Contradiction" and "On the Correct Handling of Contradictions among the People."

37. See Norman Levine, *Dialogue within the Dialectic* (London: George Allen and Unwin, 1984), 317–47 and 363–91, for the debt Mao owed to "Hegelianized Leninism" for his ideas as well as the ways in which he moved beyond it. Frederick Wakeman Jr., in his *History and Will: Philosophical Perspectives of Mao Tse-tung's Thought* (Berkeley: University of California Press, 1975), offers a discussion of the debt Mao may have owed to native sources.

38. Mao Zedong, "Talks at the Chengtu Conference" (March 1958), in *Chairman Mao Talks to the People*, ed. Stuart Schram, 110 (New York: Pantheon Books, 1974).

39. Mao, "Talks at the Chengtu Conference," 111–12.

6

The Predicament of Marxist Revolutionary Consciousness: Mao Zedong, Antonio Gramsci, and the Reformulation of Marxist Revolutionary Theory

The Marxism of Mao Zedong has long been a subject of controversy both within the Communist Party of China and among serious students of Chinese history. Mao has been portrayed as the greatest Marxist of the mid-twentieth century, and his Marxism as the fulfillment of the Marxian revolutionary idea, the articulation in practice of Marx's theory of revolution. At the other extreme stands the view of Mao as a Chinese revolutionary whose deviations from Marxism were so fundamental as to place him outside mainstream Marxist thought.[1]

At the heart of all controversy concerning Mao's Marxism lies the problem of consciousness. Mao, as is commonly recognized, assigned to revolutionary activity a determinative status in the realization of socialism: The activity of revolutionaries could mobilize society in the cause of socialism even where the class basis for socialist revolution was missing; it could also bring about the establishment of socialist society without awaiting the foundation of an advanced technological base. Key to revolutionary activity was, needless to say, revolutionary consciousness, which occupied a supreme status in Mao's thinking. Consciousness, to Mao, was not simply a reflection of social reality, but a mode of comprehending and changing it.

Why Mao endowed the problem of consciousness with a crucial significance for revolutionary practice remains obscure, buried under fruitless efforts to match his Marxism against his Chineseness. In the following discussion, I suggest an answer to this question that seeks to root Mao's appreciation of the problem of consciousness in the confrontation of Marxism with the circumstances of the Chinese Revolution. Mao shared with many of his contemporaries a perception of the difficulties involved in reconciling the universalistic premises of Marxism with the particular circumstances and needs of the Chinese Revolution. What distinguished him was his commitment to achieving such a reconciliation. His preoccupation with consciousness was a product of his recognition of the burdens this task imposed upon the consciousness of revolutionaries.

There are striking parallels between Mao and Antonio Gramsci in their understanding of the problem of revolution. This discussion does not undertake a point-by-point comparison between Mao and Gramsci; rather, I examine certain basic aspects of Mao's Marxism in light of insights derived from discussions of the problem of revolutionary consciousness by Gramsci and by commentators on Gramsci's Marxism. I will return to a more explicit comparison of Mao and Gramsci at the end of the discussion.

Writers on Gramsci have repeatedly drawn attention to the similarities between Gramsci and Mao on Marxism. In his pioneering study of Gramsci, *Antonio Gramsci and the Origins of Italian Communism,* John Cammett first noted the kinship between Gramsci's and Mao's views on the role of the peasantry (or rural areas) in revolution, and described Mao's communism as "quite Gramscian in character."[2] Cammett's suggestion has been repeated by a number of authors. Genovese, taking his cue from Cammett, observed a "deeper link between the two—that concern for the dialectics of historical development."[3] More recently, Jerome Karabel has noted the similarity of Gramsci's "specialized and political" intellectual and Mao's "red and expert" intellectual to the new type of intellectual required for socialism.[4] Nigel Todd, following Cammett's advice, has offered a sketchy comparison of Mao's and Gramsci's views on intellectuals that reveals the potential value of comparison between the two revolutionaries.[5]

At the risk of sounding outrageous, it is possible to observe, I think, that Mao did what Gramsci thought. Mao was not given to theoretical speculation for its own sake. The considerations underlying his revolutionary practice remain imbedded in his revolutionary activity and writings, which were invariably practical in purpose. Gramsci, equally practice oriented, was nevertheless forced into speculation by the tragic circumstances of his life. The concept of hegemony, which he elaborated in his prison cell to cope with the problems of Italian politics, very often reads, at least for a novice in Gramsci's thought, as a description of Mao's activities.

Having said this, however, it is necessary to add a note of caution. There are certain dangers in comparing Mao and Gramsci. The two revolutionaries shared a common disdain for preoccupation with orthodoxy. Gramsci's statement, "Are we Marxists? Who is a Marxist? Only stupidity is immortal,"[6] parallels in its contempt for orthodoxy Mao's view of dogma as dung. Furthermore, there is still considerable uncertainty over the precise intent and meaning of Gramsci's theoretical formulations, and his Marxism is controversial, as is Mao's. The Marxism of one, therefore, does not vindicate the Marxism of the other. Still, this makes comparison more, not less, useful, since it refocuses attention from abstract, ahistorical questions of orthodoxy to questions on revolutionary practice and its implications for theory.

The same is the case with regard to the conditions and nature of revolution as the two revolutionaries perceived it. Gramsci drew a distinction between revolution in the West and revolution in the East.[7] In the West, "civil society" (the realm of private life and institutions) was well established; revolution, therefore, was as much a cultural and educational activity as it was a political one, since the conquest of civil society took priority over the conquest of the state. In the East (including Russia), revolution took a more directly political form—the conquest of state power—since civil society was, for all purposes, nonexistent. Gramsci clearly had Russia and Lenin in mind when he made this distinction. While the distinction is also applicable to China, the protracted nature of the Chinese Revolution distinguishes it from the Russian Revolution. While China did not have a civil society in the Gramscian sense (that is, a bourgeois society), the Communists in China obviously had to struggle during their long revolution to capture the hearts and minds of the people before they were in a position to conquer state power. For them, too, in other words, the cultural and the educational task appeared as a prerevolutionary rather than a postrevolutionary requirement. Gramsci's Marxism may have led to Eurocommunism and Mao's to revolutionary violence; the answer to these divergent paths must be sought in the conditions of revolution. Underlying these different paths, however, one may detect a similar appreciation of the intimate dialectic between revolutionary consciousness and culture, and the consciousness and culture of its social ambience.

THIRD WORLDISM, ORIENTALISM, AND THE QUESTION OF MAO'S MARXISM

Contrary to some students of Mao, Mao assigned to conscious activity a much more prominent status in revolution than did Marx. "Mankind sets itself only such tasks as it can solve," Marx wrote in 1858, "since the task itself arises only when the material conditions for its solution already exist or are at least in the process of formation." Any defender of identity between Marx and Mao would be hard put to demonstrate that the absence of requisite material or social conditions for the solution of political problems ever restrained him from pursuing such a solution anyway. This is not to imply that Mao was an arbitrary voluntarist who recognized no constraints on revolutionary activity, or that he ignored the context for revolutionary activity. Nevertheless, Mao's career as a revolutionary provides the most incontrovertible evidence of his belief in the ability of revolutionary activity to create the conditions for its own fulfillment.

Preoccupation with orthodoxy is not only misguided in the case of a revolutionary who thought Marxist dogma to be less useful than dung, but diminishes his creativity as a Marxist. More seriously, it ignores the significant differences from Marx in the content of Mao's consciousness, which were a product of the concrete circumstances within which Mao carried out his revolutionary activity. The argument that Mao and Marx both endowed consciousness with a role in social and revolutionary change at the formal theoretical level makes an abstract comparison that does not say much about the concrete role of consciousness in revolutionary activity. This is a serious deficiency in a Marxist analysis. It sweeps under the rug, as I will argue, the most significant elements in Mao's thinking on consciousness. Underlying this view is a "Third Worldist fantasy," a fantasy of Mao as a Chinese reincarnation of Marx who fulfilled the Marxist promise that had been betrayed in the West.

Explanations that attribute Mao's faith in revolutionary consciousness to his life-long preoccupation with subjective will, or trace it to some vague Chinese cultural legacy, are even less satisfactory because they abolish the problem as a problem within Marxism and, with it, Mao's Marxism itself. These explanations are informed by a pre-Leninist economistic understanding of Marxism that serves, on the one hand, to emasculate Marxism as a progenitor of revolutionary consciousness, and, on the other hand, to "Orientalize" Mao by encapsulating him in a Chinese cultural and political space. The economistic interpretation of Marxism renders consciousness epiphenomenal by definition. Therefore, it denies the significant role of consciousness in social change and revolution. Mao's preoccupation with consciousness appears, consequently, as an aberration of his Marxism that must be traced to sources extraneous to Marxism. Mao's individual orientation or his predisposition as a Chinese revolutionary provide a convenient, and circumstantially logical, explanation. Mao's Marxism has been orientalized both by Western students of China, suspicious of the authenticity of his Marxism because of his Chineseness, and by Chinese who, convinced of the resiliency of their cultural heritage, resist any suggestion of the impregnation of Chinese culture by an alien ideology. The culturalist interpretation of Mao, it might be noted, coincides with a politically conservative reading of Marx that limits considerably the boundaries of Marxist revolutionary activity.

The problem with such explanations is that they ignore the Marxist problematic, basic to which is the idea of class, within which Mao viewed the problem of consciousness, and which shaped his activities as a revolutionary. Fred Wakeman and Li Rui, with different emphases, have shown that Mao was indeed preoccupied with the question of subjective will from his youthful days.[8] What needs to be pointed out is that Marxism tamed Mao's subjectivism, and taught him the constraints placed on revolutionary will by social circumstances. The mature Marxist Mao who first expressed his views on this subject in the 1937 essay, "On Practice,"[9] remained conscious of the dialectical relationship between consciousness and social existence, between revolutionary activity and its material premises.

This would seem to be belied by the Cultural Revolution, which was in fact responsible for dramatizing to students of China, Mao's persistent preoccupation with the autonomy of revolutionary consciousness. The Cultural Revolution informs most discussions of Mao's so-called voluntarism. During the Cultural Revolution, arbitrary subjectivity seemed to take over once again, and led Mao to the assertion of the power of revolutionary will over material reality. The Cultural Revolutionary phase of Mao's career has recently been repudiated by Mao's successors on these same grounds, which would seem to confirm earlier analyses by students of China.

Yet this is valid only from a limited perspective on Marxism, and it remains to be demonstrated that Mao abandoned the basic Marxist premise that "social being determines consciousness" during the Cultural Revolution. We have yet to distinguish the intention that underlay the Cultural Revolution from the circumstances that perverted the intention into its own caricature.[10] In its intention, the Cultural Revolution was quite in keeping with the revolutionary goals Mao had pursued as a Marxist for all of his mature years. From the beginning, Marxism redefined for Mao the goals as well as the strategy of the Chinese Revolution. His aim as a Marxist was not simply to create a strong and independent China, but a revolutionary one as well.

Mao's idea of the "sinification of Marxism" has been used as evidence that he subsumed Marxism within his nationalism. It is clear from Mao's discussions of sinification, especially his seminal essay, "On New Democracy,"[11] however, that Mao's nationalism was quite empirical, that the Chinese nation he had in mind was yet to be created in the course of the Chinese Revolution. Marxism was to be present at the creation. Unlike sinification of old (that is, the absorption of foreign cultures and peoples into Chinese civilization, where they lost their identity), the sinification of Marxism did not imply the absorption of Marxism into a Chinese culture that could be taken for granted; Marxism was to serve as the litmus paper against which the new Chinese culture was to be tested. Hence Mao could by definition exclude from the culture he envisaged Chinese "feudal" culture as well as Western "bourgeois" culture.

If Mao nationalized Marxism, in other words, his idea of nationalism was fashioned by Marxism, and its tasks were defined by revolutionary considerations of class and class consciousness. It is sufficient to place Mao's nationalism against the nationalism of his successors to appreciate the revolutionary mold in which his Marxism cast his nationalism.

It is only when this revolutionary nature of Mao's, nationalism is overlooked, when his nationalism is equated with China's national salvation pure and simple, that the Cultural Revolution appears as a departure from Mao's previously Marxist understanding of consciousness. On the other hand, if Mao's Marxism is viewed not simply as an instrument of his nationalism but also as its determinant, the Cultural Revolution appears as an attempt on the part of Mao to move further along the path of revolution, past the point where immediate national goals had been achieved, toward the creation of a revolutionary culture. That Mao, as a revolutionary committed to China's autonomy and strength, would risk China's wealth and power in the pursuit of revolutionary goals only attests to the powerful part Marxism played in the shaping of his nationalism. From Mao's perspective, there was nothing aberrant or arbitrary about the Cultural Revolution, which remained firmly within the Marxist problematic that had guided him all along.

From this perspective, it appears that what Mao rejected during the Cultural Revolution was not the Marxist conception of consciousness, but a determinism that relinquished to technological development the task of achieving socialism. To interpret Mao's activities during this period as expression of a faith in the power of subjective will over material reality is to ignore Mao's very Marxist premise that social relations mediate between consciousness and material reality. A note Mao made on the origins of capitalism in the late 1950s, when the problems that were to culminate in the Cultural Revolution were already in his mind, is illustrative of his appreciation of this problem. Mao observes in that note that bourgeois consciousness and bourgeois social relations historically preceded the technology that had come to identify capitalism. He obviously had in mind a parallel with socialism, that socialist social relations, too, could precede a socialist technology, that socialist social relations presupposed a socialist culture and consciousness. This is quite consistent with Marxism except in its technological determinist version; indeed, Mao's note may contain the insight that technology itself must correspond to the desired social relations and not be allowed to subvert them or render them impossible, an insight that many present-day Marxists share.[12]

The notion of voluntarism is the guise in which the problem of consciousness appears in most discussions of Mao. This approach is misleading because it poses a false issue. If voluntarism is meant to be juxtaposed against determinism, it does not suffice to distinguish Mao from any other Marxist revolutionary (including Marx) since all revolutionary activity is by definition voluntary activity. If, on the other hand, voluntarism is meant to imply obliviousness to social and material constraints on revolutionary activity, it suggests an unjustified and undemonstrated conclusion that Mao's Marxism represents the degeneration of Marxism to arbitrary subjective activity. Here Mao's Marxism no longer appears as a serious problem within Marxism.

The problem appears in a different light when posed in terms of conscious activity that is both intentional and voluntary, but is not, therefore, arbitrary activity, since there is no necessary contradiction between intentionality and social existence, only a complex relationship to be analyzed and explained. When we approach the problem of consciousness in Mao from this perspective, it becomes possible to perceive why Mao should have endowed consciousness with a fundamental role in revolutionary activity.

What Mao juxtaposed was not consciousness versus social and material reality, but revolutionary consciousness against consciousness in general. Consciousness in general is the outlook on life and society that guides people in their everyday activity; it is shaped not just by immediate social and material circumstances, but by inherited cultural traditions; it is just as much a part of social existence as are the material conditions of life. Revolutionary consciousness (that is, class consciousness), on the other hand, appears in this light as part of a more all-encompassing concept of consciousness to which it bears a problematic relationship.

The revelation of this problem may be Mao's contribution to Marxism. His own appreciation of the problem was a direct product of the problems that were implicit in the confrontation of Marxism with an alien cultural and social environment. As Schram has observed, in a slightly different sense than mine: "the whole record of Mao Tse-tung's intellectual itinerary during the ensuing decades [after 1926] can be read as a persistent search for ways to combine the principle of proletarian hegemony with the vision of Chinese society which had gripped him in 1926."[13] This confrontation exposed problems that were not apparent under circumstances where Marxists could anticipate the spontaneous articulation of revolutionary consciousness that they thought was immanent in society. Marxism in China provided the redefinition of the goals and strategy of the Chinese Revolution, but it did not survive the process unchanged. In order to serve as an effective ideology of action, Marxism had to be nationalized to lose its alienness to the circumstances of the Chinese Revolution. This was the predicament of Marxism in China: to retain its identity unchanged and lose its relevance to the Chinese Revolution, or to undergo the necessary adjustment and relinquish its identity. The greatness of Mao as a Marxist lay in his recognition of this predicament, and his persistent conviction that a dialectical integration, a mutual incorporation of Marxist and Chinese goals (rather than a "combination," as Schram suggests) lay within the realm of possibility. It was this recognition, I think, that led him to endow the problem of consciousness with a significance and urgency that it did not call for under those conditions where the circumstances of revolutionary activity were less alien to its theoretical premises.

MAO AND MARXISM: SOCIAL EXPERIENCE AND SOCIAL REVOLUTION

It is necessary to view Mao's preoccupation with consciousness from the perspective of Marxist thought both to identify its roots in the Marxist problematic of revolution and to appreciate Mao's originality.

Marx conceptualized consciousness in its dialectical relationship with history, with the proletariat as its concrete referent. Revolutionary consciousness represented the development of proletarian consciousness as the proletariat became aware of itself as a class by comprehending itself in history. As the articulation of proletarian self-consciousness, revolutionary consciousness mediated the transformation of the proletariat from a politically inert class-in-itself to a revolutionary class-for-itself capable of carrying out its historical destiny. The task of the revolutionary was to present to the proletariat its image in history in order to help the proletariat fulfill its potential. Revolutionary activity was, therefore, placed in a dialectical relationship with the teleology that Marx's social and revolutionary theory presupposed.

Lenin's recognition that revolutions did not come about spontaneously through the dynamics of social forces, but were brought about by the conscious activity of revolutionaries, was a crucial redefinition of the relationship Marx had established between consciousness and history. Revolution to Lenin was not a social but a political event; it was the product not of social movements of classes but of political organization; and the revolutionary consciousness that guided revolution was not the articulation of proletarian consciousness but an attribute of revolutionaries that presupposed the proletariat as an object, rather than the subject, of revolutionary activity.

Lenin's recognition that revolutionary consciousness was not the expression of social forces, but was autonomous political consciousness that sought to remold social forces, freed Marxist revolutionaries from the necessity of waiting upon history; it also opened up the possibility of arbitrariness in the pursuit of revolution. The dialectic between theory and revolutionary activity, imbedded by Marx in history, was relocated by Lenin in the consciousness of the revolutionary. Marxist theory, divorced from its concrete social referents, could, therefore, be instrumentalized in the service of goals that bore no organic relationship to its social premise; in other words, capitalism and its revolutionary product, the proletariat, were no longer preconditions for socialist revolutionary activity. At the same time, socialism could now accommodate, or even be appropriated by goals that expressed the aspirations of a social context alien to the original social premise of Marxist theory. This rendered consciousness much more problematic than it had been to Marx, and required the revolutionary party as guardian of the integrity of revolutionary consciousness.

Mao was heir to this problem. In his case, however, the problem was much more complex than it had been for Marx or Lenin because of the tenuous status of Marxism, not just among the people of China, but among Marxist intellectuals themselves. In the first place, Marxism was an alien ideology in China. (I do not mean this in the sense of alienness to an "Orientalized" China that was a world unto itself.) In the twentieth century, China was placed in a world setting, and was absorbed into a world market of ideas just as much as it was absorbed into a world market of commodities. Marxism was one of these ideas. It was relevant to the problems of Chinese society to the extent that China's problems were identifiable with the new setting in which China was placed. Socialism in China was from its beginnings concerned with the role capitalism should play in China's development in a world dominated by capitalism.

Nevertheless, there existed a gap, as Tang Tsou has noted, between ideological development and social and political development.[14] Social being in China was much more complex than it had been for Marx or for the émigré Lenin, both of whom felt at home in European thought and politics. For a Chinese revolutionary, social being in China meant a Chinese existence as well as existence in a China situated in the world; consciousness had a corresponding complexity. The predicament of Marxist revolutionary consciousness was not just political (reconciling Marxist and Chinese political goals), it was also cultural. This predicament was underlined by the cultural inertia of the masses the revolutionaries sought to revolutionize. Contradiction, rather than dialectical integration, is the appropriate term for describing the inner tensions of revolutionary consciousness, not to speak of the relationship between revolutionaries and the masses they hope to lead. Revolution would have to be made, and a revolution in consciousness and culture was the precondition to, rather than an expression of, a revolution in material existence.

This problem became dramatically evident after 1927 when the Communists were driven to the countryside, and when Mao began his ascent to leadership. In the early twenties, the first years of communism in China, it might have been possible to have some faith in spontaneous mass uprising on the evidence of working-class revolt in China's cities. After 1927, revolution had to be made in agrarian China where, in spite of all the existing social agitation, political consciousness remained enshrouded within traditional forms of protest, and revolutionaries faced a much more difficult task in remolding peasant grievance into revolutionary class consciousness. It was to Mao's credit that he could perceive the revolutionary potential of the peasantry. Maurice Meisner has pointed to Mao's populist faith in the spontaneous revolutionary creativity of the peasant.[15] This faith, however, was not such as to lead Mao to anticipate spontaneous class consciousness or revolutionary activity from the peasant. In his classic report on the peasant movement in Hunan, Mao identified traditional social and religious authority as forces that weighed down the peasant. As in the case of his nationalism, Mao's faith in the peasantry was mediated by his Marxism. To the end of his life, Mao remained suspicious of those who believed that "the peasantry is simply wonderful," and thought it necessary to transform peasant consciousness in accordance with socialist premises.[16] Nevertheless, his Marxist conviction in the necessity of transforming the peasantry was not accompanied by disdain for the peasant, or the belief that peasant "false consciousness" must be purged through the imposition on the peasantry of Marxist consciousness. In dealing with the peasantry, educators must themselves be educated. This attitude made as much sense from the viewpoint of revolutionary pragmatism as it did from the perspective of a populist affection for the peasantry. What it meant, from the standpoint of the problem here, was that the consciousness of the revolutionary must be transformed in the process of the revolutionary transformation of the peasant.

REVOLUTIONARY PRACTICE
AND REVOLUTIONARY CONSCIOUSNESS

This brief consideration of the circumstantial peculiarities of the Chinese Revolution points to two problems. First, that under the circumstances of the Chinese Revolution, constant vigilance was necessary, on the one hand, to prevent the instrumentalization of Marxism into a mere tool of parochialized goals, and, on the other hand, to minimize the tendency to convert Marxism into a dogma that would only serve to underscore its alienness. This was a problem primarily for revolutionaries, who had to assimilate their abstract revolutionary consciousness to the concrete demands of their immediate circumstances. The predicament of the revolutionary was born out of the uneasy assimilation of Chinese to Marxist political goals.

The problem of consciousness was not, therefore, simply a problem of the formal status of consciousness as an abstract component in the Marxist theory of revolution. The formal status of consciousness in revolution was bound up with the content of revolutionary consciousness as Mao perceived it. In other words, the same forces that shaped Mao's own consciousness as a revolutionary appear simultaneously as the forces that account for the supreme status with which Mao endowed consciousness as an agent of change. As Lenin had perceived and Mao now elaborated, revolutionary consciousness was not mere static reflection of class or society; it was a dynamic material "moment" of revolutionary activity. As Mao explained in his essay "On Practice," revolutionary activity and the conceptualization of revolution were simply alternating, dialectically linked, phases of a continuing process. Theory provided the overall direction by mediating between activity and its conceptualization, but it did not predetermine "correct" action or offer prefabricated concepts that provided universal explanations without regard for particular circumstances. By the same virtue, revolutionary activity mediated between theory and empirical conditions, and integrated them into a historical process. Without revolutionary activity, theory was reduced to dogma, and empiricism to activity without direction: both manifestations of arbitrary subjectivism.

The complexity of Mao's own consciousness mirrored the predicament of revolutionary consciousness in China. Mao was accused of empiricism in the Communist Party of China; he has also been charged repeatedly with obliviousness to empirical concerns.[17] Why he should be subjected to such antithetical interpretations may be gleaned from his 1937 essay "On Contradiction,"[18] which I think is Mao's most important articulation of his perceptions of the problem of revolution. The essay at once instrumentalizes Marxist theory as a guide to analyzing empirical conditions in society, and reaffirms the possibility of revolutionary transcendence through a theoretical grasp of social and political contradictions in their most empirical manifestation.

"On Contradiction" was the culmination of lessons Mao drew from a decade of revolutionary activity. The essay was both a description of recent Chinese history as Mao perceived it, especially as he had experienced it, and a prescription for future revolutionary activity drawn from that experience. The essay was most conspicuous for its instrumentalized conception of theory, which was implicit in Mao's stress on contradiction over class as the basic unit of analysis. In this respect, it was but a restatement in the abstract of Mao's revolutionary practice over the previous decade. From his first analysis of classes in China in 1926, Mao revealed a political conceptualization of class: In his delineation of classes in China, he was interested not in a structural determination of class in terms of relationship to the means of production, but in the identification of the status of social groups in terms of hierarchy of power, and especially in terms of relations of exploitation. In other words, Mao's concept of class was based not on abstract theoretical considerations, but a utilitarian concern to gauge the potential for revolutionary consciousness and activity of different strata within the Chinese population. The opening words of his 1926 essay, "Analysis of Classes in Chinese Society," reveal the underlying intention of Mao's analysis: "Who are our enemies? Who are our friends?" The essay went on to identify fifteen "classes" in China in terms of their attitudes toward revolution. This same activist approach to class analysis guided Mao's analysis in another essay, published in the same year, where Mao identified five classes in agrarian China, as well as in the better known essay of 1933, "How to Analyze Classes [in Rural China]," which served as the basis for Communist land reform programs then and after 1949.[19] To Mao in every case class analysis was social analysis designed to identify the dimensions of conflict in society for the guidance of revolutionary activity and policy.

"On Contradiction" was the ultimate expression of Mao's view of Marxism as a theory of conflict. The essay articulated Mao's appreciation of the complexity and multitude of social and political conflict, which was much more comprehensive and intricate than is allowed for in class analysis based on relationship to the means of production. The recognition of multifaceted conflict increased the burden on revolutionary consciousness. Revolutionaries had to absorb in their consciousness all aspects of conflict in order to devise an effective strategy of action, but without getting caught up in the conflict themselves, for the latter would result in the loss of direction to revolutionary activity. In the essay, Mao attempted to bring order to the chaos of conflict by postulating that in any situation, there was a "principal" contradiction that conditioned all the other contradictions and provided a focus for revolutionary activity; it was up to the revolutionary to identify the principal contradiction and use it as the guide to action. This, however, did not exhaust the demands on the revolutionary. The idea of a principal contradiction resolved the problem of chaos on a short-term basis, but it did not provide a guard against arbitrary activity (more crudely, opportunism) on a long-term basis; in fact, it opened up the danger of the substitution of short-term for long-term goals.

It is implicit in Mao's reasoning that the revolutionary who did not look beyond the immediate situation remained deprived of the vision necessary to transcend immediate circumstances. No matter how successful a revolutionary might be in grasping immediate contradictions, without a vision of revolution, he or she remained a manipulator of conflict. The manipulator who did not have vision of the future, we might add, was condemned to manipulation by the same circumstances that he or she sought to control. It was only by keeping their sights firmly fixed on the historically principal task of abolishing class domination and oppression, that revolutionaries could transcend the immediate historical situation, and live up to the vision imbedded in theory. It is hardly surprising that the consciousness of the revolutionary must, under the circumstances, be brought to the forefront of all consideration of change.

Second, and perhaps more important, the circumstances of the Chinese Revolution required the recognition that the people of China had their own socially and culturally determined consciousness that was very much at odds with Marxist revolutionary consciousness; in other words, that revolutionary confrontation was not simply a confrontation between Marxist revolutionary consciousness and the social and material conditions of China, but a confrontation between Marxist revolutionary consciousness and Chinese consciousness as materialized in peasant life. Revolutionary consciousness could possess this consciousness or be possessed by it; this was its second predicament. Mao recognized, rightly, that the possession had to be mutual if the revolution was to be successful, but also because he *was* a Chinese revolutionary. Marxist revolutionary consciousness had to incorporate elements of its novel cultural context if it was to lose its alienness; it also had to possess and transform that cultural context. This dynamic option was closed off by those who, in the name of revolutionary consciousness, would dismiss native consciousness as primitive or false consciousness. It was ignored by those who readily fell in with peasant consciousness and lost their ability to lead.

Mao's concern with this problem was reflected in his deep awareness of the contradiction between empiricism and dogmatism in the Communist Party[20]— above all in the concept of the "mass line" that represented an effort to resolve this contradiction in the organization for revolution. Mao wrote in 1934: "We should make the broad masses realize that we represent their interests, that our life and theirs are intimately interwoven."[21] The essence of the mass line is contained in the simple statement, "from the masses, and to the masses." But the idea was considerably more complex. The mass line represented in effect the application of the idea of democratic centralism to the relationship between the Party and the masses. John Lewis has drawn attention to the parallel between the mass line as an organizational concept and the epistemological process Mao had outlined in "On Practice": perception-conception-verification (or testing through practice).[22] This parallel implies that the mass line was not a mere technique of mass mobilization, but a means of integrating the revolutionary consciousness of the Communist Party with the consciousness of the people the Party led. As theory intermediated the interrelationship between revolutionary condition and revolutionary activity in the case of the individual revolutionary, the Party pursuing the mass line mediated the interrelationship between revolutionary goals and popular interests and consciousness. In this mediation the Party, as the agent of revolutionary transformation, served as the guardian of revolutionary integrity and theoretical correctness, but it could perform its role effectively only by absorbing into its consciousness the consciousness of the masses it led.

Whatever Mao's own proclivities, the idea of the mass line made eminent sense under the circumstances in which the Communist Party led the revolution in China. That this was not mere pragmatism, or simply a mechanical conception of party–people relationship, at least to Mao, is evident in Mao's insistence on the continuation of the mass line after 1949. As Mao's writings from the early 1960s reveal unequivocally, one of the basic problems Mao intended to solve through the Cultural Revolution was the increasing alienation of the party in power from its popular constituency, especially the working people who provided its class basis. The relationship Mao envisaged, and hoped to achieve through the mass line, was not simply a mechanical relationship of interest mediation, but an organic relationship where the culture (in its broadest sense) of the masses and the party would be "interwoven," just as he envisaged the interweaving of Marxist and national aspirations at the level of political goals.

This was ultimately the meaning of Mao's sinification of Marxism, which, therefore, can also be viewed as the "Marxification" of Chineseness. What is essential is Mao's realization that the battle for revolution was as much a battle over culture and consciousness as it was over social and political power. This realization, and the practice Mao based on it, may ultimately be Mao's most important contribution to Marxist theory.

CLASS, CULTURE, AND REVOLUTION IN GRAMSCI'S THOUGHT

Gramsci's conception of hegemony expressed his recognition of the problem of revolutionary consciousness in the battle for revolution. Unless this battle for consciousness was won, Gramsci thought, the revolution would be doomed to failure: "A social group can, and indeed must, already exercise 'leadership' [that is, be hegemonic] before winning governmental power (this indeed is one of the principal conditions for the winning of such power)."[23]

In a seminal article on Gramsci, Gwyn Williams described Gramsci's concept of hegemony as follows:

By "hegemony" Gramsci seems to mean a socio-political situation, in his terminology, a "moment," in which the philosophy and practice of a society fuse or are in equilibrium; an order in which a certain way of life and thought are dominant, in which one concept of reality is diffused throughout society in all its institutional and private manifestations, informing with its spirit all taste, morality, customs, religious and political principles, and all social relations, particularly in their intellectual and moral connotation.[24]

Revolution to Gramsci was a battle for hegemony between opposing classes. A hegemonic class was by definition a class whose values suffused the society it dominated, the "historic bloc" where hegemony over culture and consciousness corresponded to the control of the means of production. Hegemony implied the domination of "civil society," without which political domination or leadership must degenerate into naked governmental coercion, which itself was an indication of the incompleteness or degeneration of hegemony. When hegemony prevails, "discipline becomes self-discipline, coercion becomes self-government."[25]

For our purposes, three characteristics of hegemony are important. A hegemonic class must of necessity incorporate into its interests the interests of other classes (or articulate the interests of other classes through its own interests) in order to universalize its economic domination. Second, it must incorporate into its culture elements of its cultural context in order to universalize its culture. It follows, third, that a hegemonic class must be a national class. The first characteristic has been cogently expressed by Chantal Mouffe. A hegemonic class, Mouffe explains, is

> a class which has been able to articulate the interests of other social groups to its own by means of ideological struggle. This according to Gramsci, is only possible if this class renounces a strictly corporatist conception, since in order to exercise leadership it must genuinely concern itself with the interests of those social groups over which it wishes to exercise hegemony.[26]

On the question of culture, the second characteristic, Raymond Williams observes:

> Any hegemonic process must be especially alert and responsive to the alternatives and opposition which question or threaten its dominance. The reality of cultural process must then always include the efforts and contributions of those who are in one way or another outside or at the edge of the terms of the specific hegemony.[27]

Williams describes as incorporation that process whereby the hegemonic group appropriates for itself the traditions and values of a given society. Williams's description of hegemony cogently brings out the connection between class and culture:

> Hegemony is then not only the articulate upper level of "ideology," nor are its forms of control only those ordinarily seen as "manipulation" or "indoctrination." It is a whole body of practices and expectations over the whole of living: our senses and assignments of energy, our shaping perceptions of ourselves and our world. It is a lived system of meanings and values—constitutive and constituting—

which as they are experienced as practices appear reciprocally confirming. It thus constitutes a sense of reality for most people in the society, a sense of absolute because experienced reality beyond which it is very difficult for most members of the society to move, in most areas of their lives. It is, that is to say, in the strongest sense a "culture," but a culture which has also to be seen as the lived dominance and subordination of particular classes.[28]

Williams credits Gramsci with having abolished the base superstructure division in the Marxist appreciation of culture, and made culture into a constituent element of social life; in other words, materialized the notion of culture.

Finally, these considerations required that a hegemonic class must be national. "A class that is international," Gramsci observed, "has to 'nationalize' itself" in order to effect a link between the leaders and the led.[29] This led Gramsci to the idea of a "national popular" culture. Hoare and Smith, the editors of the *Prison Notebooks,* describe this idea as "a sort of 'historic block,' between national and popular aspirations in the formation of which the intellectuals . . . play an essential mediating role."[30] They further distinguish Gramsci's idea of national popular culture from Fascist or populist views on the subject. This distinction is supported, I think, by the model that informed Gramsci's idea: Lenin and the Russian revolutionaries, whom Gramsci credited with having achieved just such a nationalization of Marxism.

An elite consisting of some of the most active, energetic, enterprising and disciplined members of the society emigrates abroad and assimilates the culture and historical experiences of the most advanced countries of the West without, however, losing the most essential characteristics of its own nationality, that is to say without breaking its sentimental and historical links with its own people.[31]

Gramsci's views of intellectuals in their relationship to revolution followed from his idea of hegemony. A hegemonic class needed its own "organic" intellectuals who would be its functionaries in the world of government and culture. Gramsci described as "traditional" intellectuals those intellectuals who did not serve as functionaries of the hegemonic class; or, at least, thought that they did not do so. A basic task for a newly emerging hegemonic class (a "counter-hegemonic" class), then, was to create its own organic intellectuals and to assimilate traditional intellectuals.[32]

MAO, GRAMSCI, AND REVOLUTION

From the perspective of Gramsci's concept of hegemony, the whole course of the Chinese Revolution, but especially the late 1930s and early 1940s, when

Mao formulated his idea of New Democracy, appears as a drama enacted under the direction of the idea of hegemony. Mao, too, believed that the primary task of the Communist Party in China was to attract under its leadership the various social groups in China, but in particular the intellectuals, by demonstrating the superiority of its cultural and political leadership.[33] This was the premise upon which the whole idea of New Democracy was founded. Second, Mao's sinification of Marxism bears a close resemblance to Gramsci's idea of a national-popular culture. Both believed that Marxist revolutionary consciousness must be nationalized and lose its alienness to the national culture if it was to achieve hegemony. Third, in both cases, considerations involving the agrarian population played an important role in sensitizing them to the cultural problems of working-class hegemony. Finally, both had remarkably similar conceptions of the role of intellectuals, especially revolutionary intellectuals. Karabel's comparison of "political and specialized" in Gramsci with the "red and expert" intellectuals is especially apt. If the working class was to establish its hegemony, it needed its own organic intellectuals who would be expert enough to lead, and red enough to retain their ties with the working class. "What a tragedy it would be," Gramsci wrote in one of his letters from prison, "if the groups of intellectuals who come to the working class and in whom the working class places its trust, do not feel themselves the same flesh and blood as the most humble, the most backward, and the least aware of our workers and peasants. All our work would be useless and we would obtain no result."[34] He might have been Mao announcing the Cultural Revolution.

These similarities between Mao and Gramsci should at least caution us against the hasty attribution of Mao's Marxism to his Chineseness. Cammett has observed that Gramsci's Marxism, too, had its roots in his Italian heritage. What the two share in common is an awareness of the difficulty of Marxist revolution in a national environment not quite prepared for it. It is in the priority they gave to revolutionary practice in such an environment that we must seek the basis for the common elements in their thinking, as well as the sources of their contribution to Marxist revolutionary theory.

This parallel recognition of the problem of culture and consciousness by Mao and Gramsci adds a new dimension to the understanding of Marxist revolutionary theory, and in particular to the relationship between revolutionary consciousness and the consciousness of the culture that revolutionaries find at hand. The appreciation of this problem reveals an even greater magnitude to the problem of revolution than had been visible earlier. It was Lenin who first recognized clearly that revolution was not simply a political act, but an educational one as well. It is also clear, however, that Lenin, isolated from the masses he was to lead by his long career as an émigré, did not confront all the dimensions of the problem. In fact, even though Mao and Gramsci both claimed to be following in Lenin's footsteps, they had a much more dialectical understanding of the relationship between revolutionary consciousness and social consciousness in general.

Lenin disdained the "false consciousness" even of the working class; correct ideas had to be impressed upon the working class from the outside. Mao and Gramsci, in constant interaction with workers and/or peasants, modified and moderated the coercive implications of Lenin's approach. They recognized that class consciousness bore a problematic relationship to consciousness in general, because not all consciousness was class consciousness, and consciousness was not false for not being class consciousness. If consciousness is the articulation of social being, it contained in its constitution all the complexity of social existence, which is not merely class existence. Class interest and consciousness suffused social existence and consciousness, but did not consume it; on the contrary, class consciousness gained its concrete meaning in a particular social and cultural context, and must be articulated within the language of its cultural context in order to be meaningful. Gramsci distinguished a dominant or corporate class from a leading class.[35] A class could be dominant by imposing its class interests and ideology upon society, but it could not lead through those means. A truly hegemonic class (that is, a leading class) "articulated other interests to its own," and bathed its class ideology in the hues of its cultural environment. A class that seeks to establish its hegemony must likewise come to terms with its culture and society (which were, to Gramsci, but two sides of the same coin), and not impose upon the latter an abstract consciousness. If it is to be hegemonic, in other words, it may not capture all consciousness for its own class consciousness to the exclusion of all the cultural and ethical values it finds at hand. As it seeks to restructure society and consciousness in favor of its own interests and culture, it must learn to articulate its own class interests and consciousness in the language of the culture and society it seeks to transform.

MARXISM AT THE CROSSROADS:
THE PROMISE AND THE PREDICAMENT

This reformulation of the problems of class and class consciousness has profound implications for both the theory and the practice of Marxism. Theoretically, it calls for a reevaluation of the concept of class. The concept of class as an abstraction derived from abstract economic relations is fundamental to a Marxist sociology; but as an abstraction, it tells us little about everyday social experience. On the contrary, the assumption that a variegated and complex social existence may be comprehended through an abstract sociological concept easily leads to the substitution of the concept for social experience. As consciousness of class helps demystify much that is hidden in social experience, so is it necessary for social and political analysis to refer constantly back to social experience in order to avoid mystification of class consciousness. E. P. Thompson's observation that "class is not a thing but a relationship" is very much to the point here. If class is a relationship, class and class consciousness are not abstractions to be imposed upon society but are attributes of historically changing relationships that must be sought out in social experience as it is, and is in the process of becoming.

The implications for Marxist politics are equally profound. Mao and Gramsci were both loyal Leninists in their conception of a revolutionary vanguard party; yet, their understanding of the relationship between revolutionaries and their social constituencies contains an implicit challenge to Leninist conceptions of political organization.

In identifying class consciousness with the party rather than the proletariat, Lenin set the party apart from and above the constituency that the party claimed to represent. Lenin's conception of the proletarian party was in effect the organizational expression of the theoretical abstraction of class and class consciousness from the concrete, historical experience of the proletariat as a social class. However effectively this organization may have served as an organ of revolution under certain circumstances, it has also brought with it a host of problems, chief among which is the potential for party despotism over the very classes the party was intended to serve—a potential that has unfortunately been fulfilled repeatedly in past socialist revolutions, starting with Lenin's own revolution.

In their recognition of the need to assimilate the abstract propositions of Marxist theory to concrete historical circumstances, Mao and Gramsci also realized the need to integrate the party closely with the working classes the party sought to represent and even with classes whose interests diverged from those of workers. In a very real sense, they restored the dialectical relationship between revolutionaries and social classes that informed Marx's formulation of the problem of revolution. This realization promised, and promises, a more democratic resolution of the problems of revolution and socialism than has been possible with Leninist conceptions of politics.

How this challenge might be translated into political practice remains the basic problem of Marxist politics. As I noted above with regard to Mao, it obviously creates a predicament for Marxist identity, one even deeper than the predicament Lenin had foreseen: In coming to terms with the cluttered realities of class relations and consciousness in a complex social existence, Marxists must face the possibility of being absorbed into the very social existence that they seek to transform. At the very least, assimilation of the concrete characteristics of the social environment into Marxist political theory is likely to blur the guidelines provided by abstract class analysis, subject political activity to contingent changes in social disposition, and render considerably more tenuous the socialist vision of the future.

That may be the reason why, in spite of their difficulties with their respective Communist parties, Mao and Gramsci both held on to the Leninist conception of the party, since the party remained as the only guarantor of class identity.[36] Mao's idea of the mass line, which was intended to achieve leadership rather than the domination of the masses, may be the closest approximation to a political solution of the problems of class consciousness and identity that were created by the recognition of complexity to the relationship between class consciousness, and consciousness as the expression of complex social existence. But it is, at best, only an approximation. Though it enhanced communication between the leaders and the led, the mass line did not abolish the separation of party from people. And the line between leadership and domination is easily confused as long as power is concentrated in the hands of the party organization—as the Chinese experience past and present has shown. Socialists must still face the challenge of discovering a political strategy that is at once democratic and loyal to the vision of social and economic equality.

Neither Mao nor Gramsci formulated a political strategy that resolved these problems of socialism and revolution. But they cogently represented revolution as a continuous dialectical process with the revolutionary at the pivot of the dialectic. Mao grasped the endlessness of the revolutionary undertaking and, with it, the pathos of revolution. For either revolutionary, however, a paraphrase of the well-known statement by Marx would seem appropriate:

> People do not make their history just as they please; they do not make it under circumstances chosen by themselves, but under circumstances directly encountered, given and transmitted from the past. But people do make their own history.

NOTES

1. These extremes may be found in the symposium on "Marx and Mao" sponsored by *Modern China* in 1976/1977 (*Modern China* 2, no. 4 [October 1976] and 3, no. 2 [April 1977]). A few words about this symposium may help bring into relief the issues raised in the discussion below. Participants in the symposium offered radically different interpretations of Mao's Marxism based on different readings of Marx. But

they shared a common paradigm of Marxism that defined the boundaries for the discussion. This paradigm is informed by a base/superstructure model of society in which the superstructural elements of society (ideology, politics, and so on) arise out of and upon an economic basis (the mode of production). The question then was whether the base limited the independence of the superstructure (the most generous construal of the economic determination position), or whether elements of the superstructure could play an independent role in the determination of social change and structure. Depending on which version was accepted, Mao's Marxism was questioned or reaffirmed respectively.

I am not concerned in this chapter with judging Mao's Marxism, which is not, I think, a historical but an ideological problem. Rather, I take it as a given that Mao was a Marxist and go on to inquire into the problem of why his Marxism took the form it did, and what his Marxism means for the historical development of Marxism as a social and revolutionary theory. Marx's work, taken as a totality, is too complex and multidimensional to be reduced to an essence against which to judge later Marxists. All Marxists are true Marxists in the sense that they can trace their ideas back to Marx, and no Marxist is a true Marxist in the sense that an inevitable historical gap separates Marx from later Marxists. Any effort to reduce Marx's work to an essence must result in the substitution for the historical Marx of an unhistorical representation of his ideas produced under circumstances that are by definition different from his own. Transhistorical orthodoxies, even when they are cast in a theoretical form, serve the purpose of political legitimation but not of historical explanation.

Marxism is by now too much of a universal phenomenon to be encompassed within the boundaries set by mid-nineteenth-century European capitalism, which shaped Marx's own experience and theoretical presuppositions. What makes it possible to speak of Marxists as a distinct intellectual and political current is a language of social analysis and transformation that Marxists share. The discussion below does not seek to define Marx theoretically or ideologically. Rather, I seek to show that Mao shared with other Marxists an understanding of the problematic of social analysis and political activity that had its origins in Marx. Beyond that, the way he worked out the problems posed by Marx's formulations was determined by the specific concerns and circumstances of his particular environment, as has been the case with all Marxists after Marx.

Second, the analysis rejects implicitly the base/superstructure model of society. My concern is not with the formal status of ideology in Marx or Mao, but rather with the problem of revolutionary consciousness that melds together ideology as systematized thought with culture as lived experience. Consciousness, though not material, is rooted in the specific circumstances of material life; it does not have an independent existence outside of material life (as ideology may), nor is it simply a reflection of abstract economic or social relations. It refers to the thinking of human agency in history that seeks to transform the very conditions that fashion it. Consciousness, therefore, is not a "thing" but a dynamic concept—a product of the relationships between material conditions and ideas—that changes as those relationships are transformed through material change or human activity. The place of consciousness in Marxism, and Mao's contribution to it, should become clearer in the course of the discussion.

One final note: I am not interested here in offering a comprehensive discussion of Mao's views on consciousness and human agency as forces for revolutionary change. Those interested in the formal discussion of those ideas may be referred to John Bryan Starr's excellent discussion of Mao's Thought in his *Continuing the Revolution: The Political Thought of Mao* (Princeton, NJ: Princeton University Press, 1979). My concern is to identify certain apparent peculiarities in Mao's thinking as a Marxist and to explain them historically as a product of the integration in revolutionary consciousness of the Marxist problematic and the circumstances surrounding the Chinese Revolution.

2. John Cammett, *Antonio Gramsci and the Origins of Italian Communism* (Stanford, CA: Stanford University Press, 1967), 177n.

3. Eugene Genovese, *In Red and Black: Marxian Explorations in Southern and Afro-American History* (New York: Pantheon, 1968), 393.

4. Jerome Karabel, "Revolutionary Contradictions: Antonio Gramsci and the Problem of Intellectuals," *Politics and Society* 6, no. 2 (1976), 170n156.

5. Nigel Todd, "Ideological Superstructure in Gramsci and Mao Tse-tung," *Journal of the History of Ideas* 35 (January/March 1974).

6. Antonio Gramsci, *History, Philosophy and Culture in the Young Gramsci*, ed. P. Cavalacanti and P. Piccone (St. Louis, MO: Telos Press, 1975), 9.

7. Antonio Gramsci, *Prison Notebooks,* ed. Q. Hoare and G. N. Smith (New York: International Publishers, 1971), 238.

8. Li Jui, *Early Revolutionary Activities of Comrade Mao Tse-tung*, trans. A. R. Sariti (New York: M. E. Sharpe, 1977), and Frederic Wakeman Jr., *History and Will: Philosophical Perspectives of Mao Tse-tung's Thought* (Berkeley: University of California Press, 1973).

9. Mao Zedong, *Selected Works of Mao Tse-tung*, 4 vols. (Beijing: Foreign Languages Press, 1965): vol. 1, 294–309. Hereafter *SWMTT.*

10. It has become nearly impossible in recent years to say anything positive about the Cultural Revolution. The harsh facts that have come to light concerning the suffering it caused to individuals and groups created hostility to the Cultural Revolution even among those who were once its fervent admirers. It appears in hindsight not as an attempt at revolution, but as an episode of terror—as must any revolution that has failed to fulfill its promised goals. Under the circumstances, even the effort to explain the Cultural Revolution as a phase in China's pursuit of socialism appears as an effort to legitimize the pain it inflicted on its victims.

This attitude has created an ideological rigidity that equals in its obscurantism the unqualified reaffirmations of the Cultural Revolution in the years before 1976. Its consequences are twofold. It does not allow for recognition of any validity to the criticisms the Cultural Revolution brought against postrevolutionary socialism in China and elsewhere; for the same reason, it ratifies the claims to socialism of the socialist system as it exists. Second, to the extent that it blames the results of the Cultural Revolution upon the failings of individual leaders, it distracts analysis away from its proper focus: the systemic features of Chinese socialism, with the Communist Party bureaucracy at its center, that mediated the intentions and the results of the Cultural Revolution. The need for theoretical analysis is obviated by a moralistic condemnation of individuals that bypasses fundamental questions of socialist politics and ideology. If these questions are to be resolved, we have to take seriously the underlying premise of the Cultural Revolution that the socialist system as it exists today is not a vehicle for the realization of socialism but an obstacle to it. It may then appear that the Cultural Revolution failed not because its premises were faulty, but because the Cultural revolutionaries betrayed their own premises by using for their own ends a system alien to their professed socialist ideals. Even though they attacked this system in the abstract, they were unable to conceive any genuine alternatives to it. The result was not revolution but disorientation, which enhanced the possibilities for arbitrary despotism in a system that took dictatorship for granted.

Official ideology in China today draws a distinction concerning Mao's Thought between its Cultural Revolutionary phase and its pre–Cultural Revolutionary phase, the one to be repudiated, the other to be upheld. This distinction seems to me to be untenable. What changed after 1949 was not Mao's Thought but the circumstances of the revolution in China. The ideology of an insurgent party obviously became a threat to the Party once the Party had achieved its immediate goal of capturing political power. The basic themes of the Cultural Revolution, we might recall, were first enunciated during the pre-1949 phase of the revolution, in particular the Yan'an Period. This chapter argues that these themes represented an attempt by the Communist Party to establish the hegemony of its revolutionary ideals among its constituents. The Cultural Revolution revived these ideals to sustain socialist hegemony over a party and society that seemed to Mao to be forsaking socialist ideals with the political victory of the revolution. The deplorable consequences of the Cultural Revolution should not be allowed to conceal the fact that, from the perspective of the socialist goals of the revolution, the concern with the question of revolutionary hegemony was a fundamental one.

This problem of revolutionary hegemony was not simply a product of idiosyncracies in Mao's thinking, but is imbedded in the structure of China's socialist system. The most cogent evidence for this is provided by the resurfacing since 1976 of the very same problems that earlier prompted the Cultural Revolution. It is also noteworthy that the Party has responded to these problems with the revival of revolutionary themes for ideological education—minus the revolution. The emphasis on the need for ideological education to sustain socialist hegemony was an important theme taken up by the Twelfth Congress of the Communist Party in September 1982. (For a discussion of this problem, see Arif Dirlik, "Spiritual Solutions to Material Problems: The 'Socialist Ethics and Courtesy Month' in China," *South Atlantic Quarterly* 81, no. 4 [Autumn 1982]: 359–75.)

11. *SWMTT*, vol. 2, 339–81.

12. Mao Zedong, *A Critique of Soviet Economics*, trans. M. Roberts (New York: Monthly Review Press, 1977), 66.

13. Dick Wilson, *Mao Tse-tung in the Scales of History* (New York: Cambridge University Press, 1977), 41.

14. Tsou Tang, "Mao Tse-tung Thought, the Last Struggle for Succession, and the Post-Mao Era," *China Quarterly* 71 (September 1977): 498–527.

15. Maurice Meisner, "Leninism and Maoism: Some Populist Perspectives on Marxism-Leninism in China," *China Quarterly* 45 (January/March 1971). Meisner also observes that Mao's populism may have made him "a better Marxist than Leninist."

16. Mao, *Critique*, 146.

17. *SWMTT*, vol. 3, 13. See also Wang Ruoshi, "Lun tiaojian" [On Condition], *Zhexue yanjiu* [Philosophy Research] 6 (1979).

18. *SWMTT*, vol. 1, 311–47.

19. See *SWMTT*, vol. 1, 13–21 and 137–39 for the 1926 essay on classes in China as a whole and the 1933 essay respectively. The 1926 essay was more complete in the original. For that and the 1926 essay on rural China, see Mao, *Mao Zedongji* [Collected Works of Mao Zedong], 10 vols. (Hong Kong, 1976), vol. 1, 153–79.

20. Boyd Compton, ed., *Mao's China: Party Reform Documents, 1942–1944*, 9–32 (Seattle: University of Washington Press, 1966).

21. *SWMTT*, vol. 1, 149.

22. John Wilson Lewis, *Leadership in Communist China* (Ithaca, NY: Cornell University Press, 1963), 72.

23. Gramsci, *Prison Notebooks*, 57.

24. Gwyn Williams, "The Concept of 'Egemonia' in the Thought of Antonio Gramsci: Some Notes on Interpretation," *Journal of the History of Ideas* 21 (October/December 1960): 587.

25. Chantal Mouffe, *Gramsci and Marxist Theory* (Boston: Routledge, Kegan & Paul, 1979), 73.

26. Mouffe, *Gramsci*, 181.

27. Raymond Williams, *Marxism and Literature* (Oxford: Oxford University Press, 1977), 113.

28. Williams, *Marxism and Literature,* 110.

29. Gramsci, *Prison Notebooks*, 241.

30. Gramsci, *Prison Notebooks*, 421n65.

31. Gramsci, *Prison Notebooks*, 19–20.

32. Gramsci, *Prison Notebooks*, 5–23.

33. The following statement by Mouffe could be describing China in the late 1930s and the 1940s: "In effect, the war of position is the process of ideological struggle by means of which the two fundamental classes try to appropriate the non-class ideological elements in order to integrate them within the ideological system which articulates itself around their respective hegemonic principles." Mouffe, *Gramsci*, 198.

34. Cited in Karabel, "Revolutionary Contradictions," 123.

35. Gramsci, *Prison Notebooks*, 55n5.

36. Mao Zedong, *Chairman Mao Talks to the People*, ed. Stuart R. Schram (New York: Pantheon, 1965), 277–79.

III

THE CULTURAL REVOLUTION IN HISTORICAL PERSPECTIVE

7

Revolutionary Hegemony and the Language of Revolution: Chinese Socialism between Present and Future

A beginner who has learnt a new language," Karl Marx wrote in *The Eighteenth Brumaire of Louis Bonaparte,* "always translates it into his mother tongue, but he has assimilated the spirit of the new language and can freely express himself in it only when he finds his way in it without recalling the old and forgets his native tongue in the use of the new."[1] Revolution, the metaphor suggests, is learning. It is also forgetting; forgetting not in the sense of loss of memory, but in the sense of relegating to memory that which obstructs the assimilation of the new.

The metaphor of language offers an illuminating perspective on the tortuous course the Chinese Revolution has followed over the last three decades.[2] Learning a new language and forgetting the old has been a basic problem in Chinese politics, as is evident in the radical shifts in the language of socialist ideology. The problem does not lie in a choice between revolution and restoration; there is no dispute among China's socialists over the transformative role socialism must play in creating a new society. The dispute has been over the best way to reconcile the demands of the revolutionary vision that brought the Communists to power with the responsibilities placed upon a revolutionary party in control of state power. This has called forth a synthesis of two meanings of socialism, both of which have deep roots in the history of Chinese socialism: socialism as an ideology of revolution and socialism as an ideology of modernization. Revolution and development have long been associated in Chinese socialist thought as interdependent constituents of socialist ideology, and the historical experience of Chinese socialism shows that neglect of one almost inevitably undermines the other. There has also been a perennial contradiction, however, between an idea of socialism that

151

derives its language from a universal ideal of an egalitarian and democratic society, and one that renders socialism into an instrument of parochial pragmatic goals of national development. These alternative conceptions of socialism also have different implications for China's relationship to its past, and to the historical context out of which Chinese socialism has grown.

The contradiction is a contradiction between the language of vision and the language of economism. Unable to integrate these two languages into a new language of socialist progress, socialist ideology in China has ended up for the most part speaking two languages at once, which has confounded the speakers no less than the listeners. But it is also true that one or the other has been spoken with the louder voice in different phases of the revolution. Ideological struggle in Chinese politics expresses a struggle to capture the ideology of socialism for the dominance of one or the other of these languages. So far, neither has achieved a clear-cut victory.

The difficulties the Chinese have encountered in discovering a new language of socialism disclose a fundamental problem that Marx's metaphor overlooks. The new language is new to the neophyte who encounters it for the first time, but the language already exists before the encounter as a completed design, which the neophyte needs only to assimilate in order to express himself freely. Not so with revolution. The new society that is the promise of revolution does not appear as a completed design, but as a project to be realized. The revolutionary neophyte must create the language in which he is to learn to express himself. This makes the task more, not less, difficult. For the new language, if it is to be intelligible, can only be generated out of the language of present reality. The revolutionary consciousness that bears the responsibility for creating the new language is itself the product of the history it seeks to transcend.

Herein lies the predicament of revolution, and of socialism. The problem of language for the revolutionary is not simply the problem of acquiring a new skill, but a problem of discovering new ways in which to think about the world, its constitution and purpose. It is, in a fundamental sense, a problem of what Antonio Gramsci described as "hegemony." The struggle to create a new language of revolution is but a struggle to assert the hegemony of revolution over its historical inheritance.

A revolution, if it is authentic, must create a new language of its own. A revolution that employs the language of the society it has rejected in order to comprehend its own meaning is a revolution that has conceded defeat at the moment of its conception. To the extent that revolutionaries must translate their goals back into the language of prerevolutionary society in order to render them intelligible, they must perpetuate the hegemony of the past over the present and the future.

On the other hand, revolution is not the substitution of an arbitrary language for an existing one. The new society must transcend the old society, not merely negate it; and this it can achieve only by generating the new language out of the language it finds at hand. Even if it were possible for revolutionaries to sever their ties to the past, to start off with a blank sheet of paper as it were, a new language created out of thin air lacks the ability to articulate the social experiences upon which its vitality depends. A revolution that seeks to escape the past by refusing to speak its language is deprived of its own source of intelligibility and isolates itself from the reality it would transform. Revolution is of necessity a historical process where the revolutionary consciousness must be transformed in its own activity to revolutionize the world. The alternatives must be, on the one hand, fossilization under the pressure of the past or, on the other hand, loss of intelligibility in a present to which it is alien and, therefore, incomprehensible.

The progress of Chinese socialism after 1949 illustrates this predicament of revolutionary socialism. The Cultural Revolution of the 1960s, in a fundamental sense, was an attempt to create a new language of revolution. Mao Zedong was preoccupied with the fossilization of the revolution under the new regime, not because Chinese society ceased to change after 1949, which it obviously did not, but because it was becoming increasingly clear that the revolutionary leadership had lost sight of its socialist vision once the revolution had accomplished its immediate goals. The Cultural Revolution expressed the conviction that without a renewed effort to create a new language, the past must inevitably reassert hegemony over the revolution and divert it from the path of socialist progress.

It has become fashionable in recent years to portray the Cultural Revolution as an aberration in the history of Chinese socialism. The Cultural Revolution was to end up as an aberration, a parody of its own aspirations; but that is no reason to deny the reality of the problems it sought to resolve or the seriousness of its intentions. Indeed, it is possible to see in the failure of the Cultural Revolution the intractability of the problems that the Chinese Revolution has had to confront.

The Cultural Revolution claim that without further revolution China would inevitably gravitate back toward capitalism was a misleading one. China had never been a capitalist society in a technical sense, nor was it likely to become one after the revolution. But neither can it be disputed that there were significant social groups in Chinese society, including some within the Communist Party, whose thinking was informed by a paradigm of development to which the social goals of socialism were marginal. These social groups were potential instruments for the perpetuation of the hegemony over revolution of this paradigm. If this paradigm were to take hold of Chinese thinking, the socialist vision would be relegated to a future so distant that it would cease to have any bearing on the present. With the creation of a socialist language—a socialist society—indefinitely postponed, it was inevitable that this paradigm would come to dominate Chinese thinking, and drive the revolution away from the socialist vision that informed it. The forces and attitudes that have resurfaced with the termination of the Cultural Revolution bear ample testimonial to the validity of these fears.

Rather than an effort to institute socialism immediately, the Cultural Revolution was an attempt to create a new language of revolution that would reshape Chinese thinking on socialist development and guarantee the hegemony of revolution. Briefly, the Cultural Revolution sought to restructure the language of development by politicizing it. Its basic premise was that it was not developmental needs that must determine the course of revolution but, on the contrary, revolutionary goals that must shape the course development would take. Contrary to current charges brought against it, the Cultural Revolution did not reject development, but only development based on economistic assumptions that reduced socialist progress to economic development: that economic, or even simply technological, progress is the ultimate meaning of socialism; that social inequality and authoritarian political relations are the price we must pay for the social order necessary for economic progress; that economic efficiency must take precedence over considerations of equality and democracy in the organization of work, and the structure of social relations in general.

The Cultural Revolution sought to make a break with these economistic premises. It held that social relations must be informed by revolutionary goals; that economic development must proceed in such a way as to reinforce these social relations; that self-reliance at the local and national level was essential to break down the hegemony over China of the capitalist world economy; that social commitment must take precedence over professional ideological commitments (red over expert). The grammar of this language was dialectical: revolutionaries must remake themselves through their activity of remaking the world. Crucial to the language of the Cultural Revolution was the premise that the social goals of the revolution must not await the development of its economic basis, but must be incorporated into the very process of development.

This idea of development has an internal coherence that is at odds with currently prevalent notions of the Cultural Revolution as a product of deranged minds. Moreover, the idea draws upon a vision of socialist society that was informed by the experiences of the Chinese Revolution. Self-reliance, commitment to revolutionary goals, transformation of social relations in order to promote socialist development, and even the idea that revolution must create its own language were ideas that went back to the pre-1949 phase of the revolution, in particular the war years (1937–1945) when the Communists had developed the strategy that carried the revolution to victory. It was not the language of revolution that had changed, but the circumstances of the revolution.

The Cultural Revolution failed to formulate a strategy of revolution that would correspond to its language of development in these new circumstances. The strategy of a revolutionary party in insurgency was not appropriate to a revolutionary party in power. The problem with the Cultural Revolution was that it not only took as a given the political structure that had emerged with the revolution, but tried to use that same political structure to achieve its own ends. This structure imposed upon Chinese society a form that was antithetical to the values the Cultural Revolution espoused in the abstract. The result was a confusion born of the disjuncture between the Cultural Revolutionary language and the language of its structural context, which confounded both the proponents and the subjects of the revolution.

This was a basic reason that the social policies of the Cultural Revolution almost uniformly contradicted its verbal aspirations. The politicization of the issue of development led not to a reconsideration of the meaning of economic development, but to the use of politics to mobilize society more effectively for economic development. The liberation of labor was to end up in the conversion of labor to forced labor. The substitution of moral for material incentives led not to the abolition of incentives, but to the addition of considerations of political gain to existing considerations of material gain.

Likewise, input from the masses into politics, intended to counteract party and government bureaucratization, was converted rapidly into the subjection of the people to mindless recitation of officially sanctioned slogans and "quotations" that could only dull their political senses. As the Cultural Revolution did not question the economic ends of socialism, neither did it consider restructuring politics to abolish hierarchy. "Dictatorship of the proletariat" and the rule of the party remained as matters of faith. The attack on bureaucracy did not eliminate bureaucracy but disoriented it, which only enhanced the possibility of arbitrary despotism.

And so with the other aspects of the Cultural Revolution. Self-reliance ended up as an atavistic assertion of a revolutionary brand of nationalistic chauvinism. The liberation of imagination in culture turned into the confinement of cultural imagination in the straitjacket of political clichés. The reassertion of political commitment over expertise degenerated rapidly from an attack on the elitism of professionals to a pervasive anti-intellectualism.

The denouement of the Cultural Revolution illustrates what I meant above by loss of intelligibility in a revolutionary attempt to impose upon society a language that is the product of revolutionary vision divorced from social reality. The Cultural Revolution suggested an almost magical notion that revolution could conjure a new society simply by invoking its language.

This language, coherent in the abstract, lost its coherence when applied through the realities of power in Chinese society. The intention underlying the Cultural Revolution was coherent; not so its practice of revolution. In the end, the contradiction between an ideology derived from revolutionary vision and a social reality to which vision had little relevance was resolved by the subjection of the vision to social reality. Instead of abolishing economic and political hierarchy, as it professed, the Cultural Revolution assumed in exaggerated form the hierarchical disposition of its social and ideological context. The divorce of intention from result, theory from practice, rendered both the intention and the theory meaningless.

When in 1957 Mao Zedong described the Chinese people as "poor and blank," upon whom one could presumably write any script, he had forgotten the lessons of the revolutionary experience which he had done so much to articulate: that the intelligibility of the revolutionary message depended on its ability to speak the language of the people. The Cultural Revolution, unable to formulate an intelligible message, was to isolate itself from the people it hoped to lead. It could be sustained for as long as it was, not because it was able to establish the hegemony of revolution in Chinese thinking, but because of the threat of coercion it held against all who deviated from officially sanctioned norms. A revolutionary language, divorced from reality, and hence lacking concrete referents, could not but become a plaything at the hands of revolutionary whims. As the whims changed, so did the winds of revolution. The paradigm of revolution the Cultural Revolution offered is already overshadowed in historical memory by its betrayal of its own policies. In hindsight, it appears more an episode of terror born of power struggles among the Chinese elite than an authentic revolutionary effort.

In contrast, the post–Cultural Revolution leadership in China is convinced that the language of revolutionary society can only be generated out of the present language of socialism through an arduous historical process that builds upon the past. It has not only renounced the Cultural Revolution, but has proceeded to abolish revolution as a principle of Chinese politics.

Changes since Mao's death in 1976 have been described by Chinese leaders as a "second revolution," which has been heartily echoed among sympathizers of the regime abroad. What the future of this "revolution" might be is impossible to say, but its meaning is clear: it expresses the victory of an uncompromising economism in the understanding of socialist development that matches in its obdurateness of the Cultural Revolution to put "politics in command." Its goal is not to create a revolutionary society, but to achieve a "pragmatic" adjustment of revolution to the demands of present reality.

The present regime promotes the definition of socialism as an ideology of modernization. The new attitude is cogently captured in the following lines written by a prominent economist in 1980: "The basic Marxist approach to socialist ownership is: anything that can best promote the development of the productive forces, yes, and it may count on the support of Marxists; anything that does not, no, and Marxists will not support it; anything that actually impedes the development of the productive forces will be firmly opposed."[3] Absent from this statement and, with a rare exception from socialist ideology since 1978, is any suggestion that further change in social relations might be necessary in China's socialist progress. If there is to be further social change, it must follow the demands of economic development.

The underlying premise of this definition of socialism is that China had already become a socialist society in 1956, when the socialist transformation of production had been accomplished with the abolition of private ownership of the means of production. The basic contradiction in China since then has been the contradiction between a socialist economy and backward forces of production. The most urgent need for China, therefore, is economic development and the technological modernization that is essential to economic development. Under a socialist regime, economic development must ensure the eventual realization of socialist society.

In accordance with these premises, the regime proceeded to establish new policies designed to foster rapid economic development. These policies are well known by now: reprivatization of the economy, increased material incentives to encourage labor productivity, attack on egalitarian practices that interfered with economic efficiency, political relaxation to mobilize support for the regime, especially among the professional-managerial class, and a rapidly intensified program of technological, economic, and intellectual exchange with advanced countries of the capitalist world. The key to all these changes was the shift to a more individualized conception of economic organization and activity.

These policies do not represent a restoration of capitalism, but they do express acceptance of a paradigm of development that was the product of capitalism, and to which socialism as it exists today has become heir. Chinese leaders justify their policies through an empiricist pragmatic claim: that these policies best suit the realities of Chinese society. Poverty is not the only reality of Chinese society, however, for so are political and economic inequality. Resignation to a paradigm of development that does not address these other realities implies acceptance, even the reinforcement, of a social system that is antithetical in structure to the social goals of socialism.

This, of course, exposes the fallacy of "seeking truth from facts," as the new pragmatism is described. Pragmatism is a term without ideological content of its own, implying only the willingness to approach practically tasks defined outside of itself. It may be invoked in service of a given ideological and social system, or it may be invoked in service of a revolutionary ideology that challenges the system. To portray pragmatism as an alternative to ideology rather than as its servant serves only to universalize the ideological claims of the existing structure of power. To a socialist revolutionary, pragmatism within a hierarchical social and political structure may only mean legitimization of a structure that impedes socialist progress. A revolutionary pragmatism must seek practical ways of transcending the existing system, not a practical adjustment to it. Socialists have tried to escape the dilemmas created by their "pragmatism" by explaining such pragmatism as a necessity of a transitional period. The cliché of "transition" does not do away with the reality, as Rudolf Bahro has said of Eastern Europe in his *The Alternative in Eastern Europe*, that the very structures that are relied upon to guarantee socialist progress may themselves become the biggest obstacle to socialism.[4] Policies that reinforce these structures must of necessity undercut the very promise they hold forth.

The notion of pragmatism mystifies the ideological and social implications of the new policies in China. These policies clearly give priority to reasons of state over the call of revolution. The Chinese conception of socialism today is that of a bureaucratic-managerial society, where a bureaucracy of experts plans and administers social order and development. The Cultural Revolution had attacked this bureaucratic conception of socialism. Conflicts over bureaucracy since then have not involved the question of the political place of bureaucracy under socialism, but rather have revolved around the questions of bureaucratic efficiency and integrity. To this end, Chinese leaders seek to improve the quality of China's bureaucracy through better education of bureaucrats, transfer of power to experts, and better management techniques. This technical administrative conception of politics corresponds to their conception of economic problems essentially as problems of the technology of production and management.

If the regime takes the bureaucratic organization of society for granted in its conception of socialism, its economic policies promise to further reinforce existing hierarchies in Chinese society. The idea that as long as a socialist regime remains in power, economic development will automatically abolish inequality, is the product either of a premeditated myopia, or of an ideological blind spot where the regime's social basis is concerned. Present developmental policies are informed by the premise that economic inequality is the only means to achieve development: inequality here implies not simply inequality in income, but inequality in the management of production and social power. The regime believes that development is contingent upon the creation of an economic-political elite that will supervise the process of development. This elite has already come to identify the interests of society as a whole with its own interests as a social class. Economic development under the guidance of such an elite is not likely to create a democratic and egalitarian society, but to reinforce hierarchy. If current tendencies continue, moreover, this elite will increasingly share an ideological affinity with the global economic and technocratic elite, which will only enhance its distance from the population it "manages." Already, the language of this elite is the language of management: efficiency, productivity, labor discipline, expertise, administrative skills, etc. Chinese students today study administrative and policy-making skills in the United States and Japan, even as China imports capitalist technology and methods of organization that are designed to control labor, not to liberate it. What is good enough for capitalism, evidently, is good enough for socialism.

The forces unleashed by the new policies have created a predicament for China's socialist system. Economism, taken to its logical conclusions, is at odds not only with the socialist revolutionary vision, but with the existing socialist system as well. The regime's idealization of economic development has licensed opposition to party rule and its ideological basis, socialism, on the grounds that they interfere with efficient development. The uncompromising economism of the initial period of the new regime has been qualified by the revival of ideological issues, which seeks to restore the vocabulary of revolution to the language of socialism. Over the last five years, there has been an increasing concern with ideological education to create a "socialist spiritual civilization." These concerns were incorporated into official policy in the Twentieth Congress of the Communist Party in September 1982. In the words of then-Party Secretary Hu Yaobang,

> Socialist spiritual civilization constitutes an important characteristic of the socialist system and a major aspect of its superiority. In the past, when referring to the characteristics of socialism, people laid stress on the elimination of the system of exploitation, public ownership of the means of production, distribution according to work, planned and proportionate development of the national economy, and political power of the working class and other working people. They also laid stress on another characteristic of socialism, the high development of the productive forces and a labor productivity higher than that under capitalism as both a necessity and the end result of the development of socialism. All this is undoubtedly true, but it does not cover all the characteristics. Socialism must possess one more characteristic, that is, socialist spiritual civilization with communist ideology at its core. Without this, the building of socialism would be out of the question.[5]

Hu's speech did not call for a reevaluation of the regime's development policies, but simply added a "spiritual" to the "material" aspect of development. There is no true dialectic here, only the simultaneous pursuit of two formally distinguished aspects of socialist development. The language of spiritual mobilization is not the language of revolution but the language of social control. The so-called Five Stresses and Four Beauties, which have been enunciated as the behavioral norms that the spiritual mobilization campaign seeks to establish give a good idea of the order the regime seeks to achieve. The Five Stresses refer to stress on civil manners, propriety, cleanliness, order, and morality; the Four Beauties, to the beautification of spirit, language, behavior, and environment.[6]

There is no question that the new stress on ideology represents a shift in the regime's approach to socialism. The question is the meaning of this shift. Some of the themes of the campaign for spiritual mobilization are quite reminiscent of the themes promoted by the Cultural Revolution. But there is a crucial difference: the goal of the new campaign is not to create a new paradigm of socialist development, but to secure and consolidate the economistic paradigm that continues to shape the regime's thinking on development. In other words, it does not seek to supersede the economistic paradigm, but to guarantee its welfare by counteracting the adverse tendencies it has created. This is confirmed by the most recent manifestation of the regime's efforts to contain the contradictions created by its economic policies: the so-called new authoritarianism *(xin quanwei zhuyi)*, which seeks to keep in check the social, political, and cultural consequences of economic individualism through an authoritarian political structure. The inspiration for "new authoritarianism" is rooted not in any socialism, but in the experience of right-wing dictatorships in East and Southeast Asia (Taiwan, South Korea, Singapore) that have achieved economic miracles without the benefit of democracy.[7]

Contrary to much wishful thinking, the discrepancy between revolutionary vision and social reality continues to haunt Chinese politics today, as it did under Mao Zedong. The difference is in the meaning of the vision in politics. The revolutionary vision no longer serves as a principle of politics, but only as ideological legitimacy for policies that are antithetical to the promise they hold forth. Unlike during the Cultural Revolution, when political incoherence arose out of the discrepancy between the language of revolution and the language of the existing political structure, today it is the discrepancy between the language of the existing political structure and that of economism that lies at the source of political incoherence. The Cultural revolutionaries had accused the Party of having become an obstacle to revolution; the basic charge brought against the Party at present is that it obstructs economic development. While the regime has moved toward restructuring power to meet the demands of the economy, it has also chronically revived the language of revolution to keep these demands in check.

That the new regime has had to revive revolutionary idealism to defend its evidently antirevolutionary policies underlines the "pragmatic" significance of revolutionary idealism in Chinese politics. The revolutionary vision of socialism carries the weight it does in Chinese politics not because it offers a remote promise, but because the socialist revolution played a significant practical role in China's national integration and development, which all Chinese socialists recognize. The concrete contributions of the revolution to popular welfare and national autonomy make it a powerful symbol around which to unify a society where the bonds of "socialist unity" remain more apparent than real. Chinese leaders may abandon the vision at their own risk. It is also clear, however, that in this "pragmatic" role, the vision promises not liberation but consolidation of a hierarchical system that is fashioned by the economistic assumptions that dominate Chinese socialism today. The socialist vision, in other words, serves to guard politics that negate the meaning of socialism as social vision.

The problem of creating a language free from the hegemony of inherited paradigms of development, and yet adequate to reforming existing social reality, is a universal problem of socialism. This is not surprising. Socialism as a political idea seeks to transcend capitalism. But the idea is itself a product of capitalist society; not simply an outgrowth of capitalism but a dialectical product born of capitalism in opposition to it. Still, the language of capitalism infuses the consciousness of socialists who, though rebels against capitalism, share many of its premises with regard to the purpose and process of historical development.

This is as true of socialists in the capitalist periphery as it is in the core capitalist states of Western Europe, Northern America, and Japan, though it is not as evident in the case of the former. Socialists in advanced capitalist societies have willingly subordinated their socialist vision to the hegemony of capital. The language of socialism in these societies appears as a language of corporatism, which represents but the assimilation of the vocabulary of socialism into the language of capitalism. Socialists of the periphery have upheld the vision of a revolutionary socialism; but there, too, the hegemony of capital has persisted in the language of national development, although the use of a national idiom in these cases often disguises the continuing reality of this hegemony.

Indeed, socialists in these societies have often turned to the national idiom as a source from which to generate an autonomous language of socialism free from the cultural hegemony of capital. The danger here, of course, has been the risk of assimilating socialism to the national language in the very effort to assimilate the national idiom to the language of socialism. Such a nationalized socialism may serve to ward off control by global capital, but it no longer carries the meaning of socialism as a universal ideal of human liberation. On the contrary, it may assume the colorings of its precapitalist environment both socially and in its conception of politics. This is to some extent what happened in China during the Cultural Revolution.

Keeping global capital at a distance, moreover, does not mean abolition of the hegemony of capital. Too much emphasis on the burden of the precapitalist past in shaping socialism in these societies conceals the dynamic forces that shape socialism, and the role socialism plays as a transformative ideology. Socialism has been as much a product of capitalism in peripheral societies as it was in the capitalist core: a product, in the one case, of the autonomous development of capitalism, and, in the other, of its worldwide diffusion. It is ultimately from the intrusion of capital that socialism has derived its political relevance in peripheral societies.

In either case, the socialist goal has been to transcend capitalism, not to escape back from it into a precapitalist past. The effort to assimilate the national idiom into the language of socialism is itself motivated by the search for a locally acceptable language of socialism. Socialism is not a plaything at the hands of some unconscious traditionalism, therefore, but a transformative ideology that seeks to create a postcapitalist society out of the dialectical synthesis of the national idiom with the language of development. For the same reason, socialism appears in these societies not only as a vision of equality and democracy, but as an ideology of development. The burden of development, achieved in core societies by capitalism, falls here upon socialist shoulders.

It is this burden that ushers in the hegemony of capital over the socialism of peripheral societies which, in spite of its intended goal to ward off global capitalism, draws its inspiration from a paradigm of development that is the product of capitalism. This has meant the incorporation into socialist language of the grammar of capitalist development.

The fact that in these circumstances class struggle is placed in the context of a national struggle against global capital, moreover, creates the predicament that the nation may overshadow class as the locus of socialist activity. When this happens, socialism is reduced to an instrument in the cause of national development which, in a world under the material sway of capital, must result in a "pragmatic" adjustment of socialism to the hegemony of capital. This mode of development, Rudolf Bahro suggests, is better described as "noncapitalist development" than as socialist development. Some Chinese socialists used this term in the early part of the century to describe a nonrevolutionary socialism that would bypass capitalism to achieve more efficiently the goals of capitalist society. The language of noncapitalist development is not a socialist language but a dialect of capitalism. This is the language that dominates Chinese socialism today.

The Chinese experience with socialism is the most recent example of the difficulties that have confronted socialism historically. What is clear from accumulated experience is that if socialism is to retain its viability as an alternative to capitalism, it must create a language of its own. This requires, first and foremost, a reconsideration of the meaning of development that, at present, is fashioned by a paradigm of development rooted in capitalist assumptions on the ends and meanings of human progress. It also requires, therefore, that socialists abandon the illusion of present-day socialism as the end, rather than the beginning, of the history of socialism.

Such a language, to be intelligible, can only be created out of the language of the present. But to be authentically revolutionary, it must derive its grammar from the language of the future: a language that articulates the vision of a social existence free of exploitation and oppression. Without such a language, socialists must be deprived of an identity to call their own.

NOTES

1. Karl Marx, *The Eighteenth Brumaire of Louis Bonaparte* (New York: International Publishers, 1967), 15–16.

2. This chapter deals with the general problem of interpreting socialism. There is another, equally significant, aspect to the problem of language: its use in the articulation of social interest. Socialism in China provides the common language of politics but is subject to discursive appropriation by different groups in society, which interpret it in accordance with their own group interests and ideology. The different interpretations of socialism point, in other words, to contradictions in the social situation out of which they spring. It may be worth pointing out that the tendency of some groups in China today to derogate socialism may have less to do with the "failures" of socialism per se than the animosity to socialism of groups who, in order to realize their group interests and fulfill their ideological aspirations as a group, indiscriminately blame all of China's woes on socialism. The various conflicting discourses on socialism, in other words, point ultimately to social conflicts, including class conflict. The economistic interpretation of socialism discussed in this chapter also coincides with the social interests and ideology of the professional-managerial groups in Chinese society who seek to render it into the "hegemonic" interpretation of socialism for the society as a whole. Other essays discuss the resistance to this hegemony of groups that stand to lose by it or do not share its ideological assumptions for a variety of reasons.

3. Yu Guangyuan, "The Basic Approach to Socialist Ownership," *Beijing Review* 49 (December 8, 1980).

4. Rudolf Bahro, *The Alternative in Eastern Europe* (London: New Left Books, Verso edition, 1981), 6–14 and chapter 2.

5. Hu Yaobang, "Create a New Situation in All Fields of Socialist Modernization," *Beijing Review* 25, no. 37 (September 13, 1987): 21.

6. For further discussion of this campaign, see Arif Dirlik, "Spiritual Solutions to Material Problems: The 'Socialist Ethics and Courtesy Month' in China," *South Atlantic Quarterly* 81, no. 4 (Autumn 1982): 359–75.

7. For a contemporary discussion of this controversial idea, see "'New Authoritarianism' Seen in Chinese Actions," *New York Times* (February 28, 1989): A13. For a subsequent compilation, see "The Chinese Debate on New Authoritarianism," ed. Stanley Rosen and Gary Zou, special issues of *Chinese Sociology and Anthropology* 23, nos. 2, 3 (Winter 1990–1991 and Spring 1991).

8

The Two Cultural Revolutions: The Chinese Cultural Revolution in the Perspective of Global Capitalism

The Great Proletarian Cultural Revolution in China was a world-historical event. To describe it as such does not require that we overlook its tragic consequences for many in China, condone its comic operatic excesses, or agree with all or even a large part of its economic, political, or cultural policies; world-historical events almost by definition are traumatic events with ambiguous consequences, that may or may not deliver the promises that motivate them but almost inevitably grind down those who stand in the way of the urge to redirect history. But it does require that we recognize the Cultural Revolution as an expression of deep-seated problems of its historical circumstances, not just its immediate historical circumstances in China, but the global circumstances with which the national problems were linked inextricably. It also compels us to recall that within those historical circumstances, the aspirations of the Cultural Revolution resonated globally with a widespread and urgent quest for answers to those problems.

It may be stating the obvious to describe the Cultural Revolution as a world-historical event. In its time, and well into the late 1970s when it was officially denounced in China, the Cultural Revolution was widely recognized as one of the most important events of the second half of the twentieth century. Since then, however, and especially over the last decade, there has been a consistent effort to discredit the Cultural Revolution—and the Chinese Revolution as a whole—by reducing its history to histories of cannibalism, or the sexual peccadilloes of Party leaders, in particular Mao Zedong, whose image as a promoter of revolution has been replaced now by an image as a transmitter of sexual perversities. Rather than confront critically the issues raised by the Cultural Revolution, such rewriting of its history seeks to erase its memories as a historical event through trivialization or moralistic condemnation—in much the same way, we may note, that the Cultural revolutionaries sought to erase their opponents from history. This may not be very surprising; ours is an age that seeks to forget the two-century history of revolutions not just in China but globally. The turn to the right politically that is at work in the erasure of revolutionary history is reinforced in the case of China by a persistent Orientalism that refuses to recognize authentic temporality to Chinese society, but instead perpetuates a retrograde culturalism that is relentless in its search of evidence to authenticate its own congealed images of China. A society without history, such Orientalist representations imply, obviously cannot produce world-historical events. It is this erasure of history that necessitates a recovery of the Cultural Revolution as a historical event—not just to confront *it* critically but, perhaps even more importantly, to restore a critical self-awareness to our own evaluations of it, so that we may be able also to confront critically the many problems of our times that are swept under the rug in the very erasure of revolutionary pasts.

The discussion below focuses on three aspects of the Cultural Revolution that I think qualify it as a historical event of primary significance: as a new departure in the history of Communist revolutions, as an expression of Third World socialism in the immediate aftermath of worldwide decolonization, and the social ideology it promoted which challenged accepted norms of economic and political development in both capitalist and Soviet-style socialist societies. These same features also account for the popularity that the Cultural Revolution enjoyed globally during the two decades (1956–1976) of its duration. I am not concerned in this chapter with the internal consequences of the Cultural Revolution, which I have described elsewhere.[1] I may suggest here, however, that contrary to the claims of former admirers of the Cultural Revolution who have now turned against it, there is a connection between the impact of the Cultural Revolution as a historical event of global significance and the evaluation of its internal consequences. So long as the Cultural Revolution was viewed as an event of world significance, there was a tendency to overlook evidence of its less desirable consequences. The prominence of the latter at the present, conversely, may be a product not of new evidence per se, but of its demotion as a historical event, which has helped bring to the surface its more sordid aspects. I will return to this question below.

WHAT WAS GLOBALLY SIGNIFICANT ABOUT THE CULTURAL REVOLUTION?

The Cultural Revolution was first and foremost a significant event in the history of Communist revolutions. Once the term "Cultural Revolution" had been popularized by the upheaval in China, it would be applied in other cases of Communist Revolution as well. The term, and the aspirations to which it pointed, made eminent sense: if socialism represented a new mode of production, it made eminent sense both that the new mode of production should produce a new culture appropriate to its goals, and that the revolutionary leadership should pursue the creation of such a new culture in order to consolidate the new relations of production. The Cultural Revolution in either case followed logically from the Marxist premise that there was a necessary correlation between cultural life and the material conditions of existence. New men and women were indispensable to the new mode of production.

In the years since the Cultural Revolution in China, such usage of the term "Cultural Revolution" has been extended beyond the experiences of socialist revolutions to the experiences of revolutionary transformations in general—beyond Marxist conceptions that equate revolutionary transformations with changes from one to another mode of production. Thus, the term "Cultural Revolution" has been used to describe cultural changes corresponding to transformations within the same (capitalist) mode of production,[2] transformations that accompany the emergence of the modern nation-state,[3] and even changes in attitudes toward everyday matters.[4] In other words, while pointing to problems of specifically socialist transformation, the idea of cultural revolution, has also opened up new ways of perceiving cultural transformations.

This enlargement of the scope of Cultural Revolution may be testimonial to the intellectual influence of the Cultural Revolution in China (even among those who might no longer associate the term with the historical event), but it is important nevertheless to recall the concrete meanings the term carried in its immediate historical circumstances. The Cultural Revolution in China dramatized three important problem areas in socialist revolutions that need to be specified. First was its challenge to the prevalent thesis that socialist revolutions (and revolutions in general) must inevitably be "deradicalized" as they were institutionalized. This thesis, based upon the earlier experience of the Soviet Union (especially Stalinism), held forth that once the generation that had carried out the revolution disappeared from the scene, the revolution would be routinized and bureaucratized, losing its utopianism against the exigencies of power.[5] The Cultural Revolution in its time stood as a refutation of this idea. In this sense, it needs to be distinguished from earlier efforts, such as those in the Soviet Union in the twenties, to create a new culture appropriate to socialism. While it shared this goal with its Soviet precedents, the Cultural Revolutionary ideal of creating a new culture was tied in with an effort to resist the "deradicalization" of revolution.[6] Secondly, this same concern was to culminate during the Cultural Revolution in a revolution against the revolution itself, which would go a long way toward the popularization globally of the Chinese against an earlier Soviet model of socialism, that answered a widespread search for a democratic against a dictatorial social-ism. While the Cultural Revolution sought to create new socialist men and women for a new kind of society, the means it utilized to that end were much more radical than anything witnessed earlier, because these new men and women were to be created against the bureaucratic inertia of the new regime itself. The Cultural Revolution set itself against the old culture, but it did so by questioning the new "revolutionary" culture of the Communist Party bu-reaucracy itself. In this respect, its goals appeared to be truly revolutionary, directed not only against the hierarchical regimes of capitalist society, but against socialist hierarchies as well, which resonated widely with global dis-satisfactions against the bureaucratization that seemed to characterize moder-nity in its capitalist as well as Soviet socialist manifestations. The antibu-reaucratism and antielitism of the Cultural Revolution was an important element in giving birth globally to new Communist movements that sought to break with earlier models of Communist politics.[7]

Finally, the Cultural Revolution dramatized within Marxism a new concep-tion of the relationship between culture and a new mode of production, and, by extension, politics and the mode of production. As I noted above, while Marxism presupposes some correspondence between a new mode of produc-tion and a new culture, there is some ambiguity in the theory as to whether the new mode of production produces a new culture, or whether there is some au-tonomy in the realm of culture in facilitating the new mode of production. Not satisfied with the cultural consequences of the new relations of production that had been established by 1956, and bent upon carrying the revolution further, radicals in the Communist Party (led by Mao Zedong) in some ways had no choice but to settle on culture as the next realm of revolutionary activity. In the process, they were to recognize to the realm of culture an unprecedented mea-sure of autonomy (in Marxist terms), so that culture would come to bear the burden for the transition to socialism. It matters little in this context whether this autonomy recognized to culture was a product of China's historical legacy, the legacy of a guerilla revolution in which ideological struggle played a cen-tral part, or the logic of theory confronting the consequences of a socialist rev-olution legitimized by the same theory itself (the material transformation of social relations, in other words, failing to create a new culture automatically). The consequences are clearer: cultural transformation, rather than a function of socialist transformation, must play a key role in producing a socialist soci-ety. This autonomy of the cultural against the economic or the social, resonated with changes under way globally in the 1960s, to which I will return below. Suffice it to say here that it also underlined the importance of the political and ideological aspects of the revolution, against mechanical transformations in the mode of production understood economistically or technologically, which pointed in new directions of action that broke with earlier assumptions of modernization in either its capitalist or socialist guises.

To view the Cultural Revolution simply in its relationship to the history of Communist revolutions, and hence in terms of a struggle between the First and Second Worlds of post–World War II sociology, is insufficient, because what imbued the Cultural Revolution with its concrete historical characteristics may be the ambiguous status of Chinese society in the twentieth century, even after the victory of the Communist Party; as a society that belonged in the Second World by virtue of its socialist revolutionary history, but also in the Third World by virtue of its political, economic, and cultural relationships to the world of capitalism in EuroAmerica. It is important to recall that the Cultural Revolution coincided historically with decolonization in the Third World, and that, until the advent of the geopolitically inspired Maoist Three Worlds theory of the 1970s, the Cultural Revolution identified ideologically with the colonial world against both the EuroAmerican world of capitalism and Soviet-style "social imperialism." The juxtaposition of the rural Third World against the metropolitan First and Second Worlds was important, I think, both to the new departures in Cultural Revolution socialism, and to its ideological claims on the procedures of revolution.

Especially for its seeming anachronism with the present, Lin Biao's "Long Live the Victory of People's War" must be viewed as one of the most important documents of the Cultural Revolution, because it crystallized both the hostilities and the aspirations against the worlds of industrial capitalism and socialism of the newly emerging nations around the globe, and resonated with the ideology of national liberation struggles, of which the Chinese had been the most successful to date. It matters little whether or not it was ideologically justifiable from a Marxist perspective on socialism or revolution, which was its presumed theoretical basis; though it is arguable that it carried to its logical conclusions a Third Worldist socialism that had appeared first in the Second Congress of the Communist International in 1920. What is relevant is that Lin applied globally a paradigm of the Chinese Revolution itself, which had captured the cities from the countryside, and brought to the fore the fundamental meaning of that revolutionary experience: the primacy to any consideration of the world of agrarian against industrial societies. The hostility, unfortunately, would overshadow the more meaningful message: that a resolution of global problems would require the resolution of the problems of agrarian societies, just as the resolution of economic problems in individual nations, especially Third World nations, called for the resolution of the economic problems of the majority population of peasants.[8]

The significance of this piece for the purposes here was not that it called for war on industrialized societies, or that it stressed emphasis on agrarian societies, but that the call itself expressed the sense of empowerment in Third World societies that accompanied decolonization. This same sense of empowerment is visible in the articulation at the time of different notions of development than those that prevailed under either capitalist or Soviet-style socialist strategies of development. The Maoist paradigm of development was possibly the most powerful of the alternative notions of development which came to the fore as the new National Liberation struggles sought for ways to bolster economically their newfound political sovereignty. This paradigm proposed (a) that development policies take as their point of departure the necessity of all-round development nationally, and, (b) that this could be realized only by delinking from the capitalist world-system.

The first premise was enunciated clearly in Mao's classic 1956 essay "On the Ten Great Relationships," which called for attention to contradictions created by "uneven development" nationally. The second premise was enunciated throughout the Cultural Revolution years by the stress on national self-reliance, and the avoidance of material or ideological dependence on the outside world. It followed logically from the first premise in its analytical assumption that involvement in the capitalist world system would inevitably substitute the economic demands of this world system for the needs of a national economy. It may be worth emphasizing here that these "Maoist" premises had deep roots in the Chinese Revolution. The implications for the national economy of involvement in a capitalist world economy already had received intense attention among Chinese Marxists in the 1920s.[9] As these premises were reenunciated in the 1960s, they exerted immense influence in thinking on Third World development, of which the work of the distinguished development economist Samir Amin may be exemplary.[10]

Aside from the structural implications of this new paradigm of development, finally, were the substantive issues it raised, with profound social implications, that resonated with contemporary concerns in both advanced capitalist or socialist and Third World societies. A slogan such as self-reliance, that was central to Maoist developmental ideology, implied not just avoidance of dependency, but also called for active participation on the part of the people in the process of development. Its social implications were profound. Against their marginalization in earlier conceptualizations of development (capitalist or Soviet-socialist), self-reliance recognized the "people" as both the motive force and the end of development. No longer to be left in the hands of experts, development conceived along these lines brought the "people" into the center stage of the developmental process. In order for such a process to work, it was necessary also to place collective values over private ones, for cooperation and everyday negotiation were crucial to the achievement of social goals. Politically, the process required participation in collective decision making on a daily basis, creating unprecedented possibilities for grassroots democratic participation in social life. The laboring population, that is to say the majority of the people, would be responsible also for managing its own productive life. At the most fundamental level, the insistence on self-reliance was premised on a recognition of the subjectivity of the people, and their ability to manage their subjectivities in accordance with social goals.

In its idealistic reading, "putting politics in command"—a condition of self-reliance-implied the priority of public over private values. The type of individual who could live up to this absolute priority of the public over the private was obviously one who had overcome internally the force of social divisions that generated individualism; be it class and gender divisions, the division of labor, hierarchies of experts and nonexperts and, at a most fundamental level, the division between mental and manual labor. Creating such individuals required the appropriate social settings, but it also required individual effort at cultural self-transformation, because of a dialectic between social and cultural transformation. It required social institutions that would promote the welfare of the people, and enable their loyalty to collective institutions; but it would also require individuals who, rather than take advantage of such institutions, would devote themselves to fulfilling their promises.

I would like to stress here one aspect of the Maoist institutional vision that has received much criticism from the perspective of economic efficiency, but was nevertheless quite significant in its consequences for social and political organization. This was a conviction in the necessity of integrating agriculture and industry, so as to overcome the structural division between agriculture and industry, or rural and urban societies, that seemed to characterize modern societies. This was one of the institutional innovations of the disastrous Great Leap Forward in 1958, but like other aspects of Maoist developmental thinking, its origins lie in the history of the Chinese Revolution. While the Communists had sought such integration out of necessity in revolutionary Yan'an years, when they had no choice but to produce for themselves, the idea itself was one that first appeared in Chinese radicalism in anarchist writings in the first decade of the twentieth century (inspired by the writings of Peter Kropotkin). In anarchist writing, it is also important to note, the idea of integrating industry and agriculture to create self-sufficient local communities found a parallel in the creation of well-rounded individuals, who combined mental and manual labor, and thus overcame the class divisions that grew out of the division of labor. Needless to say, for anarchists, who eschewed nationalism, the primary goal was to avoid the alienation of modern industrial society in a reaffirmation of community. As it was appropriated into Maoist ideologies of development, these anarchist ideals were also linked to strategies of national autonomy and development.[11]

Even so, however, the anarchist juxtaposition of nation and community may have something to tell us about Maoist conceptualizations of society, and the contradictions that they contained. The idea of self-reliance, of which these institutional innovations may be viewed as expressions, is a multi-layered idea. It did not aim just at national autonomy through self-reliance, but autonomy at every level of society, down to the locality (which is what is disturbing from an economistic perspective that stresses "comparative advantage"); so that local societies themselves had to seek to be self-reliant, without relying on the outside, symbolized in Cultural Revolution years by the accomplishments of the Dazhai Brigade in Shanxi. Here, too, there is a conflict between the vision of autonomous communities and the existence of a hierarchical Party bureaucracy with the power to dispose of resources according to its own notion of political, social, and national good. But the distinction is important. Self-reliance was a means not just to national economic autonomy, but also to community formation. Its utopian aspirations could attract even those who otherwise did not share in the goals of a Chinese nationalism.

There was a downside to all of these promises, especially under conditions of unequal power, which the Cultural Revolution in the end would exacerbate rather than eliminate, but that is not the question I wish to pursue in this context, where I am more concerned with the appeals of these Maoist ideas globally.[12] The paradigm of development offered by Cultural Revolution Maoism seemed not only to answer the needs for simultaneous economic development and social cohesion in emergent postcolonial societies, but also the widespread alienation produced by development in economically advanced capitalist and socialist societies. It is not surprising that the Cultural Revolution should have spawned a new radical literature on development that rejected economic efficiency in the name of participatory development and democratic management.[13] Neither is it very surprising that it should have proven to be appealing even to those who had little reason to be favorable to its revolutionary goals, conservatives who saw in the social achievements of the Cultural Revolution the promise of new kinds of social cohesion and commitment to social goals.

THE CULTURAL REVOLUTION IN CONTEMPORARY PERSPECTIVE

Before I suggest a contemporary framework for evaluating the Cultural Revolution historically, a few words may be in order to clarify my conceptualization of the Cultural Revolution. My understanding of the significance of the Cultural Revolution as a historical event has drawn on elements that fall outside of the Cultural Revolution as it appears in official periodizations in

China; an event of three years (1966–1969) duration, as in the resolution of the Ninth Party Congress in 1969, or the "ten years of disaster" (1966–1976) in the official views of the post-Mao regime. It might be suggested even that, in pointing to the revolutionary roots of Cultural Revolution development policies, I have rendered the Cultural Revolution into a crystallization of the Chinese Revolution as a whole—which, it may be recalled, was the claim of the Cultural Revolution itself. The latter in particular may suggest that the historical significance I assign to the Cultural Revolution is little more than a repetition of the claims on history of the Cultural Revolution.

I have explained elsewhere[14] why I think it is proper to view the Cultural Revolution in terms of the two-decade period from 1956 to 1976. I will not dwell on this question, therefore, except to point out that such a periodization is not intended to deny that the Cultural Revolution had history, or that everything that happened during the 1966–1969 or 1966–1976 periods might have been predictable from problems that first emerged in the aftermath of the Eighth Party Congress in 1956. I do think, however, that the Cultural Revolution provided the sharpest articulation of those problems, and was responsible for dramatizing them globally. It was through their articulation during the Cultural Revolution that Maoist social and economic policies exerted their global influence.

A similar argument may be made with regard to the relationship between the Cultural Revolution and the Chinese Revolution as a whole. Contrary to the claims of the Cultural Revolutionaries, the Cultural Revolution did not represent the culmination of the Chinese Revolution as the only revolutionary alternative produced by the revolution. It is even arguable, in the perspective of the revolution, that there was more than one Maoism, and that the Cultural Revolution propagated certain tendencies within Maoism against other tendencies that were equally identifiable with Mao's policies in earlier phases of the Chinese Revolution.[15] To Mao's successors, obviously, the Cultural Revolution represented a betrayal of the goals of the Chinese Revolution.

Nevertheless, in the policies it propagated, the Cultural Revolution did express themes that were as old as the history of the Chinese Revolution, some of them even preceding the origins of Communism in China. And it is arguable that the Cultural Revolution drew its significance and its unique characteristics as a world-historical event from its articulation of these themes. Without its roots in the Chinese Revolution, which endowed it with plausibility, the Cultural Revolution indeed might not have amounted to much more than a power struggle within the Communist leadership, or the peccadilloes of Oriental potentates. This may also be the reason why the post-Mao leadership has sought to separate the Cultural Revolution from the history of the revolution, denouncing the Cultural Revolution while preserving memories of the Chinese Revolution for its own legitimacy. Conversely, it also accounts for the efforts of antirevolutionaries in China and abroad, who have linked the Cultural Revolution to the Chinese Revolution as a whole, hoping thereby to discredit not just the Cultural Revolution but, through such a linkage, the Chinese Revolution as a whole.

A genuinely critical evaluation of the Cultural Revolution, I would like to suggest here, must proceed by recognizing its historicity; by which I mean both a recognition of its significance under its historical circumstances, and also a recognition that with the transformation of those historical circumstances, the Cultural Revolution appears as a remote historical event, that left behind little but memories of misdeeds and oppressions. But it is not necessary, in order to understand the Cultural Revolution critically, to erase memories of what it meant to contemporaries. Such erasure in fact obviates the need for critical understanding not just of the Cultural Revolution, but of past and present ways of thinking about it. In the case of those who were victimized by the Cultural Revolution it would be asking too much to expect them to think of it critically, but surely that is only part of the reason for the contemporary urge to degrade memories of it totally. While there was never any shortage of those who would condemn the Cultural Revolution on moral or political grounds, they have been joined over the last two decades by Chinese participants in the Cultural Revolution who were complicitous not only in its ideology but its misdeeds, foreigners who would forget their earlier admiration for the Cultural Revolution, and many others who seem to perceive in the vulgarization of its memories the means to producing best-sellers for the world market. Ideology and a consumptive voyeurism have come together in curious ways to obviate the need to speak about this event with any degree of intelligence, let alone critical intelligence. I do not wish to engage here in an analysis, however important it may be, of the transformation in the literature on the Cultural Revolution that we have witnessed over the last two decades. I merely wish to raise the question of why, hailed until two decades ago not only by radicals but even by conservatives as a paradigm of revolutionary (and developmental) achievement, the Cultural Revolution is presently denounced and degraded in this fashion, with nothing to say to the present. My answer to the question is abstract and speculative, intentionally so in order to encourage discussion that accounts for historical memory, but may also offer some promise of rescuing criticism where the Chinese Revolution is concerned from its current intellectual degradation.

If the Cultural Revolution seems irrelevant today, it is because the problems it addressed are no longer significant problems. This is quite obvious where it concerns the first two items in my discussion above. In its day, the

Cultural Revolution appeared significant as a breakthrough in the history of socialist revolutions, or revolutions in general, in defiance of the inevitability of "deradicalization." At a time when socialism, and the whole idea of revolutionary politics, have been relegated to the past, a breakthrough in revolutionary politics carries little meaning, let alone historical significance. Much the same could be said with regard to the Cultural Revolution as an expression of resurgent Third World politics. In the immediate circumstances of the Cultural Revolution in the 1960s, the idea of a Third World carried significant weight in global political discourse. In our day, when it is hardly possible to speak of the Third World as a coherent idea, let alone a promise, it makes little sense to speak of a revolutionary Third World alternative to accepted paradigms of development.[16] Third Worlders, including Chinese in the People's Republic, are anxious to remake themselves in the image of the First World (there is no longer a Second World to speak of, contrary to the claims of remaining socialist regimes), and the societies of the Third World, where they have not made it already into the ranks of developing economies, are in shambles, apparently in need of new colonial aid for their sustenance.

These changes are not changes on an ideological plane, but are products of transformations within global relations. I have suggested elsewhere that the whole history of socialism as we have known it, no less than the history of the Third World, need to be comprehended in their relationship to transformations within capitalism.[17] Colonialism, and socialism as a response to it, especially in the Third World, were products of one phase within capitalism. While capitalism as a mode of production persists, contemporary capitalism is quite different in the global relations that it calls for than the capitalism that produced the Third World, or sought to contain the socialism that was its own product. This new phase in capitalism, whether it is called Global Capitalism, Late Capitalism, post-Fordism, or Flexible Production or Accumulation, has made irrelevant earlier conceptualizations of global relations, as well as of the relations of exploitation and oppression informed by those conceptualizations. EuroAmerican transnational corporations may still be dominant globally, but they have been joined by others, some of them originating in the former Third World. There may still be dominant nations, but it makes less sense than before to speak of imperialism or colonialism, when the nation-state has lost much of its power to corporations that are transnational, both in personnel and culture. And, most importantly in the context of this discussion, it makes little sense to speak of national economic autonomy, when the paradigm of development based on the national market has been replaced by a paradigm of development that calls for export economies and porous national boundaries as a condition of development. The nation-state, indispensable to the economic operations of capital in an earlier stage, now finds itself under attack as an obstacle to the same operations. Capital still rules, but under a different regime, one that seeks to be inclusive rather than exclusive.

These structural transformations within capitalism would produce their own Cultural Revolution, which is what I have in mind in the reference in the title of this chapter to the "two cultural revolutions." As theorists such as Fredric Jameson and David Harvey were the first to point out, the new phase in capitalism was to demand and produce its own culture, which may be encapsulated conveniently by the term "postmodernism."[18] This other cultural revolution, a cultural revolution of capitalism, interestingly coincided with the Chinese Cultural Revolution, although few were aware at the time of its eventual significance. It may be interesting to recall, in historical hindsight, that the launching of the Cultural Revolution in China, with the developmental policies it promoted, coincided almost to the year with the establishment of the export zones in Kao-hsiung in Taiwan and Masan in South Korea. It might not have occurred to radical critics of modernization and capitalism at the time that the future lay with the latter rather than the former. But that is exactly what has happened. And national autonomy in economic development has receded before the onslaught of export-oriented economies symbolized by these zones. The success of these economic zones, needless to say, would be made possible ultimately by new technologies that made possible the transnationalization of production. It was these same technologies that would make possible the new cultural revolution in capitalism, central to which is its self-representation as producer of images and information rather than of commodities (which still need to be produced, albeit in Third World locations, while the First World takes over as the "brain center" in designing the world). What the capitalist Cultural Revolution produced ideologically was culture as an end in itself, rather than as culture as a means to something else, such as community.

Viewed in this perspective, what is striking about the Cultural Revolution in China was that it was directed at the problems of a world that was already in the process of being replaced by another world that was dictated by the transformative power of contemporary capitalism, that was far ahead of what its critics imagined—whether they were located in the First, Second, or the Third Worlds. The Cultural Revolution, as a product of the revolution against imperialism, or First World domination of the Third World, spoke to problems inherited from the past, when the First World of capitalism was already in the process of creating new global relations, and corresponding social and cultural relations, that made those problems irrelevant. The contradictions between modernism and antimodernism in Mao Zedong Thought, at the moment of their enunciation, were already incorporated in postmodernist conceptualizations of the world which since then have proven to be of immense capacity in their ability to contain contradictions; so that business can utilize Maoist strategies in planning for the market while radicals continue to argue about appropriate responses to cliché-ridden conceptions of capitalism.

Whatever its failings as ideology and practice, the demise of Maoism as it appeared during the Cultural Revolution was a result not just of its own failings as a revolutionary ideology, but of its increasing irrelevance to an emergent world of capitalism that was radically different than the one that had produced Maoism. Cultural Revolution Maoism represented not a solution for the future, as it was taken to be at the time, but a last gasp of a past that was already irrelevant to a present that had overtaken it.

Does the Cultural Revolution, or more precisely, the revolutionary Maoism that the Cultural Revolution drew upon, have anything to say to the present? I think so. The repudiation presently of Maoist alternatives in modernity is part of an overall repudiation of radical alternatives to capitalism. We need to remember that, while transformations in capitalism may have rendered irrelevant earlier socialist challenges to its domination, capitalism is still capitalism, and these very same transformations have produced, and are in the process of producing, problems that await urgent resolution. Some of these problems are as old as the history of capitalism, others are products of new departures in capitalist production and organization. The resolution of these problems must take the present as their point of departure, but that is not to say that the past does not have anything to offer to the present. Recalling earlier revolutionary challenges is necessary to overcoming the ideological hegemony of capital. But it is not only for ideological reasons that the past is important. The revolutionary Maoist vision of society in particular—what I described above as the substantive issues that Maoism raised with regard to local society—may be relevant in surprising ways to confronting problems of contemporary capitalism.

Recent years have witnessed a reorientation of radical activity globally from an emphasis on the nation-state to an emphasis on local movements. The disillusionment with the inability of socialist states to resolve social problems is certainly an element in this reorientation. That disillusionment itself is part, however, of a broader loss of faith in the state in capitalist as well as in formerly socialist societies. While the nation-state is by no means dead, as some would suggest, for the last two decades states worldwide have been anxious to shed many of the responsibilities they had assumed earlier for the welfare of their populations. This has been accompanied by an increasingly visible alliance between states and transnational capitalism; so that once again the state appears nakedly as a promoter of the interests of capital, sometimes against the interests of the populations whom they claim to represent. While the "privatization" of the state has been proceeding at different rates in different places, depending on the ability of the populations to resist it, such privatization nevertheless represents a global tendency against an earlier conception of the nation-state as a defender of the public against private interests. This, too, is a product of the new phase of capitalism. In this sense, the fall of socialist states—the most extreme form of the priority of the public over the private—since the late 1980s may be viewed as part of a global process that includes the capitalist state as well.

One by-product of this weakening of the "public state" is the weakening of an earlier role that the state played as an intermediary between the transnational forces of capitalism, and the needs of local societies; so that local communities face more directly than before the demands of a global economy. The increased stress on local society in recent years, in other words, is a product not just of loss of faith in the state, or in state-oriented solutions to social problems, but of the very operations of transnational capital that draw localities out of their isolation, utilize them to their own ends, and abandon them when such localities no longer serve those ends. The very operations of capital, it may be suggested, produce the local as we know it presently. In response, local societies have to fend for themselves as well as they can without reliance on the help of the state. This need has been quite important in fostering local movements.

I am not suggesting here that local movements can afford to be merely local. In order to be effective, local movements have to seek translocal alliances—not just nationally but transnationally—to counter the global powers of capital; under the circumstances of global capitalism, the welfare of working people at any particular location, say, in the United States or China, may be much more interdependent than earlier. But the new situation suggests that radical defense of people's welfare has to take the local as its point of departure.

This is where, I think, memories of the Chinese Revolution in its Maoist guise may have much to offer to the present. As I noted above, the Maoist vision as articulated during the Cultural Revolution linked the fate of the local to the national, but that vision was informed in the history of the Chinese Revolution by a prior alternative anarchist vision that disassociated the local and the national, and gave priority to the needs of local society apart from, and against, the nation-state. In its stress on "self-reliance" at the level of local society, the Maoist vision contained this idea of local autonomy. Its products are well known. Especially important has been the institutionalization of integrating agriculture and industry at the level of local society, which was to produce a unique social configuration not just in Maoist but also in post-Mao China, that has accounted in many ways for the ability of Chinese society, in contrast to other formerly socialist societies, to withstand the socially destructive forces of capitalism while opening up to the capitalist world-system.

This social configuration also owes much of its success to the experience of revolutionary years which may have created conditions of corruption and the abuse of power, which seem to receive all the attention these days, but that were also to breed habits of self-reliance, collective activity, and cooperation between local political leadership and the population at large.[19]

What is interesting is that while the regime in Beijing retains its coercive powers, and is quick to claim for itself the developmental successes of Chinese society, much of this success is in fact due to the ability of the many localities in China to fend for themselves. While it would be misleading to state that the Communist regime in Beijing and the development of local society in China should be viewed in isolation from one another, an analytical distinction may nevertheless be useful that points to two conflicting paradigms of development in China. One is that to which the state is central, that guarantees to the Communist regime, and the new managerial class it cultivates, a position of power in the global economy and politics, but promises little beyond an authoritarian state capitalism. The other is one that is based in local society, that draws on an earlier revolutionary legacy of local development that gives priority to the welfare of the people over the power of the state, and points to a democratic socialism. What is radical politically about the latter alternative is also that, while it obviously does not reject the state, it calls for a reevaluation both of the territorial scope of the state (as expressed in new regionalisms) and the scope of its powers. In other words, it calls for a reconsideration of the boundaries and the responsibilities of the state against the claims of the present regime to define the nation, and claim it for its legitimacy.

Thanks to its revolutionary legacy, rather than the antirevolutionary authoritarian propensities of the current Communist regime, in other words, Chinese society not only continues to offer a model of alternative modernity that challenges the hegemony of capitalism, but also offers concrete resolutions of problems that are products of the reconfiguration of global relations under contemporary capitalism. The legacy of the Maoist vision may be more visible in China than elsewhere, but there are suggestions of it in other local movements around the world; not just in Third World locations (from India to Chiapas) where the language of self-reliance promotes the defense of local community against the ravages of capital, but also in First World societies, where it invokes memories of living communities against the "virtual communities" of global capitalism.

The Cultural Revolution may or may not lay claims to be the only, or even the most accurate, representation of the Maoist vision, which was itself rooted in the history of the Chinese Revolution. It dramatized for the world the power of that vision. That it will haunt the memories of many for generations to come may be sufficient to qualify it as a world-historical event. But it was not merely a ghostly event. Try as we might to exorcize its memories, it haunts us because, in its very historicity, it spoke to problems that are also part of our legacy. Like it or not, it will be with us so long as we demand solutions to those problems.

NOTES

1. See Arif Dirlik, "Cong lishi jiaodu kan 'wenge' de zhengzhi yiyi" (The Politics of Cultural Revolution in Historical Perspective), in *Xianggang shehui kexue bao (Hong Kong Journal of Social Sciences)*, no. 7 (Spring 1996): 21–48.

2. Fredric Jameson, "Post-modernism, or the Cultural Logic of Late Capitalism," *New Left Review*, no. 146 (July/August 1984): 53–92, where a Cultural Revolution describes both the emergence of a bourgeois culture of modernism and the emergence of postmodernism that breaks with the latter, but still within the context of a bourgeois mode of production.

3. Philip R. D. Corrigan and Derek Sayer, *The Great Arch: English State Formation as Cultural Revolution* (Oxford, UK: Oxford University Press, 1985).

4. Stuart Hall, "Negotiating Caribbean Identities," *New Left Review*, no. 209 (January–February 1995): 3–14.

5. This was actually a liberal argument against conservative anti-Communism, which implied, against Cold War presumptions, that it would be possible to deal with Communist regimes on the basis of geopolitical considerations. An important, and influential, example is to be found in Robert C. Tucker, *The Marxian Revolutionary Idea* (New York: Norton, 1969).

6. Maurice Meisner in his various writings has emphasized this aspect of the Cultural Revolution. For examples, see "Stalinism in the History of the Chinese Communist Party," in *Critical Perspectives on Mao Zedong Thought*, eds. Arif Dirlik, Paul Healy, and Nick Knight (Atlantic Heights, NJ: Humanities Press, 1997), and "Deradicalization," in *Marxism and the Chinese Experience: Issues in Contemporary Chinese Socialism*, eds. Arif Dirlik and Maurice Meisner (Armonk, NY: M. E. Sharpe, 1989).

7. See A. Belden Fields, *Trotskyism and Maoism: Theory and Practice in France and the United States* (New York: Praeger, 1988) for a detailed discussion of the reception and impact of Maoism on Communist movements in France and the United States. For the global impact of Maoism, see the essays by William Duiker (Vietnam), Orin Starn (Peru), Sanjay Seth (India), J. Victor Koschmann (Japan), and Emerita D. Distor (Philippines), in *Critical Perspectives on Mao Zedong Thought*, Arif Dirlik, Paul Healy, and Nick Knight, eds. (Atlantic Heights, NJ: Humanities Press, forthcoming). See also the unpublished paper by Nick Knight, "Maoism Down Under: The Theory and Tactics of the Communist Party of Australia (Marxist-Leninist)."

8. While the essay seems silly from a contemporary perspective, when agrarian societies have been marginalized, the books significance was recognized immediately.

See Chalmers Johnson, *Autopsy on People's War* (Berkeley: University of California Press, 1973) for a "refutation" of Lin's arguments by an influential U.S. political scientist.

9. See Arif Dirlik, "National Development and Social Revolution in Early Chinese Marxist Thought," *China Quarterly* 58 (April–June 1974): 286–309, for an account of the Chinese Marxist debates on this question.

10. Of Amin's many works, the most thorough may be *Delinking towards a polycentric World* (London: ZED Books, 1990). Amin, of course, was not alone. The example of the Chinese Revolution and Maoist development policy also exerted influence on important thinkers such as Immanuel Wallerstein and those associated with him in promoting "world-system analysis." It is also important to note that the Maoist development model in its concerns resonated with the contemporary dissatisfaction with modernization "theory," expressed mainly but not exclusively in world-system analysis and the "dependency theory" emanating from Latin America. In other words, the Maoist paradigm was part of a search globally for alternatives to modernization theory.

11. See Arif Dirlik, *Anarchism in the Chinese Revolution* (Berkeley: University of California Press, 1991), and Ming K. Chan and Arif Dirlik, *Schools into Fields and Factories: Anarchists, the Guomindang, and the National Labor University in Shanghai, 1927–1932* (Durham, NC: Duke University Press, 1991) for discussions of anarchist views on local society.

12. See the essay referred to above, "The Politics of Cultural Revolution in Historical Perspective," for a critical evaluation.

13. Stephen Andors, *China's Industrial Revolution: Politics, Planning, and Management, 1949 to the Present* (New York: Pantheon, 1977), and Charles Bettelheim, *Cultural Revolution and Industrial Organization in China: Change in Management and the Division of Labor* (New York: Monthly Review Press, 1974), for two of many examples.

14. Dirlik, "The Politics of Cultural Revolution in Historical Perspective."

15. See Edward Friedman, Paul Pickowicz, and Mark Selden, *Chinese Village, Socialist State* (New Haven, CT: Yale University Press, 1991) for an argument that the Cultural Revolution broke with the more reasonable and effective policies of an earlier period. For the contradictions within Mao's own thinking, see Dirlik, "Xiandai zhuyi he fanxiandai zhuyi: Mao Zedongde Makesi zhuyi," in *Zhongguo shehui kexue jikan*, 5 (15 November 1993): 37–49 [tr. of "Modernism and Anti-Modernism in Mao Zedong Thought]. See also Dirlik, "Hou shehui zhuyi?—dui 'Zhongguo tesede shehui zhuyi'de fansi," in *Haiwai xuezhe lun "Zhongguo daolu" yu Mao Zedong*, eds. Li Junru and Zhang Yongwei (Shanghai: Shanghai shehuikexue yuan chuban she, 1991) [translation of "Postsocialism? Reflections on 'Socialism with Chinese Characteristics'] for a discussion of Maoism in its New Democracy versus Cultural Revolution versions.

16. For the Third World in the contemporary age, see Arif Dirlik, "Three Worlds or One, or Many: The Reconfiguration of Global Relations under Contemporary Capitalism," in *Nature, Society, Thought* 7, no. 1 (1995): 19–42.

17. Arif Dirlik, *After the Revolution: Waking to Global Capitalism* (Hanover, NH: University Press of New England for Wesleyan University Press, 1994).

18. Fredric Jameson, "Post-modernism," op. cit. fn. 2, and David Harvey, *The Condition of Postmodernity: An Enquiry into the Origins of Cultural Change* (Cambridge, MA: Blackwell Publishers, 1989).

19. For further discussion, see Roberto M. Unger and Zhiyuan Cui, "China in the Russian Mirror," *New Left Review* 208 (November/December 1994): 78–87.

9

Revolutions in History and Memory: The Politics of Cultural Revolution in Historical Perspective

I reflect below on certain questions that are presented by recent evaluations of the Cultural Revolution of the 1960s in China. The Cultural Revolution was an intriguing and significant historical event in its own right. What makes it particularly significant in the present context is that questions of the Cultural Revolution invite questions concerning the entirety of the Chinese Revolution and, by extension, the problem of revolutions in general as phenomena of modernity. The question ultimately is what to do with revolutions in a postrevolutionary age that in its self-image postulates a break not just with the history of revolutions, but with a modernity that was as much a producer as the product of revolutions?

While I make some effort below to disentangle problems of the Cultural Revolution from its contemporary representations, my primary concern in this discussion is with the latter. There are two aspects to my concern with these representations. First is the question of memory and history where revolutions are concerned. How to reconcile memory with history has emerged as a major concern over the last decade or two, most importantly with regard to questions of the Holocaust and World War II, but also over questions of revolutionary legacies. While there has been much discussion of the status of memory in history, there has been relatively little discussion that I am aware of that addresses directly the question of *historians'* memories. The Cultural Revolution presents interesting problems in this regard for my generation of historians who, provoked into radicalism by the Cultural Revolution (among other events of the 1960s), nevertheless have had a tendency in recent years to "forget" this intellectually formative event. The questions raised by this "forgetting" may not be encompassed, I suggest below, under technical historiographical questions of documentation, historical revisionism, etc., but are bound up with important transformations of the present, which have called into question not just the Cultural Revolution, but revolution as an idea. In our day when "settling accounts with the past" seems to be quite widespread, it is important I think for historians to settle accounts with their own forgotten memories. Such confrontation is important for historical work itself because it calls for elucidation of the relationship of historians' memories to their historical evaluations and explanations. It is possible after all for historians to have too much memory of the experiences that have shaped them as historians, that might make for a nostalgic resistance to changed perspectives. It is also possible, at the other extreme, to dismiss past perspectives as irrelevant, not on some "objective" ground but out of a desire to forget past perspectives that have become uncomfortable due to changes in the historian's environment and consciousness. The question here is not just one of the relationship of the historian's present to the construction of the past, which is a perennial problem, but also a question of the relationship of the historian's present to his/her own past at a time of apparent discontinuity between the present and the past.

The question of historical memory and forgetting is not, needless to say, just an academic question, but is quite consequential for the ways in which we comprehend and act on our presents. Charles Maier has cautioned historians to ask "about the interests of the stakes involved in memory: the psychological or existential stakes and then the political stakes. For memory does not come in a social or political vacuum."[1] Neither memory nor forgetting is entirely innocent—nor is the historical consciousness that they inform. A central question for the present, I think, is how to distinguish critical memories of the past that also allow for a critique of the present from those memories that conform to the predispositions of the present, and serve to legitimize contemporary configurations of power. Revolutions are particularly significant in this regard; the relegation to the past of a phenomenon for long associated with uncompromising futuristic progressivism inevitably provokes questions about contemporary notions of the relationship between the present and the past. It also helps, I hope, to disturb some of the self-complacency of the present about the past that it has in its self-image left behind.

I reflect by way of conclusion on some of the contemporary changes that may help explain the recent turnabout in attitudes toward the revolutionary past, from revolutions as forces of social transformation and liberation to revolutions as producers of backwardness, oppression, and terror. My point of departure is a question that springs from my own experience as a historian of China, but hopefully has broader implications: Why is it that revolutions, which seemed to make eminent sense only decades ago, no longer seem to make any sense? The question provokes other questions that pertain at once to history and the historian. Is it the conditions that have been transformed so drastically, revealing revolutions in all their senselessness, or is it we who have changed, so that we can no longer make sense of a phenomenon that seemed eminently sensible to many for two centuries? I think one could make a case either way, but I argue below that how the case is made is quite significant in its implications for the present. Revolutions may be historicized, or forgotten, in different ways. In the substance of the discussion below, I query the implications for the present of the manner in which revolutions are "forgotten" these days—which requires that we also "forget" a great deal about the present. One of my concerns here is to disturb the categories, among them "authoritarianism," which serve presently to contain complex phenomena of the past; I invoke revolution above all to reconsider contemporary "strategies of containment" that "contain" not just the past but also radical possibilities at the present.

I argue below that while the historical perspective provided by the present enables new critiques of the past, a claim to a genuinely critical historiography may be sustained only if the critique of the past returns as its ultimate goal to the critique of the present. I hope by the banality of this premise to underscore its importance to a contemporary "regime of discontinuity,"[2] when it is practiced mostly in the forgetting, especially when it comes to the revolutionary past. That the historian makes history is hardly fresh news, especially with the postmodern stress on the author that, in its denial at the extreme of any reality to the past beyond its discursive construction, lodges history firmly in the present, however elusive that may be. It is all the more remarkable then that those who would deconstruct the past rarely extend the deconstruction to their own practices; not in some narcissistic sense of authorial self-deconstruction, which seems to represent the limit of critical self-reflection in our day, but in the more significant sense of the relationship of discursive practices to the structures of power of which discourses are at once products and producers. Another banality that might be recalled to some critical effect in discussions of revolution is the existence of a relationship between representation and power; specifically, the ways in which contemporary representations of revolution not only may resonate with the self-images of contemporary configurations of power, but also stand as articulations of the power of those same configurations over the present and the past. While a sense of rupture with the past privileges more than ever the present over the past, it also conveniently places the present beyond the reach of any critical insights that may be gained from the critique of the past. With all their contradictions, revolutions may still be recalled, I suggest, to serve a much needed critical purpose, and help rescue quite justifiable, and necessary, criticism of the past from intended or unintended complicity in legitimizing—perhaps even preparing the ground for—contemporary structures of power.

But the issue of revolution involves more than critical scholarship, or even criticism of existing forms of power. For all their flaws, shortcomings, failures, and occasional horrors, revolutions provided alibi for possibilities of fundamental social, political, and cultural transformation—and, in the case of socialist revolutions, the possibility of alternatives to a capitalist modernity. This may be a fundamental reason that revolutions are presently under condemnation not just for their acts of terror, but for the radical discourses that are held responsible for the terror, which discredits not just the revolutions in history as discrete historical events, but the very idea of radical structural transformation; including the social and political phraseology of radical change from class to equality and even democracy. This itself is not particularly novel; it did not take the "linguistic turn" in social sciences to reveal that speaking about revolutions, or invoking the terminology of radical transformation, might speak revolutions into existence. The Guomindang regime in China in the 1930s blamed the success of Communism on loose talk about social phenomena. More than one U.S. politician in recent years has warned about speaking too much about classes lest such talk conjure classes into existence. The diagnosis of the linguistic turn that revolutionary discourses may have conjured revolutions into existence is not novel, but pervasive compliance with a linguistic turn that denies to revolutions any significant social and political basis may be revealing of the conservative turn in postmodernist/poststructuralist social science.[3]

To recall revolutions, similarly, is not merely to single out one or another revolution for its virtues or vices, but to keep open the possibility of alternative forms of social existence and organization. From radical perspectives, it is arguable that the fall of state socialisms have allowed for the recognition once again of certain kinds of radical social visions, grounded in everyday life, that have been as undesirable to a modernizationist socialism as to capitalism. Also, while the state socialist projects of the past may have failed to achieve the most fundamental of their promises, it is not clear that their revolutionary legacies are therefore little more than curiosities from a forgettable past. I would like to suggest that in transformed ways that account for the failures of the past, the legacies of revolution, and the search for alternatives that it inspired, are very much alive in our day in movements that seek to achieve from the bottom up what state socialisms sought to realize through the agency of bureaucratic states. These movements articulate a critique not just of past authoritarianism, but the authoritarianism (among other things) that is built into the very structures of contemporary capitalism, to which democracy often means little more than market democracy, while markets provide at the same time unprecedentedly powerful means of supervision and control. Preoccupation with the flaws of the past may indeed blind us to the democratic impulse in revolutions which now finds expression in different forms in contemporary social movements. The presence of these movements—as contemporary incarnations of earlier visions of democracy and social justice that also repudiate, however, earlier means to achieve those ends—also makes it possible to recall the past as a resource without falling into a conservative or reactionary reaffirmation of the past. These movements serve as reminders that contrary to celebrations of historical discontinuity, both in the structures of power and oppositions to them the present and its past are linked quite intimately. It is not only in oppositional social and political movements that the legacy of revolutionary pasts is visible. The discourse on development at the highest levels of contemporary politics and power has slowly disintegrated as it has sought to come to terms with alternatives to capitalism that, while they may not have been direct products of revolutionary regimes, and even subject to suppression by the latter, nevertheless found their most powerful articulation in the demands for revolutionary change.[4]

Revolutions as we have known them may quite well be phenomena of the past. The social forces that made revolutions possible have largely disintegrated, and no amount of revolutionary discourse is likely to conjure into existence political identities that made revolutions possible; this may include national as well as class identities. On the other hand, the conditions that called forth revolutions in the past have hardly disappeared—either in terms of structural conditions, or in the dislocations of life by the forces of capitalist modernity which if anything are more powerful and unpredictable than earlier. These dislocations now give rise to identities of another type which in their most visible forms shift opposition to existing forms of power onto other terrains, most powerful among which these days would be the terrains of religion and ethnicity. Alongside these oppositions which are highly divisive and, to this author at least, productive of new forms of oppressive abstractions, however, are movements based in everyday life that seek to sustain and rejuvenate in transformed forms long-standing community ideals. If I may resort to a political language that has been abandoned too readily in the rush to forget revolutions, revolution has been hijacked in recent years by forces of the Right. One fundamental reason for recalling revolutions of the past is once again to empower those movements of the Left that retain commitments to visions of democracy and social justice.

The Cultural Revolution in China offers an important case for exploring some of these questions, both because it is still within living memory, but also because of its complexities that still render it relevant to the present. The Chinese Revolution was at once a socialist and a Third World revolution, where nationalist and socialist goals reinforced and contradicted one another, class issues clashed with those of the state, and developmentalism came into conflict with the agrarian loyalties of a guerilla revolution. In the end, the Chinese Revolution presented itself as an alternative both to capitalism, and to socialist modernizationism as represented by Soviet socialism. The Cultural Revolution proclaimed in the final phase of the revolution (which retrospectively has shaped understanding of the entire Chinese Revolution) was a "revolution within the revolution," to recall Regis Debray's pithy phrase, that revealed the contradictions that beset all revolutionary regimes. In spite of the upheaval and ultimate terror of the Cultural Revolution, moreover, the Communist Party leadership has refused to abandon professions of faith in socialism even as it has opened the country ever more radically to capitalism; whatever we may make of this socialism which I have described elsewhere as postsocialism, it has interestingly allowed for some latitude of policy and experimentation that may account for the remarkable ability of the regime to survive and to flourish, at least for the time being. A most significant aspect of this latitude is the rather interesting flexibility of both the regime and of the population toward the revolutionary past, which differs significantly from the urge to erase memories of the revolution among most China scholars, and some Chinese intellectuals, and may account for continued anxiety concerning China's future.

The issues that I take up below are best stated through a paradox that the Cultural Revolution presents in historical hindsight. The Cultural Revolution was launched to prevent a slide from socialism to capitalism, which Mao Zedong and his supporters perceived as an immanent possibility. Since the end of the Cultural Revolution, this is indeed what has happened, as Chinese society under Deng Xiaoping (one of the prime targets of the Cultural Revolution) has been incorporated into a capitalist world system, and is by now socialist only in name, and the persistent dictatorship of the Communist Party. In other words, the prognosis that justified the launching of the Cultural Revolution has been born out by subsequent history. Why is it, then, that the image of the Cultural Revolution that prevails in most quarters in China and abroad is that of a historically meaningless and deviant undertaking, that had little purpose beyond satisfying the craving for power or the perverse ideological attachments of its leaders and proponents?

There is probably more than one answer to this question; but whatever the answer or answers may be, it is necessary, I think, to account for two sets of problems. One set relates to the failings of the Cultural Revolution itself. Revolutions are tragic events even when they succeed in achieving their goals; a revolution that fails is likely to leave behind only memories of the naked oppressions and cruelties that revolutions inevitably unleash. In this particular case, that Chinese society has reverted to capitalism since the Cultural Revolution not only does not serve to legitimize it historically, but only underlines its futility. What stands out in historical memory is the wasteful and arbitrary cruelty it visited on millions of people.

To leave the matter here, where it is usually left these days, is to be entrapped in the ideology of the present, that seeks to erase in a teleology of the present memories of past alternatives that envisioned different historical outcomes than that which has eventuated. A genuinely critical appreciation of the Cultural Revolution is one that needs to understand it critically against its own claims and deeds, but without entrapment in this ideology of the present. Hence we need to account for a second set of problems that are epistemological; that pertain to our ways of knowing China, our understanding of revolutions (socialist or otherwise) over the last two centuries and, last but not least, the conceptions of the present and the future that inform our understanding of the past. This task is all the more crucial in light of changes in the world situation over the last decade, when the fall of socialisms around the world and the seemingly undisputed global hegemony achieved by capitalism marks off our world from the world of the Cultural Revolution—to the point where it seems difficult to imagine even that there might have been a time when there were those audacious enough to envision a world different from the world of the present. This new ideological disposition reinforces the image of futility and arbitrariness left behind by the failures of the Cultural Revolution, making it almost impossible to speak about it critically as a historical event.

It is these two sets of issues that I take up below. I have two goals. First, I undertake to evaluate the Cultural Revolution historically, within the context both of the modern Chinese Revolution and the global history of which the revolution was an inextricable part. And second, to inquire into the relevance for the present, across the divide that I referred to above, of the political problems and aspirations that the Cultural Revolution expressed, which carry a significance not only beyond the whims and ideological predispositions of individual leaders, but a significance beyond the boundaries of China itself.

THE VIRTUES OF AMBIVALENCE, OR THE PROFOUND AMBIGUITY OF THE CULTURAL REVOLUTION

Ambivalence usually implies moral and intellectual uncertainty or even worse, a cowardly refusal to take a position on a problematic issue. It may, however, also serve another, less ignoble, purpose: to avoid entrapment in ideologically shaped moralities or intellectual positions in order to leave the door open for the possibility of other moral and intellectual positions.[5] Much of the problem with past and present interpretations of the Cultural Revolution lies in a refusal of ambivalence in favor of clear-cut positions that have ideologically suppressed one aspect or another of this complex historical event.

Over the last three decades, interpretations of the Cultural Revolution in the United States have gone through roughly four phases, each phase drastically revising or reversing the judgment of the previous phase. The interpretation that prevails presently, ironically, is closest to the initial responses to the Cultural Revolution in 1966. When news of the Cultural Revolution reached the outside world in late Summer 1966, the immediate interpretation placed on it was that of a power struggle in the communist leadership that in its extremeness and unprecedented nature confirmed the madness of the whole enterprise that was the Chinese Revolution.[6] In the radical atmosphere of the late 1960s, this interpretation was challenged almost immediately by radicals, including a new generation of radical China scholars, who saw in the Cultural Revolution a Third World renewal of the promise of revolutionary socialism that had been betrayed in the Soviet Union. While conservative critiques of the Cultural Revolution never disappeared, by the early 1970s, this radical version was in the ascendancy. Following President Nixon's visit to China, this unquestioning positive assessment of the Cultural Revolution spread beyond radicals to conservatives, who went even further than the radicals in lauding the Cultural Revolution; Richard Nixon himself credited the Cultural Revolution under "Chairman Mao" with instilling in the Chinese people the Protestant spirit of commitment and hard work that had been lost among the original Protestants in the United States.

The enthusiasm of this second phase was to vanish almost overnight after 1978. As enthusiasm shifted to Deng Xiaoping's reform policies, both in scholarly and journalistic circles the image of the Cultural Revolution turned, following the assessments in China, into "ten years of disaster," that had taken a heavy toll both in terms of human lives, and on China's economic development. Now reporting from China, U.S. reporters wrote books showing that beneath the image of rosy-cheeked Red Guards lay a much harsher reality for the lives of the people, scholars began to uncover evidence that the developmental claims of the Cultural Revolution had been false, and the new socialist ethic that had so impressed visitors of the 1970s gave way to the image of a population rendered listless and immobilized by political conflict and incoherence at the top. Earlier enthusiasm for Mao and the Cultural Revolution gave way to an even more exaggerated enthusiasm for Deng Xiaoping and his "democratic" policies. Whether or not post-Tiananmen assessments of the Cultural Revolution deserve to be described as a fourth phase is problematic, for in many ways they represent an elaboration of, rather than departures from, the assessments of the 1980s. Following the Tiananmen Tragedy, and especially the nearly abandonless opening of China to capitalism after 1992, it is not so much the image of the Cultural Revolution that has changed, but the image of the Chinese revolution as a whole, as the Cultural Revolution now became emblematic of the bankruptcy of the revolution as a whole (this theme was already on the emergence by the late 1980s). The Tiananmen Tragedy burst illusions about Deng Xiaoping, who now joined Mao in the pantheon of "China's new emperors." The accumulation of memoirs by Chinese who had suffered under the Cultural Revolution confirmed the effects of the Tiananmen Tragedy, making the whole history of post-1949 China (if not earlier) into one sorry story of corruption, ineptitude, and waste. It is not just the Cultural Revolution, but the revolution of which it was one manifestation, and the regime that claims the legacy of that revolution, that is presently the object of American suspicion and hostility. On the other hand, in some areas such as economic development, there has been a tendency in recent years to qualify the uniformly negative assessment of the 1980s concerning economic achievements of the Mao years.[7] This latter has not affected the assessment of the Cultural Revolution in other areas.

The history of representations of the Cultural Revolution remains to be written, but it is possible to observe that in spite of their divergent interpretations of the Cultural Revolution, these four phases share one thing in common: the refusal to acknowledge the ambiguities of the Cultural Revolution as a historical event, and to incorporate such ambiguity in analysis. While there is no question that there has been an accumulation of evidence to call for new interpretations of the Cultural Revolution, these shifts in interpretation are not explainable on the basis of evidence alone. What we make of the Cultural Revolution depends on how we view it, and the latter is not just a matter of evidence as it involves considerations of our perceptions of China and the world. There was always enough evidence of silliness and cruelty, if only in the language of the Cultural Revolution, and yet it was ignored so long as positive assessments prevailed. On the other hand, presently evidence of silliness and cruelty seems to be the only kind of evidence that counts, ignoring the concerns which had justified earlier positive assessments. The refusal of ambiguity presently is even more serious in its consequences than earlier. Even at the height of the positive assessments of the Cultural Revolution, there were always conservative voices that insisted on alternative assessments, making for some diversity of interpretation. In contrast, presently, the memories of the Cultural Revolution that prevail are uniform in their condemnations of it as a historical event. My call for ambivalence, under the circumstances, is intended to counter this situation. I will make a brief case in its justification here, to illustrate how it may enable a less ideological and more critical historical evaluation of the Cultural Revolution.

What we mean by the Cultural Revolution is itself problematic, as it entails questions of where we draw the boundaries of the Cultural Revolution in its temporality. Different periodizations of the Cultural Revolution throw up different kinds of problems. If we take the Cultural Revolution in its most restricted, official sense, it refers to 1966–1969, and the image it yields is of chaos, mindless idol worship, political factionalism at the top and social conflict at the bottom, gratuitous violence, and an escape from the world at large. If we take the Cultural Revolution in the sense that the post-Mao official periodization takes it, as "ten years of disaster" from 1966 to 1976, the image becomes that of political factionalism at the top, and systematic oppression of dissidents at the bottom with, however, quite different characteristics than the 1966–1969 period in terms of Party–society relations, development policies, relationship to the world, etc.

While this latter periodization accounts for the consequences of the "official Cultural Revolution," however, it ignores the concerns and the problems that went into the making of the Cultural Revolution, which take us back to the fateful year of 1956, when it was declared in the Eighth Party Congress that China had successfully achieved "the transition to socialism." It was conflicts over what was to be done next, with a concern for serious transformations in the global context, that were to culminate in the Cultural Revolution—not inevitably, but step by step as certain policies and conflict over policies brought about the upheaval of the mid-1960s. If stress on the first two periodizations foregrounds issues of personality and power, this broader periodization makes it necessary that we deal also with issues of policy. We may note, also, that in this periodization, what we understand by the Cultural Revolution pertains to what we make of the "socialist phase" of the Chinese Revolution since, by the regime's own reckoning, the period before 1956 was still the period of "transition to socialism" (or "New Democracy," I would suggest), and the period after 1976 witnessed the step-by-step abandonment of socialism, contrary to claims of "socialism with Chinese characteristics." This broad periodization, finally, raises the question of the relationship between the Cultural Revolution (or the socialist phase of the revolution), to the revolution as a whole.[8]

The profound ambiguity of the Cultural Revolution arises from a deep contradiction between the policies it professed and promoted, and the consequences of those policies at the ground level, which were indeed as problematic as its detractors claim. To briefly rehearse those policies, which were once the cause for adulation of the Cultural Revolution in China and abroad, they sought, in the first place, to "delink" China from the capitalist world-system in order to guarantee progress toward socialism; based upon an understanding of an inevitable entrapment in capitalism that would follow from any serious involvement in the capitalist world-system.[9]

These policies, secondly, were intended to move China in a direction of socialism that broke with the example of the Soviet Union. As Mao noted in his reading of the texts on the Soviet economy, the process of socialist development required close attention not just to the forces but even more fundamentally to the relations of production.[10] Ignoring this problem had produced in the Soviet Union a new class structure based on the hierarchy of bureaucracy and expertise. Attention to relations of production was necessary to counter such class tendencies, as well as to evolve more democratic forms of management both in agriculture and in industry that required popular participation in decision making. The latter required also that more attention be given in development to popular mobilization over technology and technique. Under Chinese circumstances, this also meant a continuing emphasis on the peasantry in the process of development. In accordance with Mao's conviction in the necessity of spatial evenness in development, as expressed most cogently in his, "on the Ten Great Relationships," a consequence of this emphasis on the peasantry and the countryside was to bring industry to the villages in order to forestall an urban/industrial versus rural/agricultural bifurcation. Close attention to local circumstances, rather than bureaucratic fiat from the center, was basic to all these policy formulations.

Thirdly, crucial to either set of policies was an emphasis on "self-reliance" at all levels, from the national level to minimize material and intellectual dependence on advanced countries, to the level of the individual in order to foster individual creativity in service of public goals; "self-reliance" as an idea was inseparable from a commitment to placing public ahead of private interests. Growing out of earlier revolutionary experiences, especially in Yan'an where the slogan of "self-reliance" had first emerged, the stress on self-reliance also addressed a fundamental problem of all Third World societies whose political sovereignty had been compromised by continuing financial and technological dependence on the capitalist and the socialist blocs. Internally, it addressed the thorny question of creating a public consciousness in the process of development.

Finally, the idea of Cultural Revolution itself addressed the question of creating a new culture appropriate to a new, socialist, mode of production. Such a culture could not emerge overnight, but required continuing revolution so that development would take a genuinely socialist course, rather than move in the direction of capitalism or the hierarchical bureaucratic socialism of the Soviet Union. Cultural Revolution referred not just to transformation at the level of "high" culture, but more importantly the transformation of everyday culture. It also required the elimination of institutional factors (all the way from bureaucratism to an undue emphasis on expertise to "bourgeois right" in economic remuneration) that stood in the way of developing a more egalitarian and just society.

These policies were enumerated in one official document after another from the late 1950s to the 1960s.[11] Taken together, they added up to the promise of an alternative mode of development, alternative both to capitalism and to Soviet-style socialism. In the circumstances of the period they made eminent sense, and still do, especially if we look at what has happened to Chinese "socialism" under Mao's successors, which has confirmed the direst predictions of the period; from reversion to capitalism to new class formations to the emergence of a hedonistic consumer culture—except for one thing: China and Chinese in general have gotten richer, which everyone would seem to be enjoying tremendously.

To recall these policies at the present, however, is not to fall in line with the ideological claims of the Cultural Revolution, as many were wont to do earlier. Some of the problems of the Cultural Revolution were evident even when it was an object of uncritical admiration; idol worship, distempered language, wanton violence were all there to warn the observer that there was more (or, if you like, less) to the Cultural Revolution than revolutionary slogans. It was not that the evidence was not there, it was that at a time when revolution seemed to be the order of the day, the available evidence was easier to dismiss as silly, or marginal to the main business of revolution. Now that we have a much better grasp of what transpired at the ground level, it is possible and necessary to judge the intentions against the consequences.

"Delinking" from the capitalist world economy was never complete, and it was too short-lived to produce any significant results. If its goal was to create a well-rounded economy that answered the needs of the Chinese people rather than the distorting requisites of involvement in the world economy, too many other factors were involved—technical and political—to achieve that goal in such a short period. The policy was also intended to cow those in China who believed that economic and technological development required assistance from the outside; it may have been successful in this regard for a short period, but already by the 1970s the question was a moot one. If the idea that Chinese could go it alone inspired enthusiasm and technical creativity for a short period; the obverse side was to encourage chauvinism, xenophobia, and self-righteousness, that cut Chinese off from the world intellectually and culturally—not just the capitalist world, but also from new ways of thinking about Marxism and revolution. Most seriously, China never "delinked" from the capitalist world-system ideologically; developmentalist assumptions that had their origins in capitalism (and were evident throughout in aspirations to surpass capitalist countries in production) were an important factor, I will suggest below, in undermining the promise of an alternative kind of socialism.

The question of social relations (or relations of production) was to prove to be even more problematic. While insistence on the need to pay close attention to social relations was both theoretically and politically justifiable, the Cultural Revolution leadership never came up with any sophisticated analysis of the question of social relations under socialism in general, and China in particular. Throughout, there was a tendency to reduce all social relations to class relations, which are but one manifestation of social relations in general. To make matters worse, the leadership was unable to provide a convincing class analysis of Chinese society, that could serve as a guide to action, beyond clichés about socialist and capitalist roaders. The question of class was complicated in China by an interaction between prerevolutionary social and ideological relationships that persisted into the new regime, the new "caste" system of rankings imposed upon the population after 1949 in terms of their relationship to the revolution, and the structure of power created by the communist regime itself. Given this situation, it was not at all clear against whom class struggle was to be conducted. As Richard Kraus observed in his study of this problem, for lack of clarity on the question, the concept of class became the site of the struggle which it was supposed to guide. How this worked out in practice has been demonstrated in another excellent study of the Cultural Revolution, Hong Yung Lee's *The Politics of the Chinese Cultural Revolution*. Depending on the winds of change, class could be defined economically, politically, organizationally, or ideologically. At its worst, class was reduced to a biological category in the so-called "blood-line theory," that rendered class into a matter of lineage.[12] Rather than guide a coherent struggle, class, like other things during the Cultural Revolution, became a tool to justify contingent power struggles. Under the circumstances, efforts to establish new production relations in other areas, such as new management practices, were also confounded by lack of clarity about what constituted proper socialist behavior; and were immobilized by uncertainty about what might come next. Terms such as socialist and capitalist did not provide guidelines either, as they were reduced from concepts to handy labels, to be manipulated in power struggles even by those who had little idea as to what they meant.[13]

The question of property relations, in other words the problem of collectivization, also needs to be recalled with a critical eye. While the formation of collective production units in agriculture, and productive and living "units" (*danwei*) in urban areas from the late 1950s on was a necessary step toward socialism, under conditions of centralized power, they, too, played an ambiguous role. In his recent interesting study, *Policing and Punishment in China*, Michael Dutton observes sharply the coincidence of utopianism and social control in such units.[14] While this may be a problem of all community, the problem is obviously exacerbated when the community is under the supervision of a power outside of itself, which also raises questions about the claims during the Cultural Revolution to an alternative mode of development.

This is quite evident on the third aspect of the Cultural Revolution I enu-merated above: self-reliance, which was key to the political, economic, and cultural goals of the Cultural Revolution. While certainly appealing as an idea, especially in its insistence on giving priority to public over private in-terest, under conditions where the state reserved for itself the embodiment of the "public," and committed itself to a productionist ideology, "self-reliance" could also serve as a cover for exploiting the labor of the people. There is plentiful evidence of that also, even in work that is favorable to the Cultural Revolution. "Grasp revolution, promote production" was another common slogan of the Cultural Revolution, that implied the instrumentalization of rev-olution in the cause of production. The other side of the coin was minimizing consumption in the cause of public commitment. In either case, putting pub-lic interest ahead of private ones could easily be converted into sacrificing all individual and local interest in favor of a "public," which served as a euphe-mism for the state and the Party. The claim that the state of the people cannot exploit the people is not very convincing, based more on a "social imaginary" of the state than on actual relations between state and society.

Similar critiques may be offered with regard to problems of Cultural Rev-olution, and the idea of continuing the revolution: theoretically convincing, but quite problematic in actuality. Cultural Revolution, orchestrated from above, easily degenerated into cultural despotism. It silenced all alternative cultural activity in the realm of high culture. At the level of everyday life, the transformation of life habits was tied in so closely with Mao-worship that it converted the quest for self and social improvement into a zealous bigotry that bore all the marks of religious intolerance, that could justify the worst acts of cruelty against opponents. The shifts in policy at the top, confounding the zealousness that was prevalent initially, also bred cynicism, giving rise by the end of the Cultural Revolution to pervasive opportunism in the name of the revolution.

Finally, the question of continuing revolution, on which rests the claims of the Cultural Revolution to being a revolution. There was much about the Cul-tural Revolution that was indeed revolutionary in aspiration, but in light of what I have written above, its actualities must be qualified seriously. Did the Cultural Revolution, launched in the name of a struggle against capitalism and bureaucracy, have any serious vision of an alternative society; more specifically, a society without the Party, which would imply also a society without "the dictatorship of the proletariat?" In Karl Marx's vision of post-capitalist society, there were two competing models for progress to socialism: "the dictatorship of the proletariat model," and the Commune model, inspired by the Paris Commune of 1871. The Paris Commune might have provided a genuine alternative to "the dictatorship of the proletariat." But while there was discussion during the Cultural Revolution of the Commune, and the possibility of communal reorganization appeared in 1967, Mao himself was to back away from this alternative model, and reaffirm his commitment to "the dictatorship of the proletariat," which was to result over the ensuing decade in the restoration of Party rule, and the punishment of those who had dared to voice opposition to the Party. The memory of the Cultural Revolution as a revolution was tainted by the acts of its leadership before its opponents got around to questioning it.

William Hinton, the foremost chronicler of the Chinese Revolution, has written that "the Cultural Revolution that had seemed, from a distance, to be

> a watershed in history—a breakthrough that would enable people to shake up the superstructure of old China, all the inherited institutions and culture of an entrenched feudalism, and remold it into harmony with the new communal relations of production, a harmony that could propel production forward—now seemed to have degenerated into a most bizarre and Byzantine free-for-all, a no-holds-barred factional contest for power from top to bottom, where nothing mattered but getting the best of the opposition, and all means to that end seemed justified. If capitalism was an economic jungle, socialism, if that was what existed in China, looked like a political jungle.[15]

If the Cultural Revolution was based on questionable premises, betrayed its own goals, and visited untold suffering on the people, why bother to dwell on the intentions that underlay the Cultural Revolution, or the ambiguities arising from the discrepancy between intention and result, one might ask, which is indeed the prevailing attitude toward the Cultural Revolution.

The explanations engendered by this attitude are quite problematic themselves. The intentions that inspired the Cultural Revolution are a matter of historical record, and for a while at least inspired considerable enthusiasm; recalling them is a way not only to recover the historical record in China, but also a way to confront the lineage of our own contemporary historical explanations. Unless it can be demonstrated that the policies in and of themselves inevitably led to the opposite of what they were intended to accomplish, it is necessary to explain the conditions that led to the consequences. The Cultural Revolution as here conceived had a history, a history that was the product of the interaction between policy and circumstance, theory and practice, socialist goals and material conditions.

The question is not merely academic. Ignoring these intermediating factors, and discrediting the intentions by holding them directly responsible for the consequences, is a means to burying not just the Cultural Revolution, but also the revolutionary problematic that inspired it in the first place. Ironically, those intermediating factors which may have done much to distort the initial aspirations of the Cultural Revolution are still in place, while the aspirations are systematically "forgotten." Before I return to a consideration of those factors, a few words may be in order here concerning the problems presented by contemporary representations of the Cultural Revolution.

THE PAST IN THE PRESENT: OUR WAYS OF SEEING CHINA

As I noted above, contemporary interpretations of the Cultural Revolution do not differ significantly from the initial responses to it in 1966, except that they have been enriched by the testimonial of Chinese witnesses and victims. The latter contributes to our understanding in significant ways, but the representations based on them are not without serious problems.

Most devastating may be that literature, popular and influential, that depicts a society so bizarre and corrupt at all levels that it becomes meaningless even to speak of problems of revolution.[16] In the name of capturing Chinese realities at the everyday level, this literature offers lurid tales of sexual perversion and cannibalism that serve well to sell books to a voyeuristic reading public, but also dissolves serious political issues into Orientalist representations of a China immune to the ordinary (and normal) operations of politics. While in at least one case the veracity of such accounts has been challenged, also implicating scholars involved in the production of the account,[17] the problem with this literature in general is not veracity but its contribution to a discourse that renders irrelevant basic questions of historical explanation. If I may use an unkind analogy, to understand the Cultural Revolution (or Chinese politics) on the basis of such works is not very different than going to *People* magazine as a source for understanding American society and politics.

This literature, secondly, has confirmed a tendency, apparent since the mid-1980s, to use the depredations of the Cultural Revolution to discredit the Chinese Revolution as a whole. The first work that I am aware of to make this connection explicitly was Anne Thurston's *Enemies of the People*, which attributed pervasive vindictiveness in individual behavior during the Cultural Revolution to a century of ethical degeneration brought about by the revolution.[18] This work was not alone; the enthusiasm over Deng Xiaoping's policies before the Tiananmen Tragedy burst the bubble, was accompanied by a feeling among many, specialists and nonspecialists alike, that China had returned to a normal path after more than a century of revolutionary deviation of which Mao and the Cultural Revolution had been culminations.

While it is quite legitimate and necessary to point to the connections between the Cultural Revolution and the revolutionary process that had brought the Communist Party to power, there are two problems with the way in which this connection is approached, indeed with the whole problematic of the Chinese Revolution as it appears in these works. First, both the Cultural Revolution and the Chinese Revolution are treated as if they were sui generis products of the internal dynamics and characteristics of Chinese society without any reference to the global context of the revolution—and the problem of imperialism—which was of so much concern both to Chinese revolutionaries, and to an earlier generation of scholars. Secondly, while China scholars have long argued (misleadingly, in my view) that socialism in China was little more than a euphemism for a national search for "wealth and power," when it comes to the depredations of the Cultural Revolution, or its "roots" in the Chinese Revolution, this connection is forgotten, to lay the blame at the feet of socialism, rather than a socialism contaminated by nationalism (although, to be fair, there have been those to suggest that such depredations may be explained in terms of "nasty" strains within China's cultural legacy, which contrasts remarkably with the praise bestowed on Chinese culture, also a product of the 1980s, when it comes to explaining capitalist development in Taiwan or Singapore!).

While the attitudes above may be viewed as rehearsals of an earlier orientalism, that are effective in burying historical problems presented by the Cultural Revolution but too vague themselves in their culturalism to explain anything, more intriguing are explanations of the Cultural Revolution in terms of power relations, that address questions of immediate context. How the structure of power established after 1949 may have been complicit in both the origins and the consequences of the Cultural Revolution is a fundamental question. It ought to be distinguished, however, from those views that reduce the question of power to personal power; that view the Cultural Revolution and its policies merely as a cover for factional power struggles, or the efforts of a waning Mao Zedong to recover the power he had lost after the Great Leap Forward. Mao may have lost prestige after the Great Leap Forward, so that others were not as prepared as before to follow his bidding, but there is little evidence to prove that he lost the ability to coerce his opponents by force, if necessary (he did, after all, have Lin Biao and the military). This also raises the question of style, which has been an insistent question since the Cultural Revolution; in other words, if Mao was engaged in a Stalinist purge of his opponents, why did he not use Stalinist means to do so, but instead resorted to mass mobilization, which made considerable sense in terms of the legacy of the Chinese Revolution. Finally, and most importantly, there is the question of policy. Politics, all politics, is about power, to be sure; but except in the most unscrupulous cases, the search for power is connected with certain policy positions. In the Cultural Revolution, too, there were policy positions; if they are denied now (in China and abroad), that may have more to do with the denial of historical logic to the Cultural Revolution—to an assumption that under such bizarre conditions of Oriental politics, ordinary assumptions of politics do not apply. As the quotation above from Hinton suggests, those bizarre conditions may have been a product, rather than the premise of the Cultural Revolution; in other words, it is important once again to remember the historicity of the Cultural Revolution, that it assumed certain characteristics in its unfolding.

I will return to the question of power below. Before I do that, it is necessary here to confront one body of evidence against the Cultural Revolution that would seem to be irrefutable in its testimonial: the proliferating memory literature written by the victims of the Cultural Revolution. This body of literature, in what it has exposed of the workings of the Cultural Revolution at the ground level, would seem to leave no doubt that the policies of the Cultural Revolution were quite irrelevant to its workings, only providing a cover for petty struggles for power. While the emotive power of this literature is such that it seems obscene even to raise questions about it, we nevertheless need to make certain distinctions, and point to certain ambiguities with regard to this literature as well.

First, there is the question of whose memories? one would not expect memoirs written by victims to convey anything but the most devastatingly negative portrayals of the Cultural Revolution. But what about other kinds of memoirs? In a recent discussion of this literature, Mobo Gao notes that the occasional memoir that offers a less condemnatory account of the Cultural Revolution is not well received.[19] One could go further and suggest that there has been a suppression of memories of the Cultural Revolution which, while recognizing its undesirable outcome, insist on accentuating the positive in terms of policy. One recent example is Qin Huailu's *Ninth Heaven to Ninth Hell,* a story of the Dazhai Brigade (a model of self-reliance during the Cultural Revolution) and its leader, Chen Yonggui.[20] A hero of the Cultural Revolution, Chen Yonggui was discredited subsequently through a systematic campaign. Likewise the Dazhai Brigade, earlier a model of collective agriculture, was to come under attack as soon as policies were adopted for the privatization of agriculture. Qin's book, which seeks to clear the names of Dazhai and Chen Yonggui against their detractors, was not permitted publication in China, and was smuggled out of the country for its English publication.[21] The case of Dazhai may be unusual (after all, it was the supreme agricultural model), but the case is an instance of the politics of memory in China and, therefore, abroad. Peasants, at least some peasants, remember Mao and the Cultural Revolution (though not Lin Biao, the "gang of four," etc.) differently than in the memoirs that have recently dominated our consciousness. Peasants in the Chinese countryside have converted Mao into a Buddha-figure, and erected temples to him.[22] This is not to say that we should ignore the wrongs described by the victims of the Cultural Revolution, but simply to note that historical assessment must come to terms with other kinds of memories as well. Even memories of intellectual victims of the Cultural Revolution are not free of ambiguities. Again I will take a recent example, Ma Bo's *Blood Red Sunset*.[23] This account of a young intellectual (son of the famous writer, Yang Mo) rusticated in Inner Mongolia is a devastating account of the arbitrary and corrupt power of Party cadres who could inflict harm on others with impunity, all the time mouthing the slogans of the Cultural Revolution. Ma Bo was victimized by such cadres, and condemned for years to a horrendous life. At the same time, this is an unusually frank account, which lets the reader know that, whether or not he deserved the fate he got, the author of the memoirs was capable himself of vile and corrupt behavior. His horrendous experience of punishment nevertheless leads to a personal transformation; so that the Ma Bo at the end of the account is a much more sympathetic person than the Ma Bo at the beginning, who starts his revolutionary activities in Inner Mongolia by attempted murder of a "capitalist-roader" Mongolian herdsman, and the actual murder of his dog. The reader of the account may draw his or her conclusions on how to respond ethically to a story such as this one; I will only note here that the account both proves the premises of the Cultural Revolution (class differences, urban-rural differences, hostilities between Party and intellectuals, the corruption of the cadres), and the manner in which the Cultural Revolution itself was to become a source of intellectual, moral, and material corruption.[24]

Mobo Gao writes that "when a memoir is written at a time when the prevalent framework of discourse is different from that of the time when the memoir is written about, events and even feelings can be restructured without the writer's knowledge. It is true that personal suffering and violent brutality did occur during the Cultural Revolution. But explanations of why they occurred and how people felt about them can be restructured."[25] Much the same could be said of most writing on the Cultural Revolution in our day. One way of overcoming this problem, which is a general problem of history, is to judge the Cultural Revolution against its own claims, which also requires that we give credulity to the claims themselves, rather than rendering them into verbal masks for something else. It is to this question that I return.

BACK TO AMBIGUITY: WHERE DID THE CULTURAL REVOLUTION GO WRONG?

The consequences of the Cultural Revolution were inevitable, I will suggest, but the inevitability was historical, rather than being implicit in the policies promoted. It is simply that given the ideological dispositions of the regime, and the material structure of power it had put in place after 1949, those policies could not be realized, and were likely to lead to the consequences they did. Mao's tragedy was that given the conflicting roles he assumed, he was bound almost of necessity to betray the revolution that he launched.

I suggested above that ideology (both in a narrow political sense and in the broadest sense that Karl Mannheim assigned to it, as life-outlook, or *weltanschauung*), the legacy of Orientalism, and even market forces contribute to the making of contemporary representations of the Cultural Revolution. Even where there is agreement on the "factuality" of facts, which is not always the case, what significance we assign to competing facts, and how we contextualize them, remains problematic; and so do our evaluations.[26] I acknowledge readily that my own comments on the Cultural Revolution, including the insistence on ambivalence, is infused with ideological assumptions in both of the senses above. If I place a positive evaluation on the policies that informed the Cultural Revolution, it is because I think they had something important to say about socialism as it existed; about the necessity of socialism both as a critique of capitalism and a source of alternative conceptualizations of human development I have few questions. These same assumptions infuse my critical comments about the Cultural Revolution: about its developmentalist ideology and its reductionist assumptions about social relations, socialism and capitalism; about its exploitation of the notion of "self-reliance"; about its chauvinistic nationalism; about its conceptions of Cultural Revolution and revolution. Some of these criticisms are informed by my own objections to nationalism or the fetishism of development, which are quite contrary to the assumptions and aspirations of many under capitalism or socialism as we have known it, in the First World or the Third World; they may indeed be most objectionable to those in the Third World, living under conditions of poverty, who see in national striving the way out of such poverty. Likewise with my statements about self-reliance or culture, which may seem the most irrelevant to the majority peasant population in a country like China, who have to work hard no matter what, and may not feel terribly deprived by not having access to other cultures (although they may feel different presently, now that television and Hollywood have entered the everyday lives of Chinese peasants as well!).

With this in mind, let me offer a few considerations that I think are fundamental to the evaluation of the Cultural Revolution. First, the Cultural Revolution was doomed to failure because the policies that motivated it, if they were to be workable, required a different social and political context than the structure of power that had been put in place after 1949. The most important of these policies were legacies of the Chinese Revolution. The assumption that these revolutionary policies could be kept alive under a postrevolutionary regime that had ensconced itself in power seems in hindsight somewhat anachronistic. If they were to be instituted, the post-1949 regime would have had to be transformed, which was not the intention of the Cultural Revolution and maybe was inconceivable given both the national and the international context. The Cultural Revolution has been attributed, among other things, to Mao's utopianism. It is possible to suggest from this perspective that Mao was insufficiently utopian, for he was unable or unwilling, because of his own ideological assumptions, to think beyond the "dictatorship of the proletariat" or the developmentalist nation-state. As a consequence, rather than challenge the existing structure of power as the Cultural revolutionaries professed, Maoist policies ended up as instruments in a competition for the conquest of power within the existing structure; a competition that the Cultural Revolution did much to unleash.

Secondly, the power structure itself has, of course, been the intractable problem of all socialist regimes: a new power structure is necessary to the transformation of social relations, but how to render power subservient once again to the new social relations without opening the way to the resurgence of older social relations? The contradiction goes even deeper: with the overthrow of existing social relations, what is put in place are not new social relations, but organized power; is it possible to return from a politics of organization to politics as the expression of social relations without jeopardizing the future of the revolution?

The power structure that was put in place after 1949 represented the invasion by the Communist Party not only of political, but social, space as well; indeed, the distinction was abolished as society was reorganized according to a social imaginary that was an expression of the Party's own power. Party omnipotence can be exaggerated; the new centralized, hierarchical bureaucracy that infiltrated society was subject like all bureaucracies to routinization, and the slackening that attends it; the bureaucracy itself was not immune to infiltration and influence from below (expressed in continuing concern with localism). Still, it is difficult to ignore that, if we take into account the Party and its subsidiary organizations, one in every ten Chinese (of all ages and genders) belonged to at least one organization. Furthermore, the designation of class ranks imposed upon society as a whole the Party's political conceptualization of society, creating something akin to a caste system. If in ordinary times, bureaucratic slackening and/or moderate policies could leave some social space outside of organized control, the Party could always strike back, as it held in its hands the instruments of control and coercion; frequent mobilizations beginning shortly after 1949, whatever their other intentions, also served this purpose.

Even without the explicit or direct use of coercion, the power of the Party was anchored in an ideology that made the Party into a frame of reference in all activity. Three consequences of this power structure may be noteworthy: (a) It abolished all "public" space outside of the Party. Especially important with reference to Cultural Revolution policies was the abolition of local autonomy. The stress on the local remained throughout, and local initiative was recognized in terms of economic development, but, as Christine Wong writes of the rural industrialization program, "it was a program initiated from the top, which determined the scope and objectives of rural industrialization. The conflicting aims of local participation and central control interacted to produce a situation in which control often became divorced from responsibility, with unforeseen but extremely undesirable outcomes."[27] William Hinton spells out the political consequences of the abolition of the local:

> Hemmed in by institutional feudalism at the top of the hierarchy, Mao failed to give effective support to the popular institutions of self-government sprouting at the base, the place where democracy, however limited, had the most chance of success . . . higher bodies routinely usurped the sovereign power that should have resided in elected village congresses or revolutionary committees. . . . Nobody—not even Mao, apparently—was willing to trust villagers with substantive local power, and this made it all but impossible short of major, centrally led mass movements of the sort initiated from the Party center—for people on the land to challenge the bureaucracy at all. Once the movements ebbed, traditional rule always reasserted itself.[28]

(b) A by-product of the continued invasion of the local from the top was to impose a bureaucratic uniformity on rural China, which led to the abolition in policy of differences among localities, which recognition had been a strength of the Communist Party in revolutionary years, and continued to receive emphasis in formal policy statements. Such a recognition would have done much to alleviate both the political and the economic despotism of the new structure of power. (c) One final consequence of the new structure of power worth emphasizing was its effect on individual personality and behavior. The structure created an urge to satisfy the power structure so as to be able to join it which, rather than nourish a cooperative culture, led to behavior that oscillated between slavish compliance and aggressiveness, and religious faith and cynicism, encouraging an almost irrational degree of competitiveness under the guise of public commitment.[29] The political structure, in other words, bred "nastiness."

Third is the question of the challenge to this structure in the name of Maoism. Given the problems of this structure, and the obstacles it presented to socialism in any meaningful sense, the challenge was understandable, but what was the nature of the challenge itself? We know that this power structure, with all the tensions and resentments it contained, was the initial context for the Cultural Revolution. We also know that when this same power structure was threatened in the heat of the Cultural Revolution, Mao himself was to lead a quick return to its restoration. What was the challenge about then? For all the documentation we have of rapid changes during the Cultural Revolution, and the succession of power takeovers and the declaration of new organizational forms, for lack of any serious theoretical elaboration or articulated vision, it is difficult to say what the challenge amounted to. All we know is that against the Liu Shaoqi/Deng Xiaoping line of the early 1960s, which assigned to the Party a supervisory-managerial role while opening up some social spaces outside of the Party's daily intervention, Maoism proposed a more fundamentalist and thorough integration of politics and society, integration both from the top and the bottom, that presupposed greater participation in politics from the bottom, but also opened up the possibility of a more thorough political infiltration of social space. Is it possible to suggest that if Maoism was utopian, it was a utopianism directed not against the existing power structure, but a utopianization of that very structure; an experiment designed perhaps to fulfill the premises of that structure? There is some reason to think so since, when during the Cultural Revolution occasions arose of genuine challenge to the existing structure of power by the socially disaffected (including disaffected workers) as during the January revolution in Shanghai in 1967, or the anarchistic *shengwulian* protests against the Party later the same year, these alternatives were quickly rejected; there was, in other words, no apparent plan to transform the political organization in accordance with social demands. Political mobilization served under the circumstances to complete the unfinished task of Party-state-society integration which disorganized the political organization but also, under the circumstances of power hierarchy and inequality, resulted inevitably in the abolition of all private social space, the terrorism of power, and the surfacing of divisions and resentment that had been barely contained so long as the political organization had retained some coherence. Frequent power takeovers by competing factions, and the declarations of a new revolutionary forms of government that accompanied them, in practice added up to little than occasions for factional revenge on opponents. It is noteworthy that these power takeovers, while they claimed local initiative, in actuality followed directives from the center. Putting "politics in command" may have inspired public commitment, individual initiative and creativity; but in the end, rather than bring about the organic unity it was intended to achieve, it led to its opposite, exaggerating divisions. The politicization of everyday life "automatically raised every incident to a level of higher principle like 'class struggle.'"[30] As William Hinton writes of such "higher principles,"

> the most damaging excesses had their roots in Mao's constant reiteration of such slogans as "Never forget class struggle" and "Grasp class struggle, and all problems can be solved." While these calls laid bare the essence of the overall situation and defined the principal contradiction besetting society at each stage of development, they did little to illuminate most of the problems that came up from day to day. Cadres who treated all contradictions as class conflicts raised them artificially to absurd levels of antagonism, created "class enemies" where none existed, and ended up fighting battles that they never should have fought.[31]

Mao was only part of the problem. To use a distinction that the historian Harry Harootunian has employed with regard to the role of the Japanese emperor in politics, it is useful I think to distinguish Mao as a principal of politics from Mao as a principle of politics. Mao, of course, did serve as a political agent, playing a role in the initiation of the Cultural Revolution, as well as intervening personally at crucial points. But more important may be the part that Mao played as a principle of politics. To most Chinese Mao was either a remote figure, an object of adulation, or a body of texts, most notably, the Little Red Book, of little importance as a theoretical text, but most significant as an inspirational one. As a principle of politics, Mao was open to interpretation, and many of the conflicts of the Cultural Revolution may be viewed also as conflicts over the interpretation of Mao. In this sense, while Maoism was offered in the Cultural Revolution as a challenge (and an alternative to the existing structure of power), in reality it was open to interpretation and appropriation by all sides, including the power structure that it purportedly challenged—which was possible because, while the texts invited "revolution," the revolution was premised on the preservation of the existing power structure. This is not to absolve Mao of responsibility, for in the end he turned to the support of that power structure when it was challenged. It does enable an explanation of the conflict conducted in the name of Mao Zedong. The reception of Mao, and the different uses to which Maoism was put during the Cultural Revolution, indicates the existence of deep social divisions and resentments which the Cultural Revolution did much to bring to the surface. Rather than resolve those divisions, the Cultural Revolution may have exacerbated them. In the end, it was to be a casualty itself of those divisions.

The fourth problem is an ideological one; what I will describe as "developmentalism." Developmentalism was not a peculiarity of Mao and the Cultural Revolution; it has its roots in a Marxism that accepted the premises of capitalism concerning human need, was perpetuated in the Soviet Union under Lenin and Stalin, and continues today in China under the post-Mao regime. It needs to be specified as a problem in connection with the Cultural Revolution because, I think, that it distorted policies of "self-reliance," greater popular initiative in development, balanced development, and even cultural policies. My premise here is that those policies could have led to positive outcomes only under conditions of local autonomy and decision making, which would have enabled a primary emphasis on the local community, and the needs of the people as they perceived and defined them, and shifted emphasis to a negotiation of difference and inequality rather than their exaggeration—which was to undermine all sense of community. Culturally speaking, developmentalism, which is wedded to the idea of an inexorable move away from the past, rules out the possibility of drawing on the past as well as the present in defining the future.

The question here is not whether or not all development is undesirable, but rather the criteria for development. While the Cultural Revolution placed much verbal emphasis on the people, and Maoist economic policy was not without real benefits for the people as Hinton, Bramall, Wong, and others have argued, the developmentalism that I am referring to here had its sources on the one hand in a productionist interpretation of Marxism, and on the other hand in considerations of national wealth and power. This may not be a problem for the kind of "socialism" that has been pursued under Deng Xiaoping, but it does present a problem in light of the premise of Maoism that attention to relations of production should have priority over the forces of production in the creation of socialism. What exactly those relations of production should be was never spelled out clearly, but if local community and initiative were to be essential components of such new relations of production, as the Maoists intimated, subjecting the local community to central directives rather than guaranteeing it some kind of autonomy was not the best way to achieve that goal.

Finally, a problem that is often ignored in our day, even though it was central to earlier evaluations of the Cultural Revolution: the problem of nationalism in relation to the global environment. As I have intimated already, considerations of national wealth and power did not disappear in the Cultural Revolutionary preoccupation with rejuvenating the revolution for socialism but, if anything, assumed a more exaggerated chauvinistic form. The Cultural Revolution, however, was launched at a time of genuine crisis in China's relationship to both the United States and the Soviet Union. Now that China has been incorporated into a capitalist world system (although still not without friction), it is easy to "forget" that it was not Maoist paranoia but real and declared threats to China from both powers that played an important part in this crisis. The war mentality that this situation created was quite apparent during the Cultural Revolution in everything from economic policy to the language of politics.[32] Given the revolutionary tradition of the Communist Party, in which the language of politics had never been clearly distinguishable from the language of war, this may not seem very peculiar; but the sense of crisis created by the military threat from abroad certainly played a part in reinforcing the militarization of politics, and the chauvinistic turn in Chinese nationalism. We may never know exactly what part these factors played in the initiation and the course of the Cultural Revolution, but it may be said with some confidence that they need to be factored into any consideration of how the goals of socialism were distorted by the sense of crisis that they expressed.

With an event as momentous as the Cultural Revolution, which touched the lives of all in China, and destroyed many, it is easy to confound historical explanation with the justification for the movement. On the other hand, it is necessary also to consider the consequences of not making some effort at explanation. It is difficult to write about the Cultural Revolution because it was a traumatic event. It is also difficult not to write about it because it had a great deal to say, in both its promises and its betrayals, about the world in which we live. Distancing it to an alien time and space is not the best way to hear the messages it conveyed as one of the most important events of the twentieth century.

How does the historian confront historical trauma, and still retain the will to historicize? The question forces a reminder that history ought not to be a positivistic undertaking that objectifies the past, but at best a dialogue between the historian and those who lived the past, between the historian's construction of the past, and the way that the past was or is constructed by those who lived it. If the historian has one obligation, it is to engage in a dialogue with as many memories as possible. What is inexcusable is to privilege some memories over others and, at worst, to render individual memories and experiences into a substitute for historical understanding.

In the case of events such as the Cultural Revolution or World War II, it is presently almost impossible to undertake this task of comprehensive dialogue because some memories are silent, while others are so traumatic as to make speech impossible. But there is another, more abstract, problem as well. The changes of the last decade have been so fundamental that the world of the Cultural Revolution seems to be a world quite distant in time from ours, which operated according to different rules than our world; so that the memories of individuals who lived through that world seem to be the only thing that connects them. With socialism seemingly a thing of the past, who cares about the Cultural Revolution challenge to socialism? With China a playground for capitalism, and former Red Guards turned into entrepreneurs in global capitalism, what meaning could "delinking" and "self-reliance" have? With peasants becoming millionaires, even if they are once again the object of scorn among intellectuals, why recall the ideals of collectivization? With national boundaries increasingly in question, what might have been the point about the Chinese Revolution—or imperialism?

All these questions are in the air, even if they do not appear often as points of entry into discussions of the Cultural Revolution or the Chinese Revolution, for that matter. As all the questions sought earlier to make sense of the Chinese or other revolutions fade into the past, all that remains in historical memory is the suffering of those who lived through those events; a suffering that seems all the more pointless because the events that caused the suffering have been deprived of meaning. Those events may be relegated safely to an oriental temporality and spatiality, denying their connections not just to our present, but to their presents as well. In a historical perspective that takes them seriously as events in the history of modernity, however, the same events appear otherwise: as the constituents of a final effort—the most impressive of all such efforts—to create an alternative Third World modernity based on socialism.

In the temporal and spatial distancing of the Cultural Revolution lies a danger, I think, because this same distancing, in denying the modernity of the Cultural Revolution, suppresses the problems of modernity as well, which are still part of our present. In his discussion of the Holocaust, Zygmunt Bauman has argued that far from being a throwback to the past, the circumstances that led to the Holocaust were very much a part of the history of modernity.[33] Those who would speak of the Cultural Revolution as a holocaust might keep his reminder in mind. If the Cultural Revolution was indeed an event comparable to the Holocaust, the question of modernity was very much complicit in its outcome; the Chinese Revolution itself was very much an assertion of Chinese modernity, and the Cultural Revolution was a phase of that process. In the discussion above, I have sought to bring out this aspect of the Cultural Revolution: how modernizationism economically, socially, politically, and culturally was very much on the agenda of the Cultural Revolution, and distorted the aspiration to create an alternative modernity to produce the outcome it did.

There is widespread agreement on the outcome; after all, even Mao Zedong was in the end ambivalent about what he had set in motion. But the quest for an alternative modernity has not therefore ceased, because the problems of modernity which were part of the Cultural Revolution have not gone away in spite of brave declarations of "the end of history" that would have us wallow in the ravages of a capitalist modernity. And in this quest, the name of Mao Zedong keeps coming up one way or another, and so do the aspirations that inspired the Cultural Revolution. After being propelled with full force into global capitalism and consumerism in 1992, Chinese of all walks of life were

suddenly gripped by a "Mao fever" in 1993 which, however distant in its consumerism from the political days of the Cultural Revolution, points at the
least to the persistence of nostalgic memories that are not entirely innocent of
political dissatisfactions with the present. The topography of the Chinese
economy, at least partially responsible for the economic success of the last
decade, bears upon it the imprint of Maoist policies of integrating industry
and agriculture in a program of rural industrialization. Some analysts have
observed also that earlier collectivization experiences have enabled the rural
population in some areas to create new forms of cooperation on their own.[34]
Wherever these experiences may lead in the end, they are indications that earlier aspirations to an alternative modernity have not been extinguished, and
they have ties to historical memories of the Chinese Revolution of a kind different than those that capture the headlines.

GLOBALISM, HISTORY, AND MEMORY

The Cultural Revolution in its consequences has done its share to discredit
revolutions. I would like to suggest here, however, that in order to comprehend their political ramifications, contemporary representations of the Cultural Revolution need to be viewed within the context of a general repudiation of revolutions. While Maoism was once perceived as an alternative to
Stalinism, this distinction seems to have lost its significance presently when
Maoism is portrayed as another version of Stalinism, or Mao and Stalin are
held forth as examples of tyranny along with the likes of Hitler.[35] It is not only
socialist revolutions that are at issue. Critics of the Chinese Revolution draw
freely for inspiration on the work of Francois Furet. The criticism of the
French Revolution has been quite significant in shaping contemporary attitudes toward revolution; unlike socialist revolutions which all along have
been viewed with suspicion within the context of capitalist societies, criticism
of the French Revolution is far more profound in its consequences as it calls
into question one of the founding moments of modernity, thereby calling into
question all revolutions regardless of political orientation, and the aspirations
and visions that endowed revolutionary change with meaning.[36]
    Condemnation of revolution is as old as the history of revolutions. Present-
day critics of the French Revolution such as Furet recall in their criticism contemporaries of the Revolution such as Alexis de Tocqueville.[37] Those who
have suffered from revolutions, had their interests or ways of life threatened
by them, or simply perceived in revolutions the breakdown of everyday human norms obviously have no reason to look upon revolutions with a friendly
eye. While it may be possible historically to point to revolutionary traditions

marked by the various revolutions of the last two centuries, it is necessary also to remember that rather than follow a triumphal trajectory from one revolution to the next one, revolution as an idea has suffered many ups and downs in its appeal and prestige.[38] There have been all along severe critics who could perceive in revolutions little more than sources of terror and totalitarianism. To pick a few especially memorable twentieth-century examples at random, one thinks readily of Pitirim Sorokin who, in his 1942 work *Man and Society in Calamity,* included revolutions among calamities such as war, pestilence, and famine; of Hannah Arendt who in her powerful *Origins of Totalitarianism* equated the experience of socialist revolutions with the devastation under Nazism; and in the case of the Chinese Revolution, of works dating back to the 1950s, such as Karl Wittfogel's *Oriental Despotism* or Robert J. Lifton's *Thought Reform* and the *Psychology of Totalism.* These scholarly condemnations of revolution may pale in the significance of their impact when placed alongside works of fiction or semifiction by George Orwell, Arthur Koestler, Eugene Zamiatin, etc., or, in the case of China, the popular blockbuster by Richard Condon, *The Manchurian Candidate* and the movie based on it. There is little in contemporary condemnations of revolution that could surpass the powerful antirevolutionary message conveyed by these works.

What is most remarkable in our day, however, is the broad consensus over revolutions that could not be sustained even in the hottest days of the Cold War, when revolutions for all their flaws seemed to be going concerns, and could be called upon in critiques of capitalist society. The present consensus is made possible above all by the evidence of those who experienced revolutions first hand, and revolutionary leaderships that have renounced their pasts. At a time when history and memory diverge and conflict in so many ways, in the case of revolutions they would seem to confirm one another—which suggests, in the case of a recent event such as the Cultural Revolution, that there is also a great deal of forgetting at work, because only as late as two decades ago there was no shortage of memory or history to give an entirely different account of the event against its critics. Conversely, the repudiation of revolution has brought forth alternative memories. Memories of victimization and corruption which I discussed above have been supplemented in recent years by more triumphalist memories of survival, usually in the form of family narratives, and opposition.[39] When he wrote memorably in *The Unbearable Lightness of Being* that "the struggle against power is the struggle of memory against forgetting," Milan Kundera probably did not anticipate that his statement foreshadowed a surge of memory against Communist regimes from Eastern Europe to China, that became part of the process of overthrowing and, in the case of China, transforming those regimes.[40]

The reversal in memory and forgetting is interesting, and may be revealing. Where under the Communist regimes memories were of survival and opposition in "the old society," now it is the revolution that had to be survived, and "the old society" has reappeared in a completely different, favorable, light. The reversal in China began in the late 1970s with the retreat from revolution and the gradual incorporation into capitalism, which almost overnight turned former revolutionaries into conservatives, and former "capitalist-roaders" into reformers. With antirevolutionary memory surging, history has not been far behind—especially history that seeks to authenticate itself through contact with the bearers of memory.[41] There is a tendency to deprive revolution of its social legitimation; its claim, in other words, that it was a product of social forces, and gave voice to the aspirations of the oppressed in society. Revolution appears now as a political act that may even have gone against deepest social aspirations.[42] Alienation from revolution has also allowed a positive evaluation of the prerevolutionary period. As revolution is rendered into an enemy of economic and political progress, the former targets of revolution (and not just the Communist Revolution) are restored into history as the bearers of progress whose promise was extinguished by revolution—not just the modern bourgeoisie, but even the gentry and landlords of the late Qing.[43] One beneficiary of this revision of prerevolutionary history is the idea of "civil society," which purportedly was in the process of formation when the victory of communism put an end to it. Here, needless to say, history has moved beyond memory because what is at issue is no longer just what revolutions did to people, or what they failed to accomplish, but the validity of the discourses that justified and guided revolutions.

It may be instructive to take a brief detour here to place the interplay of memory and history of revolutions within the broader problematic of memory and history that has become quite prominent over the last decade or so. The concern with memory and history would appear to have different sources in different contexts—the Holocaust in Germany, the Armenian massacres in Turkey for the Armenian population in the United States, the two hundredth anniversary of the Revolution in France, World War II in the United States, Japan, and China, etc.[44] It also appears prominently in the efforts of populations, suppressed by hegemonic histories, to recover their histories through memory, as in the case, for example, of indigenous peoples. In all cases, recovering lost or suppressed identities would seem to be an important concern. So is, however, settling accounts with the past. It may be an irony of our times that there is a proliferation of memory when forgetting is increasingly a condition of existence; it is as if the past must be remembered so as to complete the break with it.

The proliferation of memory, and its enhanced status—especially through its use in media like television—implies that memory may no longer be viewed merely as "the raw material of history."[45] Viewed with suspicion by scholars since the publication of Maurice Halbwachs' classic, *The Collective Memory*, which underlined the constructedness and partialness of memory, memory has emerged as a competitor with history in opposition to the latter.[46] Memory may be both a beneficiary of loss of faith in abstract, hegemonic history, and an element in its dissolution. Individual memories all along have been part of the materials out of which we have constructed history; the contradiction between history and memory may accordingly be viewed as part of a contradiction between history, and the materials out of which we construct history. But with an increasingly pervasive feeling that history itself is little more than a construction that has served purposes of social and political hegemony, it has become increasingly difficult to sustain history's claims against memory—or, for that matter, literature. Evidence of historians "forgetting" does not help much to instill confidence in history.

Pierre Nora writes that "the loss of a single explanatory principle, while casting us into a fragmented universe, has promoted every object—even the most humble, the most improbable, the most inaccessible—to the dignity of historical mystery. Since no one knows what the past will be made of next, anxiety turns everything into a trace, a possible indication, a hint of history that contaminates the innocence of all things."[47] On the other hand, the decline of the hegemony of the past has allowed for a proliferation of memory that talks back; not just recent memory, where it is most visible, but even distant forgotten memories that have returned to challenge history. The result is a multiplication of "private memories demanding their individual histories."[48] If history often has forgotten or suppressed memories not suitable to its purposes, memory often appears as if it is immune to the history or histories that constitute it. Ironically, the confrontation of memory and history seems also to promise abolishing the difference between the two. We may view the proliferation of memory as an indication of the impossibility of history. We may also view it as the proliferation of histories; many histories that do not cohere, and have no hope of doing so, which may be the price to be paid for "the democratization of social memory."[49]

The proliferation of memory, or the fragmentation of history, has obvious political consequences. In Charles Maier's eloquent words, "the surfeit of memory is a sign not of historical confidence but of a retreat from transformative politics. It testifies to the loss of a future orientation, of progress toward civic enfranchisement and growing equality. It reflects a new focus on narrow ethnicity as a replacement for encompassing communities based on constitutions, legislation and widening attributes of citizenship."[50] The political consequences may be even more significant for revolutions, whether nationalist or socialist, that drew upon history for their justification and legitimation. While the fragmentation of history may be tied in with the eth-nicization of politics that Maier speaks of, it also has a depoliticizing effect. As we find it increasingly difficult to speak of Right or Left in politics, it be-comes impossible also to distinguish one kind of revolution from another, or even revolution from reaction. "Terror" or "genocide" take over as the com-mon element that marks all revolutions.[51]

To leave the matter here, however, is to leave unquestioned the power con-text for memory/history. The proliferation of memory may express a democ-ratization of history, among other things, but it is also quite obvious that not all memory receives equal treatment, or even finds a voice. While it may be possible these days to whitewash Nazism or Japanese atrocities in East Asia, it is not possible to find many to speak for revolutions, or get heard when they speak. I have given examples in the discussion above. Let me just add here that there are Chinese intellectuals who would reexamine and reevaluate the Cultural Revolution, who hardly get a hearing partly because of political re-strictions but also because the very idea immediately invites condensation; I myself have been made into an "Orientalist" recently for speaking favorably of some legacies of the Cultural Revolution. For those new "democratic" Chi-nese intellectuals nothing will do but total censorship of discussion. On the other hand, peasants in the countryside who seek to erect temples to the Mao they have deified are suppressed by the government, and if they find their way into discussion of contemporary politics and culture, they do so as curi-ous throwbacks to a past best forgotten. Indeed, this seems to be the judgment these days on all who would speak favorably of revolutions: voices from the past obsessed with past problems; in the words of two labor activists, "over-coming alienation, exploitation, subordination—this is stuff of times past."[52]

A historian of Germany, Wolfgang Benz, has written in another context that, "historians . . . enjoy especial success whenever the results of their re-search and their interpretations are in harmony with the longings, dreams and yearning for deliverance of the rulers and society of their times."[53] That the reconfiguration of memory is somehow bound up with the victory of the po-litical right globally seems obvious. As I noted above, while the silencing of revolutionary memories may be a characteristic of our times, there is little that is new in the representation of revolutions, which is reminiscent above all not of liberal criticism of revolutions, marked by some ambivalence, but of conservative criticisms. The former, even where they did not approve of revolutions, still recognized some merit to them, or at least viewed them in terms of social and political necessity; be it social oppression and exploita-tion, imperialism, or the pressures of modernity.[54] Conservative condemna-tion, however, has seen in revolutions nothing but perversions of humanity and politics by unscrupulous ideologues. The goal of conservative criticism, moreover, has been not only to condemn revolutions for their misdeeds, but to erase the political discourse of revolution. These are also the characteristics of contemporary condemnation of revolutions. Yet it is remarkable that such condemnation can assume an academic garb in portraying political questions as empirical ones, and get away with it. Few eyebrows seem to be raised over Francois Furet's frank acknowledgment of his politics in his interpretations of the French Revolution.[55] Since political considerations, *and* ideology, have been removed from history, the lifting off of revolutions from their social and political context does not seem to raise too many questions either. A case in point is the recent preoccupation in Chinese historiography with the question of civil society. Whatever the merits of civil society as a political goal, its introduction into the historiography of prerevolutionary China obviously has something to do with postsocialist developments in Chinese society, as well as a conservative reaffirmation of the virtues of classes that were in the past viewed as obstacles to China's development (not just by historians, but by generations of radical intellectuals). But these political questions do not seem to attract much attention. Neither does the historically quite significant question that the revolution, rather than extinguish a burgeoning civil society (if that is what it was), was a product of the incapacity of civil society to enfranchise large social groups produced by a Chinese modernity.

To describe the recent reorientation of memory and history as part of a turn to the Right may be accurate, but it is not sufficient in my view to explain the changes that seem to be at work, and itself needs explanation. While the preoccupation with memory would seem to have different sources in different contexts, the temporal coincidence is nevertheless intriguing. There may be a clue to it in Nora's reference to a connection between memory proliferation (or, as Maier puts it, "memory industry") and a "regime of discontinuity." There is good evidence to support the claim of many social scientists that we are in the midst of a break with the past; whether we conceive of it in terms of globalism versus modernity, postmodernism versus modernism, postcolonialism versus colonialism, or even postsocialism versus socialism. That the world is still structured by capitalism, perhaps to an unprecedented degree, does not negate the momentousness of the changes that have affected everything from economic and political structures, to the structures of everyday life to the most basic cultural and ethical values. The kinds of collective resistance associated with revolutions no longer seem relevant under the circumstances. Even the social fractures that informed and dynamited revolutions are in the process of transformation, as class, gender, and community identities are overwhelmed by a search for primordial identities lodged above all in ethnicity and race. As Manuel Castells has put it recently, "in a world of global flows of wealth, power and images, the search for identity, collective or individual, ascribed or constructed, becomes the fundamental source of social meaning. This is not a new trend, since identity, and particularly religious and ethnic identity, have been at the roots of meaning since the dawn of human society. Yet identity is becoming the main, and sometimes the only, source of meaning in a historical period characterized by widespread destructuring of organizations, delegitimation of institutions, fading away of major social movements, and ephemeral cultural expressions. People increasingly organize their meaning not around what they do but on the basis of what they are, or believe they are."[56] On the other hand, the transformations of the present have given rise to new problems that require new kinds of solutions.

I suggested above that there might be a contradiction presently between the proliferation of memory at the same time as forgetting has become a condition of existence, which may not be too much of a contradiction as remembering and forgetting may be but parts of the same process. Is forgetting anything but remembering differently? And what is its relationship to power? Certainly Germany and Japan, now that times have changed and with it their places in the world, seek to be remembered for other reasons than their Nazi or Fascist pasts. On the other hand, how else to remember failed revolutionary regimes but for their misdeeds, as both the structural conditions that produced them and the discourses that informed them are dissolved by the reconfiguration of the world? There is also an ethical question of the utmost importance: the question of divisiveness. While social division, too, may be a fact of life, who would want to further contribute to it by constantly drawing attention to it? Standing on the threshold of a new world that seems to be in the making, it seems both more plausible and ethically correct to reconcile, rather than to divide.

What we have witnessed over the last two decades is not the victory of the Right, but the disappearance of the Left. Along with that, we have lost the ability, I think, to imagine an outside to capitalism, and alternatives to it. It is in this context that we need to ask what it means to forget revolutions. While the conditions of life have changed, they have transformed rather than abolished the problems that in the past revolutions set out to resolve. Of Sorokin's four calamities, only revolutions seem to have disappeared, for war, famine, and pestilence are still with us. Social divisions, rather than disappear, proliferate and deepen. If we recall what revolutions stood for, it is not to bring back revolutions as they were, but to recall the possibilities of alternatives to the present.

I think that revolutions in history need to be decentered so that we may perceive the past in new ways that may also suggest options for the present. The preoccupation in our day is to erase revolutions so as to bring forth histories that justify the present; whether we call it development or civil society. A radical decentering of revolutions, however, cannot dispense with the critique of the present. From that perspective, one of the more revealing aspects of current denunciations of revolution is their obliviousness to the way in which the revolutions of modernity, having internalized the ideologies of modernity, foreclosed alternatives to modernity, or suppressed alternative visions of modernity that challenged assumptions of economic developmentalism and parochial nationalism. Interestingly, these alternatives, too, have resurfaced with the waning of revolutions, and enable critical perspectives not just on the past, but the present as well. It is important for any radical project to understand these alternatives in their relationship to the revolutions of the past—both the ways in which they continue the revolutionary tradition, and the ways in which they break with the past. The revolutions of modernity have failed to achieve the goal of liberation they promised—although they did achieve a good bit otherwise—but they are as crucial today as at any time in the past to any discourse on liberation; which may be the reason that it is the discourse of revolution, and not just its misdeeds or failures, that is the ultimate target of the contemporary condemnation of revolutions. As Margaret Thatcher once expressed a wish to "bury socialism," the dominant culture of the present seeks to bury not just revolutions but what revolutions stood for, and articulated; it is against this contemporary hegemony that the memory of revolutions must be sustained if there is to be any hope of envisioning the future differently. To quote Le Goff by way of summation, "memory, on which history draws and which it nourishes in return, seeks to save the past in order to serve the present and the future. Let us act in such a way that collective memory may serve the liberation and not the enslavement of human beings."[57]

TWO LEGACIES

I began this discussion with a plea for recognition of the ambiguities of Mao and the Cultural Revolution. I will end with an illustration of this ambiguous legacy, in locations very far from China, that shows that the legacy is still alive, and still very much ambiguous. Two radical movements in Latin America have in recent years evoked memories of Mao and the Cultural Revolution. The better known one is that of the Shining Path in Peru. The anthropologist Orin Starn writes of Abimael Guzman's Maoism:

A final theme centers on violence. Guzman cited Mao to contend that "violence is a universal law . . . and without revolutionary violence one class cannot be substituted for another, an old order cannot be overthrown to create a new one." During the Cultural Revolution, the future rebel leader visited China at least three times. The Savonarolan fervency of the Gang of Four reappeared in Gonzalo Thought [the appellation used for Guzman's thought, similar to Mao Zedong

Thought] in an all-or-nothing vision of history as a ceaseless struggle between the "glorious forces of true revolutionaries" and "the miserable revisionism" of other Peruvian socialist parties. . . . Opponents were "filthy," "parasitic," "cancerous," and "reptilian" in this social etiology of purity and danger, providing the ideological framework for the murder of hundreds of trade unionists, peasant activists, and neighborhood leaders from other political parties.[58]

The other movement is not one that claims an explicit relationship to Maoism or is widely known for such a connection. Its leaders, too, however, were products of the radical ferment of the 1960s and, according to one historian, were "Maoist in their underpinnings,"[59] although in this case their Maoism was articulated closely to local needs and culture, as Maoism theoretically should be. One of those leaders writes,

> Not everyone listens to the voices of hopelessness and resignation. Not everyone has jumped onto the bandwagon of despair. Most people continue on; they cannot hear the voice of the powerful and the fainthearted as they are deafened by the cry and the blood that death and misery shout in their ears. But in moments of rest, they hear another voice, not the one that comes from above, but rather the one that comes with the wind from below, and is born in the hearts of the indigenous people of the mountains, a voice that speaks of justice and liberty, a voice that speaks of socialism, a voice that speaks of hope . . . the only hope in this world. And the very oldest among the people in the villages tell of a man named Zapata who rose up for his own people and in a voice more like a song than a shout, said, "Land and Liberty.[60]

It is a long way from the shrill screams of the Cultural Revolution and Guzman to the gentle strains of the Zapatistas, from Mao's Faustian poetry to the earth-bound aspirations of the Indians for whom Zapata spoke, but there is a grammar that they share in common: the grammar of an alternative modernity rooted in the welfare and the interests of the people. The self-restraint of the Zapatista language, which is imbedded in a deeper self-restraint of aspiration, may also help us grasp where Mao and the Cultural Revolution went wrong— and what we might remember or reject of their legacies.

NOTES

1. Charles Maier, "A Surfeit of Memory? Reflections on History, Melancholy and Denial," *History and Memory* 5, no. 2 (Fall/Winter 1993): 136–51, esp. 136.

2. I owe the term to Pierre Nora, "Between Memory and History: *Les Lieux de Memoire,*" *Representations* 26 (Spring 1989): 7–25, esp. 17.

3. For a critical discussion of the "linguistic turn" in connection with the French Revolution, see Roger Chartier, "Discourses and Practices: On the Origins of the

French Revolution," in *On the Edge of the Cliff: History, Language, and Practices*, trans. Lydia G. Cochrane (Baltimore and London: Johns Hopkins University Press, 1997), 72–80.

4. Gilbert Rist, *The History of Development: From Western Origins to Global Faith*, trans. Patrick Camiller (London and New York: ZED Books, 1997), esp. chapters 8 and 9.

5. For the deployment of ambivalence in critiques of modernity, see Zygmunt Bauman, *Modernity and Ambivalence* (Ithaca, NY: Cornell University Press, 1991), and Ulrich Beck, *The Reinvention of Politics: Rethinking Modernity in the Global Social Order* (Cambridge: Polity Press, 1997).

6. This was the view of a distinguished political scientist at the University of California, Berkeley (Chalmers Johnson). Asked to explain to the public this puzzling phenomenon of a regime launching a revolution against itself, he could see in the event only the final confirmation that Mao had gone irredeemably mad. That postrevolutionary interpretations have confirmed what he had to say does not, obviously, mean that he was correct in his diagnosis, but only the logic of a political science operating according to the conventional norms of power.

7. See, for instance, Chris Bramall, *In Praise of Maoist Economic Planning: Living Standards and Economic Development in Sichuan Since 1931* (Oxford: Oxford University Press, 1993), and the essays in William A. Joseph, Christine P. W. Wong, and David Zweig, eds., *New Perspectives on the Cultural Revolution* (Cambridge, MA: Harvard University Press, 1991).

8. This broad twenty-year periodization of the Cultural Revolution is not mine alone, but is implicit in the works of Roderick McFarquhar, Jean-Luc Domenach, Mark Selden, Karl Riskin, etc. These scholars all perceive significant changes in the 1956–1957 period that were to culminate in the Cultural Revolution. The best argument for this periodization, however, was provided by the Communist Party, which, in its policy reversals of 1978, declared a return to the contradictions in Chinese society as defined in the Eighth Party Congress of 1956—a contradiction between the people's needs (and the needs of an advanced social formation—socialism) and backward forces of production—rather than a contradiction between classes, which had been the line to emerge from the early 1960s.

9. Samir Amin has been the foremost theorist of "delinking." The Cultural Revolution in China played a very important part in Amin's conceptualization of "delinking," as well as the thinking on socialism of important world-system analysts such as Immanuel Wallerstein, Terence Hopkins, Giovanni Arrighi, etc. See Amin, *Delinking: Towards a Polycentric World,* trans. Michael Wolfers (London: ZED Books, 1990). For Maoism in Amin's thinking, see his rereading the *Post-War Period: An Intellectual Itinerary*, trans. Michael Wolfers (New York: Monthly Review Press, 1994). For the importance of the Cultural Revolution in worldwide thinking on development issues, see the (unsympathetic) account in Gilbert Rist, *The History of Development*. For an argument that asserts the continued relevance of Maoism in the Third World, see W. F. Wertheim, *Third World Whence and Whither? Protective State versus Aggressive Market* (Amsterdam: Uitgeverij Spinhuis, 1997). For critical but sympathetic accounts from a contemporary perspective, see the essays in Arif Dirlik, Paul Healy,

and Nick Knight, eds., *Critical Perspectives on Mao Zedong's Thought* (Atlantic Heights, NJ: Humanities Press, 1997).

10. Mao Tse-tung, *A Critique of Soviet Economics,* trans. Moss Roberts, notes by Richard Levy (New York: Monthly Review Press, 1977).

11. Everything I have noted above, and more, is to be found in the excellent compilation of documents by Mark Selden, *The People's Republic of China: A Documentary History of Revolutionary Change* (New York: Monthly Review Press, 1979). Selden's introduction is exemplary of the interpretation placed on these policies at the time. See also the assessment by the economist John Gurley, *China's Economy and the Maoist Strategy* (New York: Monthly Review Press, 1976).

12. Even though they were written without the benefit of the evidence that has become available since, the works by Kraus and Lee stand to this day as among the most astute analyses of the Cultural Revolution ideology and reality. Richard Kraus, *Class Conflict in Chinese Socialism* (New York: Columbia University Press, 1981), and Hong Yung Lee, *The Politics of the Chinese Cultural Revolution: A Case Study* (Berkeley: University of California Press, 1978). Another study of the time that was quite revealing of everyday realities and compares favorably to the author's later writings is Andrew Walder, *Chang Ch'un-ch'iao and Shanghai's January Revolution* (Ann Arbor: University of Michigan Center for Chinese Studies, 1978).

13. While by now there is a proliferation of studies and memoirs that impart a good idea of how these conflicts and manipulations worked at the local level, one study I would like to single out for its complex approach to the subject is Anita Chan, Richard Madsen, and Jonathan Unger, *Chen Village: The Recent History of a Peasant Community in China* (Berkeley: University of California Press, 1984).

14. Michael Dutton, *Policing and Punishment in China: From Patriarchy to the "People"* (Cambridge: Cambridge University Press, 1992).

15. William Hinton, *Shenfan* (New York: Random House, 1983), 753.

16. I am referring here to works such as Nicholas Kristoff and Sheryl WuDunn, *China Wakes: The Struggle for the Soul of a Rising Power* (New York: Times Books, 1994); Li Zhisui, *The Private Life of Chairman Mao: The Memoirs of Mao's Personal Physician,* trans. H. C. Tai with the assistance of Anne Thurston (New York: Random House, 1994); Harrison E. Salisbury, *The New Emperors: China in the Era of Mao and Deng* (New York: Little, Brown and Co., 1992). These works, popular best sellers, have also been influential on academics, judging by some of the reviews they have received in the most prestigious publications.

17. I am referring here to a document circulated by The China Study Group in New York concerning Li Zhisui's memoirs. The document also includes a statement of protest by those close to Mao concerning Li Zhisui's claims. According to this document, Li was himself quite upset by the preoccupation with Mao's sex life in reviews of his work.

18. Anne Thurston, *Enemies of the People* (New York: Alfred A. Knopf, 1987).

19. Mobo C. F. Gao, "Review Essay: Memoirs and Interpretation of the Cultural Revolution," *Bulletin of Concerned Asian Scholars* 27, no. 1 (1995): 49–57, esp. 55. Gao notes in this regard Chen Xuezhao's *Surviving the Storm,* which refuses to denounce the Cultural Revolution. Informally, I know many people in China who, even

though they too were victimized one way or another, refuse to engage in blanket condemnation of the Cultural Revolution.

20. Qin Huailu, *Ninth Heaven to Ninth Hell: The History of a Noble Chinese Experiment*, ed. William Hinton, trans. Dusanka Miscevic (New York: Barricade Books, 1995).

21. See the preface and the afterword by Hinton for the politics of the book. There have been other efforts in recent years to discredit "model workers" of earlier years, and usually there is sex involved somewhere along the line. In 1993, another model worker, Wang Guofan of Zunhua County (Hebei), was to come under attack, again with lurid tales of his misdoings. Wang was an example of the "baresticks" Mao lauded in 1955 in his collection *Socialist Upsurge in China's Countryside*. Indeed a systematic study of the fate of earlier model workers might be quite revealing in terms of the politics of landownership in post-Mao China.

22. Thanks to a Chinese friend, Dr. Yu Keping, I have a photograph from a temple in Zhejiang, where Mao occupies the seat of the Buddha, flanked by the "Bodhisattvas" Yang Kaihui (the first Mrs. Mao, killed in 1930) and Zhou Enlai. Early in 1995, Party cadres in Hunan had to intervene to suspend the construction of a huge temple to Mao, once again to be built with peasant funds. The "Mao fever" that peaked in 1993 on the one hundredth anniversary of Mao's birth reveals also that these memories are not restricted to peasants, but are pervasive among urban populations, including young intellectuals. In surveys, Mao still comes out ahead of all competitors as the greatest man of all times. Just recently it was reported that the city of Changsha in Hunan plans to construct a Mao square, surrounded by Mao's poetry in neon lights. See *South China Morning Post* (13 January 1998).

23. Ma Bo, *Blood Red Sunset: A Memoir of the Cultural Revolution*, trans. Howard Goldblatt (New York: Viking Books, 1995).

24. In light of the preoccupation in this book with sexual corruption, and the author's often expressed resentment that girls got a better deal by using their sexuality, it may be worth noting here that a different spin may be put on the issue of sexuality. At least for young women, according to a Chinese woman friend who also spent these years in Inner Mongolia, the frontier provided possibilities of liberation (including sexual liberation) that were not available in a place like Beijing. This does not excuse the sexual dalliances of Party cadres, but suggests that the ethical atmosphere of the frontier may have made a difference.

25. Mobo Gao, "Review Essay," 51.

26. The post-Mao regime, if only out of concern for its own legitimacy, has been much readier than scholars abroad to recognize the problematic nature of the evaluations of Mao and the Cultural Revolution. For a remarkably honest recognition of these problems, as well as of history writing as a process of negotiation (both in terms of "facts" and politics) see Deng Xiaoping, "Remarks on Successive Drafts of the 'Resolution on Certain Questions in the History of our Party since the Founding of the People's Republic of China' (March 1980–June 1981)," in *Selected Works of Deng Xiaoping (1975–1982)* (Beijing: Foreign Languages Press, 1984), 276–96. The Party leaders also know that much of the carnage during the Cultural Revolution was perpetrated by those in power, whose power would survive the Cultural Revolution, as Maurice Meisner has pointed out in a number of works.

27. "The Maoist 'Model' Reconsidered: Local Self-Reliance and the Financing of Rural Industrialization," in *New Perspectives on the Cultural Revolution*, 183–96, esp. 195.

28. Hinton, *Shenfan*, 766.

29. Anita Chan, *Children of Mao: Personality Development and Political Activism in the Red Guard Generation* (Seattle: University of Washington Press, 1985).

30. Qin Huailu, *Ninth Heaven*, 305.

31. Hinton, *Shenfan*, 765.

32. The importance of war preparation in determining economic policy has been analyzed cogently in Barry Naughton, "Industrial Policy during the Cultural Revolution: Military Preparation, Decentralization, and Leaps Forward," in *New Perspectives on the Cultural Revolution*, 153–81.

33. Zygmunt Bauman, *Modernity and the Holocaust* (Ithaca, NY: Cornell University Press, 1989).

34. Zhiyuan Cui has documented this phenomenon in many works. For an example see "Particular, Universal and Infinite: Transcending Western Centrism and Cultural Relativism in the Third World," in *Progress: Fact or Ilusion*, ed. Leo Marx and Bruce Mazlish (Ann Arbor: University of Michigan Press, 1996). See also Dev Nathan and Govind Kelkar, "Collective Villages in the Chinese Market," *Economic and Political Weekly* (May 3, 1997): 951–63 and (May 10, 1997): 1037–47.

35. See, for example, Daniel Chirot, *Modern Tyrants: The Power and Prevalence of Evil in Our Age* (New York: Free Press, 1994). For an eloquent criticism of such views see Maurice Meisner, "Stalinism in the History of the Chinese Communist Party," in *Critical Perspectives*, 184–206.

36. Edward Berenson, "The Social Interpretation of the French Revolution," in *Debating Revolutions*, ed. Nikkie R. Kiddie, 85–111, esp. 86 and 107n5 (New York: New York University Press, 1995). "New" perspectives on the Chinese Revolution are offered in the special issue of *Modern China* 21, no. 1 (January 1995). The perspectives offered here indicate eloquently that changes in attitude toward the revolution may not be explained simply by recourse to new evidence; it is probably less accurate to say that new data have changed historians' interpretations than to say that historians, having changed, have begun to see data differently. Otherwise, how can one explain an observation in the special issue by a senior historian, an enthusiastic proponent of the Chinese Revolution in earlier days, that "the revolution was not a liberation but (foremost) was the replacement of one form of domination with another" (Joseph Esherick, "Ten Theses on the Chinese Revolution," *Modern China* 21, no. 5 [January 1995]: 45–76). It is hard to imagine that it would take a practicing historian thirty years to see the domination in the Communist regime! See also Marie-Claire Bergere, *The Golden Age of the Chinese Bourgeoisie, 1911–1937* (Cambridge and New York: Cambridge University Press, 1989) for a more honest admission concerning change in outlook and its relationship to historical evaluation. For a repudiation of revolution by two distinguished Chinese intellectuals, who also point to connections between the French and the Chinese revolutions, see Li Zehou and Liu Zaifu, *Gaobie geming: huiwang ershi shiji Zhongguo* [Good-bye to Revolution: Retrospect on Twentieth-Century China] (Hong Kong: Cosmos Books, 1996), esp. 129–36,

where the authors discuss not the Communist Revolution, but the nationalist revolution led by Sun Yat-sen, and suggest that Sun's choice of the French over the English path to revolution was a mistake (131). The French Revolution's relationship to later socialist revolutions has been on the minds both of Marxist historians and contemporary conservative historians such as Furet and Simon Schama. See Berenson, "Social Interpretation of the French Revolution," 92–93, and Michel Vovelle, "1789–1917: The Game of Analogies," in *The Terror*, vol. 4 of *The French Revolution and the Creation of Modern Political Culture*, ed. Keith M. Baker, 349–78 (Oxford: Pergamon Press, 1994).

37. Patrick H. Hutton, *History as an Art of Memory* (Hanover and London: University of Vermont Press, 1993), 144. See also Mona Ozouf, "The Terror after the Terror: An Immediate History," in *The Terror*, 3–39.

38. For fascinating illustrations see Ronald Paulson, *Representations of Revolution, 1789–1820* (New Haven, CT: Yale University Press, 1983).

39. I am referring here to such works as Jung Chang, *Wild Swans: Three Daughters of China* (New York: Simon and Schuster, 1991) and movies such as *Blue Kite* (Tian Zhuangzhuang, 1993), and *To Live*. For opposition narratives see Rubie S. Watson, *Memory, History and Opposition Under State Socialism* (Santa Fe, NM: School of American Research, 1994), especially the essay by Paul Pickowicz, "Memories of Revolution and Collectivization in China: The Unauthorized Reminiscences of a Rural Intellectual" (127–47). The family narrative literature has also spilled over to the United States through the works of Amy Tan and others.

40. Watson, *Memory, History and Opposition*. See also Kathleen E. Smith, *Remembering Stalin's Victims: Popular Memory and the End of the USSR* (Ithaca, NY: Cornell University Press, 1996).

41. See the essay by Pickowicz cited above (note 39) where the author begins his discussion by stating that "between 1978 and 1987 I traveled five times to Raoyang county" (128). The number of trips to the source also appears prominently in Edward Friedman, Paul Pickowicz, and Mark Selden, *Chinese Village, Socialist State* (New Haven, CT: Yale University Press, 1991). Here, too, there is an interesting parallel to earlier, highly positive accounts of the revolution. For an example see Committee of Concerned Asian Scholars, *China: Inside the People's Republic* (New York: Bantam Books, 1972), which was an account of the first trip to China by a group of American scholars in 1971 (Pickowicz was a member of that group).

42. This is the argument, for the post-1949 period, offered by Friedman, Pickowicz, and Selden. See also Ralph Thaxton, *Salt of the Earth* (New Haven, CT: Yale University Press, 1997). For a broader judgment along similar lines, see Joseph Esherick, "Ten Theses" (Modern China). This also has been the major thrust of revisions of the French Revolution by Furet, etc. See Berenson, "Social Interpretation of the French Revolution." The strong anti-Marxist thrust in such interpretations is rather transparent in the rejection not only of a social foundation to revolutions, but also in the repudiation or downplaying of the issue of class. For an explicit example of the latter see *Putting Class in Its Place: Worker Identities in East Asia*, ed. Elizabeth Perry (Berkeley: University of California Institute of East Asian Studies, 1996). It is ironic that social history, which was long tied to radical causes, should now find service in

the repudiation of radical possibilities. Social history has fallen upon hard times. For a fascinating discussion of how a depoliticized social history has been used by some German historians to deflect attention from Nazism, see Mary Nolan, "The *Historikerstreit* and Social History," in *Reworking the Past: Hitler, the Holocaust, and the Historians' Debate*, ed. Peter Baldwin, 224–48 (Boston: Beacon Press, 1990).

43. For a work that acknowledges an explicit connection between the waning of revolution and its own undertaking, see Marie-Claire Bergere, *The Golden Age of the Chinese Bourgeoisie*. For the origins of a "public sphere" with the late Qing gentry, see Mary Backus Rankin, *Elite Activism and Political Transformation in China, 1865–1911* (Stanford, CA: Stanford University Press, 1986). The confusion of "the public sphere" with "civil society" is most readily apparent in the recent writings of Prasenjit Duara, who has discovered "civil society" in the Chinese idea of *fengjian* (commonly, "feudalism") and in the activities of late Qing gentry. For Duara, it is nationalism that aborted the rise of civil society in China. The nostalgia for the past appears in accompaniment to the repudiation of revolution. For a critique see Arif Dirlik, "How the Grinch Hijacked Radicalism: Further Thoughts on the Postcolonial," *Postcolonial Studies* 2, no. 2 (1999): 149–63. For a debate on civil society in China, see the special issue of *Modern China* 19, no. 2 (April 1993). For a critique of the ways in which the idea of civil society is deployed in the historiography of China, see Arif Dirlik, "Civil Society/Public Sphere in China," in *Zhongguo shehui kexue jikan* [Chinese Social Sciences Quarterly] 3 (1993): 10–22.

44. For an overview of debates over the Holocaust, see Peter Baldwin, ed., *Reworking the Past*. A work that reconciles with some success history and memory in the case of the Armenian massacres, see Donald E. Miller and Lorna Touryan Miller, *Survivors: An Oral History of the Armenian Genocide* (Berkeley: University of California Press, 1993). For World War II see Takashi Fujitani, Geoff White, and Lisa Yoneyama, eds., *Perilous Memories: The Asia-Pacific Wars* (Durham, NC: Duke University Press, 2002).

45. Jacques Le Goff, *History and Memory*, trans. Steven Rendall and Elizabeth Claman (New York: Columbia University Press, 1992), xi.

46. Maurice Halbwachs, *The Collective Memory*, trans. Francis J. Ditter and Vida Yazdi Ditter (New York: Harper & Row, 1980) (French original in 1950). See also Maurice Halbwachs, *On Collective Memory*, ed. and trans. Lewis A. Coser (Chicago and London: The University of Chicago Press, 1992), especially Coser's introduction, which also refers to the disorientation caused among Russian and East European populations by the necessity of forgetting the past (and remembering it differently), 21–22.

47. Nora, "Between Memory and History," 17.

48. Nora, "Between Memory and History," 15.

49. Le Goff, *History and Memory*, 99.

50. Maier, "A Surfeit of Memory?" 150.

51. Robert Melson, *Revolution and Genocide: On the Origins of the Armenian Genocide and the Holocaust* (Chicago and London: The University of Chicago Press, 1992) for an example. The substance of Melson's study inquires into the relationships between the Young Turk revolution of 1908 and Hitler's revolution, and the Armen-

ian massacres and the Holocaust, respectively. The validity of his comparison may be questionable, but what is interesting is what is encompassed by the term "revolution." His final comparative chapter casts the net even farther by bringing in statism and the Khmer Rouge, among others. Interestingly, Melson has nothing to say about the Cultural Revolution, which others have dubbed a "holocaust," presumably because his analysis of genocide rightly gives considerable weight to intention along with structural factors.

Terror itself is depoliticizing in focusing attention on criminality and mindless evil. We have had an interesting example of this effect recently. On January 9, 1998, the *New York Times* carried three stories, one on Theodore Kaczynski ("Unabomber Chaos Grows on Talk of Suicide Try," A1), one on Ramzi Ahmed Yousef ("the mastermind" of the World Trade Center bombing) ("Mastermind Gets Life for Bombing of Trade Center," A1), and one on the Denver trial of Terry Nichols and Timothy McVeigh ("Joint Trial to Be Sought in Oklahoma in Bomb Case," A14). The lineup is interesting in the diversity of political positions. Kaczynski's actions draw upon a left-wing eco-anarchist legacy, Nichols and McVeigh represent right-wing responses to recent changes in U.S. society, and Yousef is in the line of Arab nationalist violence against the United States. Yet the politics was clear only in the case of Yousef, who, much like nineteenth- and twentieth-century militant political terrorists, declared that he was "a terrorist, and . . . proud of it," for the United States and Israel left no option for Arabs but terrorism (for which the presiding judge called him "an apostle of evil"). Kaczynski obviously agonized about his status, but in the end gave in to pressures to declare him "mentally defective," much like rebels against the Russian tsars, or the Soviet state—which, however, did not spare him the same depiction as an incarnation of evil. Nichols and McVeigh, on the other hand, seem not to have made much of their politics in getting the best deal they could get, and there was little question among their victims, and many others as well, that they, too, were evil persons. The question is What might be made of this coincidence by the reader of the *Times* that day, especially since another story the paper carried that day was the degeneration of violence in Algeria to killing for the sake of killing? On the other hand, the paper had little to say about the state terrorism in Chiapas, Mexico, where forty-five people (mostly women and children) associated with the Chiapas Uprising were killed by military or paramilitary forces. The inclusion in the category of "terror" of radically different political positions on this occasion was a harbinger of things to come. It is no longer possible to have revolutions, or even seriously radical oppositional politics, as all such politics that deviate from the norms of legal order established by the powerful—above all the United States—is likely to be construed as "terror." Terror itself loses its meaning under the circumstances, being rendered into a specter that justifies oppressive and exploitative politics.

52. Gerard Greenfield and Apo Leong, "China's Communist Capitalism: The Real World of Market Socialism," *Socialist Register 1997,* ed. Leo Panitch, 96–122, esp. 96 (London: Merlin Press, 1997).

53. "Warding Off the Past: Is This a Problem Only for Historians and Moralists?" in *Reworking the Past,* Baldwin, ed., 196–213, esp. 196.

54. Sorokin, while he viewed revolutions as calamities, nevertheless recognized that they have a progressive role in history. In the China field, scholars such as John

King Fairbank, Joseph Levenson, and Benjamin Schwartz sought to come to terms with the Chinese Revolution in different ways; while attacked by a younger generation for not being sufficiently prorevolutionary, their ambivalence made for an openmindedness that is missing from their erstwhile critics, who have now mostly turned antirevolutionary. A remarkable contemporary example of such ambivalence is Melson's *Revolution and Genocide*, cited above. Having argued that revolutions create conditions for, and sometimes result in, genocide, Melson concludes by stating that "it is distinctly not my purpose to debunk the revolutionary tradition and to throw my lot in with its detractors. Though the human costs of revolutions were always high, in many important instances their results were indeed to uplift the poor, educate the illiterate, open up the social structure to merit, broaden liberty and participation, strengthen the state against foreign exploitation, and help to adapt society and economy to modernization and industrialization" (259).

55. Hutton, *History as an Art of Memory*, 144–45.

56. Manuel Castells, *The Rise of the Network Society*, vol. 1 of *The Information Age: Economy, Society and Culture* (Malden, MA: Blackwell Publishers, 1997), 3.

57. Le Goff, *History and Memory*, 99.

58. "Maoism in the Andes: The Communist Party of Peru—Shining Path and the Refusal of History," in *Critical Perspectives on Mao Zedong's Thought*.

59. John Ross, *Rebellion from the Roots: Indian Uprising in Chiapas* (Monroe, ME: Common Courage Press, 1995), 280. See also 274–75 for the origins.

60. Subcommandante Marcos, quoted in Alexander Cockburn, "Jerry Garcia and El Sup," *The Nation* (August 28/September 4, 1995): 192.

IV

AFTER THE REVOLUTION

10

Postsocialism? Reflections on "Socialism with Chinese Characteristics"

In the discussion below, I consider the interpretive possibilities of a conceptualization of Chinese socialism that is primarily deconstructive in intention,
although it may also provide an occasion for a new reading of its meaning
and, by implication, of the meaning of socialism in our day. My immediate
goal is to find a way out of the conceptual prison into which Chinese socialism is forced by ideological efforts to constrict it between received notions of
capitalism and socialism. Chinese society today is the subject of radical transformation, which is expressed at the level of ideology by an intense struggle
between two discourses that seek to appropriate its future for two alternative
visions of history. These discourses, I will argue, are both irredeemably ideological (or, viewed from an alternative perspective, utopian). Chinese socialism justifies itself in terms of a historical vision that has no apparent relevance to the present. This renders it vulnerable to negation at the hands of a
discourse, embedded in the history of capitalism, that strives to colonize the
future for its own historical vision. In the process, both discourses impose
upon the insistently ambiguous evidence of contemporary Chinese socialism
interpretive readings that may be sustained only by ignoring evidence contrary to their historical presumptions. Stated bluntly, any representation of
China's present historical path as capitalist is not just descriptive but also pre-
scriptive; in other words, such representation is intended to shape the reality
that it innocently pretends to describe. The counterinsistence that China is a
socialist society headed for communism covers up under theoretical conven-
tions a social situation that distorts socialism out of recognizable form. In his
illuminating study, *Class Conflict in Chinese Socialism*, Richard Kraus observed that class analysis "is an aspect of the class conflict it is intended to
comprehend."[1] Much the same may be said of the question of socialism in

China which, in the affirmation or the negation of the relevance to China's future of a socialist vision, is part of an ongoing struggle over the future of socialism in Chinese society—and, by extension, globally—in which the major casualty is the concept of socialism itself. The conceptualization I offer here is necessitated by a recognition that to represent present-day Chinese socialism in terms of one or the other of these categories is inevitably to become party to ideological activity that suppresses the most fundamental problems presented to existing ideas of socialism and capitalism by the momentous changes in Chinese society.

It is the concept of socialism that is of necessity the point of departure for this discussion, since it is from ambiguities in its meaning that these problems arise. In its current usage, the concept bears two primary meanings. First, it is used to depict the present condition of socialist states, what Rudolf Bahro has called "actually existing socialism."[2] Second, it is used also to describe the future state of these societies, what in theory they strive to become in order to achieve the ultimate goal of communism (this distinction corresponds to what Bill Brugger and others have described as "system" and "process").[3] The question of meaning arises out of the gap between these two usages, between system and process, reality and vision. So long as the future appears as an immanent condition for the present, so that a striving to achieve communism guides present policy, the two meanings of socialism are easily collapsed together. It is when the future and the present are separated, when the future, though it is still conceived as an ultimate goal, ceases to play a direct part in the formulation of present policy, that the question of meaning appears in its most undisguised form. Under circumstances where the present has ceased to derive its inspiration from a conviction in the immanent relevance of the socialist vision, but instead resigns itself to the continued hegemony of contemporary circumstances that are at odds with its vision, can socialism remain socialism for long, or must it be recaptured inevitably by the forces emanating from its irreducible global context, which is dominated by capitalism?

This is the point of departure for the discursive struggle over Chinese socialism today, where the affirmation of faithfulness to a future socialist vision on the part of the socialist regime in China seeks to fend off its negation by the claims to the future of a powerful ideology of capitalism that derives its plausibility from overwhelming evidence of historical success that the regime concedes in its deeds, if not always verbally. It is precisely because of the seriousness of this discursive struggle, with all the uncertainty it implies for the future, that we must not hasten to accept the claims of either discourse, to affirm or to negate the claims of Chinese socialism, either to take it at its word or to deny validity to its self-image.

It is this condition of ideological contradiction and uncertainty that I describe here by the term "postsocialism," which allows taking Chinese socialism seriously without sweeping under the rug the problems created by its articulation to capitalism, or forcing an inevitably ideological choice between its own self-image (socialism) or an image of it that denies validity to its self-image (the discourse of capitalism). The term is intentionally residual, since the historical situation that it is intended to capture conceptually is highly ambiguous in its characteristics.

By postsocialism I refer to the condition of socialism in a historical situation where: (a) socialism has lost its coherence as a metatheory of politics because of the attenuation of the socialist vision in its historical unfolding; partly because of a perceived need on the part of socialist states to articulate "actually existing socialism" to the demands of a capitalist world order, but also because of the vernacularization of socialism in its absorption into different national contexts; (b) the articulation of socialism to capitalism is conditioned by the structure of "actually existing socialism" in any particular context which is the historical premise of all such articulation; and (c) this premise stands guard over the process of articulation to ensure that it does not result in the restoration of capitalism. Postsocialism is of necessity also postcapitalist, not in the classical Marxist sense of socialism as a phase in historical development that is anterior to capitalism, but in the sense of a socialism that represents a response to the experience of capitalism and an attempt to overcome the deficiencies of capitalist development. Its own deficiencies and efforts to correct them by resorting to capitalist methods of development are conditioned by this awareness of the deficiencies of capitalism in history. Hence postsocialism seeks to avoid a return to capitalism, no matter how much it may draw upon the latter to improve the performance of "actually existing socialism." For this reason, and also to legitimize the structure of "actually existing socialism," it strives to keep alive a vague vision of future socialism as the common goal of humankind while denying to it any immanent role in the determination of present social policy.

I would like to illustrate this thesis below through a brief examination of the contradictions in contemporary Chinese socialism, and the ideological interpretations to which they have been subjected. At the heart of official socialism in contemporary China lies a contradiction that gives it its ideological shape and animates its motions. Official description of what Chinese socialism is, or should be, is encompassed within the phrase "socialism with Chinese characteristics" *(you Zhongguo tesidi shehui zhuyi)*, which has assumed the status of orthodoxy since it was presented to the Twelfth Congress of the Communist Party of China in 1982 by Deng Xiaoping, the unofficial guiding light of Chinese socialism.[4] The urgent declaration of a Chinese claim to a *Chinese* socialism that is implicit in the phrase, however, has been accompanied since then by an equally powerful urge to represent this *Chinese* socialism as a phase in a universal metahistorical vision of which the end is communism. At the Thirteenth Party Congress held in October 1987, Party Secretary Zhao Ziyang described the current stage of Chinese socialism as "the initial stage of socialism" *(shehui zhuyi chuji jieduan)*, in the transitional stage of socialism that in this metahistorical vision lies between capitalism and the final, communist, stage of history.[5]

The Marxist view of history that informs this conception of history presupposes that societies in their progress in history follow paths that are conditioned by the inner logic of their historical constitution. There is no account in this representation of how a "socialism with Chinese characteristics" will link up with the historical progress of other societies with *their* individual characteristics to end up with a conclusion to history that is universal in *its* characteristics (unless the process is intermediated, as I suggest below, by a "universal" capitalism that may transform the globe in its own self-image, which was the original Marxist idea). The representation satisfies a double need for legitimacy in Chinese socialism: socialism must have a Chinese coloring and meet the needs of Chinese society if it is to be legitimate within a Chinese context, but this socialism, if it is to remain socialism, must reserve a place for itself in a history that is not just Chinese. The resolution thus achieved of these conflicting demands for legitimacy at the level of representation requires suppression of a fundamental contradiction between Chinese socialism and its global capitalist context, between particularity and universality in socialism, and, ultimately, between Chinese socialism as a historical project and its metahistorical presuppositions.

The contradiction, if recognized, suggests that the "socialism with Chinese characteristics" may be so much ideological whitewash to cover up a national appropriation of socialism to which socialist commitment may be a theoretically necessary (for legitimation purposes) but practically marginal consideration. Indeed, Chinese socialism, always strongly nationalistic in its orientation, appears more transparently than ever today as a disposable instrument in "the search for wealth and power." On occasion, it is even possible to encounter representations of the goal of socialism in terms of the traditionalistic phrase in which an incipient reformist nationalism in the nineteenth century cloaked its goals: "a wealthy nation and a strong military."[6] To make matters worse, if "socialism with Chinese characteristics" has a substantial content—in other words, a social and political agenda—that content has appeared so far as a broadly conceived program to articulate socialism to the demands of a capitalist world order so as to achieve rapid economic development. As the phraseology of the goals of Chinese socialism recalls nineteenth-century reformism, so do some of the policies that have been proposed to achieve those goals; a case in point is the recent proposal by Zhao Ziyang to make all of coastal China into a special foreign trade zone—an eventuality the fear of which was one of the basic motivating forces underlying the socialist revolution in China.[7]

A revolutionary socialism, long conceived by China's socialists as a prerequisite to the achievement of national autonomy and development, appears today as an obstacle to that goal; and the regime has devoted considerable effort over the last decade to dismantling the social relationships and the political organization of socialism which go back in their origins not just to the Cultural Revolution, as is commonly portrayed, but to the early period of the People's Republic in the 1950s, and even earlier to the period of the revolution before 1949 when Chinese socialism acquired an identity of its own. Around the turn of the century, the Chinese who first began to advocate a socialist resolution of China's problems did so with the conviction that socialism offered the best means to China's survival in a world where the days of capitalism seemed to be numbered.[8] The attitude toward socialism that prevails today is the opposite: that China will be doomed to backwardness and decrepitude unless socialism is amended by the proven methods of capitalist development. National concerns, which during a century of revolution found their expression in a socialist vision of the world, seem today to be possible of fulfillment only in the extensive incorporation of China into a world order of which capitalism is the organizing principle. When Chinese in our day speak in defense of this shift in attitude that Chinese socialism is different from socialism elsewhere, they seem to overlook conveniently that China does not exist in a political or economic vacuum, that this difference does not imply that Chinese (or anyone else for that matter) are free to define socialism or to choose the future as they please, but that every choice implies a corresponding relationship to a global capitalism. It is impossible to establish a Chinese socialism, in other words, without at the same time opting for a certain relationship to capitalism. What is at issue here is not a Chinese prerogative to define a Chinese socialism, which I for one am not prepared to challenge, but the implications of any such definition for the metahistorical vision of socialism that Chinese socialism continues to profess as its ideological premise, and which serves as the legitimation for this socialism in the first place. The contradiction, at the very least, creates a "legitimation crisis" for socialism—in China and elsewhere.

It is this crisis that fuels the discursive conflict over Chinese socialism. The question is: does the compromise with capitalism, justified by recourse to a nationalized socialism, leave socialism untouched as a long-term goal, or does it imply an inevitable restoration of capitalism, with socialism consigned to historical memory? The question of the future of Chinese society is not to be resolved at the level of ideology. The capitalist world order into which China seeks admission to realize its national goals demands as the price of admission the reshaping of Chinese society in its own image. China, on the other hand, seeks to admit capitalism into its socialism only on condition that capitalism serve, rather than subvert, national autonomy and a national self-image grounded in the history of the socialist revolution. The outcome in actuality will depend on the form taken by the interaction between the two social and economic systems. But ideology does play a key role in the conceptualization of the relationship, if only by defining its limits; it is important, therefore, to understand the implications of the relationship for the ideology itself.

Chinese defenders of the new policies have claimed that "Westerners . . . mistake socialism with Chinese characteristics for capitalism and unbridled free enterprise."[9] "Mistake" is a misnomer here, I would like to suggest, because what is at issue is a discursive appropriation of "socialism with Chinese characteristics" for a vision of history grounded in the history of capitalism. The tendency to read into the attenuation of Chinese socialism the inevitability of a capitalist restoration is based on a non sequitur: that any compromise of a strict socialism must point to a necessary assimilation of Chinese socialism to capitalism. Such an assumption may be justified only by an ideology of capitalism which, in its projection of its own hypostatized self-image indefinitely upon a history that is yet to be lived out (and is, therefore, unknowable), forecloses the possibility of any significant alternatives to its vision of the future.

Let me illustrate this with an anecdote. In 1980, the *Charlotte Observer* published a series of articles on China on the theme of "China: The Challenge of the Eighties," sponsored jointly by the North Carolina branch of the National China Council and the North Carolina Humanities Committee. I was asked to contribute a piece to the series discussing the implications for Marxism of changes in post-Mao China. It was the shortest piece that I have ever written, but the writing took the longest of anything I have written. Part of the reason was the adjustment it took on my part to write in a style appropriate to a newspaper. But much of the time was taken by a running dispute with the editor of the editorial page, who clearly did not like what I had to say about Marxism and showed great creativity in inventing a seemingly endless series of excuses (including the ignorance of the readership of the paper of such words as revolution, colonialism, and imperialism) to deflect the basic thrust of the article, which was favorable to Marxism and argued that, given the historical experience of the Chinese Revolution, the abandonment of Marxism might have debilitating consequences for Chinese society by compromising China's economic and, therefore, political autonomy. When we were at last able to agree on a final version, I submitted the article under the rather neutral descriptive title of "Marxism and the Chinese Revolution." When the article appeared in the paper, it was under a heading that was quite contrary to both my intention and its content: "Will Progress Doom Marxism?" He had had the last word, I suppose, by telling the readers through the title how to read and interpret the article. But the vengeance did not stop there. When the series was completed, the articles were compiled in a little booklet for distribution to high schools in North Carolina. Possibly because the editors assumed that North Carolina students would not be familiar with the verb "doom," but more likely, as I prefer to view it, because they were desirous of "dooming" Marxism, the title of the piece indicated an escalation in the level of violence; it was now changed to read: "Will Progress Kill Marxism?"[10]

The episode is revealing, I think, not as an exhibit of ideological hostility, about which there is little that is novel or interesting, but for the agenda embedded in the simple title, "Will Progress Doom Marxism?" or "Will Progress Kill Marxism?" Noteworthy is the opposition that the title sets up between progress and Marxism, and its suppression of the ideological content of the word "progress." By establishing rhetorically that Marxism may be inconsistent with progress, the question suggests that Marxism has so far owed its staying power in Chinese society to backwardness. Moreover, the reader knows as well as the editor that "progress" here refers to a specific kind of progress: that associated with capitalism. Rather than state this explicitly, the phraseology represents "progress" as an abstract universal. In an explicit phrasing, the question should read: "Will Capitalism Doom Marxism?" in which case the opposition should appear as a conflict or competition between Marxist and capitalist ideas of progress. The tacit location of capitalism within an abstract idea of progress universalizes the claims of capitalist ideas of progress while underlining further the parochialism of Marxism and its alleged status as a feature of backwardness. One must also suppose that this abstraction somehow softens the murderous intent implicit in the verb "kill"; "progress" might get away with killing Marxism—for capitalism to "kill" Marxism, on the other hand, might have proven too shocking even for an eighth grader!

Not everyone may share in the bluntly expressed desire of the *Charlotte Observer* to do away with Marxism (although it was Margaret Thatcher who popularized such vindictive language in the 1980s); but the ideological negation of Chinese Marxism (embedded in a tacit and sometimes explicit affirmation of the appropriateness to China of capitalism) has been commonplace over the last few years in the nation's leading public media, as well as in academic evaluations of Chinese socialism. It shows through rewards bestowed upon Chinese leaders who advocate compromise with capitalism and, therefore (the conclusion follows automatically), promise the imminent demise of Marxism: Deng Xiaoping has been named man of the year more than once in leading periodicals for his supposed contributions to this end.[11] It shows it academic conferences in attitudes that range from the denial of historical legitimacy to socialism (of which a striking illustration is a recent tendency to view the Chinese socialist revolution as a "historical aberration" which has not only been responsible for perpetuating China's backwardness but also for the moral subversion of the Chinese people) to the denial of functionality to socialism in a world of "progress" (that socialism is a passing phase of human history since it seems to impede the kind of progress that is necessary to national survival and the improvement of life). It shows in the reduction of socialism into a proxy for some deeper urge in Chinese history, more often than not rooted in a cultural legacy that is held to be contrary to everything that socialism stands for. Socialism appears in this perspective as an intruder upon a vast historical landscape, at best an expression in disguise for some longing, more often than not for national wealth and power, that haunts that landscape. In a new preface to a recent reprinting of his *Chinese Communism and the Rise of Mao* (first published in 1951), the first scholarly study to argue cogently that Chinese communism was communism of a new kind, motivated by particularly Chinese concerns. Benjamin Schwartz observes that the book has been criticized for stating the obvious, namely, that Chinese communism was but an expression of Chinese nationalism. He defends the book on the grounds that when it was first published (in the days of McCarthyite anxieties about global communist conspiracies), this was not a generally accepted view.[12] In our day, this view is indeed the generally accepted one: that Chinese socialism has been but a disguise for, or instrument of, the national quest for wealth and power to which socialism as an ideology in its own right has been largely irrelevant; which denies to socialism even a limited impact on the definition of national goals. Where such impact is recognized, it is portrayed in negative terms: that taking socialism too seriously has undermined China's national goals. These goals, it seems, may be fulfilled only if China rejoins the capitalist stream of history from which it has been held apart by a century of socialist revolution that now appears as a historical aberration, or at best as an account of national self-delusion.[13] Any signs of the persistence of socialist qualms about joining this stream of history is readily attributed not to general Chinese qualms about capitalism—which are, after all, as old as the history of the Chinese Revolution and one of its basic motive forces—but to the continuing hold on power of aging revolutionaries (now dubbed "conservatives") who cannot seem to part with their illusions about socialism.

   While the ideological premises of this discourse may be readily evident, it does not follow that we may ignore the questions it raises, as is suggested by Chinese defenders of official socialism. Such premises are no longer restricted to "Western" critics of Chinese socialism or apologists for capitalism, but are very much an integral part of Chinese speculation over the future of Chinese socialism. Indeed, it is quite "un-Marxist," I would suggest, to claim that socialist consciousness is immune to significant changes in socialist existence, that the changing relationship between socialism and capitalism may have no significant implication for either socialist consciousness or the Chinese conception of socialism.

The socialist regime in China today insists that the compromise with capitalism represents nothing but an innovation within socialism, at most a temporary detour that is intended to consolidate socialism and carry it to a higher plane of achievement. It has good theoretical justification for its policies. Socialism appears in the Marxist conception as a postcapitalist transitional phase on the historical path to communism, and presupposes an advanced economic (and cultural) basis established during the capitalist stage of development. China, for historical reasons, never fulfilled this premise of socialism, but instead bypassed capitalism to establish socialism upon a backward economic foundation. The discrepancy ("contradiction") between advanced social forms and a backward economic basis is responsible from this perspective for the deep problems that Chinese socialism has encountered, which are also likely to obstruct permanently the transition to communism if they are not resolved. Chinese society must backtrack, as it were, to fulfill the necessary economic preconditions for socialism so as to be able to move forward once again toward communism. Historically, Chinese society at present is placed in the initial phase of socialism—the so-called undeveloped socialism. Under the circumstances, the compromise with capitalism represents not a departure from socialism but a necessary step to put China back on a historical path that will lead, through advanced socialism, to the ultimate goal of communism.[14]

There is no more reason not to take seriously the ideological intention underlying this theoretical defense of current policies of the socialist regime than there is to deny the ideological seriousness of the views I have just discussed. While the fact that this is a defense of an official socialism may cast some doubt upon it (which may be confirmed by the willingness of the leaders of Chinese socialism on occasion to go beyond the requisites of "undeveloped socialism" in their flirtation with capitalism), as a theoretical formulation it reflects the views of China's most distinguished Marxist theoreticians such as Su Shaozhi.[15] And although it is clearly a formulation that provides theoretical legitimation for compromises with capitalism, for reasons that should be apparent from the above discussion, there is no reason to read it as a disguise to cover up an insidious intention to restore capitalism in China.

The question is: is this formulation of the state of contemporary Chinese socialism any less ideological (or utopian) than the capitalist vision to which it is opposed? I think not, because the explanation of this retreat from socialist relations that had advanced beyond the means of the forces of production to sustain them, however sound theoretically, offers no account of how a socialism, having moved backward, will move forward again; how the socialist system as it exists will return to the process of socialist development, having consolidated itself further with the aid of capitalism; or the ways in which "actually existing socialism" contains within it the promise of the Communist society that it aspires to create. Indeed, the formulation utilizes theory to suppress these fundamental questions, which suggests that faith in an eventual return to socialist development toward communism can be sustained only by a hopelessly utopian vision of the future. This is a problem for all socialist societies of the present; in the case of China the problem may be even more severe because of the negative image impressed upon all suggestions of utopianism by the experience of the Cultural Revolution, which represented a historically unique attempt to bridge the gap between the present and the future of socialism. Theory may suggest that with the development of the forces of production the gap will close itself. Historical experience provides little reason to justify privileging theory over practice, which would suggest that such advance, especially with the aid of capitalist methods of development, is more likely to create social relations and structure of power with a corresponding ideology that is likely to render the vision more remote than ever.[16]

Chinese society today provides ample evidence of the likelihood of this latter possibility, and so does this very formulation itself, which radically limits the status of socialism as a motive force of historical development. I can think of no better way of arguing this point than by "reading" the justification for "socialism with Chinese characteristics" (the Chinese version of "undeveloped socialism") in the theoretical formulation above within the context of a specifically Chinese adaptation of a Marxist metahistorical design in the course of the socialist revolution in China. The contemporary formulation of the problems of socialism invokes in the listener a strong sense of déjà vu. Viewed from the perspective of a specifically Chinese discourse on socialism, this formulation represents the most recent articulation of a nonrevolutionary socialist alternative that is as old as the history of socialism in China.

I noted above that in its understanding of the social relations appropriate to the present stage of China's economic development, "socialism with Chinese characteristics" has moved past the Cultural Revolution and the collectivization of the 1950s to the earliest days of the People's Republic of China. We need to recall that the victory of the Communist Party in 1949 was viewed by the Party not as the victory of communism, or even of socialism, but as a victory of "New Democracy" or the "Democratic Dictatorship of the People." The idea of New Democracy was first enunciated by Mao Zedong in early 1940 as a specifically Chinese route to socialism (and generally as an idea that might be applicable to societies placed similarly to China within the capitalist world system). The considerations that it drew upon were as old as the history of socialism in China. Its primary concern was to integrate national considerations into a Marxist "scheme" of historical development. According to the idea of New Democracy, countries such as China which were placed in a semicolonial status in the world system of necessity followed different paths to socialism than either advanced capitalist societies or societies, such as the Soviet Union, that did not experience colonial oppression and exploitation. Before moving on to socialism, such societies had to go through a phase of development that was neither capitalist (because it was under the direction of the Communist Party) nor socialist (because it represented an alliance of all the progressive classes, including the bourgeoisie, in a struggle for national economic, political, and cultural development). Both in economic organization and in politics, the New Democratic phase of development would be a mixture of socialism and capitalist forms, with its development toward socialism rather than toward capitalism guaranteed by the guardianship of the Communist Party. With the incorporation of this idea, the familiar Marxist "scheme" of historical development represented in the consecutive stages of feudal-capitalist-socialist-communist societies was rephrased into the stages of feudal-semicolonial semicapitalist (or semifeudal)–New Democratic–socialist-communist social formations.

The idea of New Democracy represented an ingenious effort to find an equivalent to capitalist development that would not only answer the demands of socialism, but respond to national needs for autonomous development as well. What is of interest here is its conception of socialism. While the idea of New Democracy reaffirmed socialism as the goal of historical development, it rendered socialism for the time being into a guardian over a process of development that drew its economic dynamism from capitalism, which would be allowed to exist until China had fulfilled the economic conditions for socialism. This policing role assigned to socialism becomes even more evident if we remember that the idea of New Democracy drew directly on the social and political vision of Sun Yat-sen who, as the first political leader in China to introduce a socialist agenda into a national political program in 1905, deserves to be remembered not only as the father of Chinese nationalism, but as the father of Chinese socialism as well. Sun had very early on rejected capitalism as a viable development option for China and proposed socialism as the preferable path of development. Sun's idea of socialism, which I think has been a persistent one in the history of socialist thought in China, was a limited one: he was a confirmed believer in the value of competition as a motivating force of development, but since he observed from the European experience that unbridled competition created class division and conflict, he believed that socialism was necessary to keep in check the undesirable consequences of capitalism. His conception of socialism, in other words, did not require the repudiation of capitalism, only its control. He meant by socialism state policies that would be designed to guarantee such control.[17]

Although Mao's idea of socialism in his conception of New Democracy was not restricted to Sun's conception of socialism, the latter was very much part of the New Democratic phase of the revolution as he conceived it. Indeed, it is possible to suggest that New Democracy contained two contradictory ideas of socialism: as a future vision and as a guard against capitalism in a national situation that necessitated capitalist methods for national development (as well as a prerequisite to an imagined socialist future).

In the conception of Chinese Marxists today, "socialism with Chinese characteristics" represents a return to a developmental phase that is directly adjacent to New Democracy. "Socialism with Chinese characteristics" differs from New Democracy because it follows upon the abolition of private property and the socialization of the means of production which was completed by 1956 (although the tendencies toward reprivatization in the economy obviously make for serious strains in the boundary between New Democracy and the transition to socialism). But as an "initial phase" of socialism, it is also endowed in Chinese socialist thinking with many of the characteristics of New Democracy, for example, in the need to combine a market economy with a socialist economy, the stress on the need for economic development before further moves are made toward socialism, and most importantly in its class policies which recall the united front premises of New Democracy. These economic and social realities are expressed at the level of ideology in the new status assigned to socialism in historical development. The perspective provided by New Democracy confirms that "socialism with Chinese characteristics" does not envisage a return to or a restoration of capitalism; since it is New Democracy, and not capitalism, that sets the boundary to its retreat from socialism. On the other hand, the very move back in history pushes farther into the future the lofty goal of socialism, which may persist as an ideal but becomes ever more blurred in its features. The contradiction within the idea of New Democracy was from the beginning a contradiction between future vision and present reality ("utopia" and "actual conditions," as Mao put it in his essay). The difference between the early 1950s and the present with regard to policy is a difference in the interpretation and resolution of this contradiction. Mao (and the rest of the Party in the 1950s), when forced to confront the contradictions presented by New Democratic policy, erred on the side of "utopia" against the dangers of the dissolution of the vision into "actual conditions," and pushed on to socialism. The resolution at present is in the opposite direction. The role socialism occupies in "socialism with Chinese characteristics" is not that of immanent vision, pushing society further along the road to socialism, but of ideological guardian, to check the possibility of a slide into capitalism. The prominent illustration of this role is the insistence since 1982 on the infusion in Chinese consciousness of the values of a "socialist spiritual civilization" which, contrary to official claims for it as a key to realizing socialism, is most striking as a means to controlling through the medium of ideology the disruptive tendencies that have been created by the introduction of capitalist practices and values into the existing socialist structure.[18] This policing role assigned to socialism may be subversive of its status as an ideal and even as a system—since it appears in this role as a regressive element in a process that derives its dynamism from other sources, mainly capitalism. But it is nevertheless a role that needs to be taken very seriously not only because it is essential to the preservation of the socialist system, but also because the system in the eyes of many Chinese is essential to guarding national autonomy against the possibility of national dissolution into the capitalist world system.

By way of conclusion, I will explain briefly why I think "postsocialism" is more appropriate as a concept for describing the characteristics of this historical situation than other alternatives that are currently available. My use of "postsocialism" is inspired by an analogous term that has acquired currency in recent years in cultural studies: postmodernism. J.-F. Lyotard has described as the prominent feature of postmodernism an "incredulity toward metanarratives."[19] I would suggest by analogy that the characteristic of socialism at present is a loss of faith in it as a social and political metatheory with a coherent present and a certain future.

It may seem odd that I should describe as postsocialist a society that even in the eyes of Chinese socialists does not yet qualify for socialism. This is not the issue, however. The "socialism" in my use of postsocialism here does not refer to the social situation of the future envisioned in the classical texts of socialism—Marxist, anarchist, or otherwise; while this vision as political myth has served as a significant inspiration for revolutionary social change, it has also come to serve as an ideological disguise to suppress fundamental problems that have become apparent in the historical unfolding of socialism: to legitimize societies that may justifiably claim inspiration in the socialist vision but whose very structures in some ways represent betrayals of that vision and obstacles to its realization. The term socialism refers here to socialism as a historical phenomenon; the emergence of a socialist movement that offered an alternative to capitalist development and the state structures that have issued from this movement where it succeeded. It corresponds to descriptions of such societies by others as "noncapitalist development" (Rudolf Bahro) or "postrevolutionary society" (Paul Sweezy).[20] Why I prefer the term "postsocialist" over these alternative should become clear from the multifaceted suggestiveness of the term, including the challenge implicit in it to the sufficiency of "socialism" as a social vision.

Postsocialism refers, in the first place, to a historical situation where socialism, having emerged as a political idea and class-based political movement inspired by the idea, offered an alternative to capitalism; a choice, in other words, between capitalist and socialist methods of development. The Chinese who discovered socialism around the turn of the century were attracted to it because they felt that it offered an alternative to the capitalist development that had ravaged European society. While they felt that "pure socialism" (communism or the socialist vision) had already been proven to be impossible, and some compromise was necessary with capitalism, socialism provided the most desirable path for China's development.[21] In a sense one could suggest that Chinese socialism was "postsocialist" from it origins.

With the establishment of socialist states, this alternative was delineated more sharply, and so was the *problematic* of the gap between socialist vision and socialist reality; since once socialism was established in power, immediate tasks imposed by social "reality" took priority over the pursuit of the vision that inspired socialist revolutionary movements. While socialists have been able to postpone recognition of this problem by shifting hopes from one socialist experiment to another, it has become apparent over the years that the socialist vision in reality has given rise to structures of power that are not only inconsistent with idealistic anticipations, but have utilized the promise of ultimate socialism to legitimize political systems that themselves would have to undergo revolutionary transformation in order to move once again toward the socialist promise. While it is necessary to recognize that these systems are not socialist in terms of an ideal conceptualization of socialism (which makes possible a *socialist* critique of "actually existing socialism"), it is also necessary to go beyond formalistic evaluations to recognize that these systems are historical products of the pursuit of socialism and that they point to fundamental problems within the concept of socialism as a political concept; it is possible, in other words, that however noble the socialist vision of society, in practice—*given* the actual conditions of the world—it may issue only in the structures of power represented by "actually existing socialism" in its various manifestations, which share fundamental structural characteristics. I do not wish here to participate in an antisocialist criticism of these systems, which overlooks not only much that they have accomplished for their constituencies but also that the capitalist alternative itself suffers from deep problems; I wish merely to point out that they have fallen short of their ideological claims, and that this may not be accidental but a very product of the conceptualization of socialism historically: it may be that there is a fundamental contradiction between the economic presuppositions of socialism (a planned economy, abolition of markets, emphasis on use value over exchange value) and its social and political aspirations (equality, democracy, community). Some of the chapters in this volume have shown how the Cultural Revolution in China, for all its claims to communist commitment, ended up with consequences contradictory to its intentions for structural reasons. On the other hand, contemporary Chinese socialism, following a long tradition in Chinese socialism, pursues a way out of these problems by articulating socialism to the capitalist world order. To attribute these problems to the peculiarities of China or of Chinese socialism would be to overlook that "actually existing socialisms" in our day all have run into similar difficulties, although the severity of the problem may differ from case to case.

This historical tendency, that socialist states must look outside socialism in order to salvage or to sustain it, is the second characteristic of what I describe as postsocialism. I suggest that Mao Zedong, in repudiating the Soviet experience and in his uncompromising insistence on the nationalization of socialism, was every bit as "postsocialist" as Deng Xiaoping is for looking to capitalism for remedies to the problems of socialism. Both Mao and Deng, it is worth remembering, insisted on nationalizing socialism ("Chinese style socialism" for Mao), and legitimized this by arguing that Marxism needs to be adjusted to changing conditions.[22]

Third, it is the very absorption of socialism into societies such as the Chinese that from a broader historical perspective is the condition for postsocialism. The localization of socialism in its adaptation to different national contexts—what I referred to above as its vernacularization—has undermined its claims as a unitary discourse that derives its plausibility from its promise of a universal end to human history. The latter may still retain its force as a principle of legitimation, and even as a vague goal, but it is the specific historical context that in actuality gives socialism its historical shape.

The attenuation of faith in a single inexorable vision of the future is not necessarily detrimental to socialism; indeed, it creates the conditions for a more democratic conception of socialism, since it enables the imagination of the future in terms of pluralistic possibilities (this, I think, is the significance of the "Chinese" in "socialism with Chinese characteristics"). It also creates a predicament for socialism, however. The price to be paid for these possibilities may be the price that the postmodern era exacts from us all: a resignation, in the midst of apparent freedom, to the hegemony of present conditions of inequality and oppression; and the uncertainties of a history that offers no clear direction into the future. Chinese socialism, which only two decades ago boasted command of such a direction with unparalleled confidence, today finds itself in the uncharted waters of a postsocialist condition of which it is a prime example, as well as an occasion.

The contradictions within "socialism with Chinese characteristics" are products of theoretical efforts by Chinese socialists to encompass within socialism the structural ambiguities of a social situation that places an enormous, perhaps intolerable, strain on socialist ideology. The effort to articulate socialism to capitalism at the social and economic level is expressed at the level of ideology in the limitation of the ideological horizon of socialism by its very efforts to accommodate capitalism within socialism. I have argued above that the representation of this situation in terms of the conventional categories of socialism and capitalism may be sustained only by ignoring the fundamental contradiction that animates Chinese socialism today; either by dismissing the socialism of Chinese socialists, or by ignoring the implications for socialism as a metahistorical project of its assimilation to the demands of a capitalist world-system. The idea of postsocialism brings this contradiction to the center of our understanding of "socialism with Chinese characteristics" as its defining feature. It allows us to recognize the seriousness of Chinese socialism without falling into the teleological utopianism that is implicit in the word "socialism," which by itself refers not only to a present state of affairs but also to a future yet to come. It is the attenuation of this future, which does not necessarily imply a return to capitalism or the abandonment of "actually existing socialism," that justifies the description of this state of affairs as postsocialist, for without an immanent vision of the future, socialist societies may make claims upon the present but not upon the future. In my use of postsocialism to describe this state of affairs I disagree implicitly with theorists such as Sweezy and Bahro, and their preference for descriptions such as "postrevolutionary society" or "noncapitalist development." The latter may salvage socialism as a political ideal by denying the socialism of "actually existing socialisms"; but in doing so, they refuse to come to terms with the historical fate of that ideal. Terms such as "market socialism," on the other hand, are purely descriptive and contain no hint as to where such a socialism may be located historically. "Postsocialism" allows including "market socialism" or "a planned commodity economy" (both Chinese usages) in the present of socialism, but also unambiguously repudiates a future teleology while underlining the significance of the past—of the socialist context.[23] Chinese society today is *post*socialist because its claims to a socialist future no longer derive their force from socialism as an immanent idea. On the other hand, it is also post*socialist* because socialism, as its structural context, remains as a possible option to which it can return if circumstances so demand (this is what distinguishes it from a capitalist or even a postcapitalist society where such options as collectivization, socially, and a socialist culture, ideologically, are foreclosed). Even today, the socialist regime would seem to be prepared to return to economic and social practices that it has repudiated verbally (such as collectivization) if it seems necessary to do so—which is obviously a source of constant frustration to those who wish socialism in China to disappear forever and, because of their wishful thinking, have no way of explaining why the Chinese refuse to foreclose socialist options for the future.[24] Such options retain considerable power because, at least for the older generation of Chinese, socialism is an integral component of a national self-image.

The alternative that comes closest to postsocialism is Gordon White's recent suggestion that China may be evolving toward a new mode of production, which he describes as "social capitalism."[25] White recognizes that the term may not be felicitous (although it does parallel the "social imperialism" that Chinese coined to distinguish Soviet from capitalist imperialism), but the concept is suggestive. In recognizing this "socialism" as a mode of production, it avoids the ideological notion of socialism as a transition and, therefore, a temporary compromise with reality. It recognizes the system as a serious modification of capitalism; a new mode of production *does* represent a break with the mode out of, or in response to, which it has evolved. And, finally, it suggests the ideological and structural limitation of this system by the capitalist world order, within which socialism as we have known it has taken shape, and which may well serve to establish the boundaries to its further development. Socialism has now been incorporated into a division of labor within this world order; and it is unlikely that it may evolve further toward a socialist vision of society without changes in the world order itself.

My insistence on postsocialism, nevertheless, is motivated not by a desire to proliferate a new socialist jargon, but by an evaluation of socialism as an ideology, which calls forth considerations beyond the systemic analysis that guides White's conceptualization of the problem. Ultimately, postsocialism as a concept presupposes the perception of China (and of other socialist societies) in their relationship to the capitalist world context which has been the irreducible condition of socialism historically. Socialism has spread around the globe in the wake of capitalist transformation of the world; and the particular direction it has taken in different national contexts has been conditioned not only by specific national historical legacies but also by the history of the specific relationships to a capitalist world system in formation. Socialism in China was a response not to an internal capitalism, but to a capitalism that was introduced from the outside and appeared from the beginning as an alien force (but also, therefore, as a set of economic practices that China was free to choose from, or even reject, in accordance with national needs).[26] Hence the national element in Chinese socialism has always been prominent; it may even be suggested that there has been no autonomous socialist discourse in China, apart from or opposed to, a nationalist discourse on politics. Nationalism has enhanced the staying power of socialism, since socialism has offered the most plausible way to fend off the possibility of national dissolution into the capitalist world system. This appropriation of socialism into a national project, however, has also implied subversion of the claims of socialism as a metahistorical project. Chinese socialism, as a national liberation socialism, has played an important part in the disintegration of socialism as a unitary discourse, although it obviously may not be held responsible for a tendency of which it was as much a product as an occasion. Once Marxists had to give up hope in the possibility of a global socialist revolution (and it was nearly impossible, in historical hindsight, to entertain such a hope at the latest by the time of Lenin and the October Revolution), it was apparent that socialism could succeed only on a nation-by-nation basis *within* the context of a capitalist world-system. This has obviously created a deep predicament for socialist societies, vulnerable by their very economic nature to recapture by capitalism; since in an authentically socialist society, the transformation of social relations must take priority over considerations of economic efficiency. China during the Cultural Revolution was to make an effort to shut off world capitalism in order to establish a firm foundation for uninterrupted progress to socialism. The disastrous failure of that attempt has made it more evident than ever that socialist societies must make an effort to incorporate themselves into the capitalist world system without abandoning a basic structure of socialism.[27] This condition, in the period of what has been described by Marxist theoreticians as "late capitalism," is the ultimate justification for the use of "postsocialism" to describe it, because the need to find some accommodation with the capitalist world order without abandoning its basic institutional structure seems to be a permanent condition of actually existing socialism unless some drastic change occurs within the world system. To call this condition "capitalism" would be fatuous because it remains to be seen what the incorporation of socialist systems into the capitalist world order will imply for capitalism itself. For socialist societies such as China, the opening to capitalism has created new possibilities; among these may be included greater openness to economic alternatives (which may be greater even than that of capitalism, which, for all its flexibility, forecloses one important option—socialism), greater possibilities for democracy than before because of the relinquishing of faith in the immediate possibility of a coercive utopianism, and richer cultural possibilities that have arisen with the recognition of global cultural diversity, which was not possible so long as progress was conceived as a unilinear movement to uniform human destiny. On the other hand, it is also clear that within the context of a capitalist world system, the overall motions of which are shaped by a capitalism that socialism has ceased to challenge but rather seeks to accommodate, socialism can no longer claim to possess a coherent alternative to capitalism, but only a residual political identity that seeks to realize developmental goals imposed by the capitalist world system through "noncapitalist development." Postsocialism allows this situation to be described without reading into it either a capitalist or a socialist future, which, I suggested above, has less to do with the future than with a discursive struggle between present-day capitalism and "actually existing socialism" to appropriate the future.

I observed in the introduction to this discussion that the only casualty of the ideological activity to accommodate these changes may be the concept of socialism itself. It should be clear by now that the socialism to which I referred is socialism as a vision of the future, which continues to receive the homage of socialists without the power to guide the direction of socialism. This may justify predictions of the imminent demise of socialism, as some would wish, and it justifies my use of "postsocialism" to describe the present condition of socialism in China and globally. I would suggest, however, that post-socialism, rather than signaling the end of socialism, offers the possibility in the midst of a crisis in socialism of rethinking socialism in new, more creative ways. I think it is no longer possible to think of socialism as the inevitable destiny of humankind to follow upon capitalism. There may be little cause for regret in the passing of this ideological version of socialism that may serve (as it continues to do so in Chinese socialism) to counteract present uncertainty by the vision of a certain future; but there is something pernicious, as Paul Feyerabend has observed, in the notion of historical inevitability that imposes upon the present and the past the despotism of the future (much the same may be said of a vision of a future informed by the history of capitalism, which is often overlooked).[28] It is also possible to suggest that since the very origins of socialism, this ideological conception of socialism has conceived of the future not as an authentic alternative to capitalism, but primarily in terms of completing the tasks initiated by capitalism—it has, in other words, been bound by a vision of the future that is ultimately embedded in a notion of progress that was historically a product of capitalism. Freed of the commitment to such an inexorable future, socialism may be conceived in a new way: as a source for imagining future possibilities that derive their inspiration not from a congealed utopia, which postpones to the future problems that await resolution today, but from the impulses to liberation that represent present responses to problems of oppression and inequality. My use of post-socialism here is not descriptive but is intended to suggest that a radical vision of the future must move beyond what has been understood over the last century by the concept of socialism. Social and intellectual developments, partly under the impetus of socialist ideology, have revealed ever more sharply that the concept of socialism, essentially grounded in consciousness of class as the central datum of social oppression, is no longer sufficient to contain the question of social and political oppression the multidimensionality of which has impinged upon our consciousness with compelling power. To name just a few of current concern, oppression among nations, races, and genders, not to speak of state oppression of society, are not reducible to class oppression. Nor is it possible to account for such basic problems as ecological destruction, worldwide militarism, alienation rooted in a "culture of consumption," or even inequality created by a technical division of labor in terms merely of the class structure of capitalist society. Socialism as we have known it has not been able to address these questions any more effectively than capitalism; on the contrary, as the case of Chinese socialism today would indicate, the fetishism of development is so powerful that socialism has come to be judged by socialists themselves by criteria derived from capitalist development. It is an urgent task at present to reconsider the whole question of development, which requires a reconceptualization of society in terms other than prevailing ones. The question of class retains its significance, though not with the force of an earlier day, but any radical vision of the future must account for these other forms of oppression, and the social problems that are not merely products of class interests but have other sources and a life of their own.

So must we move beyond conventional ideas of socialism, without abandoning the perspective they afford, which still offers crucial critical insights into contemporary society, capitalist or otherwise. This is the ultimate purpose of my use of postsocialism to depict this state of affairs: in its open-endedness, the term may help release us from the hold of a narrowly conceived social vision and allow us to rethink socialism, in the eloquent words of Ernesto Laclau and Chantal Mouffe, in terms of the "infinite intertextuality of emancipatory discourses in which the plurality of the social takes shape."[29] The Chinese socialist experience, in the very questions it raises about socialism, provides us with an occasion to do so.

NOTES

1. Richard Kraus, *Class Conflict in Chinese Socialism* (New York: Columbia University Press, 1981), ix.

2. Rudolf Bahro, *The Alternative in Eastern Europe* (London: New Left Books, Verso edition, 1981). This corresponds to the commonplace but not exhaustive reading of socialism as a state-managed economy, in contrast to the privately managed economy of capitalism. I will not make an effort to define these terms any more precisely, since this whole chapter represents a reconsideration of the ways in which we think of these terms. Since I do not agree with the restriction of socialism to state socialism, I do not consider "socialist" any of the socialisms to which I refer, Maoist or Dengist. But I will suggest that Maoism was revolutionary in its pursuit of a "socialist" vision, whereas Dengism represents a deradicalization of Chinese socialism that seeks above all accommodations of capitalism. My emphasis here is on relationships, not on abstractly defined concepts. A word is necessary here also on the concept of "deradicalization," which Maurice Meisner has used in describing current policies in China. This concept derives from the earlier Soviet experience (see Robert Tucker, *The Marxian Revolutionary Idea* [New York: Norton Library, 1969]). While I agree with the idea, my argument here is that we must understand it in the Chinese context within a Chinese discourse, which contained a deradicalized notion of socialism from its origins; so that the current deradicalization also represents a return to the past. It is the meaning of this return that I investigate, which has something to tell us, I believe, about the seemingly inevitable deradicalization of all socialist revolutions, even though the specific form the deradicalization takes depends on the particular dis-

course in each case. It is also clear not just from the Chinese case but from the cases of other socialist societies that the challenge to socialism has moved far past deradicalization to questions concerning its viability. That capitalism may face an equally radical challenge does not obviate the urgency of the question.

3. Bill Brugger, ed., *Chinese Marxism in Flux* (Armonk, NY: M. E. Sharpe, 1987).

4. Deng Xiaoping, "Opening Speech at the Twelfth National Congress of the CPC," in *Selected Works of Deng Xiaoping* (Beijing: Foreign Languages Press, 1984), 394–97.

5. Zhao Ziyang, "Yanzhe you Zhongguo teside shehui zhuyi daolu qianjin" [Advance along the Road of Socialism with Chinese Characteristics], *Renmin ribao* [*People's Daily*], overseas edition (November 4, 1987).

6. Hong Xuezhi, "Fuguo qiangbing zhi dao" [The Path to "Wealthy Nation and Strong Military"], in *Renzhen xuexi "Deng Xiaoping wenxuan"* [Seriously Study the *Selected Works of Deng Xiaoping*] (Hangzhou: Zhejiang renmin chuban she, 1983), 204–10.

7. See Zhao's remarks in "China Plans Export-Led Economy," *Washington Post* (January 24, 1988).

8. See chapter 2.

9. Tong Gang, "Chinese Style Socialism Misjudged," in *Policy Conflicts in Post-Mao China,* eds. John P. Burns and Stanley Rosen, 37 (Armonk, NY: M. E. Sharpe, 1986).

10. *Charlotte Observer* (Monday, March 24, 1980). Also see the booklet that issued from the series published by the *Observer, China: The Challenge of the Eighties.* It is hard to tell who was responsible for the changes described here, because the booklet names a "Charlotte author Joan Dim" as "project editor."

11. By *Time* magazine in 1984 and 1985, and *National Review* in 1985.

12. Benjamin Schwartz, *Chinese Communism and the Rise of Mao* (Cambridge, MA: Harvard University Press, 1979), preface.

13. For an example written by a China specialist, see Anne F. Thurston, *Enemies of the People* (New York: Knopf, 1987).

14. See Zhao, "Yanzhe you Zhongguo teside," for this theme, which is common in much of Chinese theoretical writing. The contradiction referred to here was first formulated at the Party's Eighth Congress in 1956.

15. Gordon Chang, "Interview with Su Shaozhi," *Bulletin of Concerned Asian Scholars* 20, no. 1 (January–March 1988): 11–35. An earlier version was published in *Monthly Review* (September 1986).

16. It makes more sense at this point to view "actually existing socialism" as a mode of production in its own right rather than as a transition. For a discussion of this question, see Paul Sweezy and Charles Bettelheim, *On the Transition to Socialism* (New York: Monthly Review Press, 1971), esp. 123–35.

17. See chapter 2.

18. Arif Dirlik, "Spiritual Solutions to Material Problems: The 'Socialist Ethics and Courtesy Month' in China," *South Atlantic Quarterly* 81, no. 4 (Autumn 1982): 359–75.

19. Jean-François Lyotard, *The Post-Modern Condition: A Report on Knowledge* (Minneapolis: University of Minnesota Press, 1985), xxiv.

20. Bahro, *The Alternative in Eastern Europe.* For Sweezy, see his response to Su Shaozhi, *Monthly Review* (September 1986).

21. See chapter 2.

22. Mao described this as *Zhongguohua,* literally "making Chinese." The term commonly used is "sinification." I think this term is best avoided because of certain traditional associations that may distort Mao's usage. It was used traditionally in a culturalist sense, to denote *tonghua,* literally "assimilation." Mao's usage is premised upon a different conception of China than the traditional China as a nation. Hence Marxism may be "nationalized" into different national contexts. The usage is primarily social and political, not just cultural, and it does not presuppose a Chinese civilization as the premise of "assimilation."

23. Chang, "Interview with Su Shaozhi," for one instance. "Commodity Economy within a Socialist Context" is a variant.

24. Thus, in the face of difficulties created by privatization in agriculture, Chinese leaders have been willing to return readily to the glorification of the collective economy, as they did in the last party congress in praising the achievements of Doudian, which had refused to privatize and had been criticized earlier for its leftist conservatism. See "Bitter Harvest: Despite Recent Gains, China Is Again Facing Shortage of Grain," *Wall Street Journal* (January 19, 1988).

25. Gordon White, "The Impact of Economic Reforms on the Chinese Countryside: Towards the Politics of Social Capitalism?" *Modern China* 13, no. 14 (October 1987): esp. 456.

26. See chapter 2.

27. The idea that China could achieve national liberation only through autonomy from the capitalist system was a basic argument for the Communist revolution. See chapter 3. The Chinese experience played an important part in the reconsideration of socialism from a world-system perspective: that a socialist economy could not be genuinely socialist so long as it participated in the capitalist world economy. See, for example, Immanuel Wallerstein, *The Capitalist World Economy* (New York: Cambridge University Press, 1979). The argument here is similar to Wallerstein's, though it does not go so far as to assert that a "socialist" economy is in essence capitalist if it participates in the world economy (68–69). Nevertheless, there is a dilemma here, currently suppressed, that returns us to the original (pre-Stalinist) Marxist idea that a socialist revolution, to be socialist, must be global in scope. The obvious impossibility of this idea under present circumstances is part of the reasoning underlying the concept of postsocialism.

28. Paul Feyerabend, *Against Method* (London: New Left Books, Verso edition, 1986), introduction.

29. Ernesto Laclau and Chantal Mouffe, *Hegemony and Socialist Strategy: Towards a Radical Democratic Politics* (London: Verso Books, 1985), 5.

11

Looking Backward in the Age of Global Capital: Thoughts on History in Third World Criticism

It is not out of a frivolous urge to pun that I have borrowed Edward Bellamy's title as the title for this discussion. I would like to think out below, in however cursory a fashion, some problems related to the question of history in contemporary cultural criticism. I would like to do so, moreover, with reference not just to our intellectual environment in the United States but also to that of China (my area of specialization), especially because the continued claims made in China to socialism or Confucianism—that is, to an exceptional status within contemporary capitalism—bring into relief certain problems in cultural criticism. Bellamy's title, and the work to which it points, make possible a statement of the problem of history in cultural criticism within the context of contemporary capitalism—a form of capitalism that more than ever before requires that we view the question of culture as a global question. For reasons that should become apparent below, Bellamy's text, in its very distribution historically in the two geographical areas of concern, serves as a medium through which to globalize questions that are on the surface parochial to one society or the other. Marxism might have served the same purpose, but possibly not as well, and given Marxism's tribulations these days, it makes some sense for the moment to give it a rest.

LOOKING BACKWARD

Edward Bellamy's *Looking Backward,* published in 1888, tells the story of a young Bostonian, Julian West, who is frustrated by the poverty, disorder, and degeneration of society under the impact of industrial capitalism and is deeply disturbed by the complacency of the social elite in the face of this misery.[1] Going into a hypnosis-induced slumber, he wakes up in the year 2000 to find a totally transformed, and perfect, world, where all the problems of the previous century have been resolved. Bellamy looked "back" upon his society from an imagined future that is, temporally speaking, our present. The temporal location of his utopia in this present provides a convenient point of entry into our history, allowing us to ask why our times did not turn out to be as he, and others like him, imagined and to raise questions about the relationship of our past to our present that are urgently in need of answers.

Bellamy imagined a late twentieth-century world that had left behind it for good the problems created by capitalism. His vision is most striking because of its incongruence with the world as we know and experience it. Not only have we not left behind those problems but, through transformations as dramatic—though not as benign—as those that he imagined, we have added new problems to old ones and globalized those problems in an expansion and fulfillment of the processes at work in the late nineteenth century. When *we* look back upon the century that separates our times from Bellamy's, what we see is not a resolution of the problems of capitalism but an extinction of visions such as Bellamy's that held out the hope of future alternatives. Bellamy may have phrased his vision in the idiosyncratic language of aristocratic Bostonian wishful thinking of the late nineteenth century, but the future he envisioned was only one instance of imaginings about the future that were pervasive in his times and continued over the ensuing century, until very recently; though he refrained from calling himself a socialist and his vision was in basic ways antisocialist, his views would nevertheless he incorporated into socialist imaginings about an alternative future. What he had to say about the historical process that would bring about the future he imagined was not irrelevant either, and it was put to the test only to bring about results quite different from those that he envisaged. If only in a marginal way, the text *Looking Backward* was to contribute to the shaping of that historical process by inspiring activity, movements, and other imaginings about the future in areas that were at best at the margins of Bellamy's imagination.

I am interested here in the historical significance of *Looking Backward,* not in its content, but a few words about Bellamy's utopia might be useful for those who are not familiar with the work. The substance of the work may be described as an in-depth guided tour of the ideal society that had come into existence by the year 2000. That society may be described as a technological utopia with the social and aesthetic sensibilities of the late nineteenth-century Boston elite. It is a society without politics or conflict, especially labor conflict (and socialist agitation, one might add). All production and distribution are centralized, but individuals retain freedom of choice as to what and how they consume the products of industry. The society is based on an ideal military organization, in which laborers are members of an industrial army and give their labor willingly, as an ideal soldier would. Ignorance and greed, and therefore class conflict, have been left behind. It is also a society that has resolved the question of gender; women have their own army and constitute "a state within the state" because they are responsible for "bearing and nursing the nation's children."[2] In this society, individuals claim their share of the social wealth simply by virtue of being human. The same principles that guided this U.S. society in the year 2000 also provided the principles of international organization (at least for the advanced), in a world community that was finally free of war and conflict.

This society had come about through the "natural" evolution of industrial capitalism. The "labor question," the fundamental problem of the late nineteenth century, had "solved itself." As Dr. Leete, Julian West's guide in the new society, explains it: "The solution came as the result of a process of industrial evolution which could not have terminated otherwise. All that society had to do was to recognize and cooperate with that evolution, when its tendency had become unmistakable."[3] By the time the solution presented itself, production was already consolidated in the hands of a few giant corporations. All that needed to be done, Bellamy tells us, much like Lenin wrote shortly thereafter, was for these corporations to be nationalized to serve the public, rather than the private, good.

Upon its publication, *Looking Backward* was criticized from the Right for its idealized view of human nature and from the Left for its antilabor, antisocialist tone, as well as its celebration of hierarchy and material consumption. The popularity of the work was remarkable; it spawned Bellamy Clubs all over the United States and enabled Bellamy himself to launch his "nationalist" movement. The book sold hundreds of thousands of copies in the 1890s. In 1935, independently of one another, John Dewey, Charles Beard, and Edward Weeks (editor of *Atlantic Monthly)* named it the second most influential book of the past fifty years, next only to Karl Marx's *Das Kapital.* About the same time, the *Wilson Library Bulletin* included it among the twenty-six books of the past four hundred years that had "changed the modern world."[4] Arthur Morgan, a most sympathetic biographer of Bellamy, attributes the book's success to the fact that "the genius of Bellamy . . . took utopia out of the region of hazy dreamland and made it into a concrete program for the actual modern world."[5] More recently, a less sympathetic biographer, Arthur Lipow, has attributed Bellamy's success to its appeal to a middle class beleaguered by labor unrest, describing Bellamy's utopia as an authoritarian "barracks socialism" for the middle class.[6]

I am most interested here in something that these two biographers agree upon in spite of their wide differences in evaluating *Looking Backward*: that Bellamy's influence reached far beyond his time (and place). In Lipow's words: "The significance of Bellamyism goes beyond this [its place in the history of authoritarian socialist ideas in the United States] and even beyond its important role in the history of the American socialist movement during the formative period of the 1890s, for it not only foreshadowed later totalitarian collectivist ideologies but it was also a precursor of . . . bureaucratic statist or 'corporate' liberalism."[7] Although I do not necessarily agree with Lipow's terminology, his statement enunciates clearly two dimensions of Bellamy's relationship to efforts that were made to resolve the question of laissez-faire capitalism and that, in their failures, are part of the scenery of the past century as we look back upon it.

One of these is New Deal liberalism, an example of what Lipow has in mind when he speaks of "corporate liberalism." Bellamy's influence on the thinking of those who carried out the New Deal is confirmed (in addition to those cited above) by his biographer, Arthur Morgan, who was himself a convinced New Dealer as the head of the Tennessee Valley Authority before he became president of Antioch College. Morgan also cites the example in Franklin Roosevelt's cabinet of Adolf Berle, a close confidant of Roosevelt, whose father had been a member of the Bellamy Club of Boston and whose own views were quite "Bellamy-like."[8]

The other of these is socialism as we have known it. Bellamy's work was quite influential among those in Europe who later led a variety of social democratic movements and regimes, but the illustration I would like to focus on here is the case of Chinese socialism. Shortly after its publication in the United States, *Looking Backward* was serialized in the *Globe Magazine (Wanguo gongbao),* an influential missionary publication in Shanghai, and was available in book form by the early 1890s. The first generation of radical reformers in China was familiar with the book. Martin Bernal has suggested that *Looking Backward* was an influence in the first modern utopian works written by Chinese reformers such as Kang Youwei and Tan Sitong, whose works in turn exerted considerable influence on China's first generation of anarchists and socialists.[9] Some of the writings on socialism in the first decade of the century by the followers of Sun Yat-sen, or by independent socialists such as Jiang Kanghu, contained passages that might have come straight out of the pages of *Looking Backward.*

I do not wish to carry this line of argumentation beyond what is reasonable. In addition to the timing of Bellamy's utopia, it is this association of *Looking Backward* with two efforts to overcome laissez-faire capitalism, which are seemingly worlds apart, that makes the work an apt medium through which to view the past century—and the fate of those efforts. The point here is not that Bellamy's work "caused" the New Deal or Chinese socialism. Not only were many forces at work in the former, but Chinese socialism in later years moved in directions that had little to do with Bellamy, whatever role the latter's work may have played as a source of inspiration for its origin. The point here is that Bellamy's work, if only as a symptom, is illustrative of multidimensional diagnoses of the problems of capitalism and of efforts to resolve them. And the ultimate failure of these efforts is revealing of the distance between the future as he imagined it and the future as we have it.

It should also be obvious, moreover, that what is at issue is not the failure of Bellamy's utopia, however we understand it, to achieve realization. Rather, the issue is whether the "natural" evolution of capitalism can result in any kind of good society, as Bellamy thought. That faith is still with us, whether in the form of lingering memories of the New Deal in the United States or in the form of Deng Xiaoping's "forces of production and consumption" socialism.

This is where global capitalism comes in. We sometimes seem to forget that capitalism has a history (Marx himself sometimes forgot this, in spite of his assertions that perhaps only capitalism had a history). Unlike in Bellamy's vision, the world we live in at the end of the twentieth century is the world of global capitalism, which, evolving out of and in response to various efforts to tame capitalism, has defeated not only these efforts but has created a situation where the only alternative futures left to be imagined seem to be the paradise or the inferno of capital. In the celebration over the fall of actually existing socialisms, it is often overlooked that what has been extinguished is not just socialism, but New Deal "corporate liberalism" as well (which is what makes Bellamy a more apt metaphor than Marx in "looking backward" from our times). Global capitalism made socialism untenable. It also eroded, and continues to erode, the New Deal legacy of a regulated capitalism. It makes it difficult, if not impossible, to think of the world in terms of earlier categories such as nation or Third World, which were basic to both socialism and regulated capitalism. It has globalized the division of labor, creating a global elite and a global working class. It has globalized the commodification of culture. It has scrambled up notions of space and time. The only center that remains globally is located in transnational corporations. Richard Barnet, in his recent *Global Dreams,* tells us that three hundred corporations, all originating in what used to be the First World, account for 25 percent of all productive assets in the world.[10] What has been universalized are "global dreams." In the meantime, three- to four-fifths of the global population have been marginalized, rendered irrelevant to either production or consumption. Capital, having finally captured the globe, seeks to reconfigure local societies, classes, genders, and ethnicities with its own "global dreams" in a final move to extinguish all possibility of resistance. It not only appropriates the language of cultural resistance by commodifying it but, with its monopoly over cultural production, subverts cultural criticism by obliging it to incorporate the vocabulary of commodities in its language.

When we look back from the late twentieth century, it is not just Bellamy's text that seems a quaint relic of the late nineteenth-century American imagination, but the whole possibility of alternatives to capitalism that his generation, in the United States and elsewhere, imagined. Our problems may still be the problems of his day, but the solutions of his day seem to belong irretrievably in the past, relegated there by their failures in the intervening century, which makes them quite irrelevant to our present.

To recall the text in our times only underlines our distance from all the imagining about alternative futures during the century that separates our times from Bellamy's. So long as we remain cognizant of this distance, without which recollections of the past may serve little purpose beyond a reactionary nostalgia, however, a critical appreciation of our own present may be impossible without recalling these alternative imaginings—especially now that the future has been deprived of all coherence except as a proliferation of postcontemporary moments.

Before I engage this question of the relevance of the past, however distant, to critical appreciation of the present, I would like to share certain of my observations, recorded in my journal during a recent trip to China and presented in the order (sort of) in which they were recorded. Students of cultural studies in the United States are quite familiar with the problems of postmodern consciousness, its relationship to global capitalism (whatever name it may go under), and what this relationship may mean for radical criticism. My observations on China, however crude analytically, are of some help in illustrating, I hope, that the last bastion of socialism, as its leaders would like to think of it, is very much part of this same world.

KARAOKE SOCIALISM, OR FRAGMENTS
OF CULTURE IN CONTEMPORARY CHINA

Karaoke

A new kind of sign has appeared in Guangzhou since I was last there four years ago: Kala in Chinese characters, followed by OK in Latin letters. It takes a few restaurants, and constant repetition to myself, to figure out that it is Karaoke. Spreading from Japan, via Taiwan and Hong Kong, the term has become a ubiquitous sign in China of incorporation into an East Asian cul-

tural domain—as well as a sign of a new East Asian presence in global culture.

The People's Liberation Army

On the train from Zhengzhou to Beijing, I share a compartment with two PLA [People's Liberation Army] officers returning home from a meeting in Central China. Talk turns to Mao Zedong Thought. Observes the younger of the two: "At least Mao Zedong had some thought. Our current leaders have nothing that could be construed as thought (yidianr sixiang ye meiyou)."

The PLA is making good use of the media to improve its public image, which hit a low point in 1989. It is all over television. One TV show is reminiscent of a show on U.S. TV in the 1960s: What's My Line. *Three people dressed up as pilots. The task of the panel (that includes some PLA officers) and the audience (that includes many PLA soldiers, men and women) is to guess which is the real pilot. Reminds me of that old poster about the Pentagon having to have a bake sale to purchase bombs and planes.*

A friend closely connected to the PLA tells me of its form of corruption these days. Officers sell license plates to private entrepreneurs for their cars. A general's plate goes for 50,000 yuan, a colonel's for 40,000 yuan, and so on down the line. No wonder there are so many PLA license plates around. Back in the United States, a TV report on Chinese spying in the United States relates that the PLA and the Chinese armed police are busy with trade in this country; they have imported a million automatic rifles over the past year. Their shops also serve as covers for spying.

Imperialism and Culture

Report on a one-day conference on "Cultural Interaction" held at Beijing University early August 1993. Umberto Eco is the featured speaker. A Chinese participant in the conference, a professor from Beijing University, gives a paper on the need to reevaluate imperialism. According to the report, the Chinese scholar argued that although imperialism had negative aspects, these negative aspects must not be overemphasized. Imperialism was also important in facilitating cultural interaction and, therefore, enrichment. Some participants in a conference in Shanghai a few years ago had decided already that Shanghai should be viewed as a beachhead not of imperialism but of modernity.

This new consciousness is significant. It may enable a distinction of anti-imperialism from the cruder rejection of everything foreign at an earlier time and make possible a confrontation of Chinese modernity. But is that where it is headed?

This conference was sponsored by the Italian government. Italy, according to a recent report in a new publication, Construction and Investment, *has the second highest volume of trade with China of all the EC [European Community] countries.*[11]

Opening Ceremonies of the Seventh National Games, Xi'an, Early September, 1993

We had just visited Qin Shi Huang's tomb, with its terra-cotta army, which is still an awesome sight on a second visit. In the evening, I watch the broadcast from Beijing of the opening ceremonies of the Seventh National Games. There is heightened anticipation for these games all over China because the Olympic Committee decision concerning Beijing as a possible location for the 2000 Olympics is only weeks away. Students who only four years ago filled Tiananmen Square with calls for democracy have been demonstrating in favor of the Chinese bid for the Olympics. More irony. The head of the Chinese Olympic Committee is Chen Xitong, the former head of the Beijing Party committee, just a couple of years back described by students as a butcher for his role around 4 June 1989.

The Games are a dress rehearsal for the 2000 Olympics. The ceremonies open with a number in which the dancers are dressed in the uniforms of Qin Shi Huang's terra-cotta army. The symbol of imperial despotism rendered into the point of departure for Chinese culture. Minorities of various kinds appear in succession, singing and dancing of the brilliant future that awaits China. The last number is a dance of science fiction coneheads dressed in golden space suits. These are the kids who had been rehearsing throughout the summer on the campus of Capital Normal University.

It turns out that the charm of the ceremonies, enhanced by their elementary school amateurism, disguises a serious historical reinterpretation that is in progress. The performances are unified by their imaginary location in the northwestern reaches of the Yellow River, the route of the Silk Road, which is represented now as a symbol of China's openness to the World—past, present, and future (the slogan for the 2000 Olympics, on banners plastered all over Beijing, was: "A More Open China Awaits the 2000 Olympics"). The minorities are there to prove that Chinese society has always been a cosmopolitan society, a product of the historical mixing of different nationalities and cultures.

Are the ceremonies somebody's response to the TV series He Shang *(River Elegy) of a few years ago, which used the Yellow River as a symbol of Chi-*

nese parochialism and despotism and was one of the cultural landmarks on the way to June 4?

Salt City

A TV variety show celebrating the salt workers of Yancheng, Jiangsu. The show gets underway with the theme song from Bonanza. *It proceeds with performances in song and dance that celebrate the longevity and durability of Chinese culture ("the tree with 5,000-year-old roots"). The styles are mixed: Chinese operatic singers/tenors from the Red Army Chorus. The centerpiece is a celebration of the "salt of the earth," the workers of the salt mines. About twenty young dancers act out the "salt of the earth." Dressed all in black, they do a rap number. More songs and dances. The show concludes with more theme music from* Bonanza.

Buddhism

In the Shanghai station I encounter a group of Buddhists (origin, destination unknown). One of them is wandering around as Buddhist monks do, hands clasped in the back. I notice his sneakers. Written on the sides, in large letters, is the brand name: Playboy. I mention it after my return from China to Victor Mair, who is a specialist on the history of Buddhism in China. Victor tells me that at a major Buddhist seminary in Nanjing, the popular courses of study these days are hotel management and business English. That may explain why the monks at Xixia Temple in Nanjing came out of their quarters to chant their prayers every hour on the hour. Good for tourism (not just foreign). Mair also tells me that the area around a major Buddhist monastery in Tibet has been razed to be made into a parking lot. Circumambulation of the monastery (three times) was part of the ritual before prayers. Do they wind their way through Toyotas now? Whose cars?

The Past as Spectacle, Packaged

There are two theme parks in the most famous of China's special economic zones, Shenzhen, that the public relations people on Central TV seem to be very proud of. One is the Chinese history theme park, the other the aborigine theme park. The history theme park contains all the major tourist landmarks in China, from the Great Wall to the Great Buddha of Mt. Omei. In an English-language broadcast on Central TV, the American host working for the station announces: "China is a great country with a four thousand-year history. Can you believe that you can grasp this history in half an hour? That is what we will provide you with over the next half hour." Even a half hour is not necessary in the end. Because the same program also takes the viewer around the aborigine theme park, which contains villages in replica of a whole host of aborigines. One of the aborigines interviewed by the host tells him that he is very happy to be able to provide visitors with authentic portrayals of his people.

There is something self-defeating about the commnodification of the past, if the goal is to make money. The past, packaged and commodified, can be moved anywhere. Tourists from the United States no longer have to go to China to experience the Chinese past. A replica of the history theme park is now available in Florida.

The Chinese, the vast majority of whom cannot go abroad anyway, now can also experience the world right at home. A weekly TV program, Corridors to the World, *makes available to Chinese spectators the "exotica" of the world. Even better, for the people of the Capital anyway, there is a new theme park only sixteen kilometers from Tiananmen Square, where "Beijingers can tour the world in a few hours." According to a December report in* Travel China, *China's major tourism paper in English, the park contains all the famous spots of the world, Chinese and foreign, from the pyramids ("built of 200,000 white marble bricks, each as large as a bar of soap") to the Statue of Liberty. History is open-ended, too. "According to a park spokesman, some ground has been kept open. Those who want to add scenic spots from their countries can contact the park." The paper does not say how much it costs for countries to buy their way into world history in its most recent location.*[12]

History

On a visit to the Institute of Modern History of the Chinese Academy of So-cial Sciences, I raise the question of new paradigms that may be necessary now that the older paradigm centered on the revolution is in crisis. There is deep suspicion even of the notion of paradigm, which most of the historians present take as a possible new source of despotism over the study of the past. I ask them if "modernization," which seems to guide so much historical study these days, is a paradigm; they say no. But the real confrontation comes when I ask why Chinese historians pay so little attention to questions of ethnic or gender oppression and no longer discuss the question of class. One historian, a specialist on Chen Duxiu, the founder and first secretary of the Communist Party, launches a highly emotional attack on ideas that caused so much divi-siveness and suffering. We make up when I suggest that class, too, needs to be historicized.

Against the reductionist historiography of an earlier day that was blind to everything other than class, that wrote the modern history of China as a history of the Communist revolution, and the history of the Communist revolution as the biography of Mao Zedong, there is a refreshing openness in Chinese historiography today to other kinds of questions, to a possibility of disagreement over alternative modes of inquiry and explanation. State discourse on history is schizoid: It affirms the older history for legitimation of the Communist Party, but it also encourages a counterdiscourse to legitimize the break with the Maoist past, to justify Deng Xiaoping's "wager on the strong." This gives historians an opening, a space within which to pursue their own questions. But these questions seem to shy away from all hint of contradiction. Sensing that modernization is the order of the day, historians invade the opening with their own anti-Marxist, elitist ideologies; the "subalterns" as the subjects of history are pushed aside in a scramble to restore to history the primacy of modernization and the modernizers and even of those once viewed as oppressors of the "people," so long as they contributed to China's "wealth and power." In the process, modernity and modernism are stripped of all complexity, all sense of the possibility of alternatives. Is history more open, or is it simply that the Deng Xiaoping line has overcome the Mao Zedong line here as well?

Historians I encounter all say that there is little interest in the past among their undergraduates: no relevance to the present, no money in it. During the Summer of 1993, Beijing University announces publicly that in the future theoretical subjects will be downplayed in favor of practical ones. Among historians, the favorite topics these days seem to be China's opening to the West in the nineteenth century, the Guomindang, chambers of commerce, and bandits. They tell me that these topics are relevant to the present and, therefore, easier to publish. A friend who was studying Song dynasty science when I last saw her in 1989 has now turned to the study of banditry in the Song. Contribution to modernization appears to be the guiding principle in choice of dissertation topics by graduate students. Nanjing University holds a conference in November on the blooming field of "republican studies"; where the stress is on the Guomindang contribution to modernization. The conference is financed by a Taiwan "capitalist."

The turn is not just against Marxism in historical studies. The vast majority of books on the shelves of history sections in bookstores are biographies of emperors and generals, Chinese and foreign leaders. In 1902, the important reformer-thinker Liang Qichao wrote that the Chinese had never developed a national consciousness because Chinese history had been written as stories of kings and generals.[13] What does the new trend say about historical and national consciousness? Chinese historians all complain of manuscripts sitting in their homes because publishers will not touch anything that will not make money—which, according to the historians, means anything serious. It is no longer socialism but capitalism that constricts historical inquiry and consciousness.

A footnote: The People's Daily *(6 April 1994) reports that on 5 April, ceremonies presided over by Li Ruihuan were held at the Temple of the Yellow Emperor, which was constructed recently at the supposed site of the Yellow Emperor's grave in Qiaoshan, Shaanxi. Jiang Zemin and Li Peng contributed their calligraphies. A century of Chinese historical scholarship into myth and history in China's past wiped out instantly by the state's re-creation of ancient myths. But state discourse is only part of the problem. Anxieties about national identity, commercial interests in tourism, and a revived chauvinism all predispose numbers of Chinese to receptiveness to the state discourse. The* People's Daily *report is subtitled "The Sources of Chinese Civilization Are Distant, Its Course Long; Fondly Recall the Ancient Ancestor, to Re-create Its Splendor." The ceremonies were attended also by overseas "Compatriots," and a youth chorus from Taiwan provided the music. According to the report, overseas "Compatriots" have already contributed 13 million yuan for the repair of the emperor's tomb.*

Disneyfied history is an American invention. The state of Virginia just committed 130 million dollars for infrastructural expenses in preparation for a U.S. history theme park near Washington, D.C. A historian commenting on the theme park worries about the arrangement of history in the park, not bothering to wonder what it means to place "history" in a theme park in the first place. Disneyfied history erodes critical sensibilities here, too. Commercially produced historical spectacle in China, however, is backed by state discourse, which makes it all the more powerful in abolishing all critical space in which to think about the past. Is historical entertainment turned into political myth a sign of creeping fascism?

Runzhi Restaurant

In Nanjing there is a new Mao Zedong theme restaurant. The tiny restaurant has a little statue of Mao (the one with flowing overcoat, hand waving to invisible masses), flanked by two panels of quotations from the first two lines of the song "The East Is Red": "The East Is Red/The Sun Is Rising." On its TV screen, the restaurant features Mao Zedong karaoke videos. When the restaurant opened in the summer of 1993, one critic queried: "If a Mao Zedong cafe is allowed, then is a Marx bar okay, too?"[14] "Why not indeed," it is tempting to answer, "when socialism has become karaoke socialism, why not a Marx bar, too?"

THE NEW CONFUCIANISM AND ORIENTALISM

China today is a society where everything seems to be for sale. The slogan cheerfully adopted by managers of the Yangzi Gorge Dam last summer was "Come to the Gorges and Make Money." Universities are converting campus walls into shops and restaurants. Professors are "going out to sea" (a euphemism for business). The PLA is selling license plates. And the Party is selling everything. The modal person is the hustler. "It is more capitalist than capitalist societies," a Chinese friend says. It is also less coherent and more corrupt, it might be added—as befits a frontier economy.

It seems almost trivial under the circumstances to speak of the commodification of culture in contemporary China. Since Deng Xiaoping called for "consumption as a motor force of production" on his southern trek in spring 1992,[15] a consumption fever has joined the many other fleeting "fevers" in Chinese society. In a society where wages are still extremely low, who consumes the high-priced commodities (by Chinese standards) that now fill proliferating stores is a mystery. The stores are full of people. Friends say that most are window-shoppers, that no more than 3 percent of the population can and does join in the craze for consumption. The explosion in TV ownership means that culture, as it is peddled by TV programming, may be one of the cheaper and more universal items of consumption. The commodification of culture is not due to economic reasons alone. Some Chinese leaders realized in 1989 that the bad image of the Communist Party in the aftermath of June 4 had been the result of a failure in public relations. They have achieved, in the meantime, a public relations revolution of sorts (aided, no doubt, by foreign public relations firms that have been entering the China market). Culture is also good for public relations: showing the world how much China has opened up and telling the Chinese public that the opening only proves the durability and superiority of China.

The unspeakable Mao himself has become the object of this two-pronged (economic and political) commodification. Ideas associated with the Mao period have little relevance to anything these days. But Mao as commodity has been everywhere for the last few years with the "Mao Zedong Fever." The regime decided in 1989 to reassert Mao against unruly students. In the meantime, peasants and workers, dissatisfied with the inequalities and corruption bred by the reform, have made Mao into a literal deity. Dissatisfied students have all of a sudden gotten curious about Mao. Now there is a market to meet this multifaceted demand. Books about Mao, movies about Mao, Mao emblems for the poor, Mao gold coins for the rich, Mao watches, Mao clocks, and, of course, Mao tapes and videos were especially prominent in 1993, the one hundredth anniversary of Mao's birth. The BBC (British Broadcasting Corporation) reports that Mao theme parks may be next. Commodification takes away the political edge from any ideological residues that may be left from the Mao years. It also salvages Mao for legitimation purposes while obviating the need to confront issues of the Maoist past.

China is the most recent frontier of global capitalism, and so far the most fecund (though the Vietnamese "bullet train" threatens to become a competitor). In 1987, at the Thirteenth Party Congress, then Party Secretary Zhao Ziyang advocated opening up all of coastal China to foreign investment (to prevent that eventuality had been one of the goals of the Communist revolution). In the Summer of 1989, Zhao lost his post. His successors, however, were to go beyond what he might have imagined. Especially after Deng traveled south and declared that he liked what he saw, the country was caught up in an "investment fever." "Internationalization" is now the word.

The culture of capitalism that invades this new terrain is both a product of China's incorporation into capitalism and a necessity of its infrastructural preparation to attract capital. On the surface, the invasion is liberating. Commodification is a medium of freedom to the Chinese population after decades of controlled consumption. And what could be wrong with it if karaoke socialism enables that population to sing its way to socialism—not with the sterile songs of the Mao era but with the polyphonous tones of global capitalism?

Cultural disorientation might be one answer, but probably not a very accurate or useful one, besides being patronizing (are Chinese more "disoriented" than anyone else?). There is some disorientation, to be sure. What Chinese leaders would like to represent as another manifestation of "socialism with Chinese characteristics" in the cultural realm is most striking for its salad-bowl eclecticism; not cultural hybridity but cultural dissonance might best describe the contemporary production of culture. Besides, for all the claims to "Chineseness," neither in motivation nor in form is there anything particularly "Chinese" about the new cultural products, which are recognizable only as very contemporary products, on a local terrain, of a global consumer culture that erases the distinctiveness of the local by commodifying it. Claims to "Chineseness" appear at best as efforts to contain the corrosive effects of commodification in a society where the present betrays no visible links to a past or an imagined future—except in the assertions of future power.

The material terrain for these cultural developments may be revealing about the cultural activity as well. When Deng declared that he liked what he saw in Shenzhen and, by extension, Hong Kong (since Shenzhen is but an extension of Hong Kong, for all practical purposes), the urge became to reproduce Hong Kongs all over China so that, in the words of one cynical commentator, "all of China could be turned into one big Hong Kong." Deng was to decide subsequently that Hong Kong might be too unruly as a model. In 1993, he apparently sent a high-level official to report on Singapore as a possible model for China's internationalization. Word has it that this was what he settled on; whether subcontinental China can become a Singapore is highly problematic, but the choice of model is revealing nevertheless.

Singapore represents a new model of capitalism not just to the Party leaders in China. It is one of the "little dragons" (tigers to some) in Asia; it has been held up as a model of "authoritarian capitalism" or, oxymoronically, "communitarian capitalism."[16] To provide the new model with a theoretical identity, Singapore under its former premier Lee Kwan Yew also became a major exporter of Confucianism as a source of East Asian development.

The claim is testimony both to the globalization of capital and to seams within global capitalism. Singapore, along with that other modern city-state, Hong Kong, is an example par excellence of the globalization of capital; from a center in the entrepôt trade of the British East India Company, it has been transformed with post–World War II technologies into a gathering place for global high-technology production and distribution, as well as a financial center. It may be an indication of the essential homelessness of global capital, however, that in spite of the origin of most high-tech corporations in Europe, Japan, and the United States, their location in Singapore can justify local claims to a different kind of capitalism. As capital has been globalized, it has to some measure assumed the garb of local cultures, which shows in recent discussions of "economic cultures" or different "cultures of capitalism."[17] In the case of the so-called dragons, Confucianism appears as the unifying local feature of capitalism.

This "new Confucianism," while it claims continuity with earlier efforts to revive Confucianism in twentieth-century China, is nevertheless little more than a restatement of the problems of Confucianism in the language of capital. There is little about it, in other words, that suggests an alternative to capitalism, be it in terms of social relations or human relationships to nature. Rather, it seeks to replace the earlier Weberian argument about Confucianism as an obstacle to capitalism (on the grounds of the differences in the above relationships) with an argument that Confucianism is a source of values that promote capitalism. Capitalism is its frame of reference, and it is to this framework that the argument articulates Confucianism; the result is that Confucianism appears in the argument not in its differences from a culture of capitalism but as a different culture of capitalism.

The point here is not whether Confucianism, or Chinese cultural legacy, may have anything to contribute to development, but rather the dehistoricization in the argument both of Confucianism and of capitalism. To take up the latter first, it is quite possible that Confucian values, and the institutions informed by those values, might have impeded an autonomous capitalist development or capitalist development in its earlier phases, while being suitable to capitalism at another phase and within a new institutional and global context. The hierarchical familial values that are often held out as characteristics of Confucianism, as well as a Confucian emphasis on education, may well be functional to a global capitalism, where the need simultaneously for global control and local flexibility seems to favor organizationally a combination of the transnational corporation, on the one hand, and the small firm, on the other hand. Kinship or pseudokinship values, loyalty and teamwork, and high levels of education may well meet the needs of this organizational setup better than the individualistic values of an earlier day. Chinese capitalists are not any the less "capitalistic" for being Chinese. They merely add a repertoire of commercial practices and values derived from China's past to the existing repertoire of capitalism, which enriches and expands the possible choice of economic practices. (Is this also their advantage these days over Euro-American capitalists who have a narrower repertoire to work with?) Capitalism has always been good at absorbing all kinds of knowledge. Euro-American capitalists did not just expand over the globe, they did so by absorbing "local knowledges" along the way. Now Chinese capitalists are adding their "local knowledge" to the legacy of capitalism.

The problem, therefore, is not the relevance of native Chinese practices to capitalism, but the absence from these arguments of an account of the history in capitalism. The proponents of Confucianism may disagree with Weber's conclusions, but they follow even more than the Weberian essentializing procedures in their arguments. Dehistoricizing procedures are even more evident in the treatment of Confucianism, which, deprived of its intellectual complexities, is often reduced in these arguments into a timeless set of characteristics of one kind or another. Indeed, Confucianism more often than not appears as a repository of what are said to be characteristics of Chinese or even East Asian cultures. This in not new with Confucianism. Lionel Jensen has argued that Confucianism as a discourse was an invention of the Jesuits in China,[18] and we might add that over the two millennia of Confucianism it has been invented and reinvented in state discourses, until it was finally rendered into a synonym for Chinese society in the twentieth century. It is now being reinvented in its articulation into capitalism. It is also worth noting here that this reinvention is not just the doing of Chinese scholars; Tu Wei-ming, an outstanding proponent of the new Confucian idea, readily concedes the origins of this reinvention to the work of visionary developmentalists such as Herman Kahn and Peter Berger.[19] (Just as, as a success story, "authoritarian capitalism" draws upon the developmental ideas of Samuel Huntington.) Confucianism in this new guise is indeed functional to a capitalism in need of a hegemonic ideology over labor, women (who make up a large part of the labor force), and others. (According to a Singaporean scholar who must remain nameless here, Lee Kwan Yew has expressed regret on several occasions for having encouraged women's education.)

For Chinese scholars, however, the Confucian revival may carry an anti-hegemonic significance as well, in the assertion of the relevance of Chinese cultural values against an earlier Euro-American denial of their relevance in the modern world. In this sense, it also appears as an assertion of the new-found power of Chinese, and East Asian, societies. It is Euro-American managers these days who are anxious to discover in Confucianism (or in a variety of "Eastern" classics ranging from the *Yijing* to military tracts of one kind or another) the secrets of East Asian success. This success seems to confirm the uniqueness of East Asian cultures—but the same cultures ironically seem to be portable. (Gobalism, indeed.)

I would like to stress here that in its intellectual procedures, as well as in many of its conclusions, the Confucian or the East Asian argument reproduces what we have come to call "Orientalism." The stipulation of a cultural essence, the location of the essence in some classic or some institution (such as the family, the examination system, whatever), the dehistoricized and de-socialized understanding of culture, and even the obliviousness to contemporary history (accompanied by a suppression of its own origins in contemporary history) very much mark the Confucian argument as an Orientalist argument that is the product of collaboration between Euro-Americans and the "Orientals" themselves. This Orientalist discourse also draws its power from a collaboration between the state, global capital, and intellectuals who, themselves products of a new world situation, articulate in an old cultural language their own status within this world situation, while suppressing their complicity with new forms of hegemonic power.

The Singapore connection as a developmental model may have something to tell us about cultural developments in China as well. As with the Confucian revival (which, needless to say, has also found its way to China, not just in theory but in tourism as well), the assertions of ties to a past going back to the Yellow Emperor connect Chinese culture to a contemporary global situation. This is visible in the revision of Chinese history to prove that China has always been an open and cosmopolitan society (an Italian delegation was told by its hosts that Chinese-Italian friendship was a continuation of the legacy of Marco Polo), which relieves foreigners of their anxieties about investing in a China that might reclose any time.[20] It also shows in the forms of cultural production, which blend "Eastern" and "Western" forms and frame patriotism with the theme music from Bonanza.

The apparent cosmopolitanism of cultural production, however, also disguises simultaneous assertions—in strong tones of national chauvinism—of a Chinese exceptionalism that, refusing to engage the recent revolutionary

history, finds its outlet in cultural abstractions of a remote past. The chauvinism here may be simply an exaggerated expression of pride in the achievements of a Third World society that, playing by the rules of a new world situation, has been able once again to assert its own subjectivity and to reinvent
old myths to express itself. But is that the whole story? What of the repudiation of revolutionary history, which in the past also served as an account of
national achievement? Does it make no difference that culturalism has taken
over from revolution as the trope of national self-assertion? What does the
choice of trope indicate in terms of China's place in the world and a vision
for the future? Above all, can this self-assertion be grasped in its full contemporary significance without reference to a new world situation?

China's opening to the world appears in much of this cultural production
as the replay of world cultures on Chinese national terrain, which then cata-
pults that terrain into the future as a developmental model for others to follow. There are claims on the past as well. An example is recent discussion of
the "Chinese" origins of American Indians, inspired by DNA research in the
United States showing conclusively the Asian origins of the native populations of the Americas. According to one author writing in a popular newspaper, the Americas were populated by remnants of the Yin dynasty escaping
from the Zhou conquerors at the end of the second millennium B.C. "Yin"
then became the origin of the word "Inca." Since Shanghai was the point of
departure for the Yin emigrants to the Americas, the author concludes with a
celebration of a brilliant role in the Pacific once again for a resurgent Shanghai (this occurred right about when Deng referred to Shanghai as still a new
model for the rest of the country).[21]

Cosmopolitanism in these manifestations does not turn into an assertion of
global equality or even a form of globalism but instead becomes a medium
for the expression of national power. This has shown up also in geopolitical
language in assertions of a "Greater China" or a "cultural China" (which
reaches far beyond East Asia in its compass, to encompass all kinds of Chinese all over the world). It shows in cultural production in a renewed emphasis on what might be summarized as "Asia first, and in Asia, China first." In
this guise, too, representations of Chinese culture bracket the historicity of the
very concept of China, and the past in its very reaffirmation is worked over
by the language of the present.

Socialist China worked over by global capitalism, in other words, has become a promoter of Orientalist notions of China, which have now been appropriated as the characteristics of Chinese society, often in the very language
of Orientalism (including the term "Oriental" itself). China has no history but
culture (or history only as the repeated manifestation of a "5,000-year-old
culture"), and that culture is not subject to social appropriations and produc-

tions but is proof of a national, if not racial, homogeneity. While theorists in the United States speak of the end of nations and problematize culture as a social construct, there are no comparable doubts in China either about the nation or about culture. We may assert that this discourse, promoted by the state, disguises deep anxieties at a time when there is every sign of political and economic disintegration as China is incorporated into a global capitalism, but for the time being it is this formerly socialist and Third World society that has become a major promoter of Orientalist images of itself.

This question of an "Oriental" society producing Orientalism points to the complexities of the question of culture in China today. The commodification of culture promotes Orientalism in its very need to package Chinese culture into a consumable and reproducible entity. But Orientalism, whether in the form of Confucianism, of which there are advocates in China as well, or in more abstract statements, is also a product of newfound economic and political power. An essentialized Chinese culture becomes a cultural expression and explanation of material success. It also serves as a means to contain a reality within which Chinese may be successful, but "Chineseness" is very much a problem in the diasporic dispersal of the Chinese.[22]

Orientalism itself may be a complex phenomenon in a Chinese perspective. The TV series *He Shang* utilized Orientalist images of China to criticize the existing system (accompanied by the revival among historians of an interest in "Oriental despotism"). It is interesting that critics of the series, in China as well as in neighboring Chinese societies, attacked it not because it was antisocialist but because it was derogatory about Chinese culture. Now the critics have taken over the Orientalist images in a reassertion of the superiorities of Chinese culture. Against that, some offer "Occidentalism" (a reverse Orientalism in which a timeless West is held up in critique of a timeless China) as a critical position.[23]

HISTORY IN CULTURAL CRITICISM

Confined to a discursive space that is theoretically at odds with the comparative tenets of contemporary cultural studies, the sinologist holds on to the language of the nation-state as his weapon of combat. This is one of the major reasons why "history," in the sense of a detailed, factographic documentation of the local, the particular, and the past (understood as what has already happened and been recorded), enjoys such a prioritized disciplinary status in East Asian cultural politics. The hostility toward the critique of Orientalism currently heard in some East Asian scholarly circles is a direct consequence of this language of the nation-state.[24]

The Orientalist has a sibling whom I will, in order to highlight her significance as a kind of representational agency, call the Maoist. Arif Dirlik . . . sums up the interpretation of Mao Zedong commonly found in Western Marxist analyses in terms of a "Third Worldist fantasy"—"a fantasy of Mao as a Chinese reincarnation of Marx who fulfilled the Marxist promise that had been betrayed in the West." . . . Whereas the great Orientalist blames the living "third world" natives for the loss of the ancient non-Western civilization, his loved object, the Maoist applauds the same natives for personifying and fulfilling her ideals. For the Maoist in the 1970s, the mainland Chinese were, in spite of their "backwardness," a puritanical alternative to the West in human form—a dream come true.[25]

My colleague shares the predicament of Mead and Levi-Strauss insofar as the stereotypical "native" is receding from view. What confronts the Western scholar is the discomforting fact that the natives are no longer staying in their frames . . . what I heard was not the usual desire to archaize the modern Chinese person but rather a valorizing, on the part of the Western critic, of the official political and the cultural difference of the PRC [People's Republic of China] as the designator of . . . "authenticity." If a native from the PRC espouses capitalism, then she has already been corrupted. An ethnic specimen that was not pure was of no use to him.[26]

The Tiananmen Massacre of June 1989 brought modern Chinese history to a standstill. This is the standstill of catastrophe. If Chinese history in the past century and a half has been a series of catastrophes, the events of June 4, 1989, marked their summation in the form of a mindlessly internalized violence directed against civilians by a government which barely forty years ago had stood for hope and emancipation from the corruption of the Chinese tradition.[27]

These quotations are from *Writing Diaspora*, a collection of essays by Rey Chow, a literary and cultural critic with whom more often than not I find myself in agreement. I do not intend to analyze these texts in detail but merely to comment on the questions they raise with regard to a problem that I would like to address briefly: the problem of the past in cultural criticism. I have selected these quotations because they illustrate how the very selection of focus in analysis may blur, if not suppress, what I take to be historical questions of primary significance for contemporary cultural criticism.

First, the question of Orientalism, which runs through three of the four quotations above, should be addressed. Rey Chow herself is aware that "the natives" themselves are quite capable of producing Orientalism, but she brackets that awareness that, if rendered explicit, would have introduced into her analysis a problem that complicates current approaches to the question of Orientalism. This problem is implicit in what I have said earlier: What do we do with Orientalism when the "Orientals" have become its promoters? Cultural criticism in recent years has focused on Eurocentrism as an, if not *the,* object of criticism. But how do we deal with a situation when ideas, attitudes, and intellectual procedures that may have been products of Eurocentrism historically are appropriated by the "natives" themselves in reassertions of new-found power? My earlier observations on contemporary China were not intended to engage in gratuituous China-bashing, but rather to underline this problem. I might add to what I have already said another observation: Those foreigners who seem to be most welcome in China are not those who would advocate a critical understanding of the Chinese past and present but are those who share in the ahistorical homogenized notions of Chineseness; in other words, they are the purveyors of Orientalist attitudes. Not only is China a promoter of Orientalism, therefore, but it sustains it abroad in a new guise.

It seems to me, therefore, that whatever role Euro-American Orientalism has played in shaping contemporary consciousness globally, it is no longer sufficient in cultural criticism to focus on Eurocentrism as *the* problem. The problem of Orientalism is a problem in global culture, and in order to deal with it, cultural criticism has to adopt a global perspective rather than merely juxtapose nations and regions in cultural production.

Second is the related question of the past, which, like the question of Orientalism, underlies all Chow's statements quoted earlier. It is present in the statement about "Maoism" as a "sibling of Orientalism," which is also interesting because it draws on a statement of mine. Although Chow does not misrepresent what I wrote, she cites it out of context in ways contrary to my conclusions. There is no question that Maoist fantasies have been an element in leftist thinking; for a while, it was even pervasive among other fantasies of the Left about the working class, peasantry, and other oppressed groups, which now go under the general heading of "subalterns." Rather than recognize an autonomous consciousness within these groups and try to understand what they say and want, leftists of all stripes have imposed their own fantasies, revolutionary longings, and abstractions upon them. In this sense, it may be possible to speak of a leftist Orientalism. However, declaring such fantasies (or, should I say "visions") as a "sibling" to a hegemonic Orientalism and therefore totally suppressing the liberating impulses that informed them is also to bury that strain on the Left that recognized Third World national liberation movements as an integral part of a global political agenda. My statement was intended to underline the material circumstances that differentiated Maoism (as a Third World, national, and vernacular Marxism) from European Marxism; I sought to repudiate neither the Marxism of Mao nor Marxism. Chow's condemnation of a leftist Orientalism not only ignores crucial issues of Third World Marxism, but it does so by relegating those issues to the past, as part of an Orientalist legacy. Obviously Rey Chow does not think that Maoism, or any idea associated with it, should have any relevance to the present. I happen to think that it does—above all in the Maoist

insistence on the need to imagine alternatives to Euro-American developmental models.

But Maoism is relevant in another sense. However we may evaluate it as
an ideology, as an integral part of our immediate past, Maoist ways of thinking about the world and the Maoist challenge to Eurocentrism (including
Marxist Eurocentrism) are part of a legacy that has expanded our ways of
thinking about the world. That Maoism in practice produced some horrendous
results may lead to a wish to bury that past, but the question is what else we
would be burying with it, and how burying that past plays into the hands of
the contemporary hegemony of a Eurocentric developmentalism. I may note
here something that I have argued elsewhere at some length: that certain ideas
of Mao, especially those ideas associated with guerrilla warfare, would seem
to be alive in the marketing strategies of global capital, which utilizes them
to sustain its hegemony.[28] Finally, since Chow is very concerned in general to
recognize a contemporary presence for the "natives," it might be noted that as
China is absorbed ever more deeply into a global capitalism, Maoist aspirations in transformed form have enjoyed a revival in China, not so much in the
discourse of the state as in popular transformations of Mao into a bodhisattva-
like savior.[29]

The repudiation of the past is even more dramatically evident in Chow's interpretation of the events of June 4, 1989. Although the very trauma caused
by those events may justify her response, it does not seem to me that it justifies suppression of the questions raised by the event, chief among them an intellectual and cultural incorporation into global capitalism (which is a matter
apart from whether or not the protestors sought to overthrow the Communist
Party in favor of capitalism). This is quite evident in Chow's interpretation of
June 4 as the summation of modern Chinese history, which now appears as a
piling up of catastrophe after catastrophe, rather than a revolutionary history
that sought liberation from imperialism and brought forward significant social aspirations. What is being buried in the statement, in other words, is not
just the Communist Party, with which I have little sympathy, given what the
Party has become, but revolution itself and with it all the categories, such as
"imperialism" and "class," among others, that until recently were fundamental categories in the analysis of oppression and liberation (once again, I am
referring to the suppression of a problem, which obviates the need to engage
those categories as problems).

Finally, Chow, it seems, objects not only to the uses of the past but to history as epistemology. The first quotation cited earlier states explicitly that the
stress on history is a manifestation of continuing Orientalism in the China
field. If Maoism is a "sibling" of Orientalism, history appears here as its
handmaiden. What is negated, once again, is not just a hegemonic objectivist

version of the past, but the past as a realm of inquiry that might have something to do with a liberationist or a critical project. It may be trite but useful to recall here that historical practice informed by Marxism (including Third World Marxisms, such as Maoism) has played a central role over the last half century in bringing to the surface of historical consciousness all those groups, from workers and peasants to women and indigenous peoples, as subjects of history; cultural criticism takes these groups (now generalized as subalterns) for granted while denying the original impulse that propelled them into our thinking about culture. Conversely, as in contemporary Chinese historiography, the suppression of that impulse and, with it, questions of subalternity in history reduces cultural thinking to Orientalism, or to that preoccupation with "kings and generals" to which I referred earlier.

Chow's own work provides examples of the ways in which obliviousness to historical questions may undermine criticism. She is not beyond falling into an Orientalist mode, as in her analysis of the relationship between the state and intellectuals in China, which she presents as an unchanging relationship from the beginnings to the present—in the process calling on the testimony of *Time* magazine, which long has been a purveyor of Orientalist interpretations of China. The refusal to come to terms with history shows at the other end in her silence on the fate of the protesters of 1989 in the years since, when Chinese intellectuals have emerged not only as enthusiastic proponents of China's incorporation into a global capitalism but have done so in complicity with the state that they opposed in 1989.

The third and final question the statements raise is the question of the "native." Given her stance on the questions of Orientalism and history, it may not be surprising that Chow's observations on Eurocentrism and the "native" also suffer from a bracketing of historicity. To repeat what I have already said, Rey Chow is quite aware of the possibility of "native" complicity in the production of Orientalism and, in the particular case of China, of the suppression by Chinese intellectuals themselves of "Chineseness" as a problem. But her exclusive focus on Eurocentric Orientalism blurs the problem of the Orientalism of the "Oriental." A criticism of the native for being "capitalist" might indeed constitute denial to the native of a contemporary presence, but whether such denial of contemporaneity carries the same meaning to Chow's "colleague" as it did to Mead and Levi-Strauss is another matter. It is quite possible that what is at issue in the former situation is not the "authenticity" of the "native," but rather the native's complicity in an oppressive global situation. To suggest that the reference point for evaluating the "native's" capitalism is the PRC state is misleading, as "capitalism" no longer suffices to distinguish the "capitalist" native from the state in the context of contemporary China; indeed, it makes the "native" complicit in the power of a state of which Chow is critical. It is possible that Chow ignores this problem because, somewhat ahistorically, she identifies the PRC state with the Maoist past regardless of how much it may have broken with that past. What she fails to bring to the surface of analysis is this question: What should we do when the "native" emerges as an oppressor or an active agent in a structure of oppression? The "capitalist" Chinese is not just an object of a Eurocentric "gaze" but a "subject" who, in complicity with the state, appears today as an exploiter (in the name of "socialism with Chinese characteristics" or a more straightforward assertion of national/racial power) not just of other Chinese but, in the sale of cheap and "flexible" Chinese labor to global capital, of laborers elsewhere. Chinese labor practices, held up to others for emulation, become part of a global structure of oppression and exploitation not only in the Third World but also in the First. To represent the contemporary "native" in terms of earlier global relationships indeed does little but suppress the questions raised by contemporary global configurations.

The fundamental question here is how to deal with a moment of radical change in time and space with a vocabulary and frames of reference of another time. Ironically, whereas Chow is anxious to repudiate absolutely earlier discourses or politics, her own approach to the question fails to account for new meanings generated by the new historical situation. The fundamental question thrown up by this historical situation, put starkly, is: Is it Eurocentrism that is presently the primary problem for cultural criticism or is it capitalism, with its own history, that is no longer to be identified with its European origins?

Cultural criticism has yet to confront a new global situation of which it may well be a product. This new world situation has been created by radical changes in the global political economy, by the emergence of a global capitalism that has transformed the economic, political, and cultural configurations of an earlier day. Ironically, it is in this situation created by global capitalism, when the globalized economy impinges irresistibly and globally on everyday life, that cultural criticism appears most reluctant to address questions of political economy. Two consequences are especially noteworthy.

One is what I will describe as a kind of solipsism in cultural criticism, by which I mean a tendency to view the world of cultural criticism as the world. Cultural criticism in recent years has raised many issues of the utmost importance by questioning earlier understandings of such categories as imperialism, the Third World, nation, class, and culture, as well as by introducing new categories into analysis. It has also brought in a new understanding of spatiality and temporality, of the local and the global, of encounters between nations and peoples. What is a problem, however, is a tendency to assume that the realities of cultural criticism are the realities of the world and that others share in these perceptions of reality, especially powerful others. The world of cultural criticism repudiates totality even as corporate managers are at work on plans to globalize power; it repudiates utopianism and the future, whereas a "handbook for managers" states that "analyzing your present culture is like going to history class, when you could learn more valuable stuff from studying the future";[30] it repudiates the past, though Henry Kissinger and Zbigniew Brzezinski still speak of Russia in Cold War terms. The world of cultural criticism declares an end to centers, but Richard Barnet tells us that three hundred transnational corporations control 25 percent of all "productive assets" in the world; it tells us that nations are dead when the United States and Japan are locked in combat over national markets. The world of cultural criticism tells us that "Chineseness," in the very conditions of diaspora, is an end rather than a starting point of definition, while the Chinese are singing that they are the children of the Yellow Emperor destined for global glory. The world of cultural criticism holds that cultures are porous when ethnic groups around the world are engaged in genocide in the name of cultures; it speaks of the politics of identity and location when a global capitalism is in the process of marginalizing and casting out into a never-never land the majority of the population of the globe regardless of location—in the United States, China, India, or the so-called basket cases.

The problem is not that cultural criticism is wrong. I picked the examples above *because* I think that cultural criticism has had much of value to say about those issues. The problem is that cultural criticism does not seem to look beyond itself to another world, with the consequence that there is a blurring of lines between what goes on out there and what should be going on, between analysis and wishful thinking. In a conference I attended recently, one participant coming from the "real" world of the Social Science Research Council reminded the participants about the "real" world. This is not my intention. The question is not that the world of cultural criticism is not "real." It is rather that there are other worlds out there that are also real, in addition to having more power. To the extent that cultural criticism ignores the global framework that is also its framework, it remains oblivious to these other worlds. The consequence is a failure to delineate its own position within this world, so as to carve out a location for resistance. Indeed, in some of its versions, cultural criticism renders it impossible to speak about politics, when politics still rule the world.

The other consequence, related to the first, has been to cast criticism adrift in the uncertain waters of ideology: To the extent that cultural criticism theorizes the world without a sense of its own location within it, it begins to speak itself in the disorganizing language of global capital, while its own insights are quickly absorbed into the language of global hegemony. This is especially

evident in Third World cultural criticism. I have argued this out at length elsewhere with reference to the so-called postcolonial criticism, so I will not repeat it here.[31] Suffice it to say that "postcolonial criticism," as part of its project of repudiating metanarratives, has been anxious also to repudiate
questions of political economy and past conceptualizations of the world as
well as questions of political struggles that were informed by these metanarratives. As a result, what is intended as criticism often reads as a celebration
of the social and cultural products of global capitalism compared to earlier
radical positions, and critique becomes indistinguishable from ideology.

My comments above, as well as my criticism of "postcolonial" criticism,
imply a relationship between history as epistemology and the critique of political economy. It is this relationship that I would like to pursue a bit further
here, with reference to my comments on *Writing Diaspora*. I do not know if
Rey Chow identifies with postcolonial criticism's repudiation of metanarratives, but in her emphases on her own hybridity and marginality, in her preoccupation with Eurocentrism, in her repudiation of the past, and in her hostility to Marxism, she would seem to share in some of the premises of
postcolonial criticism. I will thus return to my comments on her statements in
my discussion of the problem of history as a general problem in cultural criticism. I am especially interested in Chow's discussion of Orientalism and her
repudiation of the Chinese Revolution.

If ignoring political economy deprives cultural criticism of its ability to locate itself spatially, extending a similar denial of political economy to the understanding of the past (as in the so-called post-Orientalist histories) cuts off
criticism from the legacy of radical struggles of the past, throwing into question its own temporal location. The question is a tricky one, since insistence
on memories of the past is usually characteristic of a conservative position.
For a historian of China, insistence on memories of the Chinese Revolution
raises two questions. First is the question of nostalgia. Chinese society and
politics have gone through radical changes over the last two decades, and for
a historian like myself, who started his career in the middle of the cataclysmic
upheaval of the Cultural Revolution, there is indeed the possibility of hang-
ing on to the past out of a kind of personal and professional nostalgia, just as
earlier generations of Chinese historians held on to memories of the Qing dynasty (after the revolution of 1911) or of Republican China (after 1949). To
make matters worse, the nostalgia is for a past when the Chinese "native" was
placed at a disadvantage vis-à-vis Euro-American domination compared to a
present in which the "natives" have asserted themselves, which makes it typ-
ical of Orientalist nostalgia—mixed possibly with some envy at the Chinese
success at a time of apparent decline in Euro-American power. To say that this
time around the nostalgia is different because it is for socialism or revolution

does not make it any the less conservative, especially at a time when both socialism and revolution appear as aspects of a past now irretrievably gone.

The second question is that of the very epistemological status of history, especially for a historian who shares in the postmodernist argument on history as representation, without privileging claims to the truth of the past. For a historian of China, and perhaps any historian in the late twentieth century, this postmodern insight does not come as fresh news. The repeated rewriting of history has been an integral ideological feature of the Chinese Revolution, best articulated in the 1981 comments by Deng Xiaoping on the Official Resolution on Party History, in which Deng offers an account of the political negotiations that were very much a part of producing a post-Maoist history of the Communist Revolution.[32] It is conceded similarly in *Pasts and Futures, or What Is History For?* by Jean Chesneaux, the distinguished French Marxist historian, who eschews a materialist faith in the truth of history to argue for the relationship between political vision and historical representation.[33]

The point in recalling the past, however, is not to privilege the epistemological status of history or to keep alive a past that is already gone. An insistence on the relevance to the present of recalling radical visions and struggles of the past need not imply imprisonment of the present in the past, any more than an insistence on the relevance of political economy implies an economic or class determination of cultural criticism. In this regard, I disagree also with Aijaz Ahmad's recent critique of cultural criticism in his *In Theory.*[34] Ahmad's insistence on political economy and the centrality of the question of class needs to be taken seriously, perhaps more seriously than ever before, because with global capitalism it is possible for the first time to speak of global classes. But Ahmad, in his repudiation of past categories such as imperialism and the Third World, is at one with postcolonial criticism in flattening out unequal and uneven relationships across the globe. In spite of his recognition that a new global situation has come into existence, moreover, he does not place this situation in any kind of historical perspective or confront the questions raised by it, hence the ease with which he carries solutions as old as Marx (but skipping over Lenin and Mao) into the present.

Global capitalism has indeed created a new situation. The structure of production has been transformed and, with it, older global relations, which calls for new modes of understanding. The appearance of a new division of labor has transformed relations between societies, disorganized the nation-state, and produced a new cultural situation. Although the First World may still be the First World, the very transnationalism of First World corporations implies that terms such as First and Third World are no longer to be understood simply in terms of fixed global locations. Nations are still there, but they are no longer to be understood simply in terms of fixed political boundaries. Classes may be there more than ever; however, they are no longer to be understood simply in terms of economic relationships but require the mediation of other categories of analysis, from gender to ethnicity. Cultural differences and hegemonies are still there, but they are no longer to be understood simply in terms of European subjects, versus native objects. Capitalism is still there, but capitalism, too, has history, and it is not to be understood merely in terms of its past.

Capitalism is there nevertheless, and one of its features in its new phase is a claim to global totality as well as to monopoly over the future, now that all alternatives of comparable scope to its historical claims seem to have been abolished, and the only obstacles to its total victory that remain seem to reside in puny local resistances that emerge out of fractures in the totality that are produced by its very motions. These resistances do offer a point of departure for cultural criticism as well, but not without a careful consideration of some fundamental questions. Can cultural criticism be satisfied with a local consciousness against the global consciousness of capital? It may not make sense to speak of societies or cultures in an earlier vocabulary of metanarratives, but can such speech ignore the totalizing that is its condition? Can we speak of Orientalism as if it were still the Orientalism of yesterday, where the native Other was produced by the European Self, without regard to the fact that a China worked over by capital itself produces Orientalism due to a new location in global capitalism? Can we repudiate the legacy of socialism and revolution in China and elsewhere as merely an account of catastrophes, without a simultaneous awareness that what is being buried with them is a possibility of resistance to global hegemony on its own global terrain—which may be exactly the reason that the culture of global capital places the past in history theme parks, organized according to its own consumptive vision? Orientalism persists in our day not in "factographic" accounts of the "Orient" but in the commodified representations of its exotica in theme parks and in the ideological pantheon of global capitalism, of which the "Orient" has become an integral constituent. Rather than the end of Orientalism, what we may be witnessing today is its victory under the auspices of global capital, with the very complicity of the "natives" themselves. If capitalism is in a new phase, the new phase is nevertheless continuous with the past, as an overcoming of the obstacles that were produced by its own activities. Similarly, a cultural criticism that is cognizant of political economy must come to terms with past criticism that predicated its solutions on the primacy of capitalism. The question here is not to revive but to engage the past. That is the possibility effectively obliterated when cultural criticism renders its own radical legacy into a mere account of catastrophes that are best forgotten, while formulating its problems in terms of its immediate historical situation, which confines its vision within the ideological horizon of global capitalism. Ironically, the contemporary hegemony of global capital over the present and the future may have left the past as the sole source of critical perspectives. As Jean Chesneaux writes in *The Brave Modern World,*

> By definition, the past will not return, and only those who have lost confidence and seek refuge in nostalgic dreams can call for a return. But invoking the past as a critical reference is something quite different, based as it is on the past not because of its previousness, but because of its otherness. Since it offers us *another quality of life*—a life which actually existed and not an idealistic and utopian vision—the detour by way of the past helps us *to relativize the present,* resist the tendency to surrender to the present, and recover the sense of duration of time and, hence, a concern for the future.[35] [emphasis in original]

The catastrophes of the Chinese Revolution need to be remembered, if only to avoid their repetition. But so must the history of which those catastrophes were not just agents but products. That history was shaped by a capitalism that, dislocating all societies from their own parochial trajectories, was to relocate them in a global temporality that permits no escape from its dominion except into oblivion. But that history was also shaped by alternative global visions of socialism or Third Worldism that promised humans the ability to once again take control of their lives. The contradiction between vision and history provided modernity with a vital tension, a space in which to imagine other possible futures. What is at risk today is that space. Take, for example, "developmentalism," a commitment to material and technological development that is fundamental to the ideology of capitalism past and present. Developmentalism was also the legacy of capitalism in socialism, but it appeared in the latter as a contradiction, at odds with the socialist promise of human control over life, which in the end distorted both the promise of liberation and the course of development. What is gone today is that promise. Without it, however, developmentalism has turned into a fetishism of change so powerful that merely to question its goals is to risk relegation into an irredeemably reactionary past since it has claimed for itself totally the present and the future.

Cultural criticism, instead of confronting this urgent predicament, joins in the celebration of this present and the demise of alternative visions of the future that once seemed to be real possibilities. The result is to yield the future to a global capital engaged in homogenizing societies globally. In the absence of alternative visions, the only resistance to such global homogenization seems to come from a reassertion of older ethnic and cultural identities with similarly universalistic pretensions (expressed through older ideologies, be they Confucianism, Islam, Hinduism, or whatever, now essentialized in their articulation to global capitalism), which substitute for the promise of liberation the celebration of cultural practices that legitimize oppression of one kind or another and express themselves in deadly ethnic competition and conflict. The utopianization of a culturalist nationalism or ethnicism, already a danger under nationalized socialisms but held in check by the very vision of socialism, now has reemerged with a vengeance. The choice that faces us all seems to be between either a global capitalism that promises an illusory cosmopolitanism or an ethnic or nationalist fascism; the two even manage some collaboration against alternative possibilities of social organization that may make possible genuine "diversity in unity."

I am referring here to the "local" as the site of struggle. There is resistance still, or perhaps I should say there are many resistances. The location for resistance to global power and homogenization these days would seem to be local resistances, whether of indigenous peoples or of local communities that seek to rework their historical legacies into social alliances that can guarantee survival and dignity in a reassertion of local subjectivities against their manipulation by capital, by states, and by the purveyors of new culturalisms. Jean Chesneaux offers one way to theorize such local resistances. In *The Brave Modern World,* he describes the contemporary situation as an "off-ground" situation, playing off the euphemism of global capital about "offshore" economies, which refer to those economic sites that are beyond the control of states, regardless of where they are located with respect to the sea. In an "off-ground" situation, neither material nor spiritual or intellectual life has any relationship to its immediate locality; rather, an "off-ground" existence refers to a situation where location in global networks defines place and, therefore, time. Theme parks, Confucianism, or even the Yellow Emperor—not to speak of much in contemporary cultural criticism—derive their significance in this conceptualization from their interconnection with global political, economic, and cultural networks, from the abstract relationships between their various constituents, rather than from the answers they provide to the needs of their immediate material environments, the needs of everyday life. Indeed, in their very globalization, they become part of the forces that threaten to erase the multifaceted needs of everyday life. Radical social theory itself, to the extent that it feeds off global networks, becomes complicit in the production and reproduction of this "off-ground" existence.

The answer that Chesneaux's metaphor invokes is deceptively simple: to "reground" thinking in everyday life. This is deceptive not only because it is difficult to imagine an everyday life that is free from the oppressive burdens of the past but also because local resistances are vulnerable to the extent that they seek to overcome their own mythological underpinnings by subjecting such understanding to the scrutiny of the present. Moreover, even if that hurdle were to be overcome, these resistances, however promising, probably do not have much chance unless some way is found of establishing global alliances to empower them. That would also require constant attention to the global context of local struggles in global capitalism, as well as in the struggles globally of classes, women, ethnicities, and cultures. Recalling the past with these new struggles in mind is a task that awaits cultural criticism—one that may rekindle its dormant political energies.[36]

The Cultural Revolution in China may have represented the dying gasps of an earlier form of resistance to capital, and June 4, 1989, may have symbolized the pains of a China being incorporated inexorably into a global capitalism. The distinction, in the very radicalness of the difference, may also serve as a reminder of what these two events might have in common. What they have in common is also what makes necessary the relevance of history to cultural criticism. It is with this understanding that I read the following well-known lines:

> Historical materialism wishes to retain that image of the past which unexpectedly appears to a man singled out by history at a moment of danger. The danger affects both the content of the tradition and its receivers. The same threat hangs over both: that of becoming a tool of the ruling classes. In every era the attempt must be made anew to wrest tradition away from a conformism that is about to overpower it. . . . Only that historian will have the gift of fanning the spark of hope in the past who is firmly convinced that *even the dead* will not be safe from the enemy if he wins. And this enemy has not ceased to be victorious.[37] [emphasis in the original]

LOOKING BACKWARD—AGAIN

When Edward Bellamy looked forward to our times in 1888, he saw a utopian society where capitalism had been transformed into something that looked very much like a socialist utopia. When we look at our times in 1994, it does not seem that what he envisioned for the year 2000 is even close; if anything, we may be closer by far to his times than to his utopia. What has been lost in the meantime is historical vision—and the hope for alternative futures that the vision expressed.

For all its ironies in the context of the discussion here, I offer by way of conclusion the following lines from *Looking Backward*:

> I asked Mr. Bartlett the other day where we should emigrate to if all the terrible things took place which those socialists threaten. He said he did not know any

place now where society could be called stable except Greenland, Patagonia, and the Chinese Empire. Those Chinamen knew what they were about, somebody added, when they refused to let in our Western civilization. They knew what it would lead to better than we did. They saw it was nothing but dynamite in disguise.[38]

NOTES

1. Edward Bellamy, *Looking Backward: 2000–1887* (New York: New American Library, 1960).

2. Bellamy, *Looking Backward*, 176.

3. Bellamy, *Looking Backward*, 49.

4. Arthur E. Morgan, *Edward Bellamy* (Philadelphia: Porcupine Press, 1974), ix–x (originally published 1944).

5. Morgan, *Edward Bellamy*, ix.

6. Arthur Lipow, *Authoritarian Socialism in America: Edward Bellamy and the Nationalist Movement* (Berkeley: University of California Press, 1982), 9.

7. Lipow, *Authoritarian Socialism in America*, 2.

8. Morgan, *Edward Bellamy,* xii.

9. Martin Bernal, *Chinese Socialism to 1907* (Ithaca, NY: Cornell University Press, 1976), 24–26.

10. Richard J. Barnet, *Global Dreams: Imperial Corporations and the New World Order* (New York: Simon & Schuster, 1994), 15.

11. Zhong Yi, "ZhongYi jinghuo hezuo dayou fazhan qiantu" [Broad Prospect of Sino-Italy Economic Relations and Trade Cooperation], in *Jianshe yu touzi* [Construction and Investment: A Guide of Investors (sic)] (January 1994): 19.

12. Wang Xuelin, "Beijingers Can Now Tour the World in a Few Hours," *Travel China* (November 25–December 9, 1993): 4. The same issue has an interesting report on Confucius for foreigners.

13. Liang Qichao, "Xin shixue" [The New History], *Yinbing shi wenji* [Selections from the Ice Drinker's Studio], vol. 4 (Taipei, 1960), 1–31.

14. *South China Morning Post* (August 19, 1993).

15. Deng Xiaoping, "Xiaofei shi fazhan shengchanlide dongli" [Consumption Is the Motor Force for Developing the Forces of Production], *Renmin ribao* [People's Daily] (June 7, 1992).

16. Lester Thurow, "Head to Head," *New Perspectives Quarterly* 9, no. 1 (Winter 1992): 41–45. As I was finishing this article in May 1994, it was reported that Lee Kwan Yew's *Selected Works* had been published in China recently and even celebrated in the Great Hall of the People, an honor usually reserved for highest-level Party officials.

17. Stewart R. Clegg and S. Gordon Redding, eds., *Capitalism in Contrasting Cultures* (Berlin: Walter de Gruyter, 1990). One article in this collection is appropriately titled, without any indication of irony, "The Cash Value of Confucian Values."

18. Lionel M. Jensen, "Manufacturing 'Confucianism': Chinese and Western Imaginings in the Making of a Tradition," (Ph.D. diss., University of California, 1992), chapter 1.

19. Wei-ming Tu, "The Confucian Dimension in the East Asian Development Model," in *Conference on Confucianism and Economic Development in East Asia* (Taipei: Chung-hua Institution for Economic Research, 1989), 63–86, esp. 63–64.

20. Zhong Yi, "ZhongYi jinghuo hezuo dayou fazhan qiantu."

21. Feng Yingzi, "Liangqian nian qiande da yimin" [Great Emigrants of Two Thousand Years Ago], *Xinmin wanbao* [New People's Evening Paper] (January 23, 1994): 13.

22. Rey Chow, *Writing Diaspora: Tactics of Intervention in Contemporary Cultural Studies* (Bloomington: Indiana University Press, 1993), chapters 4 and 6. An argument similar to the one I present here has been offered for the case of Taiwan by Yang Congrong, "Dongfang shehuide 'Dongfanglun'" [Oriental's "Orientalism" (sic)], *Dangdai* [Contemporary] 64 (August 1991): 38–53, esp. 40–41.

23. For an extended discussion of Occidentalism, see Chen Xiaomei, *Occidentalism: A Theory of Counter-Discourse in Post-Mao China* (New York: Oxford University Press, 1995).

24. Chow, *Writing Diaspora*, 5.

25. Chow, *Writing Diaspora*, 10.

26. Chow, *Writing Diaspora*, 28.

27. Chow, *Writing Diaspora*, 74.

28. For a discussion of this point, see Arif Dirlik, *After the Revolution: Waking to Global Capitalism* (Hanover, NH, and London: Wesleyan University Press, 1994).

29. See Zhang Zhanbin and Song Yifu, *Zhongguo: Mao Zedong Re* [China: Mao Fever], 3rd ed. (Hunan: Beiyue wenyi chuhanshe, 1992) for this and Mao fever in general. See also Yu Keping, "The Politics of Mao Zedong in Reform China" (unpublished manuscript). I am grateful to Dr. Yu for sharing this manuscript with me.

30. Price Pritchett and Ron Pound, *High-Velocity Culture Change: A Handbook for Managers* (Dallas: Pritchett Publishing, 1994).

31. Arif Dirlik, "The Postcolonial Aura: Third World Criticism in the Age of Global Capitalism," *Critical Inquiry* 20 (Winter 1994): 328–56.

32. Deng Xiaoping, "Remarks on Successive Drafts of the 'Resolution on Certain Questions in the History of Our Party Since the Founding of the People's Republic of China'" (March 1980–June 1981), *Selected Works of Deng Xiaoping, 1975–1982* (Beijing: Foreign Languages Press, 1984), 276–96.

33. Jean Chesneaux, *Pasts and Futures, or What Is History For?* (London: Thames and Hudson, 1978).

34. Aijaz Ahmad, *In Theory: Classes, Nations, Literatures* (London: Verso Books, 1992).

35. Jean Chesneaux, *The Brave Modern World: The Prospects for Survival*, trans. Diana Johnstone, Karen Bowie, and Francisca Garvie (London: Thames and Hudson, 1992), 173–74.

36. For a more thorough discussion, see Arif Dirlik, "The Global in the Local," in *Global/Local: Cultural Production and the Transnational Imaginary*, ed. Rob Wilson and Wimal Dissanayake, 21–45 (Durham, NC: Duke University Press, 1996).

37. Walter Benjamin, "Theses on the Philosophy of History," in *Illuminations*, ed. Hannah Arendt, 255 (New York: Harcourt, Brace and World, 1968).

38. Bellamy, *Looking Backward*, 33.

12

Markets, Culture, Power: The Making of a "Second Cultural Revolution" in China

Over the last two decades, but especially since 1992, the marketization of society in the People's Republic of China (PRC) has led to changes that have been described on more than one occasion as a "second cultural revolution."[1] It is arguable that this second cultural revolution is incomparably more far-reaching and deep-seated in its consequences than the failed Cultural Revolution of the 1960s that sought to place China on an irreversible path to socialism. The effects of the PRC's incorporation in a global capitalist economy (or, conversely, the incorporation of a capitalist economy in the PRC) are visible everywhere—from transformations in management practices to the emergence, most conspicuously, of a consumer society. It has transformed the architecture of major urban centers, where at the ground level of urban thoroughfares no less than in the contours of the skyline the institutions of global capital from international hotel chains and department stores to corporate headquarters are a dominating presence. It has changed life at the everyday level in transforming habits of consumption—of culture no less than of the commodities of everyday life. Nor are the changes urban only. Rural PRC, too, except in the remotest regions, readily reveals the effects of the new market economy, or the expectations generated by it, real or imagined—if only in the infrastructural preparations waiting to find a place on the pathways of markets and capital.

In the discussion below, I reflect through the interface of the PRC with the world of global capitalism on a question that has moved to the forefront of cultural discussion over the last ten years or so, accompanying the surge of interest in globalization during the same period: the question of cultural homogenization/heterogenization with reference to the globalization of

285

capitalist markets. This question in turns leads to a broader problematic of modernity. In recent years, modernity has become a site of cultural contention. European and North American modernities, which long provided a model for the rest of the world and pointed to the shape of its future, no longer carry the authority that they commanded earlier. Ironically, at the very moment of its victory over its socialist competitors, capitalist modernity finds itself beleaguered by a refragmentation of the world in which once marginalized cultures ("traditions") have enjoyed a resurgence in the very interior of modernity, making their own claims upon the modern. Recognition of this situation, I think, distinguishes the new discourse of globalization from an earlier discourse of modernization.

This situation finds expression in the idea of "multiple modernities." In his introduction to a recently published special issue of *Daedalus*, entitled "Multiple Modernities," the distinguished analyst of modernity and editor of the issue, Shmuel N. Eisenstadt, writes that the idea of "multiple modernities"

> goes against the views long prevalent in scholarly and general discourse. It goes against the view of the "classical" theories of modernization and of the convergence of industrial societies prevalent in the 1950s, and indeed against the classical sociological analyses of Marx, Durkheim and (to a large extent) even of Weber . . . that the cultural program of modernity as it developed in Europe and the basic institutional constellations that emerged there would ultimately take over in all modernizing and modern societies. . . . The actual developments in modernizing societies have refuted the homogenizing and hegemonic assumptions of this Western program of modernity. While a general trend toward structural differentiation developed across a wide range of institutions in most of these societies . . . the ways in which these arenas were defined and organized varied greatly . . . giving rise to multiple institutional and ideological patterns. These patterns did not constitute simple continuations in the modern era of the traditions of their respective societies. Such patterns were distinctively modern, though greatly influenced by specific cultural premises, traditions and historical experiences. All developed distinctly modern dynamics and modes of interpretation, for which the original Western project constituted the crucial (and usually ambivalent) reference point.[2]

Eisenstadt recognizes that the question of modernity presently entails far greater complexity than can be encompassed in any holistic or essentialist idea of culture. Nevertheless, his discussion, as well as the other contributions to the special issue, are at one in approaching the world in terms of various "culture areas," which are then investigated for the claims they make upon modernity. Missing from the substance of the analyses are serious confrontation of problems presented by the location of culture, which no longer is to be identified with civilizational or even national units, as well as the increasingly problematic nature of the idea of culture itself, subject as it is to new pressures of political and economic commodification. Most important, however, is the obliviousness of these analyses to the context of current disputations over modernity in the political economy of globalization, which provides a common ground for these disputations—both in empowering cultural claims on modernity, but also by containing cultural conflict within limits set by common interests and practices.

The discussion here has two goals. First is to place the homogenization/heterogenization question within a historical perspective; more specifically, within the perspective of an earlier modernity/tradition juxtaposition, including the revolutionary paths to modernity. While I disagree with the homogenization argument, at least the way it is usually phrased, the main thrust of my critique is directed at arguments that favor the heterogenization perspective. These arguments rest frequently on a "modernity of tradition" premise which valorizes tradition differently than in an earlier modernization discourse, but does not therefore constitute a fundamental break with that discourse. They may be viewed more accurately as revisions of modernization discourse in response to the demands of a neoliberal globalism, which no longer perceives in different traditions obstacles to a capitalist modernity, but rereads them to confirm the universality of capitalist modernity, albeit with local variations. Such arguments rarely make an effort to account for the content of the traditions in question, and more often than not offer by way of supportive evidence little more than trivial signs of the persistence of tradition. The culturalism that characterizes such arguments distracts from necessary attention to the fundamental transformations that are at work globally.

Equally important, secondly, is the status of the very idea of culture under the circumstances. Given the neoliberal willingness to accommodate different cultural environments in order to transform them more effectively, it is increasingly more difficult to distinguish culture as a historical legacy from culture as an object of conscious manipulation in marketing and management. Rather than bulldoze their way into new markets, transnational corporations have chosen for sometime now to acculturate themselves into new environments, transforming their operations, but by no means relinquishing their power to change the world in accordance with corporate interests and strategies. This, needless to say, is most easily accomplished through the creation of a globalized work force, that is at once multinational and multicultural. It is not surprising, therefore, to find "native" elites who, while they insist on the importance of the traditions from which they claim to hail, are also engaged in activities that promise to eradicate those traditions as *traditions*. The importance of this multinational elite in the creation of a new global capitalist culture is often ignored by cultural critics who focus on more narrowly defined groups of intellectuals and overlook the power of this elite to set the terms for the discussion of culture in our day. The close attention to the problem of culture in either cultural criticism or corporate strategy may be revealing of a loss of faith in the ability of material or social transformation to do the job of creating a new society; an insight which the original Cultural Revolution did much to dramatize and disseminate. On the other hand, that neither implies the autonomy of culture, nor that it may be viewed in isolation from the political economies, and contexts of power, with which it is entangled in intricate ways.

Aside from the fact that I am a specialist on modern China, and, therefore, a little less ignorant about China than elsewhere, there are two main reasons why the PRC provides a fecund location for examining the question. First is the weight of China's cultural legacy. We do not have to take seriously the various dehistoricized claims made for the longevity of Chinese culture by Chinese or others, which often add up to little more than clichés, in order to recognize that the claims themselves make for a cultural orientation, and, consequently, behavior shaped by the ideological force of those very claims; in other words, a compulsive urge to add "Chinese characteristics" to almost anything (from socialism to capitalism to consumerism) to assert that Chinese must be unique no matter what the evidence to the contrary. Secondly, the case of China is interesting because of the historical experiences of Chinese society with market cultures in the twentieth century: from the experience of capitalism as imperialism through arguably the greatest experiment with a socialist renunciation of markets and capitalism to incorporation into capitalism. This complex experience makes for an ambivalence toward the culture of capitalism and capitalist markets; so that even as China is drawn into a global capitalist economy, and makes claims to impending supremacy within it, there is evidence of continued resistance to being identified as one more emerging capitalist society with its own market repertories; resistance in which cultural memories, nationalist longings, and socialist habits are intertwined inextricably.

For these two reasons, among possibly others, the confrontation of the PRC with the market forces of global capital provides a revealing instance of cultural conflict and complicity in the global political economy; where homogenization/heterogenization appear not just as processes that follow some economic or ethnographic logic, but as products of the deployment of culture as a means of grasping difference and manipulating it in which there is a visible complex dialectic of agency and structure. This may render culture meaningless as a category of analysis; at the very least, it points to the meaninglessness of approaching the question without reference to its context in economic and political power. Above all else, it makes it necessary to consider the question within the context of a globalized capital which constrains what we understand by difference, where resistance to cultural homogenization may offer little more than assimilation by other means.

What I have in mind here may be illustrated by the very irony in the use of the term "cultural revolution" to describe contemporary changes, that brings into relief the difference of our times from times past. It is arguable that the Cultural Revolution of the 1960s played an important part in paving the way for the present by making culture into an object of manipulation, and an instrument for the political transformation of Chinese subjects. But whatever we may think of its causes and consequences, and its often arbitrary deployment of culture, the Cultural Revolution was intended nevertheless to carve out a path to socialism that imagined an outside to capitalism (and what was deemed to be its socialist version in the Soviet Union). The appropriation of the term presently for incorporation into global capitalism, on the other hand, refers not only to social and cultural transformation, but also signals the abandonment of any possibility of alternatives; the impossibility, in other words, of imagining outsides to a globalized capitalism. This, I think, is an indicator also of the contemporary limitation of the boundaries of cultural discussion as in the homogenization/heterogenization juxtaposition, where "heterogenization" comes to serve as a stand-in for what might have been conceived earlier as an outside, where terms such as hybridity and heterogeneity come to express not radical difference, but pleas for the recognition of difference, or perhaps even simulated difference—where difference is imaginable only as variation on a theme that we have come to call "capitalism."

McDOMINATION AND McASSIMILATION[3]

There is little disagreement among writers on the evolving market economy in the PRC that a revolutionary transformation has occurred over the last two decades in the popular orientation to the market and market values, evident most importantly in a "consumer revolution."[4] While there is little reason to question the importance of this "revolution," or even, in the absence of some unforeseen disaster, its irrevocableness, some caution is necessary nevertheless in assessing its extent, depth, and durability. Against the relentless effort to instill a productionist ethic in the Chinese population during Maoist years, when consumption was reduced to a bare minimum for the majority of the population, any reorientation toward consumption values is bound to appear as a radical break with the past. We need also to take into account the considerable hype about the consumption turn in Chinese society that characterizes the writings on the subject of marketers and advertisers who have an obvious interest in a rosy portrayal of the future of consumption in the PRC.

To speak of a consumer revolution in the PRC is not necessarily to suggest that China has become a consumer society like the United States or Japan, or even Taiwan, Hong Kong, and Singapore. For one thing, while the government has released the forces of consumption to promote economic growth, it remains suspicious of the social consequences of consumer values, most importantly individual self-expression, as may be gleaned from periodic efforts to control the content of advertising.[5] Perhaps more fundamentally, China remains a poor country, and there are immense class and regional differences in the ability to consume.[6] During visits to the PRC over the last decade when I have asked of friends and acquaintances from different walks of life who consumed all the expensive (by Chinese standards) commodities with which stores seemed to be overflowing, the standard (and almost clichéd) answer has been, "three percent of the population." The emergence of a consumer society has accompanied economic changes toward a market society and privatization that have cut deeply into services provided by the socialist state, intensifying anxiety about the future. With a precarious welfare safety net (from employment to retirement, from housing to school and health services), much of the Chinese population has to be careful about spending—as the leadership found out during the recent economic crisis in East and Southeast Asia, when it was frustrated in its efforts to get the population to spend in order to forestall an economic recession. These contradictions are captured in the description of the PRC by the prominent marketing expert, and indefatigable crusader for globalization, Kenichi Ohmae, as "the most dynamic and difficult, and yet the last remaining, consumer utopia of the world."[7]

Having said this, there is little reason to doubt the importance of the consumption turn in the PRC. The question concerns rather the nature of the transformation: whether this market revolution signals the assimilation of Chinese society to a globalizing consumer culture, or the assimilation of market culture to Chinese society in a process of the localization of the global. There is good evidence that, as in the rest of the world, Chinese society as it turns into a consumer society, faces the prospect or threat of "McDonaldization" and "Coca-colonization," which have become symbolic in the literature on cultural globalization of the spread globally of the values of U.S. society. On the other hand, there is equally compelling evidence of resistance to this prospect that takes complex forms—from cultural and economic nationalism to efforts to contain global commodities by endowing them with local meanings and tastes.

For all its particularities, most important among them being the official willingness to intervene in matters of popular tastes and values, the case of the PRC is not all that different from those of other societies that face globalization in the guise of Americanization. While answers to the homogeneity/

heterogeneity question vary widely, the variation is limited by the common ground they share in the assumption of the globalization of cultures. Few would care to argue these days that there remain spaces immune to the cultural forces of capitalism, even if in many cases participation in the capitalist economy may be more by way of induction than direct involvement. The question then resolves itself into two oppositions. On the one hand are those who argue that the spread of capitalism globally implies, for better or worse, the invasion of the globe by the cultural forces of capitalism, and the erasure of cultural difference. For its celebrants, such cultural homogenization is to be welcomed as it brings us ever closer to the promise of a global village, albeit under the guidance of slogans of "markets and democracy" emanating from a hegemonic center.[8] To critics, on the other hand, homogenization is nothing less than the pervasion of capitalist, especially U.S., junk culture in the world, and represents nothing less than a new phase of imperialism, now in the guise of cultural imperialism.[9]

At the other extreme are those who concede the reality of globalization, but argue nevertheless that globalization is never a simple one-way process, and may in fact double back on hegemonic cultures.[10] In its "softer" version, this implies that the recipients of cultural globalization are never passive, but impose their own meanings on received culture, and translate it into local idioms, to produce hybrid cultures that sustain difference; a process that is often identified, mistakenly, with indigenization, without accounting for the fact that the indigenous, or the local, is impossible to grasp presently without reference to the global in the local. The "harder" version of this argument not only reaffirms heterogeneity, but claims also that globalization turns the table back on hegemonic cultures by enabling challenges to their monopolistic claims to modernity in the form of alternative modernities that draw upon different (and once marginalized) traditions.[11] The one version leads to "multiculturalism," which is but a liberal version of the "global village," the other to the "clash of civilizations." In either case, globalization signals the end of universalism, which is now exposed as the imposition on widely different societies of parochial values of the "West," associated more often than not with the single term, "the Enlightenment." Capitalism, on the other hand, becomes the common fate of humankind, subject to local variations.

Most writers on the "consumer revolution" in the PRC with whose work I am familiar are inclined toward this latter position: that consumption is conditioned by the political and cultural circumstances of contemporary Chinese society. Thus one author, highly critical of the emergent consumer society, writes that, "heavily influenced by affluent East and Southeast Asian neighbors, the current wave of mass consumption in China is assuming characteristics which set it apart from the more established pattern in the West. I will refer to it as 'Confucian consumerism' because it bears the imprints of China's long-standing values concerning families and human relations."[12] A similar view is to be found in another author, this time an enthusiastic proponent of consumer society, and himself a marketer, Conghua Li. He writes that "consumers seem to buy things for the same reason everywhere, except in China, where status is culturally nuanced. How status is defined, and how and where it fits into spending patterns is unique and changing. It is unique to regions, as well as to specific categories of consumers. To understand the meaning of status in China today, and how it influences spending, requires some understanding of the nation's social and cultural values."[13] Like Bin Zhao, Li stresses family values, interpersonal relations and the emphasis on status as distinguishing features of Chinese society.

What all this means in practice may be illustrated concretely by the transformation of global commodities as they are domesticated in Chinese social and cultural spaces. A recent study of McDonald's in Beijing by Yunxiang Yan observes that, "in Beijing . . . the Big Mac was rapidly transformed into a form of haute cuisine, and McDonald's became a place where people could gain status simply by eating there. A scrutiny of social interactions in Beijing McDonald's reveals that what appears to be the same institution represents two radically different things in the two societies. These differences are so profound that the presumed 'American style' of the Beijing restaurants has itself been transformed; McDonald's has become a caricature of its intended symbolic association. It represents a localized, Chinese version of Americana."[14]

The author perceives five aspects to this transformation. First, an "intriguing point" that "localization was precisely the goal of McDonald's management in Beijing." The company presented itself as a Chinese company on the grounds that it was 50 percent Chinese owned, used beef and potatoes purchased in the PRC, and all its employees were Chinese (with three of them holding foreign passports). It also participated in community affairs and activities of local schools, delegated employees to help out the police with traffic, and hoisted the Chinese national flag every morning. Secondly, in contrast to McDonald's in the United States, McDonald's restaurants in China allowed their customers to hang out, making themselves hospitable not only to prolonged meals but also to family affairs as well as teenage romantic assignations. McDonald's cleanliness as well as reasonable prices made the restaurants attractive for such affairs, which the management sought to enhance by organizing art exhibitions, etc. Thirdly, as in the United States, McDonald's emphasized its affinity with the family by decorating its walls with posters and slogans espousing family values. Fourthly, the restaurant stressed human interactions, adding to Ronald McDonald, "the uncle," "aunt McDonalds," female receptionists "to take care of children and talk with parents." Finally, aware of the value placed on "the little emperors," the highly spoiled products of the single-child policy, McDonald's lavished special attention on these children. One important innovation was to promote educational activity in the restaurants by organizing essay contests, special children's programs, and activities designed to give children a taste of and an acquaintance with American culture.[15]

Localization is also visible in the marketing and advertising of cosmetics and beauty products. Since the 1980s Caucasian ideals of female beauty in the guise of white skin, big breasts, and tall bodies have exerted considerable influence in Chinese ideals of beauty, and have fueled sales of beauty products.[16] While efforts to achieve a Western feminine look sometimes take gross forms of surgical transformation of the body, among their less baneful products may be the ubiquitous presence in South China of Avon ladies.

A recent examination of these new ideals of the female body recognizes this new turn in Chinese conceptions of beauty, but argues that rather than view them as an invasion of Chinese conceptions of beauty by "white, Western, and wealthy" values, we need to pay closer "attention to hybridity, Creolization and local resignification of global beauty ideals."[17] The discussion concedes that there has been a transformation in both views of skin color and breast size. Skin color, which had been a marker of class difference in premodern China, has now turned into an ethnic marker, distinguishing Caucasians from Chinese. There has been a similar shift in the valorization of breast size, with larger breasts now signifying not only a shift in ideals of bodily beauty, but a sign of modernity as well. Against the effects of advertising, mostly of "Western" products, promoting whiteness and larger breast size, Johansson juxtaposes advertisements of Chinese products and writings critical of the infatuation with Western ideals of beauty, which not only point to the somewhat undesirable side effects of the former, but reiterate native ideals of beauty that emphasize smoothness of skin and hairlessness. According to contemporary defenders of Chinese civilization, even the ideal of big breasts had existed in Chinese society, but had been aborted by Confucian ethics. He writes that "ads for skin whitening creams and skin-care products . . . [reveal] a symbolic web of visual and textual references to domesticity, traditional China, traditional femininity, fear of nature and fear of change. In my view, these ads can be interpreted as reflecting a discourse about how Chinese self-identity is being threatened by global consumerism. Confronted with the threat from Western influences and the hegemony of Western beauty ideals, protection, caution and a high standard of conduct are called for to preserve the 'beauty' of Chinese identity."[18] It is a short step from this statement to the author's conclusion that "contemporary Chinese beauty ideals have many origins, both historically and geographically. Their complexity refutes any notion that they are merely the outcome of a 'conspiracy' of the Western media and beauty industry. Not only are fair skin and large breasts ideals in China that pre-date contemporary Western-style consumer culture, but these seemingly monolithic Western beauty ideals are also re-interpreted into local terms."[19] For all its postcolonial rhetoric, or perhaps because of it, Johansson's argument is informed ultimately by a traditional/modern juxtaposition, where the confrontation with the modern does not simply produce historical transformations but resignifications of the modern in local contexts. Here Johansson simply follows the lead of those Chinese sources which insist, as I noted above, that no matter how much China or Chinese culture changes, "Chinese characteristics" must nevertheless prevail—even if it has become increasingly difficult to determine what those characteristics may be in the midst of radical social and cultural transformation, national and local. These "Orientalist" formulations are empowered now not by Eurocentrism, as in an earlier day, but by a liberal embarrassment at its legacies, as well as Chinese "self-orientalizations."[20]

Apparently taken with "hybridization" and "local resignification," which he seems to view as unquestionable truths of cultural transmission, Johansson is oblivious to the point of naiveté, to any need to distinguish "consumer nationalism," or hostility to foreign products, from the indigenization of either commodities or of discourses of beauty. A third text I would like to discuss here, while not significantly different in the conclusions it draws from Johansson's, nevertheless points to the importance of such a distinction.[21] Despite its title, "The Coca-colonization of Chinese Society," it is broader in compass than the texts discussed above because, in addition to food and beverage, it reflects also on cosmetics and household industries. The title is appropriate nevertheless in referring us to that most popular of American products, which is not only the most recognized foreign brand in the PRC, but has managed to hold on to one-third of the market for beverages there despite fierce competition from its rival, Pepsi-cola.

As in the case of the other discussions above, the author of this article also underlines the importance of the status associated with foreign commodities in determining consumption; which endows these commodities with new meanings in their new marketing context. The "indigenization" of foreign commodities, however, has been complicated by an emergent consumer nationalism, which makes it difficult to distinguish cultural resignification as a phenomenon in the "social life of things," to quote Arjun Appadurai, from the conscious manipulation of meaning in the marketing of commodities, which also commodifies nationalism and localism as they are rendered into characteristics that inhere in commodities.[22] The reassertion of Chinese nationalism in the form of pride in native culture, combined with increased competition from Chinese companies, has led to a transformation in attitudes toward foreign commodities that have become visible since the mid-1990s. In the protests against the NATO bombing of the Chinese Embassy in Belgrade in May 1999, one placard read: "I'd rather die of thirst than drink Coca-cola, I would rather starve to death than eat McDonald's."[23] It may not be surprising that these symbols of Americanization (along with Kentucky Fried Chicken), attractive in ordinary times, should turn overnight into targets of anti-Americanism. The nationalizing or localizing of commodities may be viewed as part of the process of resignification, but we need to note that national and local characteristics, as they are commodified themselves, also become available for manipulation in the service of all commodities, Chinese or foreign.

Chinese nationalism has not subdued the appeal of foreign commodities, but it has introduced new complications to the market even among post-Mao youth. The first McDonald's opened in China in 1992 (following Kentucky Fried Chicken by five years), and McDonald's appeal has risen unabated. Coke has continued to expand, taking over Chinese soft drink companies in the process. And the Chinese elite's appetite for luxury commodities (from French Cognac to Mercedes Benz) has continued to grow as it has concentrated in its hands an ever-growing portion of the country's wealth. At the same time, however, there has been an intensification of competition between foreign products, or the products of foreign companies, and similar products produced now by Chinese enterprises. Anecdotally, when I was in the PRC in 1989, Kent cigarettes, which (admitting to a sin) I smoke, carried great prestige in China; to the point where I remember a Chinese friend complaining that plumbers who came to his house to fix his plumbing refused to complete the job until they had been rewarded by a carton of Kent's. When I returned to China only four years later, I was lectured by a taxicab driver that I should switch from Kent's to Chinese brands, which he claimed were much higher in quality. Of course, by that time, it was almost impossible to distinguish the Chinese from the foreign. As some of the so-called "Chinese" cigarettes were in fact products of foreign enterprises in China, or of jointly owned companies, a new generation growing up in the new consumer society already thought that a company such as McDonald's was in fact Chinese.

Nevertheless, this has become an issue with respect to both origin and quality. As Chinese consumers have become more sophisticated, they have learned to distinguish high quality foreign products from foreign products dumped on the Chinese market. And as Chinese companies have become more sophisticated in both production and advertising, they have learned to compete with foreign brands, also using an emerging consumer nationalism to advantage. There are now "Chinese" versions of everything from McDonald's to Kentucky Fried Chicken ("American style fried chicken with Chinese characteristics"). Since many foreign name-brands have also moved their production to low-wage countries like China, it is also very difficult to distinguish an "authentic" name-brand from a name-brand sold in China for a much lower price, as they represent pretty much the same product.

What is foreign and what is Chinese, under the circumstances, becomes highly problematic. So does, for the same reason, the relationship between "indigenization," in the sense of "cultural resignification," and an economic or consumer nationalism that seeks for advantage in a capitalist market by appealing to nationalist sentiments. The question bears with an immediacy on the question of homogenization/heterogenization, or the production of "hybrid" or "third cultures."[24] Are they viewed best in terms of cultural processes accompanying globalization, or do they represent the conquest of culture by a globalizing capitalist economy, which not only has mounted an assault on societies worldwide through advertising, etc., but in the very process of responding to different market demands also seeks to shape those demands through the manipulation of culture—which is no longer something that exists outside of capital, but part of its very own self-definition?

MARKETING CULTURE IN THE CONTEMPORARY PRC

I would like to approach this question through a text to which I have referred several times already as a source both of information and interpretation, *China: The Consumer Revolution* by Conghua Li. Li is described on the cover of the book as a member of the Deloitte and Touche Consulting Group. The book is intended as an analysis of the emerging consumer society in China, for a readership whose interests are assumed to be practical: how to invest and make money in China. The endorsements for the book include academics as well as businessmen; from Kenichi Ohmae, formerly from a marketing and public relations firm in Japan, who acquired his reputation as a foremost promoter of globalization, and now holds a chair professorship of public policy at UCLA, to chair professors at the Harvard School of Business to chairmen or vice-chairmen of prominent marketing organizations. I will repeat Ohmae's endorsement here because it is of particular interest: "Conghua Li's book gives outsiders a fascinating insight into what is happening China's consumer market today. . . . The puzzles of the Chinese consumer are explained in a way that nobody has previously attempted. This is a must read for those who have their stakes vested in the most dynamic and difficult, and yet the last remaining, consumer utopia of the world."[25] It is hard to tell from the endorsement whose "consumer utopia" China might be, but the message is quite clear otherwise.

Li himself offers hints of his own experiences in the text. As far as it is possible to tell from these references, he grew up in the PRC of the Cultural Revolution, studied in the United States in the 1980s, and now makes a living in Canada as a Deloitte and Touche associate. His acknowledgments for the book include a long list of PRC officials who helped him out with his research, as well as academic and business leaders in Canada and the United States who commented on his analyses. What he has to say about his undertaking may be revealing of the complexities of the question at hand: "I am confident that the consumer trends and their business implications examined in this book will remain relevant until at least year 2010. Some may question my confidence, and the conclusions I draw from available facts and statistical references. Of course, no one knows what the future will bring. I do, however, have a deep understanding for the country of my birth and its people. Furthermore, my view of China has also been shaped by many years of professional experiences in the West, and a far ranging analysis of the present scene in China, both statistical and first hand."[26]

This "insider's" account of the consumer revolution in China stresses both the particularities of Chinese culture, and its regional variations. What is most interesting about the book is the prolonged discussion that Li provides of what he terms "the s-generation," the products of the single-child policy presently reaching adulthood, who have experienced consumption at its most lavish. These "little emperors," as they are popularly known, have been objects in their years of growing up not only of the most lavish attention by parents and grandparents, but have had all their whims met by parents anxious to secure for them futures of wealth and fortune. Li estimates that as much as one-third of family income is spent on the "little emperors'" consumption and education. As they reach adulthood presently, they promise further consolidation of the consumer economy. But they also represent a new generation with values quite different from those that guided their parents, including a self-centeredness that departs significantly from the earlier emphases on family values and interpersonal relationships that marked "Chinese culture."[27] No wonder that the author inserts a note of caution about the unpredictability of the future beyond the year 2010!

For all its emphasis on the need for recognizing the local assimilation of global practices, Li's book is most impressive for the transformations it identifies; not just in the guise of generational change but of society as a whole where even the sixty plus generation has begun to alter its habits of consumption. Most remarkably, perhaps, Li betrays no awareness that his own activity (both as marketing consultant and as author of such a text) may serve as one more moment in these transformations. Unlike conservatives who may bemoan the loss of native values with the emergence of a consumer society, or the domination of consumption practices by an orientation to foreign commodities, Li's own effort is intended to show the way to his clients to further penetrate the Chinese market. In his words, the "book sets out to explore and discuss the dominant trends in China's consumer market, and offers current facts, figures, and analysis in the hope that this information may help guide your China business strategy. The approach is structured to assist those companies wishing to enter China, as well as those already established in China and wishing to expand. It is also relevant to both domestic and international companies. I believe that, for any consumer business, success will only come if business strategy is rooted in a solid understanding of the consumer."[28] The goal of understanding the consumer, we might add, is to create better consumers, which Li makes no effort to disguise.

When Li uses the term "Chinese culture," he uses it in an operational or situational sense, including past legacies but past legacies in the process of daily transformation by forces of the market. One section in his last chapter, which gets down to the nitty-gritty business of concrete advice, is entitled, "Adopt Chinese Values." While the section begins with the observation that "Chinese society . . . draws everything into itself, consumes it, then transforms it into something organically Chinese," it is hard to see what may be "organically Chinese" about the example with which he follows up on that statement: that while in the 1980s Chinese consumers preferred "American-style washing machines (with vertical spinning mechanism)," by the 1990s the preference had shifted to "European-style washing machines (with horizontal rolling tunnel mechanism)" because "they believe that this kind of machine is better suited to their ever upgrading quality of clothes, because this mechanism saves the fiber from severe twisting during the washing process." "The trend remains the same," he concludes, "but the symptom has changed."[29]

This dressing of marketing considerations in the garb of a language of culture may serve Li well, as his book is intended to offer an "insider's" understanding of the Chinese market, and the emphasis on the particular cultural characteristics of the Chinese consumer enhances that claim, serving not only as a guide to marketing but an advertisement for the book itself. But it is by no means an exclusive feature of this particular book or its author. As the discussion above of academic studies of the Chinese market should indicate, the confounding of marketing activity with cultural hybridization or resignification also characterizes work that does not share Li's interests as a marketing consultant. We may recall here Yunxiang Yan's "intriguing point" that localization seemed to be the goal of the management of McDonald's in Beijing; which ceases to be "intriguing" the moment we recognize that domestication in different locations has been a strategy for some time now of global corporations seeking to expand their markets; as is recognized by James Watson's introduction to *Golden Arches East*, where he quotes James Cantalupo, President of McDonald's International, to the effect that "the goal of McDonald's is to become as much a part of the local culture as possible . . . people call us a multinational. I like to call us *multilocal*."[30] What is really intriguing is the reluctance of both the editor and other contributors to the volume to inquire further into what localization and hybridization might mean under the circumstances. Much the same may be observed of the other works cited above which, despite good evidence of the manipulation of culture, nation and locality in marketing, nevertheless refuse to consider the possibility that notions of cultural hybridity or resignification may be meaningless when they point not just to marketing demand but the actual manipulation of markets—whether for foreign or domestic commodities.

It is hardly a secret by now that from global media to global advertising, "First World" transnational corporations, and their "Third World" competitors are engaged in a competition for markets where culture has emerged as a prime object of manipulation in capturing markets. While this is often explained in terms of responding to culturally conditioned demand, it is equally the case that culture serves in all these cases to package commodities differently for different "cultural" markets, which does not detract from the transformative powers of the commodities, but only makes them into cultural "Trojan horses."[31] What is at work, in other words, is the ceaseless reinvention of local cultures in accordance with the marketing needs of transnational or domestic corporations—the latter utilizing the experience with native culture to gain access to transnational markets. The result is a situation in which, in Daniel Miller's words, "the close collusion over a long period of time between the development of what might be called a 'culture of business' and more general social norms . . . [is] so close that we cannot easily locate agency as cause in either the one or the other domain."[32]

Needless to say, transnational corporations are not immune themselves to the changes of which they serve as agents; that they have to reinvent themselves in the process of inventing cultures; which is visible not only in the images they promote of themselves as multilocal or multidomestic, but in actual management practices—from flexible management to deal with the exigencies of different markets to the fostering of multiculturalism (in other words, ethnically diverse management personnel) as company culture—but within limits set by the latter.[33] If this is hybridization, it is nevertheless a hybridization that does not just happen as cultural process, but hybridization that is part and parcel of the production and reproduction of the structures of global power. Issues of homogenization/heterogenization become in the process part of a broader global process of the reinvention of capitalism, and not just of postcolonial imaginings of encounters between societies.

If transnationalization seeks to overcome national and regional boundaries, it also creates a new transnational class that is marked by its participation in a global "commodity ecumene," as Arjun Appadurai has put it in another context.[34]

Without implying that participants in such an economy hold positions of equality within it, or that their relationships are free of competition and conflict, attention to this aspect of transnationalism is important nevertheless because it underlines the significance of native elites in the engineering of the consumer revolution. Where the spread of capitalist practices and consumer culture is concerned, the elite may indeed play a pivotal road. Too much emphasis on Chinese business versus "Western" business, for instance, conceals the fact that despite the use of nationalist rhetoric, Chinese entrepreneurs have been involved all along in the transformation of the economy in joint ventures, that Chinese business as it comes into its own plays a more important role in promoting consumer culture than foreign, and Chinese marketers like Conghua Li play crucial roles in guiding foreigners to the Chinese market. The elite's own consumption patterns also provide models for the emulation of the rest of the population. As Appadurai puts it, elite tastes have a "turnstile function, selecting from exogenous possibilities and then providing models, as well as direct political controls, for internal tastes and production."[35]

There is no reason why advertising, marketing, and management literature should not be discussed as discourses that produce new ideas of culture, nation, and locality; or as sites of discursive conflict between the various cultural and ideological orientations described by those terms. But it is also necessary to keep in mind in the unraveling of these discourses the stakes involved, especially the stakes of economic and social power, that discourses and discursive conflicts express. It is arguable that advertisers and marketers display a greater awareness of what is at issue in these conflicts than academics who seem to drift aimlessly over these discursive terrains, with no visible purpose other than adding case after case to the questionable assertions of postcolonial or postmodern criticism concerning hybridization, localization, or resignification; compounded by a reluctance to account for totalities and structures, without reference to which the cultural processes supposedly described by those terms lose all their connections to the world of power, telling us little beyond the power they have come to command in contemporary academic fashion.

It is difficult to account for the transformations in contemporary Chinese economic culture without referring to the fact that the Chinese population today is under a virtual assault from global advertising—which includes Chinese homegrown advertisers who are quickly learning the global tricks of trade. In the eyes of advertisers, China is one of the most important frontiers of advertising. Not only has advertising investment risen steadily, but it also involves the most prestigious international companies.[36] Moreover, the needs for advertising and marketing has brought Chinese society under greater surveillance than ever before in history; including the political surveillance of Cultural Revolution years, when the regime's goals could be achieved by having neighbors watch one another, without a very comprehensive grasp of the population as a whole on the part of the central government. Presently, by contrast, global advertisers and marketers are on their way to achieving an unparalleled oversight of the country as a whole and microlevel insights into Chinese society through their intense surveillance of popular habits and tastes, class, gender, and age differences in lifestyles, urban-rural and regional variations in culture, and even the savings of the population, including the meager savings of the majority. It is highly probable that their surveillance of Chinese society endows them with a broader and more precise understanding of cultural change in China than is the case with most academic China specialists, Chinese or foreign. Academic China scholarship has always benefited from the surveillance of Chinese society, albeit for mostly political reasons. Surveillance of Chinese society for marketing purposes opens up new opportunities for scholarship; or, at the very least, a new market for it. Do we need to add that, in contrast to the theoretically driven (or obscured) discussions of marketing and cultural change in academic work, such surveillance is driven by very practical and concrete goals: to remake the Chinese as consumers, so as to make them more willing to part with their savings, no matter how meager.

As Conghua Li says of his marketing advice, moreover, marketing and advertising do not differentiate between national and foreign companies or commodities, but between clients, whatever the nationality. We need not discount the significance of economic nationalism at the government, company, and popular level in order to recognize, nevertheless, that like culture, nationalism and localism may themselves serve as weapons in the competition for markets. Politically enforced economic nationalism is one thing, economic nationalism as marketing strategy is another, because in the latter case that strategy may be deployed by foreign as well as domestic enterprises. As domestic enterprises play up their indigenous virtues, foreign enterprises indigenize by repackaging themselves and their commodities in the guise of local cultures. Such strategies may be grasped in terms of hybridization and resignification, but they point most importantly to hybridization and resignification as strategic marketing moves that facilitate the ever-deeper penetration (I use this word advisedly) of society by the forces of capital and consumption. Indigenization may represent the attenuation of an overt invasion of Chinese society by the commodities and values of the West, so-called, but it also serves as a medium through which the practices and values of capitalist society find their way into the remotest corners of the earth. Under the circumstances, indigenization means not resistance to capital in the name of local society, but rather the takeover of its operations by native or local elites.

The point here is not to deny difference between Chinese society, say, and other societies, but rather to shift the grounds for the discussion to other locations than national or civilizational terrains. Difference itself is not a transparent term under the conditions of a capitalist economy. In the first place, difference that is a product of past legacies may be the least important consideration here. The truly important difference is that produced by the demands of capitalist production and consumption, which for their expansion require the ceaseless creation of temporal, spatial, and social differences. To cite Daniel Miller again, "capitalism, or more generally modernity, will bring new homogeneity, but equally spawn new heterogeneity."[37] This may be most visible in the case of a society such as China, where the most important contrast between the capitalist present and the socialist past is the valorization of difference, which provides a radical departure from the days of socialist frugality and control which dressed everyone in sexless green and blue in the name of socialist equality. Socialism, at least as it was understood then, required homogeneity of values as well as of representations. Capitalism, and the consumer revolution, require for their sustenance the production of heterogeneity, however superficial and symbolic.

The second issue concerning difference, following from the logic of the first, is that it is misleading to view it in terms of national cultures or neo-Orientalist civilizational values (such as "Asian values"). Capitalism has not eliminated differences in the so-called West, or even in individual societies such as the United States. On the other hand, in our day "the West is much more of an ideological than a geographical concept," subject to different interpretations in different locations.[38] The deterritorialized institutions and cultural products of the capitalist West are already integral to the constitution of most societies around the world; even where they may have lost their foreignness in popular memory and recognition. The PRC is a good example, where opposition to the invasion of "Western" consumer culture is often articulated in the name not only of an ancient cultural legacy but also the legacy of the modern Marxism-inspired revolution, which has become increasingly difficult to remember as another foreign import in its origins—much as a younger generation may think that McDonald's was originally a Chinese creation.

The homogenization/heterogenization question must lead us off the mark so long as it is conceived in terms of reified notions of national or civilizational values. There is no reason why a consumer revolution in China should lead to a cloning of the Chinese population after an American or "Western" pattern as there is no such pattern, or even to the homogenization of the Chinese population after internally generated cultural models. Indeed, the most important divisions thrown up by the consumer revolution in the PRC are not those of East or West, or Chinese and foreign, but new divisions along lines of generation, class, and region, with different access to power, wealth, and knowledge, and different relationships to the forces of globalization.

A reductionist notion of culture that equates ubiquity with homogeneity is not what critics have in mind when they speak of the attack of capital on culture; although their views are often caricatured and rendered into straw targets by the acolytes of heterogeneity. What is at issue rather is that culture is in the process of losing its autonomy as it is inducted into service in the manipulation of markets. This may seem to go against the logic of contemporary academic theories which endow culture with an autonomous logic of its own, but that may be because contemporary academic theories would seem to be more interested in refuting past (especially Marxist) notions that subjected culture to the economy, than addressing a current situation in which culture has assumed a foremost place in the arsenal of capital. "The Great Transformation"—the subjection of all life to the logic of the market—that Karl Polanyi wrote of as the revolution of capitalism is now in the process of globalization, consuming even those societies such as the Chinese which for a brief while sought to reverse it through the agency of socialism.[39] In the midst of serious national, ethnic, and religious conflict, one thing seems to endow the world with commonality: the reinterpretation of all cultural legacies to demonstrate that capitalism, and markets, have been the fates of humanity all along.

CULTURAL HOMOGENIZATION/HETEROGENIZATION: A NONPROBLEM?

Whether the world is headed for homogeneity or heterogeneity is a question that I think is unanswerable except on the basis of ideology or faith, and somewhat trivial in its intellectual consequences. I have taken it as my point of departure here in order to inquire into the possibilities of uncovering a broader context that may enable us to grasp the homogeneity/ heterogeneity opposition in their dialectical unity; as a contradiction, in other words, which implies unity as much as opposition. This requires that we shift the discussion to other grounds, from which the homogenization/heterogenization debate serves as a distraction. Zygmunt Bauman writes in a recent essay on globalization that, "not asking certain questions is pregnant with more dangers than failing to answer the questions already on the official agenda; while asking the wrong kind of questions all too often helps to avert eyes from the truly important questions."[40] The problem with the homogenization/heterogenization question is that, judging by the results, it seems to promote research agenda that are quite trivial, that seek identity in commonality, and seem to find in difference—any difference—evidence of heterogeneity—without inquiring any further whether the commonalities might be responsible for the differences, even as the differences make for the commonalities. It is remarkable how discussions of different meanings imposed on television messages or McDonald's in different contexts may overlook the elementary fact that before such differences come into play, people in all those contexts have to gather around a television set or at McDonald's, which represents fundamental material cultural transformation in the first place, or that the body has to be rendered into an object of desire before it becomes a site of discourses on beauty. The production of desire itself, we might suggest, takes priority over the different ways in which it can be satisfied; indeed, difference itself may be produced so as to preclude the possibility of the satisfaction of desire, which must be multiplied infinitely, and infinitesimally, if an ever expanding volume of commodities are to be consumed by a finite number of consumers. In the process, the subject, regardless of national or other origin, has to be made and remade constantly. Referring back to the distinction I drew in the introduction between political and economic manipulations of culture, it is possible to argue that while state manipulation seeks most importantly to create fixed subjects who are amenable to prediction and control, economic manipulation seeks exactly the opposite end: subjects who are destabilized to be voracious consumers, in search of an elusive satisfaction that is perpetually deferred. This is the subject of global capitalism—as producer, manager, or consumer.

Instead, in most discussions of homogenization/heterogenization wishful thinking, if not ideological predisposition, seems to guide choice. Cultural homogenization is most appealing to those who stand to benefit most from it one way or another; or those who see in it the promise of human coprosperity. On the other hand, a populist nostalgia for cultural difference (if not Orientalism and its mirror in parochial nationalism) seems in many cases to motivate those who find evidence of heterogeneity in everything from the discovery of "Chineseness" in roofing that adds an upward curve to its extremities, to the renaming of Coca-cola in Chinese characters that suggest that it is mouthable and enjoyable at the same time (kekou kele)—or even the excision of part of one of the legs in the "m" of McDonald's to create a Chinese imitator (which serves, I should think, as evidence not of indigenization, but of the immense debt of the indigenous to the foreign). Few commentators, academic or otherwise, seem to wonder these days why and how social transformation could come to be conceived in such trite ways, that also trivialize the meaning of what it may mean to speak of cultural difference and heterogeneity!

Whether the world is headed for homogeneity or heterogeneity depends on where we look, and what meaning we assign to what we see. And that all depends on where we stand; not just as academics or intellectuals, but also as

advertisers, management consultants, development economists, or development managers, which daily become less distinguishable from one another—
a confusion that may be responsible also for the self-limitations in the questions we pursue.

There are good reasons for this bifurcation in reading the consequences of
globalization, and they recall the old saw about the forest and the trees. Those
who focus their attention on the trees see heterogeneity everywhere, with little attention to how the forest may shape the trees; while those focused on the
forest ignore the trees and the way in which they may retain their identity
against the pressures of the forest. But the old saw may need a new twist; that
the soothsayers of either homogenization or heterogenization can any longer
imagine an outside to the forest, which makes haphazard any motion between
the whole and the parts: those who see the trees can no longer even imagine
a forest, but simply move from tree to tree, with nothing to guide them but
everyday contingencies, while those who miss the trees for the forest see the
forest from the inside out, so to speak, without any notion of what may be giving shape to the forest aside from those very motions. Arguments for heterogenization no less than arguments for homogenization are constrained by an
assumption of a cultural and intellectual space that presupposes a paradigm
(or, more severely, ideology) of globalization, and cannot imagine outsides to
it, any more than they can imagine differences other than those defined by
cultural spaces of ethnicity, nation, or race. It seems important, therefore, in
order to fully confront the question, to imagine outsides to globalization, an
imaginary location from which to perceive the trees and the forest at once,
which may be indispensable to any critical evaluation of the question itself.
Without such a perspective, any answer to the question remains constrained
in a field of limited vision, especially with regard to issues of power in globalization, and there is little to guide the analyst except for trial and error,
which is itself a negation of comprehending what is at work systemically and
systematically. For the same reasons, it remains at the mercy of the intellectual procedures of marketers, and the manipulators of market cultures. But is
it possible any longer to imagine an outside?

The question of homogenization/heterogenization is ideological at a very
fundamental level because it presupposes a conceit that we are in a position
to know the consequences of processes—chaotic ones at that—that have yet
to fulfill their histories. It is only by a denial of histories the outcomes of
which we are in no position to predict that we may say whether cultural homogeneity or heterogeneity is the ultimate fate of humankind. All we have to
work with is the present, and the present provides evidence either way, which
is tantamount to saying that the future can go anywhere, which is not saying
much. We can make educated guesses about eventualities, but those guesses

need to account for both the trees and the forest. In the meantime, claims to either eventuality become parts of the struggle that they pretend to describe as observers, shaping through their discourses, however unintentionally or perhaps even against their intentions, the world that they pretend to describe.

It may be argued that evidence of the contemporary structuring of the world may nevertheless serve as pointers to trends which render the future intelligible, at least at the level of educated guess. But that begs another, perhaps more fundamental, problem: that difference, no less than sameness, is created presently by the same agencies. The homogenization/heterogenization juxtaposition is informed by a subject/object distinction, and elicits answers that are themselves constrained by the same distinction; which range from the erasure of the object by the subject to the reaffirmation of the subjectivity of the objects of transformation in giving new meaning to the forces of transformation, indigenizing or utilizing those forces to turn the tables on their transformers. There is little consideration in these arguments of the ways in which resistance or, more proactively, a countertransformation, nevertheless contributes to the consolidation of the systemic forces that raise the question of homogenization/heterogenization in the first place—because they do not point to any possibilities beyond the totalities that envelop both. This is what I had in mind when I referred above to the triviality of much of the argument in favor of heterogenization.

Contrasts between two historical periods in China's experience with capitalism may serve to illustrate what I have in mind. There is nothing new about capitalism and capitalist markets in China. The Chinese economy long has been a market economy, though not, therefore, a capitalist market economy, and while advertising in a formal sense was not one of its indigenous products, there is plenty of evidence of the pursuit of certain commodities as being more desirable than others.[41] On the other hand, advertising did enter Chinese economic practices with the appearance of capitalism, through the agency of imperialism, and from the turn of the twentieth century, advertising practices were integral to economic life in Chinese cities.[42] How sensitive such advertising was to Chinese "cultural" habits is difficult to say, as there has been little systematic study of the subject. But it seems safe to say, if I may take a risk, that the recognition of cultural or physical difference at the time did not lead to calls for cultural hybridization, but left intact advertising intended to turn Chinese on to foreign ways, without any significant recognition that culture must be a primary consideration in marketing and advertising. In order for advertising to be effective, foreign commodities might have to be presented to Chinese consumers in a "Chinese" guise, but that by no means implied a conscious strategy of domestication and localization.[43] Chinese bodies were already objects of transformation in ads like "Dr. Robinson's Pink Pills for Pale People." The *Journal of the Shanghai Chamber of Commerce* complained in the mid-1920s that the penchant for foreign fashions had spread even to the working classes who sought after "Western" underwear.[44] I have already referred to the creation in the 1920s of new ideals of feminine beauty through advertising.[45]

If advertising did not display any particular sensitivity to native (or local) tastes in an earlier age, the indifference was even more pronounced in management practices.[46] Again, judging by the discussion of management problems in the *Journal of the Shanghai Chamber of Commerce*, it was foreign companies that showed the way to the future of management practices in China. Prominent among such management practices were those of companies such as Endicott and Johnson, with its paternalistic management practices, which impressed Chinese businessmen not for their resemblance to Chinese familism but their ability to extract greater efficiency from workers through caring for them.

Rather than assert cultural difference, Chinese businessmen in the 1920s, like the intellectuals, mostly perceived in inherited culture the source of China's weakness and backwardness. To be sure, they were economic nationalists, and longed for a stronger state that could protect Chinese business. Some of them even shared with radical intellectuals the view of foreign capitalism as imperialism that held back China's development. It was radical intellectuals, themselves the products of the new modernity, however, who responded to capitalism-as-imperialism by demands not for an alternative capitalism, but alternatives to it; that would include cultural as well as economic transformation. They found the alternative in socialism. Contrary to some tendency in contemporary historiography to emphasize the ruralness of the Chinese Revolution, the opposition to the capitalist modernity of a Guangzhou or Shanghai was not just the opposition to a new urbanism of a society that was still largely rural, but the opposition of urban intellectuals who saw in the practices of capitalism the destruction of values of society by the forces of an economy driven by no other consideration than that of profit. Unlike the revolution of the two decades after 1927, the revolutionary movement of the 1920s was an urban revolution, that pit alternative visions of the good society against the promoters of capitalism—visions in which socialist utopianism were blended in uneasy mixture with concerns for national cultural integrity. Their successors won out politically in 1949, and one of the first things they did was to put an end to the capitalist market economy, and everything associated with it, including advertising. What they did not realize, if such was to be expected, was that a national economy might need more for its integration than coordination by bureaucrats, that the national economy is as much a cultural entity as an organizational one.

The pre-1949 experience with the new capitalist culture brings contemporary developments in the PRC into sharper relief. First, a seemingly helpless object earlier of invasion by the forces of capital, contemporary China has emerged as a competitor within the new global capitalist economy, in a position even to shape its practices. Secondly, while class differences in terms of the accumulation and control of wealth may be even greater now than earlier, the increased wealth of society as a whole (which has much to do with the material and ethical achievements of the experiment with socialism) enables greater participation of the population in the consumer revolution, facilitating an unprecedented penetration of society by the forces and values of capitalism. Thirdly, under the circumstances the foreign/domestic distinctions gradually lose their meaning; especially as they retain memories of an earlier language of imperialism, which is difficult to sustain in an environment in which capitalist practices are not forced on either China or Chinese, who now make those practices their own as producers and consumers.

Under the circumstances, with an inability to imagine an outside to capitalism that is not just a Chinese but a global problem, heterogeneity seems to be the only available option in asserting difference. But this is difference that points merely to different modes of consumption, and not to any alternatives to either capitalism or consumerism. To be sure, for an older generation in particular, the assertion of difference suggests an anger at the victory of a system to which they had hoped to find an alternative.[47] Discounting such resistance from an older generation of socialists, however, the assertion of difference, at its most serious, serves as a vehicle for the expression of local identity against the homogenizing forces of capital. To complicate the problem further, consumerism may be liberating in a society like China where it enables a measure of individual expression. It is a tragedy of the Chinese Revolution that the collectivist values of an earlier generation now stand in opposition to the possibilities of self-expression that can be achieved through marketization and commoditization. It is a tragedy that is felt widely among old and young alike, at least those of my acquaintance, that finds an outlet in the easy promises of nationalism, rather than the more difficult task of finding alternatives to nationalism and capitalism, both products of a Chinese modernity. What seems to be certain is that the utopianism of an earlier day, in the formulation of Jiwei Ci, has given way to unbridled hedonism that finds expression in consumption.[48]

The preferred problem addressed in most of the literature, however, is that of cultural homogenization/heterogenization that would rather focus on the trivia of cultural transmission than cultural politics, or the politics of culture. At its most trivial, it assumes neo-Orientalist guises where placing Chinese landscapes in a restaurant or adding a curve to the roof of a building serves as evidence of "Chinese characteristics." At its most serious, it raises the question of threats to local cultures (more often than not conceived ethnically) by the forces of capital. In either case, however, the assertion of difference is very much limited by the spaces of global capitalism, and identity itself is commodified as it is confined in its expression to the commodities consumed.

CONCLUDING REMARKS

It seems to me that three questions need to be kept in mind in efforts to grasp the implications of the contemporary relationship between global markets and local societies in a long-term perspective—which is to say a perspective that demands an outside-in look on our times both temporally and spatially. First is the question of economy and society; in other words, the relationship of capitalism to its social context—both the social context that produced capitalism, and the social contexts that capitalism produces. We might call this the Karl Polanyi question, as Polanyi stated the question with uncommon clarity when he observed, following Karl Marx, that capitalism was revolutionary because it was the first system that subjected society (and, therefore, politics) to the supposedly autonomous logic of the economy. That logic seems to command even greater power in our day than his, acquiring renewed vitality from the developmentalist fever that has gripped societies globally, among which the PRC holds a most prominent place.

The second question is that of structure and agency because, while capitalism as a mode of production provides a structural totality that may condition all those who come under its domain, it is in the end human agency that creates structures, albeit human agencies circumscribed by the very conditions they would transform. These conditions are no longer simply legacies of cultural pasts, but cultural pasts already worked over by more than a century of imperialism and revolution—and a modernity understood in those terms. Currently, the globalization of capital is central to grasping these conditions, as it enables the participation in global economic practices of those who were earlier peripheral to it. The agents of capitalism are no longer just Euro-Americans, but natives of societies worldwide, who serve as the transmitters to their own societies (as well as to societies other than their own) of the values of markets and consumption. I think it is this new relationship that informs the homogenization/heterogenization question; where heterogenization serve as a means of asserting identity, but only within the limits set by the homogeneities of capital to which there is no longer an imaginable outside.

The final question is that of culture, that much disputed term that both shapes meaning, and is meaning-producing at the same time. The question of homogenization/heterogenization is ultimately a question in cultural exploration, and how cultures are received/created in our day are not only a gauge of structural transformations, but gauges as well of our relationship to the past, the present, and the future—of the worlds we would make even as we are made by those very same worlds. The world of culture is especially important because, if there is any novelty to the notion of globalization as it is understood presently, the novelty lies in the realm of culture. The present is not a time of chronicling cultures, it is a time of creating them. That may be the most important reason that the "cultural turn" has come to the fore once again; at the very moment of academic helplessness over the meaning of culture, when culture has been captured in the service of forces that always seem to be a few steps ahead of those who would reflect on it, and is tossed and turned in unanticipated directions which no longer follow the logic of history but the flexible logic of global markets and corporations. As Nicholas Dirks writes with reference to the work of Theodore Adorno on the "culture industry," "anticipating current theoretical preoccupations with cultural hegemony and discursive domination, Adorno carefully dissected the ways in which the modern subject was converted into a consumer, a consumer whose needs, interests and beliefs could be controlled and manipulated by the apparatuses of a mass media that produced pleasure (and incited further consumption) by stifling the possibility of critical reflection."[49]

The distinguished historian Joseph Levenson concluded his seminal work on China's confrontation with modernity with the observation that "what the West has probably done to China is to change the latter's language—what China has done to the West is to enlarge the latter's vocabulary."[50] That conclusion has greater validity today than it did when he pronounced it, when a revolutionary China still held out hopes of creating a new language of modernity. The struggle over sameness and difference itself presupposes a struggle over language. The terms in which that struggle is presently articulated, that pit heterogeneity against homogeneity, already point to a concession of defeat; when the search for alternatives no longer aims at the discovery of a new language of politics and society, but is constrained to competition over interpretation within the same language of markets and commodities. As modernization gives way to globalization in order to accommodate these differences of interpretation, claims to difference no longer aspire to the overcoming of the boundaries of that language but are restricted to pleas for discursive identity within it—or, at their most radical, to endless "wars of position" in an eternal present.

I do not mean to imply, in stressing the totalizing logic of global capitalism, that the future is all but determined, that it is indeed impossible to imagine outsides to capitalism. On the contrary; I am critical of the homogenization/heterogenization formulation precisely because it conceives of questions of sameness and difference within very narrow boundaries, and becomes an obstacle itself to conceiving radical alternatives to the present. Hence my emphasis above on the overlap in the approach to that formulation between academic analyses and the analyses of advertisers; the latter seeking to reshape the world in their own image by any means necessary, the former unable to transcend in their analyses the thematics established by the latter. To read these debates on homogenization/heterogenization one would think that people around the world have come to dwell in McDonald's restaurants, adding their own touches to them here and there, but without the possibility of dwelling elsewhere!

While it would be possible to make a case that the workings of capital render it into an invisible empire to which there is no outside, and alternatives to capitalism that once motivated radical movements have lost their plausibility, it is equally arguable that the domination of capital is neither all-encompassing nor seamless. For one thing, the empire is hardly invisible, but involves real human agency in its creation, which is fallible almost by definition as the agents of global capitalism are themselves often at the mercy of the unintended consequences of their own efforts to structure the world. Secondly, the "commodity ecumene" of global capitalism is just that, an ecumene that nourishes off global networks of economic and political power, but by no means covers the entire surface of the globe, or all those who inhabit it. Indeed, while it may be argued that no lives, or aspects of life, remain untouched by the operations of capital, it is also the case that global capitalism no longer seeks to incorporate all within it, but proceeds rather by marginalizing the great majority of the earth's people, who have now become irrelevant to its operations either as producers or consumers. Commentators such as Gibson-Graham have pointed to the radically transformative potential of "outsides" to global capital, where large numbers of people now seek a livelihood in those margins, formulating alternative social and economic means of existence.[51] Serge Latouche, the distinguished French expert on Third World political economy, writes of these marginal economies (the so-called informal economy) that

> The emergence of the informal economy and society is all the more significant in that it is part of the pattern of resistance, survival and endurance in the face of Westernization. Whereas the crisis of the nation-state endangers the social fabric of industrial countries and constitutes a grave threat to the very existence of the social bond, it can only liberate the vital forces and active solidarity now writhing in the fetters of nationalism and the artificial order of the mimetic state. While the techno-economic machine is showing signs of breaking down for lack

of social underpinnings, the creative energies of Third-World societies, distorted and denied by the machine's refusal to accept them, may increase tenfold. The failure of the techno-economic machine at the heart of the social fabric is bringing about the crisis of the "Western" order; but it may be a precondition for the resurgence of new worlds, a new civilization, a new age.[52]

Globalization, moreover, produces not just global integration but also global fragmentation, even of capital itself, which may make it more proper to speak of a "pan-capitalism" rather than a global capitalism. The contradictions of capital provide spaces within it that are nevertheless outsides to it, where it is still possible to imagine alternatives to capital, albeit differently than in earlier oppositional movements. This is the case not only with the informal economies that Latouche emphasizes, but also the antiglobalist movements of various kinds that have appeared not just in the Third World but the First World as well in response to the ravages of globalization, and in defense of places, the locations of everyday existence, which made their presence known forcefully in the anti-WTO protests in Seattle late last year. If it is impossible in our day to think of the local (and I don't mean just the national) without reference to the global, we need to remember that even the global is constrained to represent itself as the local—in which efforts around the world to ground the global in concrete places play a most significant part.

NOTES

1. I have encountered the term more than once in references to various aspects of change in the People's Republic's economy. It seems that everything in China, from banking to management to services, is in the process of undergoing a "second cultural revolution." For an example, see Richard W. Pollay, David K. Tse, and Wang Zheng-yuan, "Advertising, Propaganda and Value Change in Economic Development: The New Cultural Revolution in China and Attitudes Toward Advertising," *Journal of Business Research* 20, no. 2 (March 1990): 83–96. For another example, with reference to popular art and music, see "China's New Cultural Revolution," *Economist* (6 September 1997), 87. I should note also that since the terms "China" and "Chinese" have acquired immense complexity with the recognition of different "Chinese" societies, from the PRC (People's Republic of China) to Taiwan to Singapore, not to mention Chinese populations in "diaspora," I use the People's Republic of China to specify the location under discussion here (abbreviated as PRC).

2. Shmuel N. Eisenstadt, "Multiple Modernities," *Daedalus* 129, no. 1 (Winter 2000): 1–29, esp. 1.

3. I owe the term "McDomination" to a Hong Kong author, Luk Tak Chuen.

4. For a most recent, and thorough, discussion see Conghua Li, *China: The Consumer Revolution* (Singapore: John Wiley & Sons, 1998).

5. For the role consumption plays in identity creation and self-expression, see the essays in Jonathan Friedman, ed., *Consumption and Identity* (Switzerland: Harwood Academic Publishers, 1994).

6. Bin Zhao, "Consumerism, Confucianism, Communism: Making Sense of China Today," *New Left Review*, No. 222 (March/April 1997): 43–59, esp. 51–56.

7. Kenichi Ohmae, "Endorsement," on the cover of Conghua Li, *China*. There are many examples of this position. A prominent example is Benjamin R. Barber, *Jihad v. McWorld* (New York: Times Books, 1995). For a more recent argument that focuses on the attack of "capital against culture," see Walter LaFeber, *Michael Jordan and the New Global Capitalism* (New York: W. W. Norton, 1999).

8. David Rothkopf, "In Praise of Cultural Imperialism?" where Rothkopf, a member of Kissinger Associates, argues that "the decline of cultural distinctions [is] a measure of the progress of civilization," and sees in globalization a force to that end. See *Foreign Policy* (Summer 1997): 38–53, esp. 40.

9. There are many examples of this position also. For some important recent ones, see LaFeber, *Michael Jordan and the New Global Capitalism,* and Zygmunt Bauman, *Globalization: The Human Consequences* (New York: Columbia University Press, 1999), esp. chapter 4.

10. This is a position that is heard in common in much of postcolonial criticism. For an influential and frequently cited example, see Arjun Appadurai, "Disjuncture and Difference in the Global Cultural Economy," in *Modernity at Large* (Minneapolis: University of Minnesota Press, 1996), 27–47. Originally published in *Public Culture* 2, no. 2 (1990), where Appadurai asserts that "most often, the homogenization argument subspeciates into either an argument about Americanization or an argument about commoditization, and very often the two arguments are closely linked. What these arguments fail to consider is that at least as rapidly as forces from various metropolises are brought into new societies they tend to become indigenized in one or another way" (32).

11. The most famous, or infamous, illustration of this argument is that presented by Samuel Huntington in "Clash of Civilizations?" *Foreign Affairs* (Summer 1993): 22–49.

12. Bin Zhao, "Consumerism, Confucianism, Communism," 47. It might be noted here that the literature on contemporary Chinese development renders "Confucius" into one of the most abused personages in history. Confucius has been credited with the values that have helped China's recent development as well as being discredited with all the values that obstruct development. The use and abuse of Confucius is not the issue here. Of more immediate interest is the way in which this development literature has issued in a new kind of culturalism, that seeks in culture dehistoricized values that can serve as pointers to the characteristics of any one society. It is this search, most fundamentally, that issues in the invention of cultures against all the evidence of history, "poor Confucius," one is tempted to say, who, in being rendered into a symbol of Chineseness, has to suffer all the consequences of China's historical experiences!

13. Conghua Li, *China*, 5

14. Yunxiang Yan, "McDonald's in Beijing," in *Golden Arches East:McDonald's in East Asia*, ed. James L. Watson, 39–76, esp. 53–54 (Stanford: Stanford University Press, 1997).

15. Yan, "McDonald's in Beijing," 54–66.

16. This is not to say that these ideals entered China for the first time in the 1980s. They were a force already in the 1920s in the semi-colonial Treaty Ports. For a study of Guangzhou (Canton), see Virgil Ho, "The Limits of Hatred: Popular Attitudes Towards the West in Republican Canton," *East Asian History*, no. 2 (December 1991): 87–104, esp. 91–93.

17. Perry Johansson, "White Skin, Large Breasts: Chinese Beauty Product Advertising as Cultural Discourse," *China Information* 13, nos. 2–3 (Autumn–Winter 1998–1999): 59–78, 59. Johansson directs his arguments at a suggestion by Wendy Chapkiss that the spread of Caucasian ideals globally intimates a "conspicuous conspiracy afoot," but nevertheless his own arguments take the form of generalizations that go beyond a refutation of "conspiracy."

18. Johansson, "White Skin, Large Breasts," 68.

19. Johansson, "White Skin, Large Breasts," 77

20. Johansson's argument also lacks historical depth. "Contemporary Chinese beauty ideals" need to be viewed in historical perspective, as those ideals began to find their way into Chinese society a century ago. See the article by Virgil Ho, referred to above in note 16. A much more sophisticated and historically sensitive version of this argument is to be found in Louisa Schein, "The Consumption of Color and the Politics of White Skin in Post-Mao China," *Social Text*, No. 41 (Winter 1994): 141–64. Schein's argument, too, is infused with the vocabulary of postcolonial criticism. On the other hand, she is cognizant of the power of new consumption practices in the process of local resignifications and their historical reconfigurations. Speaking of the symbolism of "the white woman," she notes that while in the initial re-opening of the PRC in the 1980s it was the otherness of the white woman to the Chinese self that was the most striking, by the 1990s the "fetish of the white woman" as the other was in the process of being supplanted by "the fetish of the white woman" as commodity; in other words, fetishism of the commodity form. She writes: "When I asked Chinese consumers why the image of the white woman was so ubiquitous as a commodity *and* in the packaging of other commodities, I was sometimes told that that she represented 'modernity' or beauty. But other times I was told that there was simply no meaning intended, that commodity producers slapped on the image because *the white woman sells*" (146). We might note here that something comparable might be at work even with McDonald's and other symbols of status and "modernity": McDonald's does not just sell commodities (hamburgers, french fries, etc.), but itself becomes a commodity to be consumed.

21. Beverley Hooper, "Globalisation and Resistance in Post-Mao China: The Case of Foreign Consumer Products," *Asian Studies Review* (forthcoming). I am grateful to Prof. Hooper for permission to cite this article.

22. Arjun Appadurai, ed., *The Social Life of Things: Commodities in Cultural Perspective* (Cambridge, UK: Cambridge University Press, 1999a). For the commodification of nationalism, see Geremie R. Barmé, *In the Red: On Contemporary Chinese Culture* (New York: Columbia University Press, 1999), especially chapter 9. Barmé argues that just as the Communist Party uses advertising these days to promote itself and nationalism, advertisers (Chinese) use the Party, nationalism, and even the revo-

lutionary slogans of Mao Zedong to market their products. It has been possible in the 1990s to find everything from Mao theme restaurants to Confucius "white lightning." For some personal observations, see chapter 11, "*Looking Backward* in the Age of Global Capital: Thoughts on History in Third World Cultural Criticism."

23. Cited in Hooper, "Globalisation and Resistance," 1.

24. Mike Featherstone, "Global Culture: An Introduction," in *Global Culture: Nationalism, Globalization and Modernity*, ed. Mike Featherstone, 1–14, esp. 1 (London: Sage Publications, 1990). I think Schein is closer to the mark when she describes the disturbing of boundaries as an "imagined cosmopolitanism": "The ideology of *kaifang*—or opening—taken to the point it had reached in 1993, meant a destabilizing of contrastive Chineseness. It would be simplistic to say that Chinese had become more Westernized than they used to be; rather, the identities they were forging were decreasingly structured by an internal Chineseness versus an external foreignness. The Chinese were fashioning themselves more and more as participants in a global culture of late capitalist consumption. This process of identity redistribution, dense with local practices and cultural production, could be described as 'imagined cosmopolitanism'" (Schein, 149). Schein writes also of the part that state policies, among other forces, have contributed to the proliferation of internal differences; within the context of transnational practices, these differences further render problematic the notion of a "bounded" national identity. It is possible, under the circumstances, that consumerism without Westernization finds an escape route, however tentative, in the emulation of modernized Chinese societies such as Hong Kong. See Louisa Schein, "The Other Goes to Market: The State, the Nation, and Unruliness in Contemporary China," *Identities* 2, no. 3 (1996): 197–222.

25. Kenichi Ohmae, "Endorsement" on cover of Conghua Li, *China: The Consumer Revolution*.

26. Conghua Li, *China: The Consumer Revolution*, xv–xvi.

27. Conghua Li, *China: The Consumer Revolution*, especially chapter 2.

28. Conghua Li, *China: The Consumer Revolution*, 7.

29. Conghua Li, *China: The Consumer Revolution*, 209.

30. James L. Watson, "Introduction: Transnationalism, Localization, and Fast Foods in East Asia," in *Golden Arches East*, 1–38, esp. 12. Sometimes the preferred term is "multidomestic." For further discussion of the relationship between culture and micro-marketing, see, Arif Dirlik, *After the Revolution: Waking to Global Capitalism* (Hanover, NH: Wesleyan University Press, 1994), esp. 70–73.

31. For examples, see Barbara Mueller, *International Advertising: Communicating across Cultures* (Belmont, CA: Wadsworth Publishing, 1996), chapter 4, and John A. McCarty, "The Role of Cultural Orientations in Cross-Cultural Research and International Marketing and Advertising," in *Global and Multinational Advertising*, ed. Basil G. Englis, 23–45 (Hillsdale, NJ: Lawrence Erlbaum Associates, 1994).

32. Daniel Miller, *Capitalism: An Ethnographic Approach* (Oxford, UK: Berg, 1997), 319.

33. These practices are visible in management and marketing literature at the latest from the 1960s. For further discussion, see Arif Dirlik, "The Postmodernization of Production and Its Organization: Flexible Production, Work and Culture," in A. Dirlik,

The Postcolonial Aura: Third World Criticism in the Age of Global Capitalism (Boulder, CO: Westview Press, 1997), 186–219. For a discussion that focuses on management challenges from East Asia, including China, see Dongsui Su, Yang Zhang, and John F. Hulpke, "A Management Culture Revolution for the New Century?" *Journal of Applied Management Studies* 7, no. 1 (June 1998): 135–39. The role of culture in human resource development has also been the focus of a great deal of attention in the People's Republic of China over the decade of the 1990s.

34. Arjun Appadurai, "Introduction: Commodities and the Politics of Value," *The Social Life of Things*, 3–63, 27. Appadurai defines "commodity ecumene" as "a transcultural network of relationships linking producers, distributors, and consumers of a particular commodity or set of commodities." (Ibid.) Appadurai's term is all the more apt if we recall the original sense of the term, which, according to the classical scholar James Romm, implied "a region made coherent by the intercommunication of its inhabitants," or the "known" or "familiar" world. James S. Romm, *The Edges of the Earth in Ancient Thought* (Princeton, NJ: Princeton University Press, 1992), 37. The world of globality knows itself and its inhabitants through the circulation of commodities, which helps render it "familiar" even when not at "home."

35. Appadurai, "Introduction: Commodities and the Politics of Value," *The Social Life of Things*, 31. For a journalistic look at the spread of "American" consumption values by Asian elites, see Barbara Crossette, "Un-American Ugly Americans," *New York Times* (Sunday, 11 May 1997), "The Week in Review," 1. This is, of course, as true of local as of national elites. Local elites in China have been busy building infrastructures that might make their locations more attractive to capital, native or foreign—apparently on the principle that "if you build it they will come." According to a BBC report aired in March 1999, Chinese authorities, conceding that oppression has not done the job of eradicating Tibetan resistance, have decided to let capitalism do the job by creating a consumer society in Tibet. This report has been confirmed for the author by sources close to the Party center.

36. As early as 1979, at the very beginning of the "reform" period in China, one U.S. business columnist wrote that "advertising, the Chinese will soon find, is addictive. It's our secret weapon." Quoted in Randall E. Stross, *Bulls in the China Shop, and Other Sino-American Business Encounters* (New York: Pantheon Books, 1990), 248. While spending on advertising in China is still far behind the United States and Japan, "China is the world's fastest growing advertising market," moving from thirty-sixth place in the world to the eleventh by 1996 to an estimated fifth by the turn of the century. See "Advertising Boom," *China Economic Review* (September 1996): 10. For a historical review of advertising in China, see Jian Wang, "From Four Hundred Million to More Than One Billion Customers: A Brief History of the Foreign Advertising Industry in China," *International Journal of Advertising* 16, no. 4 (November 1997): 241–61, where the author shows that advertising revenue of Chinese media increased from around 130 million yuan in 1983 to more than 7 billion yuan by 1993, most of it going to newspapers and television. For discussions of culture in advertising, see Betsy Gelb and Yong Zhang, "Matching Advertising Appeals to Culture: The Influence of Products' Use Conditions," *Journal of Advertising* 25, no. 3 (Fall 1996): 29–46, and Rick Yan, "To Reach China's Consumers, Adapt to Guoqing [national

characteristics]," *Harvard Business Review* (September/October 1994). For the need to take a regional approach to these characteristics, see "Taking a Regional Approach," *China Economic Review* (July 1994). Advertising, too, is "going local" by finding local clients. See "Getting the Word Out," *China Business Review* 25, no. 5 (September 1998): 22–25.

37. Miller, *Capitalism*, 15.

38. Serge Latouche, *The Westernization of the World: The Significance, Scope and Limits of the Drive towards Global Uniformity*, tr. from the French original (1989) by Rosemary Morris (Cambridge, UK: Polity Press, 1996), 27.

39. Karl Polanyi, *The Great Transformation* (Boston: Beacon Press, 1957).

40. Zygmunt Bauman, *Globalization: The Human Consequences*, 5.

41. In the late 1980s, when advertising became a craze, giving birth to a new "advertising literature" *(guanggao wenxue)*, some imaginative Chinese intellectuals found signs of advertising in the poetry of the past that referred to wines and food from different regions of China.

42. Jian Wang, "From Four Hundred Million to More than One Billion Customers: A Brief History of the Foreign Advertising Industry in China," *International Journal of Advertising*.

43. For the British-American Tobacco Co., see Sherman Cochran, *Big Business in China: Sino-Foreign Rivalry in the Cigarette Industry, 1890–1930* (Cambridge, MA: Harvard University Press, 1980), 36. In a more recent paper, Cochran finds "Chinese characteristics" (this time with reference to the Chinese-owned Five Continents Pharmacy Co. in the internal decoration of one floor of the company's building in Shanghai, which was otherwise "Western." More importantly, the company succeeded, according to Cochran, because it skillfully used "Western" management techniques. See Sherman Cochran, "Chinese Agents of Consumer Culture: Five Continents Drug Stores, 1906–1937," Conference paper presented at the International Symposium on "China and the World in the Twentieth Century," Taipei, Taiwan, 6–8 January 2000.

44. For an example complaining about the spreading taste for foreign goods, see Fang Shubo, "Tichan guohuo yu guanshui yundong" [Advocating National Goods and the Customs Autonomy Movement], *Shanghai zongzhang hui yuebao* [Monthly of the Shanghai General Chamber of Commerce] 5, no. 9 (September 1925).

45. Carl Crow, an American reporter who was to end up as the head of one of the biggest advertising agencies in China, bragged with reference to changing women's fashions in China that "we brought out the first [fashion book] and . . . played our small part in revealing the most beautiful leg the world has ever seen." Carl Crow, *Four Hundred Million Customers* (New York: Harper Brothers, 1937), 41.

46. Indeed, Chinese writers at the time saw in Chinese characteristics such as familism a source of backwardness and a reason for economic stagnation. For an example, see Wang Zhiwei, "Zhongguo gongshangye puqiuzhi fangfa" (Methods for Helping Out Chinese Industry and Commerce), *Shanghai zongzhang hui yuebao* (Shanghai General Chamber of Commerce Monthly) 3, no. 9 (September 1923).

47. I know this from personal experience, but it is also recognized by writers on management who point to this older generation as problems in the new joint enterprises. More often than not, however, these problems are presented as problems of

"Chinese culture," not problems that may have been inherited from the legacies of socialism.

48. Jiwei Ci, *Dialectic of the Chinese Revolution: From Utopianism to Hedonism* (Stanford, CA: Stanford University Press, 1994). For an examination of the shift from utilitarian to hedonistic values in advertising, see Daniel A. Stout, Dennis G. Martin, and Li Zhang, "Changes in Consumption Values Reflected in Chinese Newspaper Advertising," *New Jersey Journal of Communication* 2, no. 2 (Fall 1994): 146–68. A report on "the first scientific national poll of the world's most populous country" by the Gallup organization observes that "although the Chinese have given hints of being the most materialistic people still under Communist Party rule, Gallup executives say they are surprised by the unapologetic desire for money and goods revealed in the poll." "Chinese Capitalism at Work," *Society* 33, no. 2 (January–February 1996): 3. Not everyone agrees with this gloomy evaluation of the rise of a consumer culture in China. In a recent study, Deborah Davis sees in the rise of consumption the formation of a private against the state-controlled public sphere, and the promise of civil society. See "Introduction: A Revolution in Consumption," in Deborah S. Davis, ed., *The Consumer Revolution in Urban China*, 1–24 (Berkeley: University of California Press, 2000). Such a view may be correct in pointing to the new freedoms made possible by consumption, but it is one-sided in overlooking the depoliticization of society through consumption, which renders problematic any notion of civil society. It is consistent, however, with a neoliberal understanding of civil society that abolishes any significant distinction between the market and the "public" sphere.

49. Nicholas B. Dirks, "In Near Ruins: Cultural Theory at the End of the Twentieth Century," in *In Near Ruins: Cultural Theory at the End of the Twentieth Century*, ed. Nicholas B. Dirks, 1–18, esp. 11 (Minneapolis: University of Minnesota Press, 1998).

50. Joseph Levenson, *Confucian China and Its Modern Fate: A Trilogy* (Berkeley: University of California Press, 1968), 157.

51. J. K. Gibson-Graham, *The End of Capitalism (As We Knew It): A Feminist Critique of Political Economy* (Cambridge, MA: Blackwell Publishers, 1996). For the most important discussion of globalization in terms of networks, see Manuel Castells, *The Rise of the Network Society*, Vol. 1 of *The Information Age* (3 volumes) (Cambridge, MA: Blackwell Publishers, 1996). For a discussion of globalization as a contradictory process of integration/fragmentation, see Arif Dirlik, "Globalization as the End and the Beginning of History: The Contradictory Implications of a New Paradigm," Working Papers, The Institute on Globalization and the Human Condition, McMaster University, op. cit. I am indebted to Majid Tehranian for the term "pancapitalism."

52. Latouche, *The Westernization of the World*, 115. The "informal economy," whether in Africa, Latin America, or Asia, is not to be viewed only economically, Latouche insists, as it is built on an "ethic of solidarity" that has survived the onslaught on society of the economy (114). For a fascinating example from, of all places, war-torn Somalia, see Ken Menkhaus and John Prendergast, "The Stateless State," *Africa Report* 40, no. 3 (May–June 1995): 22–26.

Index

About the Author

Arif Dirlik is Knight Professor of Social Science at the University of Oregon. His many publications include *Revolution and History: Origins of Marxist Historiography in China, 1919–1937*; *The Origins of Chinese Communism*; *Anarchism in the Chinese Revolution*; and the edited volume, *Critical Perspectives on Mao Zedong's Thought*. His most recent book is *Kuaguo ziben shidaide houzhimin piping (Postcolonial Criticism in the Age of Global Capitalism)*. A Chinese translation of *Revolution and History* was released in February 2005. *Anarchism in the Chinese Revolution* is due to appear in Chinese in 2005.